Figuring Sex between
Men from
Shakespeare to Rochester

Figuring Sex between Men from Shakespeare to Rochester

PAUL HAMMOND

CLARENDON PRESS · OXFORD

OXFORD

UNIVERSITY PRESS

Great Clarendon Street, Oxford, OX2 6DP

Oxford University Press is a department of the University of Oxford.
It furthers the University's objective of excellence in research, scholarship,
and education by publishing worldwide in

Oxford New York

Auckland Bangkok Buenos Aires Cape Town Chennai
Dar es Salaam Delhi Hong Kong Istanbul Karachi Kolkata
Kuala Lumpur Madrid Melbourne Mexico City Mumbai Nairobi
São Paulo Shanghai Singapore Taipei Tokyo Toronto

and an associated company in Berlin

Oxford is a registered trade mark of Oxford University Press
in the UK and certain other countries

Published in the United States
by Oxford University Press Inc., New York

British Library Cataloguing in Publication Data

Data available

Library of Congress Cataloging in Publication Data

Data available

ISBN 0–19–818692–4
ISBN 0–19–818693–2 (Pbk.)

1 3 5 7 9 10 8 6 4 2

Typeset in Minion
by Regent Typesetting, London
Printed in Great Britain
on acid-free paper by
Biddles Ltd,
Guildford and King's Lynn

FOR NICK

ἁπτόμενος γὰρ οἶμαι τοῦ καλοῦ καὶ ὁμιλῶν αὐτῷ, ἃ πάλαι
ἐκύει τίκτει καὶ γεννᾷ, καὶ παρὼν καὶ ἀπὼν μεμνημένος,
καὶ τὸ γεννηθὲν συνεκτρέφει κοινῇ μετ' ἐκείνου.

Acknowledgements

I am grateful to a number of friends and colleagues who have drawn my attention to relevant material, and answered my questions: Dr Michael Brennan, Professor Martin Butler, Professor Derek Hughes, Professor Harold Love, Dr James Loxley, Dr Andrew McRae, Professor Nabil Matar, the late Jeremy Maule, Professor Nigel Smith, Dr Susan Owen, Dr Patricia Palmer, and Dr Keith Walker. I am especially grateful to Professor Andrew Hadfield for reading the book scrupulously in draft and making many helpful suggestions. I must also thank the British Academy for assistance with research expenses. For permission to quote from manuscript material in their care I am grateful to the following institutions: the James M. and Marie-Louise Osborn Collection, Beinecke Library, Yale University; the Bodleian Library, University of Oxford; the British Library, London; the Folger Shakespeare Library, Washington DC; Department of Special Collections (including the Brotherton Collection), Leeds University Library; Department of Manuscripts and Special Collections, University of Nottingham; and the President and Council of the Royal Society, London.

Earlier versions of parts of the book have previously appeared in print as follows:

part of Chapter 2 as 'Friends or Lovers? Sensitivity to Homosexual Implications in Adaptations of Shakespeare, 1640–1701', in Cedric C. Brown and Arthur F. Marotti (eds.), *Texts and Cultural Change in Early Modern England* (Basingstoke: Macmillan, 1997), 225–47;

part of Chapter 3 as 'Titus Oates and "Sodomy"' in Jeremy Black (ed.), *Culture and Society in Britain 1660–1800* (Manchester: Manchester University Press, 1997), 85–101;

Chapter 4 as 'Marvell's Sexuality', *The Seventeenth Century*, 11 (1996), 87–123;

part of Chapter 5 as 'Rochester's Homoeroticism', in Nicholas Fisher (ed.), *That Second Bottle: Essays on John Wilmot, Earl of Rochester* (Manchester: Manchester University Press, 2000), 46–62.

I am grateful to the respective publishers for permission to use this material. In addition, I have adapted a few sentences from my book *Love between Men in English Literature* (Basingstoke: Macmillan, 1996), where this seemed the best way of advancing the argument.

Contents

A Note on Texts and Abbreviations

Texts are quoted in the original spelling, except that i/j and u/v have been modernized, and contractions have been expanded, so that forms such as 'y^e' and 'w^ch' are transcribed as 'the' and 'which'. Any alterations to the punctuation of the originals, and any editorial interpolations, are placed in square brackets. Shakespeare is quoted from *William Shakespeare: The Complete Works: Original-Spelling Edition*, ed. Stanley Wells and Gary Taylor (Oxford, 1986); but since it uses only through-line numbers, act, scene, and line references have been supplied from the modernized spelling version of that edition. All unattributed translations are my own.

The following abbreviations are used:

BC	Brotherton Collection, Leeds University Library
BL	British Library, London
Bodl.	Bodleian Library, Oxford
Crum	Margaret Crum, *First-Line Index of English Poetry 1500–1800 in Manuscripts of the Bodleian Library Oxford* (Oxford, 1969).
DNB	*Dictionary of National Biography*
LBM	Paul Hammond, *Love between Men in English Literature* (Basingstoke, 1996).
OED	*The Oxford English Dictionary*
POAS	*Poems on Affairs of State: Augustan Satirical Verse, 1660–1714*, ed. George deF. Lord *et al.*, 7 vols. (New Haven, 1963–75).
Smith	Bruce Smith, *Homosexual Desire in Shakespeare's England: A Cultural Poetics* (Chicago, 1991).
Tilley	Morris Palmer Tilley, *A Dictionary of the Proverbs in England in the Sixteenth and Seventeenth Centuries* (Ann Arbor, 1950).
Williams	Gordon Williams, *A Dictionary of Sexual Language and Imagery in Shakespearean and Stuart Literature*, 3 vols. (London, 1994).

Introduction

In 1996 I published *Love between Men in English Literature*, which offered an account of the literary representation of love and sex between men from the Renaissance to the 1950s. The present book develops some of the ideas from that earlier work by offering a more detailed exploration of texts from the seventeenth century, a period which is crucial but problematic for anyone interested in the cultural history of sexual relations between men. In the early part of the period, *circa* 1600, one finds poetry explicitly articulating homoerotic desire, along with plays in which homoerotic possibilities are teasingly explored. What seems to us now to be a vein of homoeroticism often colours the expression of male friendship. And yet this was also a period in which sexual relations between men were fiercely condemned by the law and the church. By contrast, *circa* 1700 it is hard to find any literature which celebrates the male body homoerotically, while at the same time there is now a self-confident, self-defining subculture, with its own meeting places (the 'molly houses') and its own language; meanwhile, one encounters an anxious insistence on the lack of eroticism in male friendships, and denunciations of 'sodomy' from groups such as the Societies for the Reformation of Manners.

How and why did the culture change so radically, and so paradoxically, over this century? This is an impossible question to answer, because in this case 'the culture' is not a coherent social milieu or literary tradition. Homosexual desire expresses itself fragmentarily, opportunistically, and there is hardly any dialogue between texts. Nor is there any readily legible relationship between literary fictions and social practices, given that those practices were punishable by death. So rather than attempt to write a survey, to construct a thesis, or to contrive a teleological narrative, the present book foregrounds the very fragmentary and elusive character of seventeenth-century writing about sex between men, attending to the essential problems of figuring sex, and figuring out what the representations mean. After an exploratory chapter, the book offers four case studies: two (centred on

Shakespeare and on the relation between 'sodomy' and political power) traverse the period and trace changes in sensibility by attending to the rewriting of texts; and two (on Marvell and Rochester) explore the complex imaginative world of individual writers towards the end of the century.

In the first chapter I address the question of how sex between men was figured rhetorically, drawing attention to two distinctive features of those literary texts which represent such desires—both those which are hostile and those which are celebratory. The first feature is the careful use of definition and indefinition. Writers wishing to voice love between men often develop strategies (such as allusions to the Greeks) which allow such desire to be identified, while also inviting readers to construe it as something other than sexual—as masculine friendship, as religious devotion. Open texts result, works which offer the reader various possibilities, space for the imagination. By contrast, writers condemning such desires as diabolical sodomy may insist upon punitive definitions, turning the complexities of real human beings into caricatures, into monsters. Definition and indefinition, the opening and closing of imaginative possibilities, are one theme of this chapter. The second theme is the construction of fictional spaces in which sex between men may be staged to the reader's imagination. Again, this may happen positively (in the creation of pastoral utopias or classical Greek settings) or negatively (in the demonizing of Italy and Turkey as locations of lust and impiety). Central to my argument in this chapter is the idea of *paradiastole*, the rhetorical trope which redefines something in other terms, a manœuvre familiar from (say) lawyers' arguments which seek to maximize or minimize a crime by careful redescription ('this was not murder, it was self-defence'). Within the texts discussed in this chapter, *paradiastole* both creates space for the homoerotic imagination to play in relative safety by permitting multiple readings, and, in bigoted texts, brands homosexual desires with the stigma of legal and religious anathema.

Chapter 2 takes up these ideas about how texts open and close possibilities and uses them to read some of Shakespeare's work. The focus here is at first on the *Sonnets*, on the rhetoric of possession and dispossession through which the poet tries to represent his relationship with the 'lovely boy', often rather desperately redescribing betrayal as fidelity, and indifference as love. Then I turn to Shakespeare's dialogue with the homoerotic poems of Richard Barnfield (not previously identified as actual sources for the *Sonnets*), and trace how Shakespeare adapts some of Barnfield's simplistic images and scenarios into his much more complex—emotionally and rhetorically complex—forms. Next I explore how Shakespeare transformed the source materials for *Twelfth Night* and *The Merchant of Venice* in ways which offer homo-erotic scenarios which were not available in the originals. The chapter concludes by showing how the complex openness of the *Sonnets* and the plays is closed down later in the seventeenth century by editors and adaptors in revisions which carefully erase any homosexual implica-tions from these texts, clarifying their language of ambiguities and purging male relationships from any possible imputation of homo-sexual desire.

Chapter 3 turns to the rhetoric of poems and plays which addressed the homosexual behaviour of political leaders. Here we see how the actual lives of historical individuals become mythologized, as their sexuality generates resources for figuring them as destroyers of the symbolic order and of the values of godly, Protestant England. The examples here range from monarchs (Edward II, James I, William III) to figures from the lower classes brought to public attention by the upheavals of civil war and political disorder: in various ways, unconventional sexuality is made to figure wider social and ideological disorder.

Chapter 4, on Andrew Marvell, brings together two kinds of dis-course, lyrical poetry and satirical propaganda. The first part of the chapter develops themes which will have become familiar from Chapter 3: the politically motivated use of allegations of homosexual behaviour. But in this case they have a special inflection, as material from a range of pamphlet attacks on Marvell repeatedly deploys the idea that he is impotent (a natural wish to hold of one's political opponent) and ambiguous or amphibious. These sexually charged caricatures are then used as the starting point for a reading of the ambiguous elements in Marvell's own lyric poetry, highlighting moments when homoerotic motifs complicate the texture of osten-sibly heterosexual poems.

The final chapter is again focused on a single writer, John Wilmot, Earl of Rochester. His name is synonymous with heterosexual liber-tinism, but I explore the ways in which homosexual interests are paraded as part of a libertine ethos, arguing that for all the homosexual bravado which we encounter from time to time in this poetry, there is actually no real homoeroticism here, in the sense of felt desire for the male body. A principal theme in this chapter is the way in which

Rochester's homosexual references were altered and removed as his poems circulated, so providing a counterpoint to the demonstration in Chapter 2 of the erasure of homoerotic possibilities from Shakespeare's texts.

This is a book of linked essays, not a comprehensive survey. In place of the cultural materialist and new historicist treatments which the subject has tended to receive in recent years, this book turns to the rhetoric of sex between men, exploring how literature creates an imagined world in which homosexual relations can be figured, and how readers responded to those creations by adapting, rewriting, and censoring those texts. I have been liberal in my quotations from seventeenth-century works, partly because the precise language through which sex between men is represented is crucial to my discussion, and partly because many of the texts, particularly those from manuscript sources, will not be readily accessible. The quotations are functional, not decorative, and will, I hope, allow readers to hear voices other than my own; and so to attend to idioms and ways of feeling which the preoccupations of the modern academy can too easily overwrite.

1

Figuring Sex between Men

Crossing the courtyard of the Hôtel de Guermantes, the Baron de Charlus catches sight of the tailor Jupien. The gaze is returned, a gaze of mutual admiration and recognition. The Baron asks Jupien for a light, and Jupien replies, 'Entrez, on vous donnera tout ce que vous voudrez'.[1] They disappear into his shop. The observer, who has known both men for a while, reflects that the Baron has been transformed by the encounter, and that his own understanding has similarly undergone a revolution: 'Dès le début de cette scène une révolution, pour mes yieux dessillés, s'était opérée en M. de Charlus, aussi complète, aussi immédiate que s'il avait été touché par une baguette magique. Jusque-là, parce que je n'avais pas compris, je n'avais pas vu.'[2] 'Because I had not understood, I had not seen', says the narrator. According to this rather Kantian formulation, we require knowledge, or at least epistemological structures, before we can see what is in front of us, before the marks become signs. Many aspects of a man's life fail to register themselves on the surface, legible to casual observers, but men who need to know how to read such signs recognize one another:

Le vice (on parle ainsi pour la commodité du langage), le vice de chacun l'accompagne à la façon de ce génie qui était invisible pour les hommes tant qu'ils ignoraient sa présence ... Ulysse lui-même ne reconnaissait pas d'abord Athéné. Mais les dieux sont immédiatement perceptibles aux dieux, le semblable aussi vite au semblable.[3]

[1] 'Enter, you will be given everything which you desire.'
[2] 'From the beginning of this scene—which opened my eyes—a transformation had come about in M. de Charlus, as complete, as instantaneous as if he had been touched by a magic wand. Until that moment, because I had not understood, I had not seen.'
[3] 'The vice (to speak according to common parlance) the vice of each man accompanies him like that guardian spirit which was invisible to human beings so long as they were unaware of its presence ... Ulysses himself did not at first recognize Athena. But the gods are immediately perceptible to other gods, and like to like.'

But to those who are disinterested observers, there seems to be nothing there to observe, until one day some chance encounter, gesture, or tell-tale phrase reveals what had hitherto been written in invisible ink, and makes meaningless marks rearrange themselves into signs and narratives: 'jusqu'au jour où sur la surface unie de l'individu pareil aux autres sont venus apparaître, tracés en un encre jusque-là invisible, les charactères qui composent le mot cher aux anciens Grecs'.[4] For the narrator, this moment of revelation forces a complete reappraisal of his relations with M. de Charlus up to that point, making him rethink words and incidents which had previously seemed without significance:

rétrospectivement les hauts et les bas eux-mêmes de ses relations avec moi, tout ce qui avait paru jusque-là incohérent à mon esprit, devenait intelligible, se montrait évident comme une phrase, n'offrant aucun sens tant qu'elle reste décomposée en lettres disposées au hasard, exprime, si les charactères se trouvent replacés dans l'ordre qu'il faut, une pensée que l'on ne pourra plus oublier.[5]

Scholars seeking to understand the representation of sexual relations between men in the early modern period have no 'baguette magique' to turn scrambled letters into coherent words and sentences. We do not always know what is a sign and what is only a mark. Part of the problem is that homoerotic desire is rarely made articulate unambiguously in texts from this period, particularly in the first person, voiced as 'I'; instead it often speaks the same language as passionate friendship. At a time when the death penalty was in force for sodomy, it was obviously expedient for writers to deploy various kinds of indefinition, using a language which permitted multiple interpretations and allowed scope for denying dangerous constructions. This also gave scope for writers to engage in the pleasures of teasing their readers with homoerotic possibilities, and for readers to

---

[4] 'until the day when, on the smooth surface of the individual who seems just like the others, there appear, traced in an ink which was previously invisible, the characters which make up the word dear to the ancient Greeks.'

[5] 'In hindsight, the ups and downs of his relations with me, everything which had previously appeared inexplicable to me, became intelligible, revealed itself plainly like a sentence which, making no sense so long as it is split up into letters arranged at random, expresses, if the characters are put back in their proper order, an idea which one can never forget.' (Marcel Proust, *A la recherche du temps perdu*, ed. Jean-Yves Tadié, Bibliothèque de la Pléiade, 4 vols. (Paris, 1987–9), iii. 8, 15–16 (from the opening of *Sodome et Gomorrhe*).)

enjoy the pleasures of teasing out half-secret meanings. Several literary conventions, notably the tropes of male friendship and Graeco-Roman myth, licensed the passionate expression of male relationships. But it may also be that in many cases distinctions between friendly and erotic feelings were not required, for social relations between men could be coloured by a warmth of verbal and physical expression which in later periods might be interpreted as improper. Homoerotic desire inhabited other discourses—the vocabularies and narratives of male friendship, or of heterosexual encounters in which homoerotic desire is allowed or even solicited through a focus on the sexual attractions of the male partner—and did so in opportunistic and discontinuous ways, so that individual readers often selected meanings from among a range of possibilities, or made readings at a tangent to the signals provided by the texts. A man might, for example, have read Shakespeare's *Sonnets* as expressing passionate homosexual love, although that is by no means the only reading which they permit; or have taken homoerotic pleasure in Shakespeare's description of the young male body in *Venus and Adonis*, so turning an ostensible narrative of heterosexual desire into a series of discontinuous opportunities for homoerotic pleasure.[6] Indefinition and discontinuity seem to have been crucial, for it was the capacity of writers and readers to refuse definition, to keep possibilities in play, that created and protected the textual spaces in which homoerotic pleasure became possible.

In reading such texts we should probably not even wish for a magic wand which makes the marks legible, placing them in 'l'ordre qu'il faut' to reveal 'une pensée'. Rather than wish for such fixed and singular meaning, perhaps we should read instead with an eye to appreciating multiplicity and ambiguity, registering the ways in which literary texts create a variety of potential spaces in which desire can be imagined.[7] Against Proust's image of the single text waiting to be decoded, we should set his own repeated insistence on the variety of human desire, on 'les intermittances du cœur', and his warning of 'la naïveté des gens qui croient qu'un goût en exclut forcément un autre'.[8]

---

[6] The homosexual Victorian scholar and critic John Addington Symonds read *Venus and Adonis* in this way: see *LBM* 167.

[7] I adapt the term 'potential space' from D. W. Winnicott's *Playing and Reality* (London, 1971); it is the area which is not wholly that of the self, nor that of the other, but a space shared between self and other in which creativity can come into play (see *LBM* 67).

[8] 'the inconsistencies of the heart'; 'the naïveté of those people who believe that one taste completely excludes another' (Proust, *A la recherche*, iii. 153, 269).

Equally, there are texts for which no one reading completely excludes another.

There is a risk that the descriptive and analytical language of modern interpreters may impose a false clarity on early modern texts. The conceptual and experiential territory mapped by the words 'sodomy' or 'sodomite' in the sixteenth and seventeenth centuries is not the same as that mapped by the nineteenth-century terms 'homosexuality' and 'homosexual', which in turn differs radically from modern perceptions of sexual relations between men: so great are these conceptual changes that to write the history of 'homosexuality' might be a meaningless enterprise, 'une question mal posée'. But it is possible to write about (if not exactly to write the history of) the representation of sexual relations between men, the work of the imagination, though even analysis of literary texts may be plagued by problems of terminology. 'Homosexual' is an anachronistic term, since it entered the language only in the late nineteenth century, and carried with it psychological, medical, and moral connotations which are quite different from those which obtained in the early modern period. We cannot altogether erase from the word's connotations the traces of these origins. It is a sufficiently awkward word in our contemporary culture, and when applied to the seventeenth century may actively prevent us from seeing.

There is, however, no simple seventeenth-century vocabulary which could be used instead. Various words were used more or less pejoratively to describe homosexual men and boys—bardash, catamite, ganymede, he-whore, ingle, minion, molly[9]—most of which refer to what is assumed to be the passive or subordinate partner. 'Sodomy' was an early modern term, but it is not clear how, or even whether, the notion of 'sodomy' belongs to a study of the representation of sex between men, let alone homoerotic desire. For, as Michel Foucault pointed out, the category of sodomy was confused and incoherent.[10] In this period 'sodomy' is not a coherent notion but a cluster of associations: it is at once too precise (a specific physical act) and too vague (a general category of moral, social, and political deviance). It can be applied not only to sex between men, but to sex between a man and a woman, or between a human of either sex and an animal; and it is deployed rhetorically as a way of establishing the unacceptable foreignness of an enemy. Its translation of desire into

---

[9] For the uses of these terms see Williams, *s.vv.*
[10] Michel Foucault, *Histoire de la sexualité*, i. *La Volonté de savoir* (Paris, 1976), 134.

subversion denies the individual a plausible subjectivity, moving him out of the kind of narrative or social space which readers could imagine themselves inhabiting.

It would be a serious distortion to use 'homosexual' as a noun in this study, because it suggests a reification which begs the very questions which this book seeks to explore, implying that early modern males based their sense of identity on their characteristic sexual preferences. Yet there seems to be no alternative to 'homosexual' and 'homoerotic' as adjectives, if we are to avoid cumbersome periphrases. The distinction between those two words is not exact, but one might use 'homoerotic' to describe feelings of sexual desire for, or erotic pleasure in the contemplation of, other men (and hence to describe texts which articulate or invite such feelings); and to reserve 'homosexual' for physical sexual contact between men. The two terms would thus distinguish between looking and longing on the one hand, and acting and possessing on the other. We also have the word 'homosocial', introduced by Eve Kosofsky Sedgwick for intense social bonds between men which are strongly affective, supportive, and competitive; but not (at least not ostensibly) erotic.[11] Homosocial relationships may set themselves up in opposition to homoeroticism; and they may be a repressed form of homoeroticism.

According to the accepted map of homosexual relations in early modern England which has been drawn by historians and literary critics, there is a marked contrast between the period *circa* 1600 and the period *circa* 1700. Alan Bray[12] argued that legal and theological discourse in the Renaissance period demonized sexual relations between men as 'sodomy', which was more of an ideological category than an erotic preference: sodomites were bracketed with Jesuits, Spanish spies, and werewolves as agents of social and moral subversion. This way of thinking provided no resources for self-definition, for a man who enjoyed sex with other men would hardly place himself in such company. Nor did it speak of love and desire, only of demonic acts. Sodomy was part of the shadow-side of human existence, a sign of moral depravity and alienation from God, an activity (or perhaps a

---

[11] Eve Kosofsky Sedgwick, *Between Men: English Literature and Male Homosocial Desire* (New York, 1985).

[12] Alan Bray, *Homosexuality in Renaissance England* (London, 1982), and 'Homosexuality and the Signs of Male Friendship in Elizabethan England', *History Workshop*, 29 (1990), 1–19.

state of being) of which anyone might be capable if sufficiently wicked. According to Bray, sexual relations between men were nevertheless common, but only became visible as 'sodomy', attracting that label, when some political or social pressure shifted the way in which they were seen: for example, a close friendship between powerful courtiers who shared a bed might be labelled 'sodomy' if the political interests of others made that expedient. In such circumstances the marks become signs, the random characters are turned into sentences. But the implication in Bray's thesis that there was a whole range of strong sexual and emotional feelings which lacked any vocabulary except the condemnatory language of officialdom does not really ring true. His otherwise compelling argument has been importantly modified by Bruce Smith, who charts a whole repertoire of literary modes through which readers were able to explore homosexual desire: these motifs included pastorals which celebrated the love between shepherds, stories of military comradeship, cross-dressing at carnival time, the relationship of master and minion, and, finally, the subjectivity of the desiring poet fashioned in Shakespeare's *Sonnets*.[13] This literature offered a gamut of imaginative possibilities, a range of social and erotic roles which a reader might try out in the private world of his imagination, and thence, perhaps, in the shared textual and physical spaces of sexual

[13] Bruce Smith, *Homosexual Desire in Shakespeare's England: A Cultural Poetics* (Chicago, 1991). For other studies of the homoerotic literature of the Renaissance see *LBM* 25–87; Mary Bly, *Queer Virgins and Virgin Queans on the Early Modern Stage* (Oxford, 2000); Gregory W. Bredbeck, *Sodomy and Interpretation: Marlowe to Milton* (Ithaca, NY, 1991); Mario DiGangi, *The Homoerotics of Early Modern Drama* (Cambridge, 1997); John Franceschina, *Homosexualities in the English Theatre: From Lyly to Wilde* (Westport, Conn., 1997); Kent Gerard and Gert Hekma (eds.), *The Pursuit of Sodomy: Male Homosexuality in Renaissance and Enlightenment Europe* (New York, 1989); Jonathan Goldberg (ed.), *Queering the Renaissance* (Durham, NC, 1994), and *Sodometries: Renaissance Texts, Modern Sexualities* (Stanford, Calif., 1992); Laura Levine, *Men in Women's Clothing: Anti-Theatricality and Effeminization, 1579–1642* (Cambridge, 1994); Rictor Norton, *The Homosexual Literary Tradition: An Interpretation* (New York, 1974); Stephen Orgel, *Impersonations: The Performance of Gender in Shakespeare's England* (Cambridge, 1996); Michael Shapiro, *Gender in Play on the Shakespearean Stage: Boy Heroines and Female Pages* (Ann Arbor, 1994); Alan Stewart, *Close Readers: Humanism and Sodomy in Early Modern England* (Princeton, 1997); Claude J. Summers (ed.), *Homosexuality in Renaissance and Enlightenment England: Literary Representations in Historical Context* (Binghamton, 1992); Claude J. Summers and Ted-Larry Pebworth (eds.), *Renaissance Discourses of Desire* (Columbia, 1993); Susan Zimmerman, *Erotic Politics: Desire on the Renaissance Stage* (London, 1992). Many of these studies focus on Renaissance drama, so I have tended to draw my illustrations from other areas of the literature.

intimacy. It offered a world of free play, with the possibility of discontinuous identity, resources for temporary and shifting modes of self-definition. For the most part these texts invite and satisfy a desiring homoerotic gaze which is part of a continuum of masculine emotional interests, creating textual spaces for homoerotic pleasure within works which principally satisfy homosocial and heterosexual interests. What these texts do not invite the reader to do is to label himself as a man with exclusive or unusual sexual preferences.

The late seventeenth and early eighteenth century, by contrast, has been identified as the point when homosexual self-definition began to take place through an emerging subculture, in clubs and meeting houses which permitted the private and collective exploration of sexual role-playing, cross-dressing, parodic rituals, and specialized slang. Towards the end of the seventeenth century the meeting places called 'molly houses' grew up in London, enabling men to enjoy sex with other men in relative safety: thus arose a self-contained, self-defining culture within the metropolitan social world; and the emergence of such men as a recognizable group prompted (or at least coincided with, for the relations of cause and effect here are unclear) a more sharply defined and targeted hostility to homoerotic desire, its subjects and its objects, in the public press. Definitions were becoming crucial; the scope for possible interpretations of individuals and of relationships was changing, as close social relations between men (particularly if they involved some element of secrecy, or association across classes) began to be seen to invite a sexual construction. The physical signs of friendship common in the sixteenth century (embracing, kissing, sharing a bed) fell out of use, no doubt partly for fear that these would be interpreted as signs of sodomy.[14] The molly houses were secret establishments, but their existence was known, and observers remarked with alarm on the contrast between some men's behaviour in the public, social world and their activities in private. Thus secrecy shared between men came to have sodomy as one of its possible significances. Alan Bray's book began to map this subculture, and his work has been extended by Rictor Norton in *Mother Clap's Molly House*, and by other social historians.[15] But this leaves the

[14] Alan Bray and Michel Rey, 'The Body of the Friend: Continuity and Change in Masculine Friendship in the Seventeenth Century', in Tim Hitchcock and Michèle Cohen (eds.), *English Masculinities 1660–1800* (London, 1999), 65–84.

[15] Rictor Norton, *Mother Clap's Molly House: The Gay Subculture in England 1700–1830* (London, 1992), and a series of works by Raymond Trumbach listed in the

perplexing question of how this later culture could have arisen from the former: how a Renaissance world of polymorphous male sexuality, in which sodomy was demonized and occasionally punished, but where varieties of homoerotic texts flourished, gave way to the eighteenth-century world of homosexual self-definition, and even a limited degree of communal self-assertion, but without the vein of lyrical homoeroticism which we find in earlier texts.

Michel Foucault noted that in France the disappearance of homoerotic lyricism coincided with the abolition of the death penalty for sodomy, and his explanation of this is suggestive for the interpretation of conditions in England:

L'époque où on brûle pour la dernière fois les sodomites, c'est l'époque précisément où disparaît, avec la fin du 'libertinage érudit', tout un lyrisme homosexuel que la culture de la Renaissance avait parfaitement supporté. On a l'impression que la sodomie jadis condamnée au même titre que la magie et l'hérésie, et dans le même contexte de profanation religieuse, n'est plus condamnée maintenant que pour des raisons morales, et en même temps que l'homosexualité... Deux expériences sont alors confondues qui, jusqu'alors, étaient restées séparées: les interdits sacrés de la sodomie, et les équivoques amoureuses de l'homosexualité. Une même forme de condamnation les enveloppe l'une et l'autre, et trace une ligne de partage entièrement nouvelle dans le domaine du sentiment. Il se forme ainsi une unité morale, libérée des anciens châtiments, nivelée dans l'internement, et proche déjà des formes modernes de la culpabilité. L'homosexualité à qui la Renaissance avait donné liberté d'expression va désormais entrer en silence, et passer du côté de l'interdit, héritant des vieilles condamnations d'une sodomie maintenant désacralisée.[16]

Bibliography. For the literature of this later period see also *LBM* 88–125; Cameron McFarlane, *The Sodomite in Fiction and Satire 1660–1750* (New York, 1997).

[16] 'The period in which sodomites were burnt for the last time is exactly the period when there disappeared, along with the end of the "libertinage érudit", a whole homosexual lyricism which the culture of the Renaissance had happily tolerated. One forms the impression that sodomy—which was previously condemned under the same heading as magic and heresy, and in the same context of religious transgression—was now only condemned for moral reasons, and at the same time as homosexuality... At that period two experiences are fused which up to that point had remained separate: the religious proscription of sodomy, and the erotic ambiguities of homosexuality. The same form of condemnation encompassed both of them, and traced an entirely novel line of separation in the territory of feeling. Thus a moral unity was formed, freed from the old punishments, put on a par in confinement, and already approximating to the modern forms of guilt. That homosexuality to which the Renaissance had given free-

While an analysis of conditions in France cannot be applied without modification to the circumstances which prevailed in England, Foucault's basic point does provide an explanation which is worth entertaining: that it was precisely the removal of sodomy from the realm of the demonic, and its transfer into the realm of the immoral, which made the literary celebration of sex between men unacceptable. But that still leaves the question of what Renaissance readers thought was being described in their homoerotic texts, if not sex between men.

The hermeneutic problem is complex. To start with, aesthetic and rhetorical tropes do not relate simply to historical social practices, and the pleasure of the text can for some readers be separated from the pleasure or otherwise of what is described. (The pleasure said by Aristotle to derive from tragedy provides an obvious example of this.) And one particular characteristic of Renaissance literature may have contributed to the possibility of reading homoerotic texts without fully registering their sexual import: images often have more than one meaning; puns are relished, including the serious, sometimes manic puns of Shakespeare's *Sonnets*; and signifiers may have a plethora of signifieds. There is an openness to allegory, the literary form in which one object may have several significations on different levels. In such texts, homoerotic desire can be figured without being exclusively figured. Restoration literature, by contrast, shies away from allegory and multiple meanings, preferring modes of knowledge which work by fixing an object empirically. The Royal Society disliked language which was capable of multiple signification.

Some comments by Katharine Eisaman Maus on the modes of signification in Renaissance drama may usefully be applied to texts from the earlier part of our period. She writes that Renaissance playwrights

inevitably encounter a gap between their limited theatrical resources and the extravagant situations they dramatize. English Renaissance theatrical method is thus radically synecdochic, endlessly referring the spectators to events, objects, situations, landscapes that cannot be shown them. We are provided . . . not with an actual sexual act but with the preliminaries or consequences of a sexual relationship . . . the English Renaissance stage seems deliberately to foster theatergoers' capacity to use partial and limited presentations as a basis for conjecture about what is undisplayed

---

dom of expression will henceforth be silenced, become forbidden, attracting to itself the previous condemnations of a sodomy which is now brought out of the religious domain' (Michel Foucault, *Histoire de la folie à l'âge classique* (Paris, 1972), 102–3).

or undisplayable. Its spectacles are understood to depend upon and indicate the shapes of things unseen.[17]

Similarly, texts which figure homosexual consummation may have to proceed indirectly—not even by metaphor, but by synecdoche, by allowing the part to stand for the whole, the courtship for the consummation. The work of the eye becomes especially important in homoerotic texts, partly because looking is a licit pleasure, where touching may not be; but also because the eye can take possession of the beloved, and so be used as a trope for sexual possession.[18] As spectators in the theatre fashion in their own minds off-stage possibilities, so readers of non-dramatic texts may be led to imagine times, spaces, and actions which lie beyond the spaces of the text itself, but are figured by some gesture of invitation. Incomplete narratives (such as that of Antonio and Sebastian in *Twelfth Night*) can thus be given beginnings and continuations *ad libitum*. This may be one important reason for the lack of closure in some Shakespearian narratives: what happens to Antonio at the end of *Twelfth Night*, or to his namesake at the end of *The Merchant of Venice*? The story is handed over to the reader. Aposiopesis, the breaking off of an expression before it is completed, is a valuable rhetorical strategy. So we need to attend closely to the figuring of sex between men, to its rhetorical exposition.

Accordingly, this book is organized around two lines of thought. The first explores how textual spaces were shaped in which homoerotic desire could be articulated and homosexual relations imagined: the ways in which potential spaces were delineated as places in which the fulfilment of such desires might be staged; the metaphors, metonymies, and similes which make the male body desiring and desirable, an erotic subject or erotic object; the classical Greek and Roman myths which give precedents to such desires and relations; and the silences which themselves may be spaces shaped by the surrounding text, waiting to be filled by the reader's imagination. The shaping of textual spaces is therefore one of this book's principal themes.

The second is the destruction of such spaces. This happens by the turning of complex, desiring human beings into sinners and demons, the turning of subjects into objects. The open, imaginative possibilities shaped by texts may be closed off in a variety of ways—through censorship and revision at the hands of officials, scribes, printers, publishers,

---

[17] Katharine Eisaman Maus, *Inwardness and Theater in the English Renaissance* (Chicago, 1995), 32.

[18] See Williams, *s.v.* eye.

adaptors; and sometimes by the writers themselves, nervously policing their own work. Ambiguities and indefinitions are clarified, sometimes punitively. This book therefore also looks at the afterlife of homoerotic texts, at the erasure of potential spaces, the closing of mind and heart.

In thinking about how these literary texts function socially, about how they translate homosexual figures (people) into homosexual figures (tropes), and how they appear to shape kinds of subject and object, two strategies mapped by Michel Foucault may be useful: the first is to ask the question, 'Qui parle? Qui dans l'ensemble des individus parlants, est fondé à tenir cette sorte de langage?'; and the second is to describe the *'emplacements'*, the sites from which one speaks.[19] Foucault was particularly interested in institutional sites such as those of medicine, and the authority which is conferred with a discourse which proceeds from such an institution; but we may adapt these questions to the much more fragmented, opportunistic, and discontinuous speech which our texts offer. When we ask 'who speaks?' in connection with the creation of a subject, we find that very few texts show themselves to be autobiographical, but many devise ingenious and subtle means of suggesting a first person singular. Drayton gives a voice to Piers Gaveston which is in some places lyrically homoerotic in his recollection of his passion for Edward II, but in other places sounds like a disapproving moralist; here the character's forked tongue is perhaps protecting the writer. Shakespeare in the *Sonnets* creates the fictional figure of the poet who desires the 'lovely boy', and exploits this minimal but crucial distance between himself and his lyrical voice; even so, we shall see that this may have given him insufficient permission to speak, or, to put it another way, an *emplacement* which was insufficiently fictional, insufficiently empowering, given his own rather low status in the social world of Jacobean England. Other writers use classical translation to provide them with a site which is culturally respectable and reassuringly foreign. In Marvell's poems, various forms of persona, ambiguous phrasing, and intertextual reference provide a site which is homoerotically suggestive but noncommittal. The libertine poses struck by Rochester can be read as a form of fiction, indeed, as a kind of miniature drama, and we shall see that subtle grammatical shifts insulate even that rather theatrical first person singular from the actual articulation of homoerotic desire.

[19] 'Who speaks? Who in the collection of speaking individuals is given the right to use this language?' (Michel Foucault, *L'Archéologie du savoir* (Paris, 1969), 68–9).

When we turn from the speaking subject to the question of how the object is fashioned, the writers who satirize the political 'sodomite'— especially James I and William III—often claim to speak plurally on behalf of the nation, asserting Englishness and the rights of the citizen against encroachment from foreign rulers, the Scot or the Dutchman, who no longer listen to their people. Their critique tends to inhabit informal sites, manuscript rather than print, but these are communally powerful platforms. Such texts implicitly create a community of male readers who are defined through their love for women and their virtuous, sometimes martial, friendship with other men; and we shall see such assumptions about a shared norm at work in the erasure of homoerotic possibilities from some of Shakespeare's texts in the later seventeenth century.

The remainder of this chapter explores two subjects which are central to the figuring of sex between men in the seventeenth century: the uses of definition and indefinition, precision and ambiguity; and the shaping of imaginary spaces in which desire might play.

DEFINITION AND INDEFINITION

Many texts about passionate relations between men move between definition and indefinition. Definition may suggest a sexual reading, while indefinition wards off the disapproval which might result. Conversely, definition may insist upon a non-sexual interpretation, while at the same time innuendo and the connotative resources of language suggestively reinstate what has formally been denied. An example of this is Shakespeare's Sonnet 20, which insists that the young man's penis is 'to my purpose nothing'.[20] But this apparent denial of sexual interest in the youth is undone by a realization that 'nothing' is slang for the female genitals.[21] Desire is often deniable; and denial may itself be an invitation, so that the formal denial of sexual interest in Sonnet 20 may be a test of the boy's disposition. Definition might proceed by including classical allusions, such as to Ganymede, the beautiful boy taken off by Zeus to be his cupbearer; or to Virgil's second *Eclogue*, which speaks of the love of Corydon for Alexis; or to Plato, sometimes invoked synecdochically to stand for the Greeks'

---

[20] Shakespeare, Sonnet 20, l. 12.
[21] *Shakespeare's Sonnets*, ed. Katherine Duncan-Jones (London, 1997), 151; and see *LBM* 79–80.

approval of sex between an older and a younger man. But while such allusions may point to the sexual element of a situation, they can also be given a non-sexual significance. Ganymede may be read as an allegory of the soul's ascent to God, leaving behind all worldly and fleshly desires.[22] Richard Barnfield defended the innocence of his homoerotic collection *The Affectionate Shepheard* (1594) by maintaining that it was 'nothing else, but an imitation of *Virgill*, in the second Eglogue of *Alexis*';[23] but *Eclogue* 2 was a notorious text, and Renaissance commentators had difficulty explaining away the apparent sexual nature of Alexis' passion.[24] And was Platonic love platonic? 'E. K.', annotating Spenser's *The Shepheardes Calender*, claimed that Socrates 'loved Alcybiades extremely, yet not Alcybiades person, but hys soule, which is Alcybiades owne selfe'.[25] But Thomas Hobbes was more sceptical about the nature of Socrates' interest in Alcibiades:

The opinion of Plato concerning honourable love, delivered (according to his custom, in the person of Socrates) in the dialogue intituled *Convivium*,[26] is this: that a man full and pregnant with wisdom, or other virtue, naturally seeketh out some beautiful person, of age and capacity to conceive, in whom he may, without sensual respects, engender and produce the like. And this is the idea of the then noted love of Socrates wise and continent, to Alcibiades young and beautiful; in which love, is not sought the honour, but issue of his knowledge; contrary to common love, to which though issue sometimes follow, yet men seek not that, but to please, and to be pleased. It should therefore be this charity, or desire to assist and advance others. But why then should the wise seek the ignorant, or be more charitable to the beautiful than to others? There is something in it savouring of the use of that time: in which matter though Socrates be acknowledged for continent, yet continent men have the passion they contain, as much or more than they that satiate the appetite; which maketh me suspect this platonic love for merely sensual; but with an

[22] George Wither, *A Collection of Emblemes* (London, 1635), 156; Alexander Ross, *Mystagogus Poeticus* (London, 1647; 5th edn. 1672), 131–2; H. David Brumble, *Classical Myths and Legends in the Middle Ages and Renaissance: A Dictionary of Allegorical Meanings* (London, 1998), 133–4.

[23] Richard Barnfield, *The Complete Poems*, ed. George Klawitter (Selinsgrove, 1990), 116.

[24] Smith, 89–92.

[25] *The Poetical Works of Edmund Spenser*, ed. Ernest de Selincourt and J. C. Smith, 3 vols. (Oxford, 1909–10), i. 17.

[26] i.e. *The Symposium*.

honourable pretence for the old to haunt the company of the young and beautiful.[27]

Hobbes, for one, had no doubt about the words to use for the motives which led philosophers to haunt the gymnasia. Redescription, the rhetorical figure of *paradiastole*, in which the character of a person or act is represented in a different light,[28] is crucial to the rhetorical procedures of such texts—both to those texts which open out imagined spaces for homoerotic desire, and to those which seek to define homosexual relations punitively.

Some key terms can be surprisingly fluid and indefinite. Frequently encountered in modern discussions of Renaissance male relationships—most particularly in accounts of Shakespeare's *Sonnets*—is the distinction between friend and lover. Critics often label the addressee of Sonnets 1–126 'the Friend', thus implicitly warding off any suggestion of sexual interest in him by the speaker of the poems. In so doing they are indeed adopting the sonnets' own vocabulary ('To me faire friend you never can be old'[29]), while passing over other terms less amenable to their preconceptions ('These poore rude lines of thy deceased Lover'[30]). But in the early modern period these words 'friend' and 'lover' each had a wide semantic field, and the two fields overlapped. They will often appear in the texts which form the subject of this book, so it may be useful to trace here the range of available meanings, citing examples from Shakespeare.[31] First, the word 'friend'.[32] At its most unemotional, 'friend' could be used to greet a stranger, particularly a social inferior, as Viola greets the Clown in *Twelfth Night*.[33] It could mean 'relation': a lady in *The Two Gentlemen of Verona* has been promised in marriage 'by her friends | Unto a youthfull Gentleman'.[34] It could mean someone of the same sex, of equal status, with whom one is specially intimate, a relationship implying comradeship, loyalty, and trust. Horatio describes himself to Hamlet

---

[27] Thomas Hobbes, *The Elements of Law Natural and Politic*, ed. J. C. A. Gaskin (Oxford, 1994), 57.

[28] For *paradiastole* see Quentin Skinner, *Reason and Rhetoric in the Philosophy of Hobbes* (Cambridge, 1996), 138–80.

[29] Shakespeare, Sonnet 104, l. 1.

[30] Sonnet 32, l. 4.

[31] This discussion is adapted from *LBM* 30–1.

[32] For the changing social meanings of friendship and its signs in this period see Bray and Rey, 'The Body of the Friend'.

[33] *Twelfth Night*, 3. 1. 1.

[34] *OED* 3; *The Two Gentlemen of Verona*, 3. 1. 106–7.

as 'your poore servant', but the Prince corrects him and redescribes their relationship as that of equals: 'Sir my good friend, Ile change that name with you'.[35] The word can be used between men and women who are in love, but not yet married or sexual partners: thus the virginal Perdita calls Florizel 'my fairst Friend' and 'my sweet friend'.[36] But 'friend' can also mean 'sexual partner':[37] Caesar says that Antony is Cleopatra's 'Friend';[38] in *Measure for Measure* Claudio 'hath got his friend with childe';[39] and Juliet—aching with love and longing as Romeo is forced to leave after their first and only night together—calls him 'love, Lord, my husband, friend',[40] where the last of those names is evidently no anticlimax; indeed, editors have described the line as a chiasmus, built around the paired synonyms 'love . . . friend' and 'Lord . . . husband'. That is the Folio text; the first Quarto uses three terms rather than four, and they seem to be arranged in ascending order of intimacy: 'my Lord, my Love, my Frend'.[41] The shifting meanings of this word are exploited in *Othello* to mark out the shifting relationships within and between the sexes: when Iago assures Roderigo that he is his 'friend' the two are of similar social status, and partners in villainy; but when Othello calls Iago—who is his military subordinate—'My Friend', this signifies the depth of dependency into which Othello has sunk.[42] And when Iago tells Othello that Desdemona has been 'naked with her friend in bed, I An houre, or more', he can be sure that Othello will understand what sort of 'friend' to his wife Cassio has become.[43] As these usages map the changing bonds within the play, so too something similar (though much more complex) happens in the *Sonnets*, which exploit these ambiguities, defining and redefining the word 'friend' through the extended play of longing, assurance, and betrayal.

The semantic field of the word 'lover' overlaps to a considerable degree with that of 'friend'. It can simply mean 'well-wisher': when Ulysses says to Achilles 'I as your lover speake' he is only claiming to be giving him helpful advice.[44] More strongly, 'lover' can mean 'one in love with someone', which according to the *OED* only happens between people of opposite sexes.[45] In Shakespeare's comedies the mooning lover is a familiar dramatic type, exemplified by Romeo or

---

[35] *Hamlet*, 1. 2. 162–3.

[36] *The Winter's Tale*, 4. 4. 112, 128.

[37] *OED* 4; Williams, *s.v.*

[38] *Antony and Cleopatra*, 3. 12. 22.

[39] *Measure for Measure*, 1. 4. 29.

[40] *Romeo and Juliet*, 3. 5. 43.

[41] *An Excellent Conceited Tragedie of Romeo and Iuliet* (London, 1597), sig. G3ᵛ.

[42] *Othello*, 1. 3. 336, 5. 2. 161.

[43] Ibid., 4. 1. 3–4.

[44] *OED* 1; *Troilus and Cressida*, 3. 3. 207.

[45] *OED* 2.

Orlando. Could the word also mean 'sexual partner', as it does today? The *OED* is innocent of this usage at any period, but 'lover' is moving towards its modern sense in *Measure for Measure*, when Isabella is told 'Your brother, and his lover have embrac'd' and that the lover is consequently pregnant.[46] In this instance 'lover' might still mean only 'one who is in love' or 'one who is being courted', but it clearly has a sexual meaning when Antony says that he will run towards death 'As to a Lovers bed', or when Juliet longs for the night which will bring her first sex with Romeo, and says: 'Lovers can see to do their amorous rights, | By their owne bewties'.[47]

Though the choice of an appropriate sense from among these possibilities may be a reasonably simple matter in the context of routine social exchanges, or emotional relationships between men and women, the uses of 'friend' and 'lover' when applied emotively between men operate in a field where ambiguity may be necessary, and definition may be undesirable or even dangerous. In which of the possible senses is the young man of the *Sonnets* the poet's 'friend'?[48] Is it the same sense in which the young man and the dark lady are 'both to each friend',[49] a phrase which occurs in an account of what is clearly a sexual relationship? When the poet refers to himself as the young man's 'Lover', or to the young man as his 'lover', in which of its possible senses is that word being used?[50] And does it mean the same in both cases? Perhaps the poet is in love with the young man, whereas the young man is only a well-wisher towards the poet, and they are not sexual partners: but that is only one possible scenario which could be constructed out of the permutations of the available meanings. Another would be that the poet begins as the boy's lover (well-wisher), becomes his lover (suitor), and ends as his lover (sexual partner). Every reader is liable to feel the nuances of 'friend' and 'lover' differently. The words 'love', 'lover', and 'friend' in the *Sonnets* have no single or unambiguous meanings, but are continually being redefined, refelt, reimagined. Shakespeare's *Sonnets* explore the half-open, half-secret domain in which a male 'friend' might also be a 'lover' in all the available senses of that word. The intricately interwoven ecstasy and desolation of the *Sonnets* are manifested partly through the poet's

---

[46] *Measure for Measure*, 1. 4. 39.
[47] *Antony and Cleopatra*, 4. 15. 101; *Romeo and Juliet*, 3. 2. 8–9.
[48] Sonnets 30, 42, 104, 111, 133.
[49] Sonnet 144, l. 11.
[50] Sonnets 32, l. 4; 63, l. 12.

realization of how transitory are the appropriate senses of 'lover', as one meaning seems to become applicable only to turn a moment later into a marker of betrayal or self-deception.

The vocabulary which was available to Shakespeare for describing sexual relations between men consisted primarily of pejorative labels for particular sexual roles, such as 'sodomite', 'catamite', or 'ingle'—none of which Shakespeare used, though he did make Thersites say that Patroclus was Achilles' 'male varlot' and 'masculine whore':[51] Thersites is the only person in the Shakespeare canon who makes such sneering definitions. The poet who would write about bonds between men which are fashioned by reciprocal emotion and desire had only the words of another world at his disposal. The literature which exploits the multiple meanings of such words as 'friend' and 'lover', and insists upon indefinition, may be carefully avoiding the kind of precision which would lead a man to execution; but it may also be exploring desires which found expression and acceptance within a continuum of masculine relationships. So long as sexual exchanges between men satisfied the participants, and reinforced rather than endangered the social fabric, why seek to define, to label, and to judge?

There were, however, many texts which sought to define sex between men punitively.[52] The following examples may help to map parts of the conceptual field. Sodomy was particularly associated with un-English and un-Christian (especially un-Protestant) figures. William Perkins, writing of the idolatry which he sees as a hallmark of Catholicism, associates physical with spiritual deviance:

we are to consider the foule attendants and companions that go with the worshippe of idols, namely adulteries and fornications. For in the judge-ment of God, they are left to bodily fornication that give themselves to that which is spiritual. Paul saith, that the Gentiles because they dishonoured God in idols, were *for this cause given up to the lusts of their owne heartes, unto uncleannesse to defile their owne bodies, and to commit sinnes against nature* (Rom. 1. 14). When the Israelites fell from God to idols, (2 King. 13. 27) oftentimes they fell to Sodomie. In Italie for their Idolatries [they] are left to themselves to permit the stewes, and to abound (as the fame is) in whordomes and fornications.[53]

---

[51] *Troilus and Cressida*, 5. 1. 15–17.

[52] Further examples are provided by Alan Bray, Cameron McFarlane, Rictor Norton, and myself in *LBM*.

[53] William Perkins, *A Warning against the Idolatrie of the Last Times* (Cambridge, 1601), 91.

Here sodomy is deployed as an example of the consequences of turning away from God, and as a form of idolatry, a kind of parody. And
given the Protestant view that Catholicism was idolatrous, and the
mass a parody of true worship, the connections between sodomy and
popery almost make themselves. Robert Milles, while identifying the
sins of Sodom as '*Pride, Fulnesse of bread, Idlenesse, Contempt of the
poore*', rather than anything sexual, moves seamlessly from his passing
observation that 'the horrible and namelesse sinne of *Sodom* hath
poisoned some' to focusing on the idolatrous practices of Catholics,
'many *Labans* with his woodden gods, close Papists at their beades . . .
such are jugling Jesuites, and secret Seminaryes'.[54] It was not without
some justification that the papacy—here ventriloquized by Dekker in
the guise of the Empress of Babylon—complained that

> our Babylonian Sinagogue,
> Are counted Stewes, where Fornications
> And all uncleannesse Sodomiticall,
> (Whose leprosy touch'd us never) are now daily acted.[55]

This is one aspect of the conceptual field of 'sodomy' which persisted
across the seventeenth century. According to *Sodom Fair: or, The
Market of the Man of Sin* (1688), Pope Julius 'did usually commit the
abominable Sin of *Sodomy*, with Two Young Noble Men, whom *Ann*
Queen of *France* had sent to one Cardinal *Robert Nevetensis* to be
educat'.[56] This pamphlet is largely an account of the heterosexual
debauchery of the popes, and the trade in indulgences and dispensa-
tions, but the point about the young noblemen being sodomized by
the Pope serves economically to reinforce Protestant abhorrence of the
Whore of Babylon at a time when the Catholic James II was busily pro-
moting his co-religionists.

The prevalence of sexual relations between men was seen as one of
the distinctive characteristics of Italy, and, in Thomas Nashe's well-
known formulation, the Englishman who ventured there might bring
back from his travels 'the art of atheism, the art of epicurising, the art
of whoring, the art of poisoning, the art of sodomitry'.[57] The Spanish

---

[54] Robert Milles, *Abrahams Suite for Sodome. A Sermon Preached at Pauls Crosse the
25. of August. 1611* (London, 1612), sigs. C4^v, E5^r.

[55] From *The Whore of Babylon* (1607) in *The Dramatic Works of Thomas Dekker*, ed.
Fredson Bowers, 4 vols. (Cambridge, 1953–61), ii. 502.

[56] *Sodom Fair: or, The Market of the Man of Sin* (London, 1688), 5.

[57] Thomas Nashe, *The Unfortunate Traveller and Other Works*, ed. J. B. Steane
(Harmondsworth, 1972), 345. For a survey of English attitudes to Italian vices generally,

too are accused of sodomy in Lewis Lewkenor's *A Discourse of the Usage of the English Fugitives* (1595).[58] Further afield, *The English Rogue* explains that sodomy was once widespread in Siam, 'to prevent which, 'twas wisely ordered, (though strangely) that the males as soon as born, should have a bell of gold (and in it a dry'd Adder's tongue) put through the prepuce and flesh'. This eminently sensible precaution, however, was evidently not a sufficient deterrent, so to encourage the men to take an interest in women, 'the women here (still the more to allure the men from that detestable and unnatural act of *Sodomy*) go naked.' The narrator, however, discovers that the practice of sodomy is still prevalent, for as he is having his way with one of the local girls, a Siamese priest, a '*Satyr-Goat-Devil* (I cannot invent a name bad enough to call him by) presently falls down upon us; and taking me thus unawares, lying on my belly, I was not able to help my self, that he had like to have performed his business.' But the priest is pulled away by the girl's companions, and tied up. Then, the narrator continues, 'taking out my knife, I could not find in my heart to spare him one inch; and that he might not have any witnesses left of what was done, I took away his testicles too'. Thereupon our hero rejoins his ship.[59] Sodomy appears to be innate in Siamese men, only controlled with exceptional methods, and still practised by their heathen priests. The source for this edifying anecdote was Francis Petty's account of the voyage of Thomas Cavendish through the south seas, where on the island of Capul he encountered the practice of driving a nail through the penis when a boy is young:

This custome was granted at the request of the women of the countrey, who finding their men to be given to the fowle sinne of Sodomie, desired some remedie against that mischiefe, and obteined this before named

---

see Andreas Mahler, 'Italian Vices', in Michele Marrapodi *et al.* (eds.), *Shakespeare's Italy: Functions of Italian Locations in Renaissance Drama* (Manchester, 1993; 2nd edn. 1997), 49–68, and for the sexual behaviour associated with Italy in the minds of Renaissance Englishmen see Williams *s.vv.* Florence, Italian fashion, Venice. For a historian's view of homosexual relations in Italy see Michael Rocke, *Forbidden Friendships: Homosexuality and Male Culture in Renaissance Florence* (New York, 1996); Guido Ruggiero, *The Boundaries of Eros: Sex, Crime, and Sexuality in Renaissance Venice* (New York, 1985).

[58] Lewis Lewkenor, *A Discourse of the Usage of the English Fugitives by the Spaniard* (London, 1595), sigs. E4^{r-v}.

[59] [Richard Head], *The English Rogue Described in the Life of Meriton Latroon* (London, 1665), 100–3.

of the magistrates. Moreover all the males are circumcised, having the foreskinne of their flesh cut away. These people wholly worship the devill, and often times have conference with him, which appeareth unto them in most ugly and monstrous shape.[60]

Petty's account weaves together various forms of the monstrous and the diabolical which Head happily embroiders into a narrative of the triumph of the red-blooded Englishmen.

On the borders of Christendom, and a major threat to it, were the Turks, and the Turks were regularly associated with sodomy.[61] Thomas Coryat noted the custom of the country in a passage which reveals a curious train of thought and association of ideas:

All the Turkes and others, that doe ride in Constantinople or Galata, doe cover the backe and buttocks of the Horse with a faire cloth. The Turkes are exceedingly given to Sodomie, and therefore divers keep prettie boyes to abuse them by preposterous venerie. A Cock and Hen of Phesants sold for sixtie Aspers, and Partridges for twentie Aspers a paire.[62]

From buttocks, to sodomy, to the price of a cock. 'Preposterous' fuses the meanings of 'inverted in position', back to front, and 'contrary to nature'.[63] When in 1685 the Turks were threatening to overrun Europe, and extirpate Christianity, the trauma of discovering that the enemy was at the gates of Vienna was figured through images of rape and buggery:

> Here, Lustful *Tarquins* tender Virgins Rape,
> Not Beauteous Boys can the lew'd Villains scape.
> Acts, not to mention with a modest mind,
> As they by Vice and Nature were inclin'd.[64]

A marginal note explains: '*Buggery much used amongst the* Turks.' The formulation in the final line is instructive: sodomy is perceived to be natural to the Turks, but at the same time a vice in which they indulge. Are they, as it were, naturally unnatural?

Tales recounted by those travellers who were captured by the Turks

---

[60] *Amazons, Savages, and Machiavels: Travel and Colonial Writing in English, 1550–1630: An Anthology*, ed. Andrew Hadfield (Oxford, 2001), 197. I am grateful to Professor Hadfield for identifying this as Head's source.

[61] See Nabil Matar, *Turks, Moors, and Englishmen in the Age of Discovery* (New York, 1999), 109–27; Williams, *s.v.* Turk.

[62] Samuel Purchas, *Hakluytus Posthumus or Purchas His Pilgrimes*, 20 vols. (Glasgow, 1905), x. 425.   [63] *OED* 1, 2; cf. p. 193 below.

[64] W. C., *The Siege of Vienna, A Poem* (London, 1685), 7.

suggest that there was more than a grain of truth in the myth. Robert Bargrave, in prison in Constantinople in 1650, found that his gaoler released him from the stocks and offered him his own 'litle Hovell' for the night, but his 'proffers of Kindness were such to mee, as are unfitt to Discourse, & horrid to remember'.[65] William Atkins recalled an incident when he and eleven other English Catholic students (forming an apostolic twelve) were captured by Turkish pirates while making their way from St Omers to Seville.[66] One night a 'Tragicall Passage' ensued:

It was that feast day of the Nativitie of the ever most undefiled Virgin Mary, joyfull to angells and men, and onlie abhorr'd by the devills and theire consorts. At the time when sunn being set and al honest mindes betaken themselves to rest, one of our master Turks whose infamous name was Arche, inflam'd with rageing lust upon the bodies of some of our more tender companie, came downe amongst us, and after many amorous lookes & gestures to prepare his way, he first blowes forth the lighte. Wee had constantlie a lamp burning amongst us in the nighte time, for light and lust are deadlie enemies. Shame foulded up in blind concealing nighte, when most unseene then most doth tyranize.

Atkins develops the tale as a Manichaean battle between Darkness and Light, Lust and Virginity. The allegorical character of his last remarks about light and lust becomes all the more apparent when we realize that Atkins has been influenced by the Renaissance tradition of sententious verse, and that he is dramatizing his plight in Shakespearian terms, for the end of this paragraph comes verbatim from Shakespeare on Tarquin's rape of Lucrece:

> For light and lust are deadlie enemies,
> Shame folded up in blind concealing night,
> When most unseene, then most doth tyrannize.[67]

The unacknowledged quotation helps to shape the frame of reference.

Arche attempts to rape several of the young men, who put up a spirited resistance, and 'by the goodness of God and the assistance of his Blessed Mother over her parthenian[68] children all behaved

---

[65] *The Travel Diary of Robert Bargrave Levant Merchant (1647–1656)*, ed. Michael G. Brennan (London, 1999), 106.

[66] William Atkins, 'A Relation of the Journey from St Omers to Seville, 1622', ed. Martin Murphy, *Camden Miscellany XXXII* (London, 1994), 235–8.

[67] William Shakespeare, *The Rape of Lucrece*, ll. 674–6. Another reader noted the sententious quality of the last two lines, which are underlined in the copy of the 1598 edn. in the library of Trinity College, Cambridge.   [68] Virginal.

themselves most valliantlie', even though Arche was 'more cruell to us then ever proud Tarquin was to chaste Lucretia'. The next night, Arche tries again, starting to rape one youth at knife-point; but as a true Catholic martyr he prefers death to submission, and cries out: 'Here, here is my throate! Quench here thy filthie lust, I will hazard the last dropp of my bloud rather than offend my God!' The Turkish sailors eventually become suspicious at the disorder below decks, and Arche's villainy is brought to light. The commanders of the vessel tell their captives

that though by the worlde they were counted & called barbarians and knowne enemies to all Christians, yet they were not so inhuman nor barbarous as to let passe such crimes unpunished, especiallie those against nature, and if they were at land (as they were at sea) the delinquent by the lawes of the greate Mahomett was to be burned alive (though they after-wards observed that this wholesome lawe is not executed amongst them).

Asked what punishment they would like inflicted on Arche, the Christians find it politic to demur, and ask simply to be left in peace. The episode dramatizes the purity of the Catholic students, under the protection of the Virgin Mary, whom only devils and the devilish could detest; and presents for our edification the heroic but passive resis-tance displayed by the youths, one of whom prefers death and purity to life and defilement. Difference of gender apparently presents no problems in constructing the young male students as versions of Lucrece facing the tyrannical and lustful power of Tarquin. The youths share Lucrece's Roman virtues of purity and honour (compounded here by these being specifically Roman Catholic virtues), while the Turk as Tarquin exemplifies the abuse of power and the inability to govern one's lust.

However, when Sir Paul Rycaut described the prevalence of sex between men among the Turks, the account which he gave presented a more complex picture.[69] Describing 'the method of the *Turkish* Studies and Learning in the *Seraglio*', Rycaut observes that the young men's reading of Persian literature provides them with ideals to emulate:

It teaches them also a handsome and gentle deportment, instructs them in Romances, raises their thoughts to aspire to the generous[70] and virtuous actions they read of in the *Persian* Novellaries, and endues them with a

---

[69] Paul Rycaut, *The Present State of the Ottoman Empire* (London, 1667), 31–3. See the discussion by Matar, *Turks, Moors, and Englishmen*, 121–3.

[70] Here 'gentle' and 'generous' both mean 'noble'.

kind of *Platonick* love each to other, which is accompanied with a true friendship amongst some few, and with as much gallantry as is exercised in any part of the world. But for their Amours to women, the restraint and strictness of Discipline, makes them altogether strangers to that Sex; for want of conversation with them, they burn in lust one towards another, and the amorous disposition of youth wanting more natural objects of affection, is transported to a most passionate admiration of beauty wheresoever it finds it.[71]

Nabil Matar points out that, for once, what is being described here amongst the Turks is a homoerotic relationship, not the sexual exploitation of a victim.[72] Rycaut stresses both the idealistic origins of the passion in a reading of noble literature which encourages 'a kind of *Platonick* love' between the young men; and, on the other hand, the practical circumstances of the absence of women which apparently diverts the boys' desires from 'more natural objects of affection'. Rycaut acknowledges the Turks' enthusiasm for Platonic love, but (as sceptical as Hobbes before him) regards this as no more than a way of excusing their lust:

the Doctrine of Platonick love hath found Disciples in the Schools of the *Turks*, that they call it a passion very laudable and virtuous, and a step to that perfect love of God, whereof mankind is only capable, proceeding by way of love and admiration of his image and beauty enstamped on the creature. This is the colour of virtue, they paint over the deformity of their depraved inclinations; but in reality this love of theirs, is nothing but libidinous flames each to other, with which they burn so violently, that banishment and death have not been examples sufficient to deterre them from making demonstrations of such like addresses; so that in their Chambers, though watched by their Eunuchs, they learn a certain language with the motion of their eyes, their gestures and their fingers, to express their amours; and this passion hath boiled sometimes to that heat, that jealousies and rivalties have broken forth in their Chambers without respect to the severity of their Guardians, and good orders have been brought into confusion, and have not been again redressed, untill some of them have been expelled the *Seraglio* with the Tippets of their Vests cut off, banished into the Islands, and beaten almost to death.

 Nor is this passion only amongst the young men each to other; but Persons of eminent degree in the *Seraglio* become inveigled in this sort of love, watching occasions to have a sight of the young Pages that they fancy, either at the Windows of their Chamber, or as they go to the *Mosque*, or to

---

[71] Rycaut, *Present State*, 31.   [72] Matar, *Turks, Moors, and Englishmen*, 122.

their washings or baths; offer them service and presents, and so engage them as to induce them to desire to be made of the retinue of him that uses this Courtship towards them, which they many times obtain, and being entertained in the service of a Master who so highly fancies and admires them, they become often sharers with him in his riches and fortune.[73]

Though Rycaut quickly redescribes this Platonic love as mere unnatural lust, he does at least bring before the reader the Turks' own way of conceptualizing these relationships. We are told about homosexual love between youths of the same age, complete with courtship strategies, jealousies, and rivalries; while the relationships between older and younger men are shown to result in wealth and security for the boys. Though this is an exotic space—the seraglio—it is recognizable space in which boys quarrel in their bedrooms, and older men watch opportunistically from windows. Rycaut's interpretation may be jaundiced, but his sense of responsibility as an observer of a foreign country leads him to present love and sex between men in an unusually realistic manner.

By contrast with the punitive definitions which associate alien races and religions with sodomy, there is a fluid, productively indefinite vocabulary for intensely affective male relationships at home. This poses problems for modern interpreters. How do we read the apparently homoerotic idiom of the exchanges between Milton and Diodati?[74] Or the 'marriage of souls' between Donne and John King?[75] Or the use of phallic symbols in Cavalier clubs?[76] Or the moment when Josias Bodley, travelling through Ireland in 1602–3 was surprised, but phlegmatic, about the way his male companions behaved one morning. The group had been sharing a bed (as was common), and were awakened by the arrival of the servants:

servi domestici, scientes quod erat tempus surgendi, in cubiculum nostrum venirent ad incendendum ignem; subito sumus omnes expergefacti, et salutavimus alter alterum (sicut mos est apud bene educatos): sed

[73] Rycaut, *Present State*, 33.

[74] See John T. Shawcross, 'Milton and Diodati: An Essay in Psychodynamic Meaning', *Milton Studes*, 7 (1975), 127–63, revised in his *John Milton: The Self and the World* (Lexington, 1993).

[75] See E. E. Duncan-Jones, 'Marriage of Souls', *London Review of Books* (7 October 1993), 4.

[76] Timothy Raylor, *Cavaliers, Clubs, and Literary Culture: Sir John Mennes, James Smith, and the Order of the Fancy* (Newark, NJ, 1994), 76.

erant ex nobis aliqui qui salutabant socios per viam de retro, quod non erat, meo judicio, valde honestum, quamvis nonnulli dicunt esse bonum pro lumbis; sed nihil male fit quod non male accipitur.[77]

The principle *nihil male fit quod non male accipitur* aptly describes the handling by contemporaries of the case of Finch and Baines.[78] Sir John Finch (1626–82) and Sir Thomas Baines (1622–80) were life-long companions, and from the days when they shared rooms in Christ's College, Cambridge, as pupils of the Platonist Henry More, to their deaths within months of each other, they were inseparable. Finch's diplomatic career and Baines's medical studies took them abroad, particularly to Italy and Turkey, where Finch was for a time ambassador at Constantinople, and where Baines died. We know that Baines at one point dissuaded Finch from marrying,[79] but the question of what happened or did not happen sexually between these two men is beyond our reach. Yet we can study the language which contemporaries used to figure this uncommon union. Robert Bargrave recorded meeting 'M[r] John Finch & his Sociat[80] m[r] Baines, two remarkeable Patternes for Learning and Virtue'.[81] An Italian observer, committing both an error of transcription and a Freudian slip, wrote that Finch was visiting Italy 'with Thomas Penis, a Briton also, whom the similarity of studies had brought together, so that they had all things in common'.[82] This stress on their studies and their virtue suggests that when such an unusual union is referred to, its scholarly foundations and its moral character need to be clarified. Baines himself emphasizes the impor-tance of virtue when asking Sir John Covell to find him a suitable boy:

---

[77] 'The domestic servants, knowing that it was time for us to get up, came into our bedroom to light the fire; at once we all awoke, and greeted one another (as the custom is among the well educated): but among our party there were some who greeted their companions the back way, which was not—to my way of thinking—very decent, although some say that it is good for the loins; but nothing is amiss which is not taken amiss': Bishop Reeves, 'Bodley's Visit to Lecale, County of Down, A.D. 1602–3', *Ulster Journal of Archaeology*, 2 (1854), 73–95, at 87. The bishop omits most of this passage from his English translation of Bodley's Latin. The imperfect tense in *salutabant* indicates that this was a regular habit: 'they were accustomed to greet' would be an alternative translation.

[78] See Archibald Malloch, *Finch and Baines: A Seventeenth Century Friendship* (Cambridge, 1917).

[79] BL MS Add. 23215, fol. 40[r], Finch to Lord Conway, 27 July 1661.

[80] 'associate, colleague; companion, comrade' (*OED*).

[81] *Travel Diary of Robert Bargrave*, 230.

[82] Quoted in Malloch, 24.

My Desire is to you, that you would seek the University & find me out some poor Lad who Understands Latin & Writes an Indifferent good Hand; I would have Him Humble & Industrious, without which Knowledge & Vertue Never grows; I would have Him Neither Ugly nor beautifull for in Either it seldome Gows;[83] T'is enough you knowe my Temper. Mʳ Brown writes to Doctour Blyth to procure another, They are both promiscuously to serve My Lord & Me in Our Chambers, & particularly one of them to be an Amanuensis for Me.[84]

It would not be difficult to read a sexual agenda into this letter, but it would surely be a misreading. The letter is hardly private, being in the hand of an amanuensis, and Baines's interest in the boy's beauty, or lack of it, is carefully presented as an index to the lad's virtue. But the example may stand as a reminder of the precariousness of our interpretations.

It is particularly notable that the two men were accepted as a couple by Finch's aristocratic family. On Baines's death, Finch reminded his brother that he 'knew all things that ever passed between us'.[85] And it appears from a letter which Baines wrote to Finch's brother-in-law, Lord Conway, that the three men had been discussing the nature of love and friendship: Baines suggests that one of Conway's arguments had been put forward not because he believed it, so much as because it allowed him to compliment the couple:

Your Lordshippe tells mee, that surely there are other causes of love then Nature, Interest, Complacency, and Correspondency, which is the similitude of souls . . . every man is pleased with Himselfe, or hath a complacency in Himselfe, if so then every man (if it stands with his Interest) Loves that in another naturally, for which Hee likes himself, then, my Lord, I conclude that similitude of soules comes under complacency; and it is more then correspondency, for a man loves a man because Hee correspondes with Him though it is not of an inward principle as complacency is . . . and thus much, my Lord as to this objection, though I thinke your Lordshippe made use of it rather to usher in your civill expressions to your Brother and my selfe then any thing else.[86]

This seems to be the work of a man who is juggling Platonist and Hobbesian readings of love. But whatever one makes of this as a

---

[83] 'Gows' may be 'grows' or 'goes'.
[84] BL MS Add. 22910, fol. 193ᵛ; 22 May 1679.
[85] Quoted in Malloch, 71.
[86] BL MS Add. 23215, fols. 34ʳ⁻ᵛ; no date, *c*.1658?

philosophical argument, it is clear that Baines is thinking aloud to Conway about what draws men together, about how his relationship with Conway's relative might be explained.

Around 1681 Finch wrote in a draft dedication to Baines:

'Tis now full thirty-six years since I began the happinesse of a uninterrupted friendship which the world never yet did equal, nor I believe will ever parallel. This alone might very well entitle you to this dedication, as a monument of our friendship. But though friendship is a thing sacred and coelestiall, yet I take gratitude to be a higher nature ... all that I doe or ever shall know, is deriv'd from those many hours of tendernesse which[87] your regard for me made you throw away from your most severe thoughts ... no wonder if our thoughts became so familiar to each other that sometimes wee forgott to whom they originally belonged ... of the twenty-six years wee spent together since wee first left England ... wee never have bin separated two moneths from each other unlesse it were in the exercising some act of kindnesse.[88]

For Finch, Baines provided an 'inimitable as well as unrequitable friendship', and the two enjoyed an 'intimate and endearing communication together'.[89] 'Friendship' is clearly the word which comes to mind most readily to describe their union, but it seems to need some qualifiers which mark it out from ordinary friendship: 'which the world did never equal'; 'inimitable as well as unrequitable'. Finch's observation that 'friendship is a thing sacred and coelestiall' perhaps draws on verses written by Baines which begin by echoing the hymn *Veni Creator Spiritus*:

> Come holy friendship from above,
>   Coelestial Branch of Royal race
> Thy father is the God of Love
>   No longer hide thy heavenly face.[90]

So Finch returns the idea to its author as a testimony of their closeness.

The union may have been without parallel, but not without imagery; though the imagery is wried a little in the effort to find

---

[87] of MS.

[88] Quoted in Malloch, 73–4.

[89] Quoted in Malloch, 74

[90] BL MS Add. 29921, fol. 69ᵛ; transcribed 1681; not in Baines's hand. The MS also includes 'The Hermit', attributed to Baines, an accomplished poem in praise of retirement which has some similarities with Marvell's 'The Garden'. Two poems by Marvell, transcribed from the 1681 folio, appear on fols. 80–1.

suitable figures. Finch compliments Baines in words which were originally addressed by Aeneas to his father Anchises,[91] and in the epitaph which he wrote for his companion he adapted Virgil's lines on Nisus and Euryalus:

> Vivam Charissimé! Memor Nostrae Amicitiae, et
> Nulla Dies Unquam Memori Nos eximet Ævo.[92]

The epitaph repeatedly refers to their friendship, *amicitia*, but also calls their union *suave et irruptum Animorum Connubium | Indivulsumque . . . Sodalitium*.[93] Henry More, in his inscription on the joint monument which was erected to the couple in Christ's College, says that their *Cor erat unum, unaq. Anima*.[94] The design of the monument, as Jean Wilson has noticed,[95] takes over motifs used in memorials for married couples, while also including emblems of virginity: the iconography denotes both love and chastity. The public face of the *connubium* of Finch and Baines carefully stressed its purity as well as its uniqueness.

The poetry of Nicholas Oldisworth (1611–45) celebrates male relationships in an idiom which adds an erotic colour to the self-consciously Platonizing language used by and about Finch and Baines. His poems circulated in manuscript, no doubt primarily for an all-male readership.[96] Several poems are addressed to 'M[r]. Richard Bacon, a hopefull Youth who was sometimes a scholar of Westminster schoole, where hee was generally praised & beloved. At last hee dyed in Travaile'.[97] They had been schoolboys together at Westminster, then Oldisworth

---

[91] *Aeneid*, 6. 112–14; quoted in Malloch, 74.

[92] Quoted in Malloch, 76: 'I shall live, dearest, remembering our friendship, and no day shall ever remove us from the memory of the age.' The source is *Aeneid*, 9. 446–7. For the passionate friendship of Nisus and Euryalus, often interpreted as homosexual, see Paul Hammond, *Dryden and the Traces of Classical Rome* (Oxford, 1999), 150–6. An anonymous contemporary used another Virgilian reference when he called Baines Finch's *fidus Achates* (BL MS Sloane 3322, fol. 166[r]).

[93] Quoted in Malloch, 75: 'a sweet and unbroken marriage of souls and undivided companionship'.

[94] Quoted in Malloch, 84: 'heart was one, and one their soul'.

[95] Jean Wilson, ' "Two Names of Friendship, but one Starre": Memorials to Single-Sex Couples in the Early Modern Period', *Church Monuments*, 10 (1995), 70–83.

[96] Though it is worth noting that one collection was prepared by Oldisworth for his wife: Bodl. MS Don. c. 24 (autograph); another collection is now Folger Shakespeare Library, Washington, MS V. a. 170. For an account of Oldisworth see John Gouws, 'Nicholas Oldisworth and MS Don. c. 24', *Bodleian Library Record*, 15 (1995), 158–65.

[97] MS Don. c. 24, fol. 9[r].

moved to Oxford, and Bacon to Cambridge for a year before enrolling at the Catholic college at Douai in 1629, aged 18.[98] At one point we find the heading 'On the death of his deare friend Mr. Richard Bacon', but the rest of the page is poignantly blank.[99] In a poem to Bacon addressed 'To his friend beyond sea', written in 1629 (*aet.* 18), Oldisworth sees the physical separation between the two men as a way of freeing their souls to achieve a spiritual communion:

> Place doth not sunder, or divide
> Our hearts, but makes them stretch more wide.
> Our passions, which before did lie
> In prison, now abroad doe flie.
> > The breadth of Place
> > Gives fancie space,
> And setts our soules at liberty.
>
> And all the Winde twixt us and Thee
> Is but a puffing Agonie
> Of sighs and Blasts which doe expire
> From the vast depth of our Desire.
> > And this is Winde
> > Of such a kinde,
> As onely blowes, not cooles the fire.[100]

But is 'spiritual' the right word? Oldisworth may write of their souls being set free, but the language of passions, desire, agony, and the fire of love is strongly erotic. Their passions were imprisoned while the two men were in physical proximity, but can now be liberated into the imagined space which both separates and joins them, the place where 'fancie' is free. But we should pause over the pronouns. 'Our' in the first stanza refers to Oldisworth and Bacon, but 'us' and 'our' in the second appear to denote those left behind in England, not only Oldisworth himself but their mutual friends. The homoeroticism links Oldisworth and Bacon but also figures a homosocial bond within the all-male undergraduate milieu. At such points our terms 'homoerotic' and 'homosocial' are too prescriptive for the nuances and complexities of the poetry which they try to describe.

A similar situation arises when Oldisworth writes of Bacon in his verses 'To the University of Cambridge. 1631'. Oldisworth imagines

---

[98] *The Record of Old Westminsters*, ed. G. F. Russell Barker and Alan H. Stenning, 2 vols. (London, 1928), i. 38.   [99] MS Don. c. 24, fol. 74[r].
[100] Ibid., fol. 9[r].

himself as Bacon's 'absent self', and asks the Cambridge under-
graduates:

> Tell us, ô tell us, yee that had the grace
> So pure an Angel daily to embrace,
> Tell us the Heav'nlynesse of those Delights,
> Wherwith hee fedd your Hearings, & your Sights.[101]

These appear to be spiritual and intellectual delights, but the language
moves between the spiritual and the sensual. We know that religious
language (at least since Petrarch) often figures sexual desire (and vice
versa); 'embrace' could be physical or conceptual; 'pure' wards off the
idea of Bacon as a source of physical pleasures, while the feeding of the
sight reinstates it. The word 'grace' has a clearly religious meaning
(especially in proximity to 'Angel'), but in the sense of 'a favour conferred' is commonly used for the granting of sexual satisfaction.[102] The
use of the first person plural rather than singular suggests that the poet
is writing on behalf of a community of admirers, not as a private friend
or lover. The passion is a passion which defines a male community.

That Oldisworth is aware of Bacon's physical as well as his intellectual beauty we see in another poem 'To his Friend beyond sea':

> Bacon, thou hardly wilt believe that Wee
> Which are so zealous in commending thee,
> Should scarce endure to heare thy publick Praise:
> Yet so it is. When any stranger sayes,
> Thou hast the active bodie of thy Father
> And thy faire Mother's face; wee had farre rather
> That hee would swear how thou wert uggly grown,
> Or how thy Teeth & Haire were not thine owne.
> Why art thou handsome. Beauty is the pride
> Not of a Gentleman, but of a Bride.
>   Truly wee hope that though thou wentst from hence
> Sweet, prety, and delightfull to the sense,
> Time will impaire thee so, that wee may finde
> Noe gifts at thy Returne, but in thy minde.
> Not that wee wish thee any kinde of ill
> (Wee for thy Welfare pray, wee blesse thee still)
> But that wee have noe other way to prove

---

[101] MS Don. c. 24, fol. 18ʳ.

[102] *OED* 8; Williams, *s.v.* It recurs in contexts which suggest that sense in some of the
following quotations from Oldisworth; and cf. Machin's use, p. 48 below.

The constancie and purenesse of our Love.
What thanks deserve wee, if wee doat on feature?
A thing, which ravishes each silly creature.
Wee dive into thy Soule, and there finde out
Jewels and Mines not dreamt-of by the Route.
  Doe, doe: continue fine. This shall bee all
Thy recompense, that where wee us'd to call
Thee our deare Brother, now another while
Our comely Sister thee wee will enstile.[103]

The poem attends entirely to a reading of Bacon's beauty. Though Bacon was 'Sweet, prety, and delightfull to the sense' when he left England, he ought to lose his good looks by the time he returns, because the loss of beauty is a guarantee of his manliness; and at the same time the loss of such beauty will guarantee that his male admirers love him only for his spiritual not his physical charms. Male beauty is dangerous, it seems, in that it effeminizes the possessor and ensnares the observer, effeminizing him too, since only a woman ('silly creature') would 'doat on feature'. Once again the first person plural creates a coterie of admirers. The love which is prized here is love of the soul; but the beauty which excites the male gaze is beauty of the body.

And there is no doubt that what Bacon's beauty arouses is desire; the word is used again in the lines 'On the picture of yong M^r. Bacon, as it is sett upp beyond sea, and enti[t]led The picture of Beauty':

Here joyned you see white snowe, and purple Fire
The one does move, the other quench desire.
Feare not or freezing or excessive heate:
The worst that can fall outt, is, but cold sweate[.]
Oh, who of such a Mixture can complaine
Where still the cure is equall to the paine.[104]

Here the youth's beauty includes a coldness which quenches the desire which it arouses.[105] But if homosexual desire is cooled by the snowy chastity of the beloved in this poem, its fulfilment is figured in 'A Sonnet'. Though 'Vertue' is the note on which the poem begins, and the second stanza invokes wisdom to array the male lover's mind, the poem celebrates the lover both sensuously and sensually:

[103] Ibid., fol. 28^v.
[104] MS V. a. 170, p. 313.
[105] I am not sure what Oldisworth intends 'cold sweat' to signify in this context.

> Fresh colours, and harmonious sounds
>   Feede his Hearing and his Sight,
> Sweete tastes, and smells, observe noe bounds
>   In flattring him with choise delight[.]
>   By the best of humane blisse
>   Lett him guesse what Heaven is.[106]

The 'best of humane blisse' which prefigures heaven suggests sexual consummation, and when the poem says that 'I and Nature all our treasure | On him, are agreed to spend', it is hard to ignore the sexual resonance of 'treasure' and 'spend'.[107]

Bacon's absence, which permitted the expression of passion in the first poem we considered, allows Oldisworth to celebrate him sensually and sexually in his poem 'On an Arbour made by Mr Richd Bacon, on the sea-shoare opposite to the Isle of Wight'. The topos of the *locus amoenus* is reworked, with the owner's absence central to the poem's conceit. The garden contains traces of Bacon, but not the man himself:

> When I approacht that happy place,
>   Where once my Friend was wont to rest,
> Each object was so full of grace,
>   Mee thought I was all over blest:
> What-ere I saw, what-ere I felt,
> What ere I heard, what ere I smelt,
>   My sences told my soule, that shee
>   Just thus in Paradise should bee.
>
> The plants there, polisht by his hand,
>   So greene, so tall, so upright growe,
> And in such dainty order stand,
>   As if their Authour they did knowe,
> Their barkes are faire, their stockes are strong
> Their leaves are sweete, their twiggs are long
>   And ev'ey branch, and ev'ey limbe
>   Retaines a certaine [   ] of Him.[108]

[106] MS V. a. 170, p. 308.

[107] 'treasure' = genitals or semen (Williams, *s.v.*); cf. Shakespeare, Sonnets 6, ll. 3–4 and 20, l. 14; *Othello*, 4. 3. 87; and see p. 75 below. The phrase 'perfume the windes' suggests an echo of Shakespeare's description of Cleopatra's barge: 'so perfumed that | The Windes were Love-sicke with them' (*Antony and Cleopatra*, 2. 2. 200–1).

[108] MS V. a. 170, pp. 322–3. A word such as 'trace' or 'mark' is missing from the last line.

The arbour empty of its master symbolizes the unattainable lover. But the lover's effect on the poet is signalled through his effect on the garden: the upright plants stand because they are 'polisht by his hand', and 'ev'ey branch, and ev'ey limbe I Retaines a certaine [   ] of Him'. The erect plants betoken sexual arousal, but the man who should turn the metaphorical into the actual is missing.

A poem addressed to a different friend, 'For a gentleman. I To yong Mr. Henry Gresley', most unusually traces the rebuttal of a sexual approach and its translation into godly friendship.[109] Beginning with a pun on Henry's name (Hal[l]/Hell), Oldisworth writes:

> Were I in heav'n, Hall, or were I with Thee,
>   (Thy presence is a heav'n to mee)
> By visions, not by wordes, I would disclose
>   Why thee, on earth, my Friend I chose.

The choice began with an attraction to Henry's physical beauty, which the poet reads as a sign of virtue:

> First, I would shew thee how thy pleasing face
>   Promis'd an Heart enrich'd with Grace,
> Through thy faire eyes, I could espie within
>   Much vertue, and scarce any Sinne.

But the poet's discovery of the lad's virtue is not altogether welcome, as Henry has evidently made it clear that there can be no question of sex (or any 'carnall' 'delight') between them—which is what, it seems, the poet had in mind until he realized that such a suggestion would shatter their friendship:

> I sawe a modestie, which did invite
>   And yet did hinder, my Delight;
> Thou wert so holy, thou to sleepe, or drinke
>   Wouldst blush, and it too carnall think:
> Oh, how thy noble Blood mounted, and flam'd,
>   When to thee first I Friendship nam'd!
> Pure friendship 'twas; and 'tis: else I should sure
>   The hell of losing thee endure.

Henry's startled recoil at the very mention of friendship suggests that the word was often used with sexual connotations, and the poem

---

[109] Henry Gresley (*c*.1615–1678) attended Westminster and Christ Church Oxford at the same time as Oldisworth, but seems to have been about four years his junior. See *DNB s.v.* Greisley.

carries traces of a conversation which seems to have rapidly toured the semantic field of 'friendship' until Henry was satisfied that he was not being asked to play Juliet to Oldisworth's Romeo. Having registered this sexual possibility, and recorded its rejection, the poem moves to an extravagant conclusion in which the poet's love for Henry is turned Platonically into a love for God:

> Tell mee, yee Cherubins, who dwell in Light,
>   Have I done well? is my Choise right?
> Have I on goodnesse my affection[110] plac'd,
>   And by a proxy God embrac't?
> Have I my JESUS, in my Harry, lov'd?
>   Is friendship now Devotion prov'd?
> If yea, then Christ smiles on our mutuall Troth,
>   And is a third Friend to us both.
> An unity here is, if noe Trinity,
>   I, thou, and Christ: Christ, thou, and I.[111]

The 'mutuall Troth', normally a term used for the plighting of marriage vows, is here a sacred friendship. The poem has effected a remarkable journey from sexual desire to Platonically sublimated desire expressed as love for God, resulting in a friendship in which Christ will forever be a third party.

In Oldisworth's poetry, erotic pleasure in another man's beauty is articulated in situations which prevent its private physical satisfaction—when the object is absent; when the passion is shared homosocially; when the friends have agreed to define their love as pure and sacred friendship. Once again, *paradiastole*, redescription, emerges as an essential figure in the rhetoric of homoerotic relations.

POTENTIAL SPACES

Among the potential spaces in which sex between men could be imagined, Catholic Italy seems to have been regarded with a mixture of attraction and repulsion. Indeed, one might say that in the conceptual space labelled 'Italy', two discourses are at play: the one, the punitive discourse of sodomy and anti-popery; the other, the homoerotic discourse which delights in finding a space where sex between men can be

---

[110] For the meaning of 'affection' see Ch. 2 n. 119 below.
[111] MS Don. c. 24, fols. 73r–v.

staged. Occasionally the two come together, as in the play *The Divils Charter* by Barnabe Barnes, which both displays the wickedness of a diabolical and sodomitical Pope, and at the same time allows a vein of homoerotic lyricism to complicate the imaginative space which the drama fashions.

Barnes's play was published in 1607, shortly after it had been staged before James I by 'his Majesties Servants', who were Shakespeare's own company. It dramatizes the life and death of Pope Alexander VI (1431–1503). Though the play is introduced by the figure of Guicciardini, thus ostensibly promising a faithful historical narrative,[112] the moralizing purpose of the drama is immediately established by the prologue:

> Behold the Strumpet of proud Babylon,
> Her Cup with fornication foaming full
> Of Gods high wrath and vengeance for that evill,
> Which was imposd upon her by the Divill.[113]

Guicciardini waves his rod three times to summon up a dumb show which presents Alexander bribing the papal conclave and then obtaining the papacy by a pact with the devil, in a Faustian bargain 'For certaine yeares agreed betwixt them two'.[114] This framing device creates a form of theatrical space which turns the characters into *exempla*, and promises an uncomplicated, moralized display. In the play's second scene, two gentlemen list the new Pope's characteristics:

> such prophane and monstrous *Sodomie*,
> Such obscure Incest and Adultery,
> Such odious Avarice and perfidie,
> Such vinolence[115] and brutish gluttony,
> So barren of sincere integritie.[116]

Sodomy heads the list of sins, and is the only one italicized by the compositor, so perhaps we are supposed to recognize this as the worst of the Pope's vices. But when Barnes actually begins to dramatize Alexander's homosexual desire, the play moves from such predictable propaganda to something much more ambiguous.

In Act 3 we meet two young brothers, Astor and Phillippo Manfredi,

---

[112] I cannot find anything in Guicciardini's history of Italy which provides a source for Pope Alexander's homosexual interests as staged by Barnes; indeed, he was notorious for his womanizing.

[113] [Barnabe Barnes], *The Divils Charter: A Tragaedie Conteining the Life and Death of Pope Alexander the Sixt* (London, 1607), sig. A2ʳ.

[114] Ibid., sig. A2ᵛ.   [115] Drunkenness.   [116] Ibid., sig. A4ʳ.

the first of whom is being courted by the Pope. There is a remarkable clash of languages at this point. Astor laments that the kind of life and liberty which he enjoys at the papal court is worse than death or servitude, and prays that

> He that with fire and Brimstone did consume
> *Sodome* and other Citties round about
> Deliver us from this soule-slaiding[117] sinne,
> To which our bodies are made prostitute.[118]

But when the Pope woos Astor, he is given the language of lyrical homoeroticism:

> *Alex.*   *Astor?* what *Astor?* my delight my joy,
> My starre, my triumph, my sweete phantasie,
> My more then sonne, my love, my Concubine,
> Let me behold those bright Stars my joyes treasure,
> Those glorious well attempred tender cheekes;
> That specious[119] for-head like a lane of Lillies:
> That seemely Nose loves chariot triumphant,
> Breathing *Paruhaian*[120] Odors to my sences,
> That gratious mouth, betwixt whose crimosin pillon[121]
> *Venus* and *Cupid* sleeping kisse together.[122]

This draws on the tradition of the erotic blazon, which is usually an itemized description of female beauty, and translates Astor into the object of homoerotic pleasure. And this is not exclusively for Alexander's benefit, as the erotic reading of the handsome young actor's features offers this pleasure to an audience which included King James. At the same time, the language has its ridiculous moments ('That seemely Nose loves chariot triumphant') which suggests that Alexander's infatuation is being satirized just enough to deflect criticism from the censorious. Alexander's language moves into another register when he explains to Astor the benefits of having an older lover:

> And though in age I love, know that desire
> In riper yeares is pure and permanent,
> Grounded on judgement, flowing from pure love:
> Whereas the love lightning from young desire,
> Fickle and feeble will not long hold fire.[123]

---

[117] Soul-slaying.   [118] [Barnabe Barnes], *The Divils Charter*, sig. E1ᵛ.
[119] Handsome.   [120] Not clear: Peruvian? Parrhasian (= Arcadian)?
[121] Pillou, i.e. pillow.   [122] Ibid., sig. E2ʳ.
[123] Ibid., sigs. E2ʳ⁻ᵛ.

The sober epigrammatic force of these latter lines would make them perfectly plausible in another context, in a handbook of conduct, or an anthology of sententious poetry such as *Englands Parnassus.*

Alexander then moves to a sexual invitation which elaborates the sensual attractions of the room which he has prepared as the setting for sex with Astor:

> see thy Chamber:
> The walles are made of Roses, roofe of Lilies,
> Be not asham'd to mount and venture it,
> Here *Cupids* Alter, and faire *Venus* hill is.
> Thy bed is made with spice and *Calamus,*
> With Sinamond and Spicnard, Arabick,
> With Opobalsam and rich gums of *Ægipt,*
> Musick *Angelicall* of strings and voyces,
> With sundry birds in sugred simphony,
> Where whistling Wood-nimphes, and the pleasant choise is
> Of Antique action mixt with harmony,
> Attend thy joyous entrance to this Chamber.[124]

The chamber is several kinds of space: an imagined space off-stage (for the Pope is leaning out of his window at this point); a mythologized place of sensual pleasures like Spenser's Bower of Bliss; and a redescription of Alexander's own body as the site of erotic pleasures: 'Be not asham'd to mount and venture it, | Here *Cupids* Alter, and faire *Venus* hill is.' An audience familiar with Spenser would know that such enticing rhetoric needs to be received sceptically; but it is nevertheless remarkable that Alexander's courtship of Astor should be conducted in a romantic and sensuous language which has the capacity to delight an audience. If this is 'monstrous *Sodomie*', it is rather appealing. And Astor himself is actually so tempted by the prospect that he has to pray for strength to resist it:

> *Ast.*   Oh blessed heavens let Sathan tempt no longer,
> His force is powerfull yet thy strength much stronger.
> He that with guilefull baites gilded untruth,
> So seekes to blast the blossome of my youth.[125]

Here is the other side of Barnes's double vision: from Alexander as romantic suitor we switch to Alexander as powerful Satan. But we note that Astor is tempted: is Barnes assuming that any man is in principle

---

[124] Ibid., sig. E2ᵛ.   [125] Ibid., sig. E3ʳ.

vulnerable to any temptation from the devil; or that any young man is liable to be interested in homosexual pleasure? Is this, as it were, part of a discourse of sodomy (of the demonic) or of homoeroticism (of the desirable)? As the Pope continues to offer sensual pleasures—fruits, wines, jewels—Astor agrees to visit him, after first attending mass. There is a gap in the plot at this point (not unusual in Barnes's disjointed play) but we infer that Astor did indeed give in to Alexander's appeals when the Pope's own son, Caesar Borgia, accuses him of keeping

> the Pearle of *Italie*,
> *Astor Manfredi* that young vertuous Prince,
> In beastly lust, and filthy *Sodomie*,
> Blasting the blossome of his toward youth.[126]

The final scene involving the Pope and the two brothers is even more remarkable in its mixture of homoerotic fascination with moral recoil.[127] Astor and Phillippo enter from a vigorous game of tennis. Tennis is a Renaissance metaphor for sex,[128] so certain homosexual possibilities are teasingly floated at the outset. The game has left them hot and sweaty, so they strip off their shirts and are rubbed down by servants, who bring them clean linen.[129] They then lie down on a bed together, and the servants leave the stage. Music plays—and music on the Renaissance stage is typically a sign of heightened emotion, often specifically evoking the lowering of one's guard against temptation, and the rousing of the senses. The boys fall asleep in each other's arms, for the Pope's henchman Barnardo has drugged the pair on Alexander's orders. The scene provides a homoerotic image and invitation: the half-undressed youths lying together on the bed, 'sweet boyes . . . | So sweetly knit in one' as Barnardo describes them as he

---

[126] [Barnabe Barnes], *The Divils Charter*, sig. G4^r.

[127] Ibid., sigs. I2^v–I4^r.

[128] Williams, *s.v.* tennis.

[129] What exactly is the spectacle which King James and his courtiers would have witnessed? The boys have entered '*in their wast-cotes*', and at this period a man would normally have worn a shirt under a waistcoat. Astor says that 'My wastcote well can witness for I sweate', and Barnardo calls for servants to bring clean linen, i.e. clean linen shirts. The actors presumably took off their waistcoats and shirts; Phillippo tells the barber, 'Rub my head first then combe it'. But it is not just his head which is rubbed, for the stage direction says: '*After the barbers had trimmed and rubbed their bodies a litle, Astor caleth*'. They presumably put clean shirts on, because Alexander later undoes them.

stands watching. Alexander enters and orders Barnardo to leave. He is now alone with the young men, who are totally at his mercy.

What he intends is not rape, but murder; but it is murder with a clear sexual charge. The ubiquitous Renaissance pun on 'die' meaning 'reach orgasm' is implicit in the stage action. He fantasizes about sending them to paradise, a paradise which will surround them with sensual pleasures reminiscent of those which he had earlier offered Astor:

> Where such sweet musick un-con-ceiveable,
> Shall entertaine your senses in sweet comfort,
> As the delight thereof shall never die.[130]

Alexander approaches the bed, pulls open the lads' shirts ('*He stireth and moveth them opening both their bosomes*', says the stage direction), and then applies an asp to each boy's bare chest, self-consciously re-enacting the death of Cleopatra. Addressing the snakes, he says:

> Take your repast upon these Princely paps.
> .   .   .   .
> And you my lovely boyes competitors,
> With *Cleopatra* share in death and fate.[131]

The boys rival Cleopatra in their beauty and their sexual appeal, which is emphasized by the way the audience's attention is drawn to their 'Princely paps', their noble chests. Alexander's address to the snakes displays pleasure in the murder, which is clearly an enacted metaphor for sexual possession:

> What now proud wormes? how tasts yon princes blood.
> The slaves be plump and round; in to your nests,
> Is there no token of the serpents draught[?]
> All cleere and safe[?] well now faire boyes good-night.[132]

The homoeroticism of this scene is complex; it will vary in actual performance, and in the uninhibited theatre of the reader's imagination. The display of the brothers' bare torsos no doubt offered visual pleasure to spectators such as King James; while the reference to Cleopatra enlists the audience's memories of Shakespeare's play and associates this tableau with the scene in which other boy actors (or perhaps the same actors) played out the deaths of Cleopatra and

---

[130] Ibid., sig. I3ᵛ.   [131] Ibid., sig. I4ʳ.   [132] Ibid.

Charmian.[133] The heady eroticism of Cleopatra is, it seems, transferable unproblematically across genders to enhance the allure of a young man. But it is also possible to imagine the play's presentation of the Pope's sexual interest in Astor as a rebuke or taunt to King James. What Barnes's play offers is a double response to the imagined homo-eroticism of contemporary Italy through the creation of a mode of theatrical space which accommodates two viewpoints: on the one hand, moralizing denunciations of sodomy—especially as it is associated with the Whore of Babylon—and the presentation of degenerate and ultimately murderous homosexual desire in an old man for a young man; on the other hand, lyrical homoerotic courtship language which only occasionally becomes grotesque, and pleasure both verbal and visual for members of the audience with homosexual interests.

But it was the classical tradition stemming from ancient Greece and Rome which provided writers and readers with the richest resources, the most extensive and varied potential space within which the homo-erotic imagination might play.[134] Platonic love—however that might be construed—was set out in the *Symposium*, which was accessible to readers with a command of its relatively straightforward Greek, or in Latin (but not English) translation. Plato was not widely read in this period, though the outlines of his ideas on love were familiar from secondary sources.[135] The Latin and Greek historians, such as Plutarch, Tacitus, and Suetonius, who were widely read in the original languages and in translation, would have informed readers about the sexual tastes of the Roman emperors, the love of Alexander the Great for Hephaestion, and Hadrian for Antinous, or the report that Julius

[133] Katherine Duncan-Jones suggests that the same actors who played Astor and Phillippo may also have played Cleopatra and Charmian, which would have added an erotic frisson for those who knew this (*Ungentle Shakespeare* (London, 2001), 304). However, there is no evidence that Shakespeare's play was ever staged.

[134] For sex between men in the ancient world (actual and imagined) see K. J. Dover, *Greek Homosexuality* (Cambridge, Mass., 1978, 2nd edn. 1989); David M. Halperin, *One Hundred Years of Homosexuality* (New York, 1990); Bernard Sergent, *L'Homosexualité dans la mythologie grecque* (Paris, 1984); Craig A. Williams, *Roman Homosexuality: Ideologies of Masculinity in Classical Antiquity* (New York, 1999).

[135] *The Cambridge History of Renaissance Philosophy*, ed. Charles B. Schmitt (Cambridge, 1988), 79–80; T. W. Baldwin, *William Shakspere's Small Latine & Lesse Greeke*, 2 vols. (Urbana, Ill., 1944), ii. 652; Stuart Gillespie, *Shakespeare's Books: A Dictionary of Shakespeare Sources* (London, 2001), 411–12; Anna Baldwin and Sarah Hutton (eds.), *Platonism and the English Imagination* (Cambridge, 1994).

Caesar had been the 'catamite' of King Nicomedes of Bithynia. Homer told of the love of Achilles for Patroclus,[136] and Virgil the love of Nisus and Euryalus.[137] Satirical poems or passages on homosexual practices and effeminate men were penned by Juvenal, Martial, and Persius; and even if some editions were bowdlerized for schoolroom use, the complete texts were available for those who were interested.[138] The pastorals of Theocritus and Virgil (especially the latter's *Eclogue* 2) spoke of the unrequited loves of shepherds, and Virgil's poem would have been familiar to any man with a grammar school education. Virgil himself was said to have preferred sex with men.[139] Lyrical expressions of homosexual desire were voiced in the first person (though not necessarily autobiographically) by Horace, Martial, and Anacreon. Sometimes seventeenth-century translations concealed or changed the gender of the original addressee: Thomas Stanley's versions of Anacreon regularly make the poems refer to women, while Cowley's are sometimes completely sexless.[140] But one anonymous translator took Martial's *Epigram* 11. 8 as the basis for a highly charged list of metaphors for his boyfriend's kisses—though the epigram has a sting in the tail:

> *Of His Boyes Kisses*
> Like Balsams chaf'd by some Exotick fayre:
> Or from a saffron feild fresh gliding ayre:
> In winter chests like Apples ripening:
> Or grounds o'r spread with budding trees in spring:
> Like silken roabes in royall presses: and
> Gumms suppled by a virgin's soft white hand;
> As broaken jarrs of Falerne wines doe smell,
> Farr off: or flowry Gardens where Bees dwell:
> Perfumers potts: Burnt Incence lost ith' ayre;

[136] Though some ancient sources made Achilles in love with Troilus: see Timothy Gantz, *Early Greek Myth: A Guide to Literary and Artistic Sources*, 2 vols. (Baltimore, 1993), ii. 601–2; Piero Boitani (ed.), *The European Tragedy of Troilus* (Oxford, 1989), 16–18.

[137] See note 92 above.

[138] On the availability and censorship of erotic classical texts see Roger Thompson, *Unfit for Modest Ears* (London, 1979), 3–6, 10.

[139] '*Virgil* was furnish'd well, with boy and bed' (*Aeneas his descent into Hell*, tr. John Boys (London, 1661), sig. A3ᵛ, citing Juvenal, *Satire* 8). See also pp. 217–18 below.

[140] *The Poems and Translations of Thomas Stanley*, ed. Galbraith Miller Crump (Oxford, 1962), 74–100, and see p. 58 below; Abraham Cowley, *Poems*, ed. A. R. Waller (Cambridge, 1905), 58.

Chapletts new fall'n from rich perfumed hayre:
What more? All's not enough: mixed all express
My deare Boys morning kisses sweetnesses.
You'ld know his Name. I'll nought butt's kisses tell.
I doubt, I sweare, you'ld know him farre too well.[141]

This is a close translation, and all the heady images have an equivalent in the Latin, which has not only prompted but in a way licensed the richly sensuous lines.

Ovid, perhaps the early modern period's favourite classical writer, told the stories of Narcissus' infatuation with his own image which he took for that of another man, of Jove's love for Ganymede, Apollo's love for Hyacinthus and Cyparissus, and Orpheus' preference for boys after the loss of his wife Eurydice.[142] Ovidian narrative, and narrative modelled on Ovid, allowed and sometimes encouraged the reader's imagination to take pleasure in the male body. For example, the renderings of the Narcissus story in the anonymous *Fable of Ovid Treting of Narcissus* (1560) or in Golding's translation of the *Metamorphoses* (1567)[143] provide descriptions of the youth which allow one to take a sensuous delight in his beauty; and since the story opens by indicating that both men and women desire the lad (Golding writes that 'The hearts of divers trim yong men his beautie gan to move'[144]), Echo can be our surrogate in the story. The moment when Narcissus, in despair, pulls off his shirt and beats his chest is an opportunity for a description which compares the boy's skin with the allure of apples, or nearly ripe grapes:

he barred all his cheste
Before the well with stonye fystes, and beates his naked breste

---

[141] *Martial in English*, ed. J. P. Sullivan and A. J. Boyle (Harmondsworth, 1996), 155–6, from BL MS Add. 27343.

[142] The stories of Orpheus, Jove, and Apollo are grouped together in *Metamorphoses*, 10. 78–219. For homoeroticism in Ovid see Jonathan Bate, *Shakespeare and Ovid* (Oxford, 1993), 48–65.

[143] *The Fable of Ovid Treting of Narcissus* (1560) in *Elizabethan Narrative Verse*, ed. Nigel Alexander (London, 1967), 27–32; *Shakespeare's Ovid: Being Arthur Golding's Translation of the Metamorphoses*, ed. W. H. D. Rouse (London, 1961), 71–5; both translating or adapting Ovid, *Metamorphoses*, 3. 346–510. By contrast, James Shirley's *Narcissus or the Self-Lover* (1646) devotes little space to any physical description of Narcissus, and does not allow the reader much homoerotic pleasure in the youth (*Elizabethan Minor Epics*, ed. Elizabeth Story Donno (London, 1963), 325–51). For other homoerotic descriptions of the nude male, including Marlowe's *Hero and Leander* (1598), see *LBM* 33–8.   [144] Ovid, tr. Golding, l. 439.

Wyth a carnacion hue, by strockes thereon dyd leave
None other wyse then apples whyte, wyth ruddy sydes receave,
Or as the growyng grapes, on sundry clusters strepe
A purpyll coler as we se, or ever they be rype.[145]

Lewis Machin, writing of the love of Apollo for Hyacinthus in 1607, relates how Apollo first saw that boy:

Thus wandring up and downe without this grove
He spyed a boy, that after game did rove,
His bowe was in his hand, shafts by his side,
His curled haire did all his shoulders hide.
A well shapt face he had, pleasing to view,
A fine streight bodie, and a hart most true,
Apollo staide and gaz'd uppon his face.[146]

Ovid's story says nothing about how Apollo first glimpsed Hyacinthus, and offers no description of him; it is Machin who introduces the work of the eye, and eroticizes the boy not only through the physical description but also by making him a hunter, for hunting is a common image for sexual pursuit.[147] (Hyacinthus is an active hunter, not merely Apollo's prey.) And while Ovid says simply

inmemor ipse sui non retia ferre recusat,
non tenuisse canes, non per iuga montis iniqui
ire comes, longaque alit adsuetudine flammas.[148]

Machin adds the boy's loving response to Apollo, their conversation, and their physical contact:

---

[145] *The Fable of Ovid*, ll. 159–64.

[146] Lewes Machin, 'Three Eglogs, The first is of Menalcas and Daphnis: The other two is of Apollo and Hyacinth', in William Barksted, *Mirrha the Mother of Adonis: or, Lustes Prodigies* (London, 1607), sig. E5ʳ. The first of the eclogues of Apollo and Hyacinthus occupies sigs. E5ʳ–E6ᵛ. I have silently corrected lower case to upper case letters at the beginning of lines, added quotation marks to clarify the speeches, and emended other punctuation as indicated in square brackets. However, this entails deciding who speaks the invitation 'Here growes hie grasse': it could be Apollo rather than Hyacinthus, for the original's lack of punctuation makes this ambiguous. Machin is discussed by Bly, *Queer Virgins and Virgin Queans*, 94–7.

[147] See Ch. 3 n. 121 below.

[148] Ovid, *Metamorphoses*, 10. 171–3: 'Unmyndfull of his Godhead, he refused not too beare | The nets, nor for too hold the hounds, nor as a peynfull mate | Too travell over cragged hills, through which continuall gate | His flames augmented more and more' (tr. Golding, ll. 180–3).

For he did dote upon this lovely youth,
Whose heart was all composde of melting ruth,
And seeing *Phebus* come, the boy did stay him,
He saide 'youth, will you walke', heede not denay him
But went along together hand in hand:
And Zephire with calme winde their faces fand,
Then *Phebus* said, 'faire youth what make you here'
'Kinde courteous stranger for to kill the deere[;]
To heare the birds to sing, the waters glide:
Tumbling in curls along a greene banke side,
More sweete content in harmlesse woods is found
Then in great Citties[:] there doth sinne abound.
But here husht quiet keepes us companie,
Free from all cares, and bad societie:
Here growes hie grasse, lets sit and make it flat,
And so beguile swift time with pleasing chat:'
So hand in hand, they sat them on the ground,
Where little birds did make harmonious sound,
But *Phebus* heart did pant and leape with joy,
When he beheld that sweete delicious boy.
His eyes did sparkle, love his heart flamde fire,
To see this sweete boy smile, is his desire.
Then with an ardent gripe[149] his hand he crusht,
And then he kist him, and the boy then blusht,
That blushing coulour, so became his face
That *Phebus* kist againe, and thought it grace
To touch his lips, such pleasure *Phebus* felt,
That in an amarous deaw his heart did melt.[150]

Machin's landscape both provides a setting for the lovers and itself figures the boy, as the very waters are 'Tumbling in curls'. This is marked out as an innocent landscape, a pastoral setting which knows nothing of the sin of the city; and yet the sexual pleasure which Apollo reaps from the boy is amply signalled, culminating in 'amarous deaw'. But the episode ends tragically, as Hyacinthus is killed by a discus. Machin's explanation of the lad's death attributes it to the gods: Apollo has neglected his duties as sun-god, and the earth no longer receives the light which it needs:

And now *Apollo* wayving towards the west,
Unteam'd his fierie steedes, and let them rest

---

[149] Grip.   [150] Machin, 'Three Eglogs', sigs. E5ᵛ–6ʳ.

Whilst he discended on this ball of earth,
To sporte with *Hiacinth* strange unknown mirth
For which the Gods were angrie, and decreed
They wold remove the cause, the boy must bleed.[151]

Why, exactly, are the gods angry? Does the 'strange unknown mirth' refer to the gender of Apollo's lover, or to the fact that the god has not previously neglected his duties? The fluid syntax permits both readings, so permitting the possibility that it is Apollo's unnatural sexual choice which is punished. Machin's eclogues have provided a richly imagined world of homoerotic satisfaction, but he seems to feel the need to end with a framing gesture which at least permits the expression of moral disapproval.

The freedom with which homosexual desire could be handled in a classical framework is illustrated by *The Most Delectable and Pleasaunt History of Clitiphon and Leucippe*, translated by William Burton in 1597 from the Greek novel by Achilles Tatius (written originally in the second century CE) and dedicated to the Earl of Southampton, Shakespeare's patron. Clitophon is in love with a girl, Leucippe, and has a younger male cousin Clinias who is in love with the boy Charicles. After various adventures the cousins meet Menelaus, who is also a lover of boys, and Clitophon asks him to explain the attraction. The resulting speech is perhaps the most extended defence of homosexual pleasure in early modern English. Clitophon asks:

'what is the cause why so many are in love with boyes?[152] surely I my selfe cannot tell, neither see any cause why?' Then answered *Menelaus*, 'what, is it not I pray you better then the love of women? boyes are more perfect[153] then women, and their beautie is of more force to delight the senses with pleasure.' 'But I pray you (quoth I) how is it more vehement? What, for because as soone as it appeareth it is gone again, neither giveth any possibility for the lover to enjoy it: but is like to *Tantalus* in the river *Stix*, that when he would drinke of the water it flyeth away from him: neither is there any sustenance left for him to receive: and that also which is drunke, is first taken away: before that hee which drinketh can be satisfied: evermore he must depart so from his lover, as if there hadde beene never no such love, or else but newe beganne, and the pleasure is mingled with a kinde of sorrow: and hee is ever drie, but his thirst can never be quenched.' Then sayde *Menelaus*: 'but you *Clitiphon*, doo not seeme to knowe which is the

---

[151] Ibid., sig. E6ᵛ.
[152] Burton omits the suggestion that this 'is now the custom': ἐπιχωριάζει νῦν.
[153] 'More open, more frank': ἁπλούστεροι.

cheefest felicitie[154] in love: that alway is most to be wished for, which
bringeth no lothasomenesse,[155] and wherewith one is never satisfied: for
those things which remaine the longer to us for to enjoy them, do take
away the delight thereof with too much sacietie, but those thinges which
sometimes are taken away, are alway newe and do daily flourish: and as
much as is taken away from them by the shortnesse of time, so much is
added to the greatnesse of the desire, and theyr pleasure doth not fade: and
wherefore is the Rose accounted the fairest of all plants, but because it
soonest doth fade away: surely I doo thinke that there is two kindes
of bewtie which is amongst mortall men, the one heavenly, the other
common;[156] which indeede are the verie givers of all bewtie: and the
heavenlie bewtie scorneth to be joyned with our mortall; and therfore
striveth to flie up to heaven: the common bewtie creepeth on the ground,
and cleave[s] to every base[157] bodie: and if you will that I shall bring you a
witnesse for this which I have sayde, marke you the Poet *Homere*, whose
verses are these:

> *The Goddes incensed with bewtie of this Boy,*
> *To heaven him brought to serve great Jove above:*
> *In filling of sweet Nectar and Ambrosian wine,*
> *Who can deny, but that the cause was love.*'[158]

So Menelaus prizes the beauty of boys precisely because it is so fleeting:
its very evanescence intensifies the pleasure which it brings. And this
passing physical beauty is transitory because it is in fact heavenly, is on
the point of being caught up into heaven like Ganymede; it contrasts
with the 'common' beauty (associated with women) which 'cleave[s]
to every base bodie'.

Menelaus then turns to a more explicit contrast between the
physical pleasures afforded by boys and by women:

But now marke you me againe, and I will shewe you what pleasure is
reaped in the love of boyes.[159] In a woman, not only her words, but also all

---

[154] 'pleasure': ἡδονῆς.

[155] 'which bringeth no lothasomenesse' has no equivalent in the Greek.

[156] The idea is from Plato, *Symposium*, 180d–181c.

[157] 'base' is not in the Greek.

[158] *The Most Delectable and Pleasaunt History of Clitiphon and Leucippe*, tr. W. B.
(London, 1597), 43–4, translating 2. 35 . 3–36. 3. I have added quotation marks to clarify
the changes of speaker. The translation is discussed by Smith, 120–2. The Greek text is
quoted from Achille Tatius d'Alexandrie, *Le Roman de Leucippé et Clitophon*, ed. Jean-
Philippe Garnaud (Paris, 1991). The lines quoted from Homer are *Iliad*, 20. 234–5.

[159] 'what pleasure is reaped in the love of boyes' for 'what concerns boys': τὰ τῶν
παίδων.

her actions, are ful of subtiltie:[160] if some be faire, they may thanke the Painters shoppe: all whose bewtie, is compacted of nothing else, then of painting, colouring, and curling their haire, and in kissing: from whom, take away this painting and counterfetting of colours, and truly you will thinke them barer then a Jaye (as the Proverbe is) when all his stolne feathers are plucked from his backe: but the bewtie of boyes is not besmeared with the counterfeyt of painting, neither spunged up with borrowed perfumes: the very sweate of the browes of a boy, doth excell all the sweete savours of Muske and Civet about a woman: and a man may openly talke and play with them and never bee ashamed:[161] neither is there any tendernesse of flesh which is like to them:[162] their kisses do not savour of womens curiositie:[163] neither beguile with a foolish error:[164] the kisses of them are sweete and delightfull, not proceeding of art, but of nature: and the very image and picture of their kisses are so sweete and pleasant, that you might very wel thinke, that heavenly Nectar to bee betweene your lippes.[165]

Menelaus prizes the sexual pleasure which boys give partly because they do not counterfeit, as women do, who plaster their faces with cosmetics, and use a prostitute's techniques to simulate love. Boys, by contrast, are wholly natural in the way they give themselves up to love. Burton's rendering is generally very faithful to the Greek, diverging significantly only when Menelaus starts to explain that sex with boys is better because it is rougher, and when in the final sentence he describes

---

[160] 'ful of subtiltie' for 'plastered over, feigned': ἐπίπλαστα.

[161] 'a man may openly talke and play with them and never bee ashamed' for 'it is permitted, even before sexual intercourse, to meet a boy at the wrestling school and to embrace him in front of everyone, and these embraces have nothing shameful about them': ἔξεστι δὲ αὐτῷ καὶ πρὸ τῆς ἐν Ἀφροδίτῃ συμπλοκῆς καὶ ἐν παλαίστρᾳ συμπεσεῖν καὶ φανερῶς περιχυθῆναι, καὶ οὐκ ἔχουσιν αἰσχύνην αἱ περιπλοκαί.

[162] 'neither is there any tendernesse of flesh which is like to them' for 'and their bodies do not make sexual intercourse soft through the softness of the flesh, but their bodies strike hard against one another and struggle for pleasure': καὶ οὐ μαλθάσσει τὰς ἐν Ἀφροδίτῃ περιπλοκὰς ὑγρότητι σαρκῶν, ἀλλ' ἀντιτυπεῖ πρὸς ἄλληλα τὰ σώματα καὶ περὶ τῆς ἡδονῆς ἀθλεῖ.

[163] 'curiositie' (i.e. ingenuity and fastidiousness (*OED* 3–4), sc. in using cosmetics) for 'knowledge': σοφίαν.

[164] 'foolish error' for 'wanton trick': σινάμωρον ἀπάτην.

[165] *Clitiphon and Leucippe*, 46, translating 2. 38. 1–5. Burton omits the final sentence: 'and in kissing you can never be fully satisfied, but the more you take your fill, the more you thirst to kiss again, and you cannot tear away your mouth until the moment when, in ecstasy, you are beyond kisses': Φιλῶν δὲ οὐκ ἂν ἔχοις κόρον, ἀλλ' ὅσον ἐμφορῇ, διψῇς ἔτι φιλεῖν, καὶ οὐκ ἂν ἀποσπάσειας τὸ στόμα, μέχρις ἂν ὑφ' ἡδονῆς ἐκφύγῃς τὰ φιλήματα.

the stages which lead the lover to orgasm, which Burton leaves
untranslated.

By contrast with Burton's close rendering, and his richly sensuous
but far from salacious vocabulary, the next Englishman to translate
Achilles Tatius shied away from this material altogether. A. Hodges,
writing in 1638, reassured his readers that 'by the exection of the two
testicles of an unchaste dispute, and one immodest expression, I have
so refined the author, that the modestest matron may looke in his
face and not blush'—assuming, of course, that this modest matron
managed to read beyond Hodges's immodest opening metaphor.[166]
Where Burton says openly that Clinias 'was in love with a young boy',
Hodges says coyly that Clinias 'had formerly beene in love'; and when
the distraught Charicles confides in his lover Clinias that his father has
arranged a marriage for him, Hodges anxiously defines the reason for
Clinias' concern: he reacts 'as if his soule had beene joyned with his,
and not onely compassionate, but really sensible of what harmes might
befall *Caricles*'.[167] When Hodges reaches the discussion between Clitophon and Menelaus, he backs away, making Clitophon say: 'I began to
tell love stories, and merry tales, at length to talke much in commen-
dation of women, but *Menelaus* who had alwayes been their enemie
spake as much against them, so at last wee fel in a large discourse concerning the dignity of their sex, which I list not here to set down.'[168] And
there he ends the chapter. In the hands of Hodges the tale has been
transposed into the idiom of Cavalier gallantry: not for nothing does it
carry a commendatory poem by Lovelace, addressed 'To the Ladies'.[169]

It was the potential space offered by classical pastoral, and particularly
by Theocritus, that enabled Charles Goodall (1671–89) to write openly
homosexual poetry.[170] The date of these pieces tests the claim that
lyrical homoerotic verse disappeared in the late seventeenth century,
but they are a special case, juvenilia which voice a young man's
passionate longings, and they were subject to a form of self-censorship.

---

[166] *The Loves of Clitophon and Leucippe* [tr. A. Hodges] (Oxford, 1638), sig. A3^v.

[167] Burton, 2; Hodges, 11, 12.

[168] Hodges, 62.

[169] Hodges, sigs. A5^v–A6^r.

[170] Goodall receives a brief notice in the *DNB* under his father, the physician Charles
Goodall (1642–1712). The poet was educated at Eton and Magdalen Hall, Oxford, where
he matriculated on 22 March 1689. He died on 11 May of the same year, and was buried
in the antechapel of Merton College. He does not seem to have been discussed by
scholars of Restoration poetry.

His work first appeared in the anthology *Poetical Recreations* (1688) when he was a 16- or 17-year-old schoolboy at Eton.[171] Five poems are included: a paraphrase on Theocritus' *Idyll* 23; a chorus from Seneca's *Agamemnon*; and three love poems to a man, called 'The Penitent', 'To Duserastes', and 'The Vow. To the same'. In Theocritus' original poem, a shepherd falls in love with another man, but the beloved will have nothing to do with him. The shepherd kills himself in despair, while the unyielding object of his desires is punished for his hard-heartedness when a statue of Cupid falls on him at the baths, and kills him. Like Creech, but unlike Dryden, Goodall retains the masculine gender of the loved one.[172] However, when Goodall came to issue his own collection called *Poems and Translations* just a few months later, he too changed the gender, and inscribed the poem 'To Idera'.[173] Perhaps in the interval between the two publications someone had suggested to Goodall that it was imprudent to write so openly of homosexual desire, especially when the translation was offered in the context of other, original, homoerotic pieces: Creech, after all, could be said to have an obligation to provide a reasonably complete and accurate rendering of the Greek.

The rewriting of the poem begins when 'By chance a noble Youth came by' is turned into 'By chance a *beauteous She* came by'. Sometimes the language of erotic appreciation seems readily transferable between the genders, as when

[171] *Poetical Recreations: Consisting of Original Poems, Songs, Odes, &c. With Several New Translations. In Two Parts. Part I. Occasionally Written by Mrs. Jane Barker. Part II. By Several Gentlemen of the Universities and Others* (London, 1688), hereafter cited as *1688*. Goodall's poems appear in Part II, 247–65, under the heading, '*The Five following Copies done by Mr. C. G. of Æton-Colledge*' (ii. 247). The book was advertised in the *Term Catalogues* for Nov. 1687. Irregularities in the lineation of pindaric verse have been regularized in the quotations.

[172] Goodall's translation appears in *Poetical Recreations*, ii. 247–54, omitting the original ending. For Thomas Creech's translation see *The Idylliums of Theocritus with Rapin's Discourse of Pastorals Done into English* (Oxford, 1684), 111–14, where it is numbered 22. The translation of this poem is dedicated to John Riley the painter; one wonders why Creech thought it a suitable gift for him. Dryden's translation, which makes the cruel beloved a woman, was published in *Sylvae: or, The Second Part of Poetical Miscellanies* (London, 1685): see *The Poems of John Dryden*, ed. Paul Hammond and David Hopkins, in progress (London, 1995–), ii. 352–5.

[173] *Poems and Translations, Written upon Several Occasions and to Several Persons. By a late Scholar of Eaton* (London, 1689); hereafter cited as *1689*. The licence is dated 25 October 1688, and the book was advertised in the *Term Catalogues* for May 1689. The translation of Theocritus appears on 28–34. 'Idera' is from ἰδέρως, one who loves at first sight.

> Marking the Beauty of his Angel's Face,
> Mix't with sweet carriage, and a heavenly grace,[174]

becomes:

> Marking the beauty of her *Angel*'s face,
> Set off with a sweet *Carriage*, and a heavenly *Grace*,
> Blest with a pleasant *Mein*, and sprightly *Air*,
> And all the dear *Enchantments* of the *Fair*.[175]

The vacuous nature of the two lines added in 1689 hardly convinces one that Goodall is much interested in the attractions of women. Indeed, when the speaker laments the beloved's lack of response, Goodall's homosexual version is much more engaged and exercised about the possibility of some response than his heterosexual rewriting:

> Choler and anger in his *Entrails* boils,
>   No pleasant smiles,
>   No *rosie Lips*, nor *blushing Cheeks*,
>   Nor languish't *Eyes* that might betray
> An inward fondness, and might seem to say,
>   I will thy mutual love repay.
>   No comfortable words he speaks;
>   Nor suffers me to ravish one kind kiss,
> That entrance to a future, and more perfect bliss:[176]

'Nor suffers <u>me</u> to ravish one kind kiss' is an interesting slip from the narrative's third person mode to the first person. No 'more perfect bliss' is imagined with the woman, who is dismissed quite briefly:

> No *rosie Lips*, no *pleasant Smiles*,
> No *blushing Cheeks*, no *languishing Eyes*,
>   That might seem to *sympathize*;[177]

Goodall also loses a sexual pun when he changes the shepherd's lament that he can find 'no liquor that can quench my flame' in *1688* to 'no Water that can quench my Flame' for *1689*: in the heterosexual version it is no longer possible for the lover's flame to be quenched by the boy's liquor—his semen.[178]

---

[174] *1688*, 247.   [175] *1689*, 28.   [176] *1688*, 249.   [177] *1689*, 29.
[178] *1688*, 252; *1689*, 32. For 'liquor' meaning 'semen' see Williams, *s.v.*, and cf. Rochester's pun on 'liquor' meaning both semen and wine: 'Since you have that for all your hast I Att which I'le ne're repine I Will take his Likour of as fast I As I can take of mine' (*The Works of John Wilmot Earl of Rochester*, ed. Harold Love (Oxford, 1999), 24).

The three other love poems printed in 1688 were all omitted in the 1689 collection. These chart the speaker's obsession with a beautiful youth called Duserastes (from δυσέραστος: unfavourable to love, hard in love), who is sometimes unresponsive, sometimes dangerously available. 'To Duserastes' shows that the desired youth is an adolescent, as yet without a beard, whose beauty is represented in conventionally feminine terms. Duserastes will lose his looks as he gets older, warns the poet in a reassignment of conventional topoi designed to persuade the beloved to yield while there is yet time:

> O Cruel, Proud, and Fair,
> Cause of my *Love*, and cause of my *Despair*.
>   When first a little sprouting *Beard*,
>   Those lovely Lips, and Cheeks shall guard,
> Not soft as Down, but rugged, long, and hard.
> When lovely *Locks*, that on your shoulders play,
>   Shall turn to the cold hoary *Grey*,
> Or, wasting *Time* shall eat 'em quite away;
>   As when too much of working spoils
>   The very heart of fruitfull *Soils*,
> And makes 'em, without *moisture*, hard and dry,
> All *Plants* and *Herbs* do wither, fall, and dye.
>   And when that lovely *Red* and *White*,
>   That in your charming *Cheeks* do meet,
>   That make the *Lilly*, and the *Rose*,
>   Their sweetness, and their colour lose,
>   Shall turn to *Wrinkles*, wan, and pale,
>   And all your other *Charms* shall fail.
>   Then as you go to gaze
>   Upon you[r] former Angel's face,
> In your too much frequented *Looking-glass*;
> Then your own *Presence* will you strive to shun,
> And thus complain in a forsaken Lover's tone.
>   Why was I ever *Young*?
>   Why was not *Beauty* long?
> Why had I ever Charms, or why are they so quickly gone?[179]

Here Goodall has silently adapted Horace's *Carm*. 4. 10, which appears thus in one seventeenth-century translation, a version which makes no effort to disguise the homoerotic basis of the poem:

---

[179] *1688*, 262–3.

Tis true (proud boy) thy beauty may presume[:]
Thank Venus for't[;] but when thy cheekes shall plume,
When manly downe shall shade thy Childish pride
And when thy locks (which dangle on each side
Of thy white shoulders) shall no more remain;
When thy vermilion cheekes (which do disdain
The glorious colour of the purple rose)
Begin to fade, being rudely stuck with haires
(Hard hearted boy) then wilt thou say with teares
(When looking for thy faire self in a glass
Thou findest another there) Ah me! alas!
What do I now perceive? why had not I
These thoughts when I was lovely smooth? or why?
To these my thoughts which I now entertaine
Doe not my Cheekes grow slik & young again?[180]

Goodall has selected one of Horace's few openly homoerotic odes as the basis for his own poem, and has added the opening address which makes explicit what is implicit in the Latin, namely that the hard-hearted Ligurinus is being courted by the poet. So once again it is the classical tradition which provides the literary resources for homosexual courtship in English, though in this case Goodall has (perhaps naïvely) dispensed with the pretext of imitation which might have made his poem more acceptable.

Being attracted to this Duserastes is dangerous, as 'The Penitent'[181] suggests, for the poet is like a gnat repeatedly drawn back to the candle flame; or in a stronger image,

> As well one may
> Touch *flaming Coals*, or with a *Serpent* play,
>   And yet receive no harm;
> As look on you unmoved by your *Charms*.[182]

Indeed, he says, 'I play and dally on *Hells* brink'.[183] Nevertheless, the speaker relates how he broke his vow to have nothing more to do with Duserastes, and, buoyed up by wine,

> Threw me head-long to his Arms,
> Where tasting of his usual *charms*,
> No *Resolution* can with-hold me.[184]

[180] Anonymous translation in *Wit Restor'd in Severall Select Poems not formerly Publish't* (London, 1658), 63–4; terminal punctuation removed from ll. 6 and 12, and other punctuation emended as marked in square brackets.   [181] *1688*, 259–61.
[182] Ibid., 260.   [183] Ibid.   [184] Ibid., 259.

In Restoration poetic idiom there is no mistaking what tasting some-one's charms means.[185]

Goodall's emphasis on the danger of succumbing to Duserastes may be a recognition of the risks of a homosexual relationship; but the hell referred to may also be a state of emotional turbulence brought about by Duserastes' volatile temperament, and not (or not only) moral danger: 'I ask not mutual *Love* in equal weight, | But only give me leave to love thee free from *hate*'.[186] And 'The Vow. To the same', concludes with the speaker hoping that in heaven 'Here shall our *love* no quarrels know, our *joys* no end.'[187] It is only in heaven that the poet can imagine a satisfying relationship with Duserastes. Or, to put it another way, heaven is a satisfying relationship with Duserastes. 'In spite of Hell, to Heav'n we will glide'.[188] Is 'Hell' here the disapproval of others? Heaven is a classical heaven, where

> in Immortal State
> Shall I on yours, and you on *Jove*'s left hand be set.[189]

So even here there is inequality between the two, and

> You shall be worshipp'd as the *God* of *Beauty*,
> To you shall Mortals pay all sacred Duty,
> My *Name* shall signifie a *Faithfull Friend*.[190]

These four poems from *Poetical Reflections* express a passionate long-ing for another youth, with clear suggestions that this longing seeks sexual fulfilment, even while they recognize that friendship may be all that can be hoped for. Though they use a classical dress, they were seemingly too outspoken to find a place in Goodall's collected poems, and were not reprinted.

Poems and Translations is an accomplished volume, especially for an undergraduate, even if it is sometimes gauche and clichéd.[191] It mainly

---

[185] 'Charms' often refers specifically to the beloved's sexual attractions during inter-course: cf. '*Naked* she lay clasp'd in my longing Armes, | I fill'd with Love and she all over Charmes' (Rochester, 'The Imperfect Enjoyment', ll. 1–2; *Works*, ed. Love, 13); 'Thy Charms in that auspicious moment try' (Dryden, 'Lucretius: The Beginning of the First Book', l. 56, on Venus entwined with Mars; *Works*, iii. 45). [186] *1688*, 261.
[187] Ibid., 265. [188] Ibid., 264. [189] Ibid., 264. [190] Ibid., 265.
[191] The collection shows that Goodall has read carefully the major contemporary poets. Much of his style owes something to Cowley, and another influence is Oldham. Besides the volume's title, which echoes Oldham's *Poems, and Translations* (London, 1683), there is the couplet poem 'Oldham's Ghost' (117–21), in which the poet appears in a dream and urges Goodall to adopt his satiric purpose and style; and a translation of Juvenal 14 which is partly in Oldham's manner (136–52). Milton is honoured in 'A

comprises poems of love and friendship which lack the desperate passion and sexual allusions of the pieces printed in 1688, but are nevertheless striking in the homoerotic inflection which they persistently give to male relations. Translations from Anacreon allow Goodall to write suggestively about the boy Cupid:

> I heard the flattering Rascal speak,
> And could not but for pity's sake,
> In such a case, open the Gate,
> Which straight my Youngster enter'd at,
> With Bag and Quiver at his back.[192]

Writing in the person of Anacreon's pet dove, the poet takes pleasure in being a go-between in Anacreon's

> affairs of Love
> With his *Bathyllus*, that dear Boy,
> (Oh, happy state that I enjoy!)
> Lovely *Bathyllus*, he that can,
> By one sweet look, ev'n conquer Man.[193]

Unlike Thomas Stanley, who in 1651 had turned Anacreon's lover into the female 'Rodantha',[194] Goodall keeps the homosexual reference.

In Goodall's original poems, the classical pastoral mode once again licenses the expression of love between men. In 'Parting with His Dear Brother, Mr. *Ash Wyndham*' Goodall exclaims that 'I love you above all things here below', and uses imagery which suggests that the friend's absence deprives the poet of sexual consummation, as 'the *Fruit*'s forbidden for a time'.[195] In another poem to the same friend, 'Solitude. To his dear Brother, Mr. *Ash* Wyndham', Goodall describes the two men, styled Thyrsis and Corydon,[196] sharing an Edenic landscape—

Propitiatory Sacrifice, To the Ghost of J— M— by way of Pastoral' (110–17), while a translation of Bion's *Idyll* 2 is dedicated to Dryden (27). (Oldham had translated Bion's lament for Adonis.) However, in the poem on Milton, Goodall regrets that 'th' ambitious *Laurel*'s dead, | *Degraded to a Mercenary* Head' (115). Since the collection, though dated 1689, was licensed before the Revolution, the derogatory allusion must be to Dryden.

[192] *1689*, 5; 'gate' = anus, 'bag' = scrotum, 'quiver' = penis (Williams, *s.vv*).

[193] *1689*, 8.   [194] Stanley, *Poems and Translations*, 79.

[195] *1689*, 41–2. Ash Wyndham (*c*.1671–1749) was admitted as a Fellow-Commoner at King's College, Cambridge in 1691 (*Alumni Cantabrigienses*, ed. John Venn and J. A. Venn, 4 vols. (Cambridge, 1922–7), iv. 436).

[196] From Virgil's *Eclogue* 7, though the names also occur separately in Theocritus.

without Eve—which '*Adam* might envy in his *Paradise*', and where
they carve each other's names on the trees:

> Or else dissolv'd in Ease, lay down our heads
>> In *Slumbers* as our *Natures* kind,
>> Bound in each others Arms
>> By *Virtue's* strictest Charms,
>> Lull'd asleep by the *whistling Wind*,
> On easie *Velvet*, fragrant *Violet-beds*.[197]

Self-consciously defining the embrace, Goodall insists that it is
'*Virtue's* strictest Charms' which entwine the pair in each other's arms;
and the insistence is necessary, given that 'dissolved' is a ubiquitous
Restoration word for lovers in a state of orgasm.[198]

'To Mr. G. L. an Ode' celebrates another male friend with the assis-
tance this time of Catullus. His face is '*Angel* all in every line of it; |
Picture of *Beauty*, and the *Stamp* of *Grace*',[199] and his absence from
Goodall is spoken of through an adaptation of Catullus' lines to Lesbia:

> Each day, my Sun, since you withdrew your light,
> Has been an everlasting Night;[200]

> soles occidere et redire possunt:
> nobis cum semel occidit breuis lux,
> nox est perpetua una dormienda.[201]

'Parting with Mr. Tho. Bebington' calls the two friends Thyrsis and
Hylas—the latter being the boy loved by Heracles. It opens with
another comparison with paradise:

> Down by a *River's side* together sat
> *Thyrsis* and *Hylas*, (such was once the *State*
> Of our *First Parents*, in a *friendly Strife*,
> Thus *Innocence* might learn to square her life)[202]

Multiple definition seems to be in play here: the boys are like the
homosexual lovers of Greek pastoral and myth; they are like Adam and

---

[197] *1689*, 72–5.
[198] For examples see Dryden, *Poems*, ed. Hammond and Hopkins, ii. 336.
[199] *1689*, 43.
[200] Ibid., 44.
[201] Catullus 5. 4–6. Jonson translated the lines thus: 'Sunnes, that set, may rise againe: | But if once we loose this light, | 'Tis, with us, perpetuall night' ('Song. To Celia', ll. 6–8).
[202] *1689*, 131. Thomas Bebington was admitted as a pensioner at Christ's College, Cambridge in 1691, *aet.* 17, so was born *c*.1674 (*Alumni Cantabrigienses*, i. 120).

Eve before the fall; and they are a pattern of innocence: the very multiplicity of definition wards off any single interpretation of this as a
moment of sexual union. Later, Hylas on the one hand swears to maintain 'the sacred *League* of *Friendship*', and on the other makes Thyrsis
promise '*Kisses* to send by every gentle *Gale*'.[203] The poem concludes
with language which figures the pair's mutual pleasure in terms which
are commonplace in Restoration poetry for describing orgasm:

> This said, ravish'd into an *Ecstasie*,
> They would in their perfection die;
> And strugling hardly to themselves can come.[204]

Cupid arrives, and pierces each lad with an arrow, but it is, reassuringly, an arrow 'dipt in *Honours Flame*'.[205]

Goodall's poetry seems to lurch between images of erotic attraction
and sexual consummation on the one hand, and protestations of
honour and virtue on the other. This may be because he is self-
consciously protecting his potential space, allowing himself the
freedom to voice homosexual desire in quasi-classical pastoral at the
price of insisting from time to time on the purity of the friendship
which he is describing. Or he might not recognize the full extent of the
sexuality of his language. Or he might see nothing dishonourable or
lacking virtue in the sexual expression of male love. But one must
remark the difference between the two publications, for in *Poetical
Recreations* he writes of a passionate love for another man, a love which
is dangerous and brings anger and quarrels as well as satisfaction; in
Poems and Translations the tone has changed to one of celebratory
pastoral which may push at the boundaries of the acceptable idiom of
male friendship, but strives to maintain a decorum. In his own collection he is more exposed to view than in the relative obscurity of the
anthology, and perhaps on reflection he thought it wiser not to reprint
the pieces on Duserastes. It looks as if we meet here a 'ligne de partage'
which separates what can be said from what cannot: the heady expression of affection in pastoral guise was acceptable, if perhaps dated by
1689; but the desperate and ecstatic poems on Duserastes, the hard
lover, fell on the wrong side of the divide, and were removed from the
record.

Like many of the texts discussed in this chapter, Goodall's poems
evolve a form of doubleness in writing about sexual desire between
men. Even within the licensed space of classical imitation, gestures of

---

[203] *1689*, 132.   [204] Ibid., 134.   [205] Ibid.

reassurance seem necessary: this is translation, this is innocent friendship. So too Oldisworth's poems translate eroticism into group solidarity or religious devotion. Frequent *paradiastole* undoes what has just been said, turns the literal into the metaphorical, sublimates flesh into spirit; but *paradiastole* is not erasure, and the sexual meanings remain legible. Through processes of definition and blurring, through the shaping of possible but not everyday worlds, a language of homosexual love makes itself heard, and a literature is formed which invites alert, nuanced, and opportunistic reading. And no texts from this period simultaneously invite and ward off a homosexual reading more intricately than Shakespeare's *Sonnets*, to which we now turn.

2

Shakespearian Figures

SHAKESPEARE'S *SONNETS*: THE RHETORIC OF POSSESSION AND DISPOSSESSION

Despite the title of this book, it would be wrong to argue a *parti pris* and be too prescriptive about exactly what is figured in Shakespeare's writing about intense relations between men.[1] This chapter will, instead, explore the kinds of imagined space which Shakespeare creates for the presentation of strong male bonds; the ways in which he adapts his sources in order to create affective and sexual possibilities where none had existed; and the rhetorical figures through which male relations are delineated. It will then conclude by examining the ways in which editors and adaptors of Shakespeare later in the seventeenth century closed down these possibilities and erased homosexual meanings from his texts.

In the case of the *Sonnets*,[2] however, 'delineation', the drawing of lines, may well be exactly the wrong word for Shakespeare's procedure.

---

[1] I have offered an introductory account of homosexual relations in Shakespeare's work in *LBM* 58–87.

[2] I have found the following edns. and commentaries particularly helpful: *Shakespeare's Sonnets*, ed. W. G. Ingram and Theodore Redpath (London, 1964); *Shakespeare's Sonnets*, ed. Stephen Booth (New Haven, 1977); *The Sonnets and A Lover's Complaint*, ed. John Kerrigan (Harmondsworth, 1986); *Shakespeare's Sonnets*, ed. Katherine Duncan-Jones (London, 1997); Helen Vendler, *The Art of Shakespeare's Sonnets* (Cambridge, Mass., 1997). For discussions of the possible homoeroticism of the *Sonnets* see *LBM* 76–87; Joseph Pequigney, *Such is my Love: A Study of Shakespeare's Sonnets* (Chicago, 1985); Smith, 228–70. In the following discussion I make certain basic assumptions about the *Sonnets*: that poems 1–126 are all addressed to or concern the same young man, who also features in some of the subsequent poems addressed to or concerning a dark lady; that the poems may not be directly autobiographical, but nevertheless engaged Shakespeare's profound emotions; and that the poems as printed in 1609 are in the order which Shakespeare intended. None of these assumptions is beyond question.

It is not that his expressions are ambiguous; rather that in the *Sonnets* he seems addicted to multiple definitions which by their sheer pro-liferation over-delineate, perpetually redescribing the young man, the poet, and their relationship. Indirections and refusals to disclose are intrinsic to the mode of the *Sonnets*, and it would be a fundamental misreading to impose a clarity upon the careful obscurities of Shakespeare's text. Sometimes indications of sexual desire are present not in the form of metaphor or simile, but as a cross-hatching of sexually charged vocabulary across the surface of a poem whose atten-tion seems to lie elsewhere.

The figuring is itself problematic, often drawing attention to its own failure, as the poet contradicts and corrects himself from one poem to another, or even within the same poem. Among the *Sonnets'* charac-teristic rhetorical figures are *correctio* or *epanorthosis*, in which what has been said is challenged and reversed: 'by this we revise either what was said or our means of saying it, and express our repentance';[3] and *paradiastole* or redescription,[4] through which the speaker tries to gain some form of mastery by producing what is generally a more comfort-ing description of the boy's character or actions, or the poet's feelings, or his place in the erotic triangle with the Dark Lady.[5] In Sonnet 96 we hear different voices describing the young man's behaviour in a variety of exculpatory ways:

> Some say thy fault is youth, some wantonesse,
> Some say thy grace is youth and gentle sport,
> Both grace and faults are lov'd of more and lesse:
> Thou makst faults graces, that to thee resort:
>
> .   .   .   .
>
> So are those errors that in thee are seene,
> To truths translated, and for true things deem'd.[6]

Such a process of translation, the desperate wishful thinking involved in deeming error to be truth, runs through the collection. Sonnet 88

---

[3] Lee A. Sonino, *A Handbook to Sixteenth-Century Rhetoric* (London, 1968), 65, quoting Talaeus.   [4] See Ch. 1 n. 28 above.

[5] For a discussion of rhetorical figures in the *Sonnets* (though not including *epanorthosis* and *paradiastole*) see Brian Vickers, *Rhetoric and Feeling in Shakespeare's 'Sonnets'* (Zürich, 1991), an expanded and corrected reprint from *Shakespeare Today: Directions and Methods of Research*, ed. Keir Elam (Florence, 1984), 53–98; see also his ' "Mutual render": *I* and *Thou* in the *Sonnets*', in his *Returning to Shakespeare* (London, 1989), 41–88.

[6] Sonnet 96, ll. 1–4, 7–8.

will 'prove thee virtuous, though thou art forsworne'.[7] And Sonnet 37
rewrites the young man's fault more radically as those 'deeds of youth'
which delight a father, and can even be called 'thy worth and truth'.[8]
Falsehood becomes truth. According to Sonnet 93, the boy is not one
of those whose 'falce hearts history | Is writ in moods and frounes and
wrinckles strange'; and so, since only 'sweet love' is written on his face,
the poet is forced to 'live, supposing thou art true', while suspecting
that he is not, suspecting that love and truth need to be redescribed as
falsehood and betrayal.[9] *Paradiastole* is sometimes a consolation,
sometimes a danger.

Typically the poetry acknowledges the sleight of hand, the desperation even, which is involved in such corrections and redescriptions.
Sonnet 42 invents a contorted reason for believing that the youth has
not betrayed the poet by having sex with the poet's own mistress, but
even as the argument is clinched in the couplet, its factitious nature is
signalled with the label 'Sweete flattery'.[10] Sonnet 35 convicts the poet
of a fault in excusing the boy's betrayal, in 'Authorizing thy trespas
with compare' through devising consolatory proverbs such as 'Roses
have thornes, and silver fountaines mud'.[11] Often apparent resolutions
or conclusions are overturned, or just set aside. Indeed, on some readings it seems that the most important word in the *Sonnets* is 'but'.
Sonnet 74 challenges the conclusion of its predecessor by opening,
'But be contented'.[12] Sonnet 13 tracks back against its own opening
within the very first line:

> O that you were your selfe, but love you are
> No longer yours, then you your selfe here live.[13]

Moreover, the status of 'love' oscillates here between nominative and
vocative: between 'but you are Love itself, and no longer your own self
...' and 'but, Love, you are no longer your own self...'. A rereading of
the first line is required as we understand the second. And many
sonnets use 'But' or 'Yet' to turn the thought in a new direction at the
start of a new quatrain, the sestet, or the couplet: Sonnet 19 turns on
'But' at line 8 and again on 'Yet' at line 13. 'But' frequently introduces
the poet's attempt to redescribe the relationship, to deny the obvious,
or to ward off defeat.

Sometimes *paradiastole* merges with *ploce*, which is the repetition of

---

[7] Sonnet 88, l. 4.   [8] Sonnet 37, ll. 2, 4.   [9] Sonnet 93, ll. 7–8, 10, 1.
[10] Sonnet 42, l. 14.   [11] Sonnet 35, ll. 2, 6.   [12] Sonnet 74, l. 1.
[13] Sonnet 13, ll. 1–2.

a key word within a line or clause. This merging of redescription with repetition may seem paradoxical, but Shakespeare often seeks redescription within the semantic field of the same word, notably the key words 'self', 'will', and 'love'. The play around 'self' (as in Sonnet 133) questions whether the poet has any selfhood which he can call his own, when his love for the boy has recreated him, sometimes transforming him ecstatically, sometimes reducing him to abject dependency.[14] And the savage punning around 'will' in Sonnet 135 fractures the autonomy of the players in this sexual drama by asking whether 'Will' as name, 'will' as desire, and 'will' as genitals have now become synonymous, with individuals reduced to interchangeable sexual objects. An extended form of *ploce* also contributes to charting the dynamics of power between the two men, as when Shakespeare repeats the image of grafting in Sonnets 15 and 37. In the former, the poet is 'all in war with Time for love of you | As he takes from you, I ingraft you new':[15] the power resides with the poet who remakes the youth in his verse, so giving him new life. In the latter, the poet likens himself to 'a decrepit father' who 'takes delight, | To see his active childe do deeds of youth', and thereby draws strength from the young man's vigour: 'I make my love ingrafted to this store: | So then I am not lame, poore, nor dispis'd'.[16] Here the poet grafts himself onto the youth's store of energy. The two images of grafting rewrite the poet, the boy, and their love. The image is potentially sexual, since 'graft' is often used to mean 'have intercourse with',[17] but maybe in these two instances this sense is held in abeyance, as a glimpsed but unrealized meaning, a wished-for but impossible outcome.

Sonnet 40 stages a virtuoso performance of *ploce* around the word 'love':

> Take all my loves,[1] my love,[2] yea take them all,
> What hast thou then more then thou hadst before?
> No love,[3] my love,[2] that thou maist true love[3] call,
> All mine was thine, before thou hadst this more: 4
> Then if for my love,[4] thou my love[5] receivest,
> I cannot blame thee, for my love[6] thou usest,

---

[14] Modernized edns. which change the original form 'my self' to 'myself' often lose an important nuance of meaning: 'myself' is purely part of a reflexive verb, whereas 'my self' posits a self which the poet calls his own.

[15] Sonnet 15, ll. 13–14.

[16] Sonnet 37, ll. 1–2, 8–9.

[17] Williams, *s.v.*

But yet be blam'd, if thou this selfe deceavest
By wilfull taste of what thy selfe refusest.   8
I doe forgive thy robb'rie gentle theefe
Although thou steale thee all my poverty:
And yet love[7] knowes it is a greater griefe
To beare loves[8] wrong, then hates knowne injury.   12
   Lascivious grace, in whom all il wel showes,
   Kill me with spights yet we must not be foes.

The various meanings of 'love' demand to be teased out:[18]

1 (*a*) sexual partners (specifically women?); (*b*) kinds of love (including sexual desire?);
2 young man whom the poet loves (sexually or not?);
3 (*a*) loving relationship; (*b*) sexual partner;
4 (*a*) affection ('for my love' = for love of me); (*b*) sexual relationship ('for my love' = (i) in place of a sexual relationship with me; (ii) as a form of sexual relationship with me);
5 sexual partner, mistress (singular of sense 1*a*);
6 (*a*) affection (the poet's love for the young man); (*b*) sexual partner, mistress (sense 5);
7 love as an ideal or power;
8 (*a*) affection (either (i) wrong is done to the poet's affection for the youth; or (ii) wrong is done by the youth out of affection for the poet); (*b*) young man whom the poet loves (i.e. wrong is done by the lover).

The display of ingenuity makes a serious, even a desperate, point. The young man has, it seems, been having sex with the poet's mistress, and in Sonnet 42 we learn that the anguish which this causes derives more from the poet's loss of the boy than of the woman. Here in Sonnet 40, the rhetoric which devises excuses for the boy's theft also contrives to imagine the sex which takes place between the boy and the mistress as a form of sex between the boy and the poet. Lines 5–6 say: 'If you have taken my mistress out of love for me, then I cannot blame you, since you are making sexual use of my love for you [which is what I wanted, albeit not in this form]'. The verb 'use' echoes Sonnet 20, which draws a distinction between the poet's love for the youth, and women's 'use' of him sexually: 'Mine be thy love and thy loves use their treasure'.[19]

---

[18] I draw partly on Duncan-Jones here.

[19] Sonnet 20, l. 14; the poem is quoted in full on p. 75 below. For 'use' = have intercourse with, see Williams, *s.v.*

Then lines 7–8 of Sonnet 40 say: 'But I do blame you if you deceive me ('this selfe'[20]) by taking this woman because of your own desire for sex with her ('wilful taste'), when you refuse to have sex with others [with the women who in Sonnets 1–17 have been proposed as suitable mothers for your offspring—or with me]'. So this intensive use of *ploce* shows us that 'love' means something slightly different each time it is used, and it is within the framework of multiple possibilities created by this rhetoric that there emerges the poet's need to be linked with the youth sexually. It is the over-delineation of 'love' which makes possible the expression of sexual desire for the youth, because each voicing of it is capable of being explained in another way.

In some poems, redescription is implicitly invited through *erotema*, the rhetorical question, as the poet asks questions to which, he knows, the youth will not respond, or will not respond with the desired answer. When Sonnet 57 opens with the rhetorical question,

> Being your slave what should I doe but tend,
> Upon the houres, and times of your desire?
> I have no precious time at al to spend;
> Nor services to doe til you require.[21]

it is repeating the Petrarchan motif of the lover as abject servant in a querulous tone which resents the dynamics of the relationship, and looks for some word or act in reply which disproves the topos of slavery.[22] Amongst the most desolate of the *Sonnets* is 87, whose *erotema* sums up the precariousness of the poet's relationship with the boy:

> For how do I hold thee but by thy granting,
> And for that ritches where is my deserving?[23]

Through its assumption that the poet is worthless and the boy calculating, the bitter question clearly implies an answer which at once belittles the poet and demeans the boy—though what the poem really longs for is a loving *paradiastole* from the boy in reply, rejecting these legal and financial images as a travesty of their bond, and redescribing their relationship in terms of generosity, trust, and unconditional love. The answer never comes.

---

[20] The reading of the 1609 Quarto and the Oxford edn., followed here, is 'this selfe'; Duncan-Jones follows Malone in emending to 'thyself', but I cannot see why the boy should be said to be deceiving himself.   [21] Sonnet 57, ll. 1–4.

[22] It also rewrites Sonnet 26, which begins, 'Lord of my love, to whome in vassalage . . . .'.   [23] Sonnet 87, ll. 5–6.

These characteristic rhetorical figures keep playing over the nature of the bond between the speaker and the youth, redefining it repeatedly and obsessively. While there are two sonnets (116 and 129) devoted respectively to formal definitions of love and lust,[24] most of the *Sonnets*' definitional work is tentative and temporary: 'Shall I compare thee to a Summers day? | Thou art more lovely and more temperate . . .'.[25] Names and comparisons are deployed only to be rejected as inadequate: 'Let not my love be cal'd Idolatrie' or 'Those lines that I before have writ doe lie'.[26] What is insistently defined and redefined is the security of the relationship and the moral and affective character of the two men's behaviour. But within all this searching for the *mot juste* to define just how and whether the youth is indeed '<u>my</u> lovely Boy',[27] the question of whether physical sex between the two is sought or granted is always just out of reach. It is symptomatic that Sonnet 20, which overtly says that the boy's penis is 'to my purpose nothing', has been read as articulating the very desire which it appears to deny.[28] And in Sonnet 110 the palpably sexual language ('affections', 'appetite', 'grin'de', 'proofe'[29]) is applied to the poet's adventures with other partners, while religious language is used of the boy ('A God in love . . . next my heaven the best'), so that the two registers are kept apart; even so, their proximity leads one to wonder whether the relationship with the boy which the speaker has betrayed is also a sexual one. Sonnet 144 begins with an apparently clear distinction between the poet's love for the youth and for the Dark Lady: 'Two loves I have of comfort and dispaire'. But which is which? Does the boy provide affectionate comfort, while the woman makes the poet despair because of his sexual attraction to her? Or does the boy generate despair by refusing to sleep with the poet, while the woman comforts him by taking him into her bed? Or does the boy comfort the poet sexually? Or do both his lovers provide both comfort and despair?

Threaded through the *Sonnets* are figures of possession and dispossession. The sequence begins by rebuking the youth for his Narcissistic self-possession, 'contracted to thine owne bright eyes',[30]

[24] See Vickers, *Rhetoric and Feeling*, 63.

[25] Sonnet 18, ll. 1–2.

[26] Sonnets 105, l. 1 and 115, l. 1.

[27] Sonnet 126, l. 1; emphasis added.

[28] *LBM* 79–80; Duncan-Jones, 150–1.

[29] For 'affection' see n.119 below; 'grind' = have intercourse with, 'prove' = try sexually (Williams, *s.vv.*).

[30] Sonnet 1, l. 5.

and continues after the speaker has avowed his own love for the lad in a series of images of private spaces in which possession might be imagined—for Shakespeare these are not pastoral utopias but dreams, or the pages of books; by contrast, there are journeys which remove the poet from the boy, and public spaces in which the relationship cannot be acknowledged. Possession is often the work of the eye,[31] and when the poet looks at the young man he sees all his previous loves gathered there:

> Their images I lov'd, I view in thee,
> And thou (all they) hast all the all of me.[32]

There is a remarkable irregular verb here which conjugates as 'I view, thou hast'. The youth has all the poet, total power over him, while the poet looks at the young man, imagining him in many different ways, but his actual possession of the youth seems limited to the work of the eye or the mind. Characteristically the language suggests but refuses to be precise about the sexuality of this possession: 'thou . . . hast all the all of me' implies sexual possession, but whether this is actual or potential, whether it is what the boy wants or what the poet is ready to grant him, is withheld from our view.[33]

Here and elsewhere, the simple verb 'have' carries much of the weight of the poems' desire for possession. Its sexual charge is clear in Sonnet 129, the definition of lust, which is said to be 'Had, having, and in quest to have, extreame'.[34] Sonnet 42 observes simply that 'thou hast her . . . she hath thee', before delivering the specious conclusion that because 'my friend and I are one, I . . . she loves but me alone'.[35] This attempt to figure, or figure out, the sexual possession of the boy by the woman is followed in Sonnets 43–4 by explanations of the way in which the poet holds the youth, which is only in dream or in imagination. At the end of Sonnet 87, which is entirely devoted to images of possession, the plain verb 'have' is defined as an imaginary possession:

---

[31] e.g. Sonnets 43, 113. For the sexual implications of the eye see Williams, *s.v.*

[32] Sonnet 31, ll. 13–14.

[33] Booth, 176–8, suggests (inconclusively, I think) that 'all' often means 'penis' (partly via a pun on 'awl', for which see Wiliams, *s.v.*), which would generate the meaning 'you have complete power over my penis'. Even if this particular reading is unconvincing, it would be hard to argue that 'all' must exclude sexual possession.

[34] Sonnet 129, l. 10. Though placed within the portion of the sequence concerning the Dark Lady, there is nothing in the actual wording of the poem which makes it refer specifically to lust for a woman.

[35] Sonnet 42, ll. 1–3, 13–14.

> Thus have I had thee as a dreame doth flatter,
> In sleepe a King, but waking no such matter.[36]

Even the couplet's disillusionment seems to modulate as we reread it. Does it say (i) that the poet's possession of the youth was always an illusion—as he now realizes; or (ii) that the poet's possession of the youth—now that it is over—seems as distant and insubstantial as a dream does to a waking man? The uncertainty over whether the having was real or imaginary once again places the sexuality of the verb 'had' *sous rature*. Like Derrida's device in *De la grammatologie*,[37] where a term is written and then cancelled, but remains legible through the cancellation, the fluid syntax and multiple rhetorical devices of the *Sonnets* allow Shakespeare to bring sexual interests into the text while simultaneously holding them at bay. Shakespeare's style characteristically forces the abstract and the concrete to exist in unsettling proximity, and throughout the *Sonnets* we never quite know whether images of possession figure mental or physical union.

The language of the *Sonnets* frequently has sexual connotations which are not consolidated into puns or metaphors, but lie as traces across the text. Take Sonnet 48:

> How carefull was I when I tooke my way,
> Each trifle under truest barres to thrust,
> That to my use it might un-used stay
> From hands of falsehood, in sure wards of trust?
> But thou, to whom my jewels trifles are,
> Most worthy comfort, now my greatest griefe,
> Thou best of deerest, and mine onely care,
> Art left the prey of every vulgar theefe.
> Thee have I not lockt up in any chest,
> Save where thou art not, though I feele thou art,
> Within the gentle closure of my brest,
> From whence at pleasure thou maist come and part,
>   And even thence thou wilt be stolne I feare,
>   For truth prooves theevish for a prize so deare.

The poet locks up his jewels, but cannot lock up the friend, who remains a prey to thieves. There is a surprising development in line 10, for one might have expected the argument to run something like this:

---

[36] Sonnet 87, ll. 13–14.
[37] Jacques Derrida, *De la grammatologie* (Paris, 1967).

Thee have I not lockt up in any chest,
Save where thou art <u>now</u>, for I feele thou art,
Within the gentle closure of my brest.

but this kind of inward, emotional possession is negated even before it is expounded: 'where thou art <u>not</u>'. And yet the elaboration of the lovely image of the boy folded 'Within the gentle closure of my brest' is a powerful one, and in its length, vividness, and warmth it counteracts and almost erases the tiny negative 'not'. The physicality of this image is clear, though it would not be out of place in a poem of friendship. Yet many of the words in this sonnet have sexual implications:[38] 'thrust . . . use . . . hands . . . wards . . . jewels . . . lock . . . at pleasure'. While the formal argument of the poem describes the ways in which the poet does not possess the youth, the language evokes both emotional and sexual possession, the former through the extended image of enclosure, the latter through the connotative power of key words.

Similar, but subtly different, is Sonnet 52:

So am I as the rich whose blessed key,
Can bring him to his sweet up-locked treasure,
The which he will not ev'ry hower survay,
For blunting the fine point of seldome pleasure.
Therefore are feasts so sollemne and so rare,
Since sildom comming in the long yeare set,
Like stones of worth they thinly placed are,
Or captaine Jewells in the carconet.
So is the time that keepes you as my chest,
Or as the ward-robe which the robe doth hide,
To make some speciall instant speciall blest,
By new unfoulding his imprison'd pride.
   Blessed are you whose worthinesse gives skope,
   Being had to tryumph, being lackt to hope.

In what sense 'had'? The opening quatrain in particular carries familiar metaphors of sexual pleasure and possession.[39] This sonnet appears to answer Sonnet 48: in the earlier poem the youth was not locked up in any closet, not even the closet of the heart; here he is locked away to be enjoyed on special occasions. But 52 is not quite a *correctio* of 48, since here it is Time that keeps the boy locked away. Yet again, the formal argument wries the poem away from the impression created by the

---

[38] As Booth notes, 211.   [39] Booth, 223.

powerful figures of possession. Possession and dispossession are woven through the same sonnet, the one turning into the other.

Perhaps the most poignant statement of dispossession is the simple, weary *ploce* in Sonnet 34:

> Though thou repent, yet I have still the losse,
> Th'offenders sorrow lends but weake reliefe
> To him that beares the strong offenses losse.[40]

The failure to rhyme underlines the inability of the poet to conjure up a way of redescribing this loss: loss, this time, is loss and nothing else.

The *Sonnets*, then, work more through intratextual than intertextual engagement: their self-conscious relation is to themselves, as poems return to earlier topics and images, undo the precarious stabilities of ostensibly conclusive couplets, regress to emotions which cannot be assuaged and constantly need to be rewritten. Intertextual engagement is less apparent. Sonnet sequences addressed to women had pro-liferated by the mid-1590s, and there were many models to follow, including Petrarch, Wyatt, Sidney, Daniel, Spenser, and Drayton. There are occasional traces of some of these writers in Shakespeare's *Sonnets*, but on the whole the *Sonnets* have only a limited intertextual engagement with this literary tradition.[41] But there is one writer of homoerotic sonnets—Richard Barnfield—who offered Shakespeare some hints for his own sequence of love poems to another man. By attending to Shakespeare's creative engagement with this predecessor, we may see more clearly some of his own characteristics.[42]

---

[40] Sonnet 34, ll. 10–12. In l. 12 the Quarto reads 'losse', which Capell and all sub-sequent editors (including the Oxford editors) except Duncan-Jones emend to 'cross'. I follow Duncan-Jones (and Booth's note, though not his text) in thinking that the repetition is expressive, and so keep the Quarto reading.

[41] Editors of the *Sonnets* have not been particularly interested in the poems' literary sources, though there are some useful pointers in Duncan-Jones's edn.; see also T. W. Baldwin, *On the Literary Genetics of Shakspere's Poems & Sonnets* (Urbana, Ill., 1950).

[42] In addition, there is Barnabe Barnes's sonnet sequence *Parthenophil and Parthenophe* (London, 1593), ed. Edward Arber in *An English Garner* (Birmingham, 1882), v. Dedicated to 'M. William Percy, Esq., his dearest friend', it begins with a group of sonnets in which a woman has taken 'my tender boy', 'a lovely virgin Boy' belonging to the poet. It gradually emerges that this boy is probably love (i.e. the poet's love for the lady), but a reading which was not particularly persistent might well gain the impression, particularly from individual poems, that Barnes is presenting a triangle of poet, boy, and mistress similiar to that in Shakespeare's *Sonnets*. Beyond this parallel scenario, some verbal echoes suggest that Shakespeare may have read Barnes: the imagery of imprisonment, bail, bonds, and pawn in Barnes's poems 8 and 11 has

Richard Barnfield's *The Affectionate Shepheard* (1594) and *Cynthia* (1595)[43] were published a year or two before the likely date at which Shakespeare started writing his own sequence.[44] There are enough verbal resemblances between Barnfield's poems and Shakespeare's for us to conclude that the latter studied the two earlier collections with some interest. Unlike Shakespeare's, Barnfield's poems are overtly sensual in their evocation of the sexual pleasure which the speaker Daphnis takes in the boy Ganymede, and the metaphors which Barnfield uses take little decoding. The opening of 'The Teares of an Affectionate Shepheard Sicke for Love. Or The Complaint of Daphnis for the Love of Ganimede' describes the speaker's first sight

> Of that faire Boy that had my heart intangled;
> Cursing the Time, the Place, the sense, the sin;
> I came, I saw, I viewd, I slipped in.[45]

The obvious evocation and alteration of Caesar's *veni, vidi, vici* is suggestive: instead of 'conquered' Barnfield substitutes 'viewd', viewing being itself a form of conquest; and while 'slippèd in' (the first disyllabic word in the line attracts added emphasis[46]) may refer back to 'the sin' into which Daphnis has slipped, it clearly also suggests sexual penetration. Here the past tense places the sexual intercourse in a fantasized past which has not actually taken place except in the imagination: past figures future. Another conceit, from the world of pastoral, using the image of Ganymede as a bee, minimally decorates the meaning of the poet's invitation to fellatio:

---

parallels in Shakespeare's Sonnets 87 and 133; and the hair of the lady being 'brown, and crispèd wiry' in sonnet 13 has a parallel in Shakespeare, Sonnet 130, l. 4. Barnes's sonnet 54 recalls how he shot the bow of love at both boys and girls. Barnes wrote for Shakespeare's company: see p. 39 above.

[43] Richard Barnfield, *The Complete Poems*, ed. George Klawitter (Selinsgrove, 1990). For critical discussions of Barnfield see *LBM* 38–43; Smith, 99–113.

[44] The chronology of Shakespeare's *Sonnets* is much debated, but some of the poems published in 1609 are probably those referred to by Francis Meres in 1598, and may therefore have been composed in the mid- to late 1590s. However, there are linguistic indications that the 1609 *Shake-speares Sonnets* includes work (either composition, revision, or both) from several periods: (1) before 1598 (up to Meres's allusion); (2) 1599–1600 (around the entry in the *Stationers' Register*); (3) 1603–4 (coinciding with an outbreak of plague and the closure of the theatres); (4) 1608–9 (coinciding with another outbreak of plague and another closure of the theatres, leading to the publication of the 1609 Quarto): see Duncan-Jones's edn., 1–13.

[45] Barnfield, 'Teares of an Affectionate Shepheard', l. 6.

[46] As Klawitter notes, 205.

> Then shouldst thou sucke my sweete and my faire flower
> That now is ripe, and full of honey-berries:
> Then would I leade thee to my pleasant Bower
> Fild full of Grapes, of Mulberries, and Cherries.[47]

Barnfield uses simple metaphor to figure the desirable parts of the male body, unlike Shakespeare, who rarely brings the body of the youth into view: 'eye' and 'heart' are often referred to by Shakespeare, but as agents in an emotional drama. (The boy's 'thing' by which he is 'prickt ... out' for sexual pleasure is cited in Sonnet 20, but in the context of a protestation that it is of no interest to the poet.) Daphnis' invitation to Ganymede is one of the points at which Barnfield is writing with a copy of Marlowe open on his table, or perhaps a commonplace book into which he has copied out some favourite lines from his mentor, for Barnfield evidently had a connoisseur's eye for the few homoerotic texts which were available in English, and Marlowe was a frequent source for him.[48] The line 'Crownets of Pearle about thy naked Armes'[49] in Daphnis' dream about Ganymede is lifted from Gaveston's fantasy about homoerotic entertainments for his lover in *Edward II*, while other lines adapt Jupiter's speeches to Ganymede, or eroticized speeches about the young Ascanius, in *Dido Queen of Carthage*.[50] Such borrowings typically constitute an invitation to some *locus amoenus*, since pastoral can offer a homoerotic utopia.[51] Shakespeare's own *Venus and Adonis* and *Lucrece* were also quarried, as was Drayton's *Piers Gaveston* for the phrase 'my bosome thy bed'.[52] So we see Barnfield constructing for himself a homoerotic canon, seeking out phrases which evoke the young male body, or which imagine a setting in which that body can be enjoyed.

[47] Barnfield, 'Teares', ll. 97–100.

[48] For Barnfield's borrowings from Marlowe and Shakespeare see Charles Crawford, 'Richard Barnfield, Marlowe, and Shakespeare', *Notes and Queries*, 9th ser., 8 (1901), 217–19, 277–9; also noted in Klawitter's edn. The lines from 'Teares' are compared by Crawford with *Dido Queen of Carthage*, 4. 5. 4–7.   [49] Barnfield, 'Teares', l. 104.

[50] Both Marlowe's plays were printed with the date 1594; *Edward II* was entered in the *Stationers' Register* on 6 July 1593; Dido was not registered. *The Affectionate Shepheard* was not registered; *Cynthia* was entered on 17 Jan. 1595. These dates suggest that Barnfield read Marlowe's plays avidly as soon as they were printed. It is possible, though unlikely given the closeness of the verbal echoes, that Barnfield noted down lines from the plays in performance; it is improbable that he could have had access to manuscript copies of both plays.

[51] For homoerotic pastoral see Smith, 79–115; Byrne R. S. Fone, 'This Other Eden: Arcadia and the Homosexual Imagination', *Journal of Homosexuality*, 8 (1983), 13–34.

[52] Klawitter, 208. For Drayton's poem see *LBM* 53–7, and pp. 121–6 below.

In turn, Shakespeare read Barnfield, though students of the *Sonnets* have overlooked this.[53] As Barnfield's Victorian editor A. B. Grosart noted,[54] lines from 'The Teares of an Affectionate Shepheard' are echoed in Sonnet 20:

> Compare the love of faire Queene *Guendolin*
> With mine, and thou shalt see how she doth love thee:
> I love thee for thy qualities divine,
> But She doth love another Swaine above thee:
> I love thee for thy gifts, She for hir pleasure;
> I for thy Vertue, She for Beauties treasure.[55]

Here the man apparently loves the boy for his virtue and his 'divine' qualities, while the woman loves him for his beauty and the sexual pleasure which this 'treasure' gives her.[56] The contrast is echoed and reworked by Shakespeare in Sonnet 20, the poem in which the speaker says that Nature has thwarted him by making the boy male:

> A womans face with natures owne hand painted,
> Haste thou the Master Mistris of my passion,
> A womans gentle hart but not acquainted
> With shifting change as is false womens fashion,
> An eye more bright then theirs, lesse false in rowling:
> Gilding the object where-upon it gazeth,
> A man in hew all *Hews* in his controwling,
> Which steales mens eyes and womens soules amaseth.
> And for a woman wert thou first created,
> Till nature as she wrought thee fell a dotinge,
> And by addition me of thee defeated,
> By adding one thing to my purpose nothing.
> > But since she prickt thee out for womens pleasure,
> > Mine be thy love and thy loves use their treasure.

Shakespeare, rethinking Barnfield's antithesis between how the male poet loves the boy and how women love him, rejects Daphnis' rather spurious Platonic claim that it is Ganymede's virtue and divine qualities which attract him, and instead of 'Vertue' substitutes 'love'.

---

[53] Duncan-Jones occasionally cites Barnfield, but as an analogue rather than a source. She also notes (47) that two poems by Barnfield were included alongside Shakespeare's in *The Passionate Pilgrim* (1599), and that Francis Meres linked the two poets in 1598.

[54] Klawitter, 210.

[55] Barnfield, 'Teares', ll. 201–10.

[56] For the sexual meanings of 'treasure' see Ch. 1 n. 107 above.

(By contrast, the virtue of the *Sonnets'* addressee is soon called repeatedly into doubt.) Shakespeare shifts the antithesis from Barnfield's focus on what attracts the lover, to a contrast between (i) love (from the poet for the boy) which is reciprocated as love (from the boy to the poet, but carefully left undefined in character and scope); and (ii) love (from women for the boy) which is returned by him in the form of sex. Shakespeare is content to leave unrevised Barnfield's rhyme of 'pleasure I . . . treasure' in the description of the women's relation to the boy, though his introduction of 'use' deftly demeans it: not only are there connotations of usury (already established in Sonnet 4), but 'use' as a noun or a verb for sexual intercourse is generally colloquial in Shakespeare—used in prose by such as Parolles, Juliet's Nurse, or Aaron the Moor.[57] Another rhyme in Sonnet 20—'dotingl . . . nothing'—also occurs in Barnfield, in a context where he is evoking the thwarted love of Narcissus for his own reflection:

> The Agget stone is white, yet good for nothing:
> Fie, fie, I am asham'd to heare thee talke;
> Be not so much of thine owne Image doating:
>   So faire *Narcissus* lost his love and life.
>   (Beautie is often with itself at strife).[58]

Sonnet 20 comes just after the subset of the *Sonnets* in which Shakespeare has accused the youth of a Narcissistic fascination with himself; and the context in which the rhyme appears in Sonnet 20 is that of an almost Narcissistic Nature who falls in love with her own creation.

Barnfield also addresses another topic which interested Shakespeare, that of the boy's beauty fading with age:

> And alwaies (I am sure) it cannot last,
> But sometime Nature will denie those dimples:
> In steed of Beautie (when thy Blossom's past)
> Thy face will be deformed, full of wrinckles:
>   Then She that lov'd thee for thy Beauties sake,
>   When Age drawes on, thy love will soone forsake.

---

[57] 'A particularly materialistic and callous term', says Eric Partridge, *Shakespeare's Bawdy* (London, 1947; 3rd edn. 1968), 210–11.

[58] Barnfield, 'Second Dayes Lamentation', ll. 260–4. This stanza might have caught Shakespeare's eye for its echo in the couplet of his own lines describing Venus' wooing of the Narcissistic Adonis: cf. 'Nature that made thee with her selfe at strife, I Saith that the world hath ending with thy life' (*Venus and Adonis*, ll. 11–12).

> But I that lov'd thee for thy gifts divine,
> In the December of thy Beauties waning,
> Will still admire (with joy) those lovely eine,
> That now behold me with their beauties baning:[59]

The line 'In the December of thy Beauties waning' is almost Shake-spearian. In Sonnet 126, the last of the sequence addressed to the young man, the poet observes that the youth has 'by wayning growne', and thereby shows 'Thy lovers withering'.[60] The 'pleasurel . . . treasure' rhyme from Barnfield and from Sonnet 20 is also repeated in Sonnet 126:

> Yet feare her O thou minnion of her pleasure,
> She may detaine, but not still keepe her tresure![61]

Time brings about the loss of the lad's beauty; but in both Barnfield and Shakespeare time is experienced differently by the poet and by the rest of the world. There is a contrast between the seasons in the natural world and the season which (because of his age or his emotional state) the speaker inhabits. 'The Second Dayes Lamentation' opens thus:

> Next Morning when the golden Sunne was risen,
> And new had bid good morrow to the Mountaines;
> When Night her silver light had lockt in prison,
> Which gave a glimmering on the christall Fountaines:
>   Then ended sleepe: and then my cares began,
>   Ev'n with the uprising of the silver Swan.
>
> O glorious Sunne quoth I, (viewing the Sunne)
> That lightenst everie thing but me alone:
> Why is my Summer season almost done?
> My Spring-time past, and Ages Autumne gone?
>   My Harvest's come, and yet I reapt no corne:
>   My love is great, and yet I am forlorne.[62]

Barnfield's Daphnis simply laments the fact that in his summer or middle age he has not yet reaped his harvest, in other words, bedded Ganymede.[63]

For the speaker of Shakespeare's Sonnet 33, the image leads in the

---

[59] Barnfield, 'Teares', ll. 211–20.
[60] Sonnet 126, ll. 3–4.
[61] Sonnet 126, ll. 9–10.
[62] Barnfield, 'Second Dayes Lamentation', ll. 1–12.
[63] Cf. Sonnet 97, where harvest time is empty without the presence of the boy.

opposite direction, for a brief moment in which love was conferred by
the boy has passed:

> Full many a glorious morning have I seene,
> Flatter the mountaine tops with soveraine eie,
> Kissing with golden face the meddowes greene;
> Guilding pale streames with heavenly alcumy:
> Anon permit the basest cloudes to ride,
> With ougly rack on his celestiall face,
> And from the for-lorne world his visage hide
> Stealing unseene to west with this disgrace:
> Even so my Sunne one early morne did shine,
> With all triumphant splendor on my brow,
> But out alack, he was but one houre mine,
> The region cloude hath mask'd him from me now.[64]

Where Daphnis is unambiguously pleading for Ganymede to surren-
der to him sexually ('Ile hang a bag and bottle at thy backe', he says[65]),
Shakespeare's poem is non-committal about the kind of possession
which is being described: 'he was but one houre mine' could refer to
just one hour of sexual intercourse, and 'one early morne' could be a
precise memory of a specific day; or these could be quasi-proverbial
expressions for the brevity of their affectionate friendship before the
youth was somehow drawn away from the poet. Joseph Pequigney,
proposing sexual connotations for 'ride' (have intercourse) and 'pale
streames' (semen), reads the poem as a fairly precise account of the
poet's sexual intercourse with the youth, and the youth's intercourse
with an unworthy rival.[66] And yet such graphic readings seem to work
against the grain of the poem. Granted, the image in 'ride' is unlikely to
be used here without any sexual connotations, since Sonnets 33–5 are
apparently about the distress caused to the poet by the boy's sexual
behaviour, but these three sonnets carefully deploy different linguistic
strategies for different aspects of the subject. For the relationship
between the two men, Shakespeare uses simile: like the sun which for a
while shines brightly and then disappears behind a cloud, so the youth
has at first shone on the poet but is now preoccupied with other relationships (Sonnet 33); like someone rashly going out of doors without
a cloak and being caught in the rain, the poet has rashly ventured to

---

[64] Sonnet 33, ll. 1–12.

[65] Barnfield, 'Second Dayes Lamentation', l. 48; 'bag' = scrotum, 'bottle' = penis
(Williams, *s.vv.*).

[66] Pequigney, *Such is my Love*, 104–8.

trust himself to the boy and been let down—or even publicly exposed, without disguise or protection (Sonnet 34); like a lawyer setting out the case against the boy, the poet deploys various arguments, but finds himself arguing more for the defence than the prosecution (Sonnet 35). But for the other relationships which the boy has been conducting, Shakespeare uses both sexually loaded metaphor ('ride . . . staine'), morally loaded metaphor ('basest cloudes . . . rotten smoke . . . loathsome canker'), and terms of moralistic condemnation ('disgrace . . . offenses . . . ill deeds . . . faults . . . trespas . . . sins . . . sensuall fault'). The anxious work of *paradiastole* is directed at finding words for the youth's actions, while the question of what once happened between poet and boy is withheld from our view. Barnfield's speaker had pleaded that Ganymede 'wilt but show me one kinde looke';[67] Shakespeare in rewriting Barnfield shows how little comfort one kind look brings.

Ganymede must share his beauty, writes Barnfield:

> Let others of thy beauty be pertakers;
> Els none but *Daphnis* will so well esteeme it:
> For what is Beauty except it be well knowne?
> And how can it be knowne, except first showne?[68]

—a strategy which recalls Shakespeare's pleas in Sonnets 1–17 that the youth should beget an heir, and use his beauty.[69] But while Barnfield's speaker recommends promiscuity, he also warns against pride, the 'foule Eclipser of that fayre sun-shine' which 'staines the fayre', 'A blemish that doth every beauty blot.' 'Ah be not staind (sweet Boy)', he pleads.[70] The verbal connection with *Sonnets* 33 and 35 is as striking as the emotional contrast. 'Cloudes and eclipses staine both Moone and Sunne | And loathsome canker lives in sweetest bud',[71] says Shakespeare: these are consolatory proverbs which attempt to assuage the pain of betrayal by making it a commonplace. Barnfield urges Ganymede not to be proud, but to use his sexuality; Shakespeare takes up his images of stain and eclipse to show the consequences of such actions.

Later Barnfield's speaker teasingly praises things which are black in order to persuade Ganymede that his fair beauty is not as valuable as he

[67] Barnfield, 'Second Dayes Lamentation', l. 31.
[68] Ibid., ll. 153–6.
[69] As Klawitter notes, 214.
[70] Barnfield, 'Second Dayes Lamentation', ll. 169–77.
[71] Sonnet 35, ll. 3–4.

believes. Did this help to suggest Shakespeare's equivocal praise of the Dark Lady, and his realization that the boy's fair appearance may conceal a darker moral nature? The whiteness of lilies is no recommendation, says Daphnis, for 'What thing is whiter than the milke-bred Lilly? I . . . Yea what more noysomer unto the smell I Than Lillies are?'[72] Once again, Shakespeare takes up Barnfield's imagery and turns it into a commentary on the boy's betrayal: 'Lillies that fester, smell far worse then weeds'.[73] In Barnfield the contrast is between the lily's visual beauty and its unpleasant smell;[74] in Shakespeare's hands—in a sonnet which starts out by thinking about those who do not act in accordance with the way they appear, and then moves on to analyse the consequences when they do act—this image becomes an instance of the general truth that 'sweetest things turne sowrest by their deedes'.[75] Again, acting on desire seems not to bring the uncomplicated pleasure which Daphnis naïvely craves.[76] These responses to Barnfield—specifically to his first volume, *The Affectionate Shepheard*—constitute a riposte to Daphnis' courtship of Ganymede, saying in effect: 'If he did look kindly on you, how long do you think that would last? Would it bring you joy? The beautiful appearance which you celebrate so casually as a sign of "virtue" may hide a nature which is rotten and rotting others.'

Perhaps Shakespeare's most overt response to Barnfield is to the first sonnet of the second collection, *Cynthia*, a poem on the relation between eye and heart which appears to be rewritten in Sonnet 46. Here is Barnfield:

[72] Barnfield, 'Second Dayes Lamentation', ll. 227–30.

[73] Sonnet 94, l. 14. Editors have noted that this line precisely echoes *Edward III*, 2. 1. 452, probably written 1592–3. Warwick's speech, in which this line occurs, has other resemblances with Sonnet 94: see [Shakespeare], *King Edward III*, ed. Giorgio Melchiori (Cambridge, 1998), 9, 91, 94.   [74] Cf. Tilley L 297.

[75] Sonnet 94, l. 13. The analysis in Sonnet 94 of those 'Who moving others, are themselves as stone' (l. 3) transposes Barnfield's epigrammatic verdict 'He loves to be belov'd, but not to love' (*Cynthia*, Sonnet 10, l. 14) into a more sinister key. For Shakespeare's further use of Sonnet 10, see p. 82 below.

[76] Pursuing his theme in praise of black, Daphnis says: 'For if we doo <u>consider</u> of each thing I That flyes in welkin, or in water swims, I How <u>everie thing increaseth</u> with the Spring, I And how the blacker still the brighter dims': ('The Second Dayes Lamentation', ll. 271–4; emphasis added). This too caught Shakespeare's eye: 'When I <u>consider every thing</u> that growes I Holds in perfection but a little moment. I That this huge stage presenteth nought but showes I Whereon the Stars in secret influence comment. I When I perceive that men as plants <u>increase</u> . . .' (Sonnet 15, ll. 1–5; emphasis added).

Sporting at fancie, setting light by love,
   There came a theefe and stole away my heart,
   (And therefore robd me of my chiefest part)
Yet cannot reason him a felon prove.
For why his beauty (my hearts thiefe) affirmeth,
   Piercing no skin (the bodies fensive wall)
   And having leave, and free consent withall,
Himselfe not guilty, from love guilty tearmeth,
Conscience the Judge, twelve Reasons are the Jurie,
   They finde mine eies the beutie t'have let in,
   And on this verdict given, agreed they bin,
Wherefore, because his beauty did allure yee,
   Your Doome is this: in teares still to be drowned,
   When his faire forehead with disdain is frowned.[77]

Here the argument is that the thief (the boy's beauty) who has stolen the poet's heart cannot be found guilty of any crime because he was given entrance by the poet's own eyes. Conscience and reason therefore acquit him, and punish the eyes with tears when the boy proves disdainful.

Shakespeare's Sonnet 46 reads like a variation upon Barnfield's conceit:[78]

Mine eye and heart are at a mortall warre,
How to devide the conquest of thy sight,
Mine eye, my heart thy pictures sight would barre,
My heart, mine eye the freedome of that right,
My heart doth plead that thou in him doost lye,
(A closet never pearst with christall eyes)
But the defendant doth that plea deny,
And sayes in him thy faire appearance lyes.
To side this title is impannelled
A quest of thoughts, all tennants to the heart,
And by their verdict is determined
The cleere eyes moyitie, and the deare hearts part.
   As thus, mine eyes due is thy outward part,
   And my hearts right, thy inward love of heart.

---

[77] Barnfield, *Cynthia*, Sonnet 1.
[78] Though there are other Renaissance poems which present a conflict between eye and heart (Klawitter, 230) the association of this conceit with that of the trial and jury suggests direct influence.

Here there is a struggle between heart and eye for rights over the boy, since both claim possession of his image. The jury, made up of thoughts ('Reasons' in Barnfield), delivers its verdict, which is a judgment of Solomon: the youth's outward appearance belongs to the eyes, but the heart is awarded 'thy inward love of heart'—a phrase which means both 'my love of you, retained within my heart' and 'your heartfelt love of me'.[79] The distance between Shakespeare and Barnfield is (in part) that Barnfield's conceit remains superficial, adding little to conventional Renaissance debates between eye and heart: the eyes give admittance to the lad's beauty and suffer when he is unkind. Shakespeare takes the opportunity to make the antithesis between eye and heart into a meditation on forms of possession, developing a mode of inwardness in his reflections on the role of the heart. But the concluding phrase 'thy inward love of heart' is a rhetorical trick which makes an ambiguous phrase refer both to the poet's love for the boy and to the boy's love for him. The latter may be wishful thinking, a rhetorical sleight of hand which reveals a touch of desperation.

If Shakespeare's Sonnet 46 is a rejoinder to Barnfield's Sonnet 1, then perhaps Sonnet 20 (quoted in full on p. 75 above) is a remaking of Sonnet 10:

> Thus was my love, thus was my *Ganymed*,
>> (Heavens joy, worlds wonder, natures fairest work,
>> In whose aspect Hope and Dispaire doe lurke)
> Made of pure blood in whitest snow yshed,
> And for sweete *Venus* only form'd his face,
>> And his each member delicately framed,
>> And last of all faire *Ganymede* him named,
> His limbs[80] (as their Creatrix) her imbrace,
> But as for his pure, spotles, vertuous minde,
>> Because it sprung of chaste *Dianaes* blood,
>> (Goddess of Maides, directresse of all good,)
> Hit wholy is to chastity inclinde.
>> And thus it is: as far as I can prove,
>> He loves to be belov'd, but not to love.[81]

Both poems develop a conceit about the lover's creation, in which there is a doubleness. Barnfield's boy has a body created by Venus, but

---

[79] Duncan-Jones, 202.

[80] The plural does not quite disguise the association 'limb' = penis (Williams, *s.v.*). Cf. a similar usage in Barnfield's Sonnet 6, quoted on p. 83 below.

[81] Barnfield, *Cynthia*, Sonnet 10.

a mind shaped by Diana; therefore he is inclined to chastity.
Shakespeare's boy is created by Nature to be a woman, and has
feminine features but male genitals. In each poem the boy has an
erotic relation to his creatrix. In each poem there is an antithesis
between the granting and withholding of sexual favours, but the
stability of the antithesis is undone. In Barnfield, the lad is 'inclined' to
chastity, but that is not synonymous with being chaste; he seems not to
love, but this is only 'as far as I can prove' ('prove' here meaning
'experience'). In Shakespeare, the boy's love is supposedly given to the
poet, and the sexual enjoyment of him to women; but the crucial verb
is subjunctive not indicative: 'mine be thy love', not 'mine is thy love'.
And the declaration that the boy's 'thing' is 'to my purpose nothing'
is ambiguous, in that 'nothing' is slang for the female genitals.[82]
Each poem draws attention to the lad's penis ('member . . . limb[s]';
'thing . . . prikt'). Each poem ends with an implicit question as to
whether the boy is sexually available to the speaker. It is as if
Shakespeare has transformed Barnfield's rather clumsy conceit about
the boy being unavailable due to a contrast between his body and his
mind into a challenge to the boy as to whether his male gender really
does make him unavailable.

If Sonnet 10 from *Cynthia* caught Shakespeare's attention for its
pondering of the boy's unresponsiveness, so too did Sonnet 6, this time
for its dream of possession. The speaker longs for Ganymede's 'sweet
Corrall lips' and the 'secret touch of loves heart-burning arrow'
(Barnfield's images are never too subtle), and then says:

> One night I dream'd (alas twas but a Dreame)
> That I did feele the sweetnes of the same,
> Where-with inspir'd, I young againe became,
> And from my heart a spring of blood did streame,
> But when I wak't, I found it nothing so,
> Save that my limbs (me thought) did waxe more strong
> And I more lusty far, and far more yong.
> This gift on him rich Nature did bestow.
> Then if in dreaming so, I so did speede,
> What should I doe, if I did so indeede?[83]

Barnfield's metaphors manage to be both coy and lubricious, and he is
interested only in physical responses. Shakespeare seems to have
turned twice to this poem: once in Sonnet 27, when he describes how

---

[82] Duncan-Jones, 151; Williams, *s.v.*   [83] Barnfield, *Cynthia*, Sonnet 6, ll. 5–14.

he thinks about the young man while alone in bed,[84] and again in
Sonnet 87, where one line from Barnfield's poem—'But when I wak't,
I found it nothing so'—seems to have generated the bitter conclusion:

> Thus have I had thee as a dreame doth flatter,
> In sleepe a King, but waking no such matter.[85]

Where Barnfield's poetry speaks of the desire of an older man to
possess a younger man, eroticizing his body and multiplying images
of physical consummation, Shakespeare's poetry moves inward,
analysing various kinds of possession and dispossession, and the
emotions which attend them, all the while self-consciously aware of
the rhetorical strategies by which the poet tries to write himself into
the boy's life.

Unlike the highly popular *Venus and Adonis*, and to a lesser extent
Lucrece, the volume entitled *Shake-speares Sonnets* was received almost
in silence when it was published in 1609.[86] Given Shakespeare's considerable reputation by this date, one suspects that this silence
betokened embarrassment or disapproval rather than indifference.
The place of the *Sonnets* within the public sphere is curious, for with
the publication of the 1609 Quarto the poems moved from the private
milieu of Shakespeare's closet to the public world of the bookseller's
stall, without, it seems, ever passing through an intermediate stage of
semi-restricted manuscript circulation around a literary circle as
happened with Sidney and Donne. Even if we accept that the book was
a reputable publication authorized by Shakespeare himself rather than
a piracy,[87] the lack of any prefatory matter apart from the eliptical
dedication ushers it brusquely into the reader's presence. With this
publication Shakespeare seems to have travelled forth without his
cloak, and misread the weather. Ben Jonson's dedication of his *Epi-
grammes* to the Earl of Pembroke in 1616, saying that 'when I made
them, I had nothing in my conscience, to expressing of which I did
need a cypher', implies that the same could not be said of another
volume with which they were both familiar.[88] The faux pas which

---

[84] Barnfield's 'Save that my limbs' seems to have generated Shakespeare's similar line opening 'Save that my' (l. 9), and his repeated 'lims' (ll. 1 and 13).

[85] Sonnet 87, ll. 13–14.

[86] Duncan-Jones, 69–74.

[87] As well argued by Duncan-Jones, 29–41, and in her 'Was the 1609 *Shake-speares Sonnets* really unauthorized?', *Review of English Studies*, 34 (1983), 151–71.

[88] *Ben Jonson*, ed. C. H. Herford, Percy and Evelyn Simpson, 11 vols. (Oxford, 1925–52), viii. 25; Duncan-Jones, 61, 64.

Shakespeare made with this publication was possibly to implicate a nobleman in its dedication without using the formal courtesies, but it was more probably the revelation of a homoerotic obsession.

Shakespeare seems to have composed and revised his sonnets over a period from around 1595 to their publication in 1609.[89] He was therefore so obsessed with the subject of these sonnets (if not obsessed with a particular young man, then certainly with the theme of a passionate attachment to a young man) that for some twelve or thirteen years he kept these poems by him, adding to the sequence and tinkering with individual sonnets. Homoerotic infatuation therefore becomes an abiding private concern for Shakespeare throughout the period which stretches from the composition of *The Merchant of Venice* to that of *Coriolanus*. But why put such poems into the public domain? Katherine Duncan-Jones proposes that the publication of these homoerotic poems was 'designed to gratify the literary culture of James's court',[90] but if Shakespeare was indeed trying to associate himself with what he perceived as a homoerotic rather than a homosocial culture, he seems to have badly misjudged the tone and ethos of the court. Perhaps as a mere player he misunderstood the functioning of signs amongst the aristocracy, signs such as Pembroke's gesture of intimacy at James's coronation in kissing the King on his face instead of his hand.[91] There is a distance between the playful physicality of the relations between nobles at court, and the impassioned expressions of the *Sonnets*, and it is improbable that the Jacobean court tolerated, let alone encouraged, such expressions. The principal problem with *Shake-speares Sonnets* is likely to have been that it offended against the precarious homosociality of the Jacobean court by putting into print for a wide readership poems which could not possibly be read as expressions of homosocial friendship. For Jacobean homosociality may have been precarious precisely because James's known predilections and his demonstrative behaviour with his male favourites threatened to cross a crucial boundary, redescribing the eroticism which coloured homosociality as an unmistakable sign of homosexual interests. Shakespeare's *Sonnets* are manifestly not poems of friendship between equals (either in years or in social status); they are obsessive; and they link the poet with the young man and the mistress

---

[89] See n. 44 above.

[90] Duncan-Jones, 50.

[91] For this incident see Duncan-Jones, 66–7. For a homosexually-charged incident involving Pembroke's younger brother, see pp. 128–9 below.

in a sexual triangle. It was one thing to print Marlowe's *Edward II*, Barnfield's *The Affectionate Shepheard*, and Drayton's *Piers Gaveston* under Elizabeth in the mid-1590s, when Shakespeare began to write his poems, but maybe the arrival of James created a different climate in which homoerotic verse was less acceptable than it had been under Elizabeth, precisely because it made the erotic element in male relations uncomfortably visible, and risked reflecting upon the King.[92]

Sonnet 87 says that the speaker has 'had thee as a dreame doth flatter, | In sleepe a King'.[93] One possible meaning of that image is that the speaker has possessed the boy in the way that King James possessed handsome young men in bed.[94] That does not have to be the line's only meaning, or its principal meaning, for it to be offensive at court. There is a comparable innuendo, and one which may actually refer to these lines, in an epigram by John Davies of Hereford, addressed 'To our English Terence Mr. Will: Shake-speare' and printed two years after the publication of the *Sonnets*, which says:

> Some say (good *Will*) which I, in sport, do sing,
> Had'st thou not plaid some kingly parts in sport,
> Thou had'st bin a companion for a *King*;
> And beene a King among the meaner sort.[95]

Though this overtly refers to Shakespeare acting kings' parts on the stage, the line of vocabulary from '*Will*' to 'parts' and 'sport' is sexually suggestive. The phrase 'kingly parts in sport' could refer to sexual roles, or to stage roles, or to the roles played out in the *Sonnets*. Was it now publicly known, or at least inferred, that Shakespeare had sexual interests similar to those of King James? Finally, one needs an explanation as to why the *Sonnets* were omitted from the 1623 Folio. The Folio was dedicated to the Earl of Pembroke, who is a likely candidate for being the dedicatee of the 1609 *Sonnets*, the enigmatic 'Mr W. H.', and a possible model for the young man of the poems.[96] It would only have

[92] It was in 1610, just a year after the publication of the *Sonnets*, that James I explicitly excepted sodomy from the offences covered by a general pardon (*Letters of King James VI and I*, ed. G. P. V. Akrigg (Berkeley, 1984), 314–15).   [93] Sonnet 87, ll. 13–14.

[94] Duncan-Jones, 284.

[95] John Davies, *The Scourge of Folly* (London, 1611), 76–7; quoted from Duncan-Jones, 86–7.

[96] Even if the dedication is to Pembroke, and the poems were worked on in James's reign, it is possible that the *Sonnets* were substantially composed in the mid- to late 1590s under the aegis of the Earl of Southampton, the dedicatee of *Venus and Adonis* (1593), of *Lucrece* (1594), and of Burton's translation of Tatius (see p. 49 above). If so, Shakespeare may have failed to register a change in the climate by 1609.

taken some Jacobean readers to have hazarded this identification for Pembroke to have felt compromised by the association.[97] To have dedicated the *Sonnets* to him again in 1623 would only have compounded the first offence.[98] This, of course, is conjecture; but *Sonnets*'s frosty reception in 1609 suggests that Shakespeare had spoken more openly and passionately than he ought, and that the sophisticated rhetoric of the poems failed to hide the true character of their desire.

SHAKESPEARE'S PLAYS AND THEIR ITALIAN SOURCES

Other ways in which Shakespeare created spaces in which homosexual desire might be imagined can be seen by comparing some of his plays with their sources, in particular, those which exploit the homoerotic possibilities of Italy.[99] Italian comedies and *novelle* supplied Shakespeare with the outlines of half a dozen plays, and generally their plots describe the entanglements of a variety of heterosexual love affairs.[100] Of course, these interested Shakespeare in their own right, but there were several elements in this material which might have appealed to a dramatist who was also preoccupied by emotional and sexual relationships between men. First, in these plays and stories Shakespeare found a kind of space which was malleable: this was nominally Italy, but it was an Italy of the mind, a comedic or romance space in which unusual happenings were possible. He would not be constrained by the kinds of plausibility demanded in London city comedy. This would have been specially important for a dramatist seeking to fashion a milieu in which homoerotic desire might be represented: it would have to be, in some sense, a world elsewhere, but still a possible world. Secondly,

[97] For the possibility that Pembroke was blackmailed over homoerotic letters written to King James, see pp. 136–7 below.

[98] Duncan-Jones (60) suggests that 'Pembroke did not need to have the sonnets presented to him if they were his already', but that seems insufficient (commercial) reason for omitting them from the Folio.

[99] For the contemporary reputation of Italy see p. 22 above.

[100] For Shakespeare's use of his sources, particularly the Italian materials, see *Narrative and Dramatic Sources of Shakespeare*, ed. Geoffrey Bullough, 8 vols. (London, 1957–75); Louise George Clubb, *Italian Drama in Shakespeare's Time* (New Haven, 1989); Robert Henke, *Pastoral Transformations: Italian Tragicomedy and Shakespeare's Late Plays* (Newark, NJ, 1997); Kenneth Muir, *Shakespeare's Sources, i. Comedies and Tragedies* (London, 1957); Leo Salingar, *Shakespeare and the Traditions of Comedy* (Cambridge, 1974); Naseeb Shaheen, 'Shakespeare's Knowledge of Italian', *Shakespeare Survey*, 47 (1994), 161–9.

disguise—and particularly cross-gendered disguise—generated the possibility of staging erotic scenes between men which at one level were safe because the audience knew that Cesario was Viola in disguise, while carrying a homoerotic frisson because the audience also knew that Cesario/Viola was being played by a pretty boy.[101] Moreover, the motif of disguise takes on new possibilities for the dramatist who is interested in forbidden desires. Thirdly, it is striking that a recurring motif in these plays from Italian sources is love threatened by the death penalty. Romeo is dead if he is caught within Verona's walls; Claudio in *Measure for Measure* is to be executed for engaging in illicit sex; Antonio in *The Merchant of Venice* accepts death as the price of helping Bassanio; and another Antonio in *Twelfth Night* risks death in a hostile city to accompany and protect Sebastian. Writing in a world where sex between men was punishable by death, Shakespeare may have had good reason to ponder these stories.

One play in which contemporary Italy features (at least nominally) is *The Merchant of Venice*, though Shakespeare has constructed that play with the help of a variety of source materials, most of which have some fairy-tale or romance qualities; its realism is only intermittent. The principal source is Ser Giovanni's collection of *novelle* called *Il Pecorone* (1558), Day 4 Story 1, which tells of the adventures of Gianetto.[102] On his deathbed, his father entrusts Gianetto to the care of his godfather Ansaldo, a wealthy merchant of Venice. Gianetto sets out on a trading expedition financed by Ansaldo, and arrives in a city ruled by a lady who has promised herself and her realm to any man who can successfully sleep with her; any man who fails must forfeit all his goods. Gianetto accepts the challenge, but is drugged and falls asleep in the lady's bed. He forfeits Ansaldo's ship with all its stores, and eventually returns home claiming to have lost everything in a shipwreck. Ansaldo finances a second expedition, with just the same results. To equip Gianetto's third expedition, Ansaldo has to sell all his goods, and raise further money which is secured in a bond against a pound of his own flesh. Third time lucky, Gianetto is warned by one of the lady's servants to avoid the drugged drink, satisfies the lady, and is duly married to her. But he forgets all about Ansaldo until reminded by chance that the fatal day has arrived for the bond to be repaid; he hurries back to

---

[101] See Stephen Orgel, *Impersonations: The Performance of Gender in Shakespeare's England* (Cambridge, 1996); Michael Shapiro, *Gender in Play on the Shakespearean Stage: Boy Heroines and Female Pages* (Ann Arbor, 1994).

[102] *Il Pecorone di Ser Giovanni Fiorentino* (Milan, 1558); tr. in Bullough, i. 463–76.

Venice, and Ansaldo is released from the clutches of the Jewish money-
lender by the same device which is used in Shakespeare's play.

A small detail shows that Shakespeare was thinking of the Italy
which forms the setting for this story as a place where homosexual
desire might be commonplace. Scholars have noted that when Jessica
escapes from her father Shylock, she dresses as a boy—quite unneces-
sarily in terms of the plot.[103] When Lorenzo sees her 'obscurd . . . | Even
in the lovely garnish of a boy',[104] he finds this 'garnish' itself attractive:
that is to say, he expresses admiration for a physical appearance which
is visually the boy actor, no longer obscured in female costume.[105]

But this homoerotic pleasure in a boy is a passing detail, albeit one
whose very gratuitousness indicates how Shakespeare's imagination
was working. More important and more difficult to read is the change
to the Italian story which Shakespeare makes when depicting the
relationship between the young man and his financial backer. Ser
Giovanni's merchant is the young man's godfather ('santolo'); he and
his father had been close friends, and Ansaldo takes on a fatherly
role *vis-à-vis* Gianetto, whom he calls 'figliuoccio' and 'figliuolo';
Gianetto in turn calls him 'padre mio'.[106] The generational gap is clear.
Ansaldo is devoted to the lad as a doting parent, but not like the other
inhabitants of Venice who all—both male and female—seem to be in
love with the boy: 'di che le donne & gli huomini ne pareuano
•innamorati'.[107] Ansaldo takes his losses stoically, and in the trial scene
says nothing. The narrative is focused throughout on Gianetto: it is his
rite of passage that the story is interested in, his predicament.

How does Shakespeare's play invite us to read the relationship
between Antonio and Bassanio, if it is not the quasi-paternal and filial
bond described in the source? Nothing in Shakespeare's text points to
any difference in age between the two men, though theatrical tradition
has often assumed it.[108] The two men clearly differ in their financial

---

[103] See Shapiro, 98–100.

[104] *The Merchant of Venice*, 2. 6. 44–5. *OED* 2 gives 'outfit, dress' as the meaning of
'garnish' here, citing only this example. While this is literally what is referred to, the
various senses associated with food indicate that the boyish appearance is an invitation
to consumption.

[105] Cf. Sebastian's pleasure in kissing Moll in boy's clothes in Middleton and
Dekker's *The Roaring Girl* (*LBM* 46).   [106] *Il Pecorone*, 31[v], 32[r], 32[v], 33[r].

[107] Ibid., 32[v].

[108] The RSC's production at Stratford in 1998 originally cast Julian Curry as Antonio,
who was of an age to be a paternal or avuncular figure to Scott Handy's Bassanio. But
one day when the role of Antonio was played by the understudy, Andrew Maud, who
was much the same age as Handy, the relationship became a union of equals, and

resources, but not in their social status. Critics have tended to argue either that Antonio and Bassanio are friends, that Antonio feels friendly but not sexual love—*philia* but not *eros*—for Bassanio; or that Antonio does indeed feel *eros* for Bassanio, and is the older man in love with the younger, the *erastes* with his *eromenos*, though in this instance with a young man who seems not fully to reciprocate.[109] But to argue one case or the other is to clarify what Shakespeare carefully left undefined. Instead of attempting such inappropriate definition, this discussion will explore how Shakespeare's dramatic language creates possibilities which are not allowed for in Ser Giovanni's text; notably the physical and symbolic spaces created by the drama, and what one might call the affective spaces formed by the play of language, often by linguistic hesitations and ambiguities. Both are Shakespeare's dramatic transformations of the Italian narrative.

Though Shakespeare is interested to some extent in suggesting the geographical spaces of Venice—particular houses, the Rialto—he also thinks carefully about the ways his characters create and inhabit social spaces. His changes to Ser Giovanni's narrative include a radical shift of interest as the play opens with the focus on Antonio's feelings, and the difficulty of articulating and understanding them:

> In sooth I know not why I am so sad,
> It wearies me, you say it wearies you;
> But how I caught it, found it, or came by it,
> What stuffe tis made of, whereof it is borne,
> I am to learne:

---

their embrace in the trial scene was unambiguously that of two men who shared a physically intimate relationship. Joseph Pequigney notes that Portia comments on the similarity of the two men, including their 'lyniaments' (3. 4. 15): 'The Two Antonios and Same-Sex Love in *Twelfth Night* and *The Merchant of Venice*', *English Literary Renaissance*, 22 (1992), 201–21, at 211.

[109] The first of these interpretations is argued by Pequigney; the second by a number of critics listed in his n. 1 on 201–2. See also two discussions of the significance of the name 'Antonio': R. P. Corballis, 'The Name Antonio in English Renaissance Drama', *Cahiers Elisabéthains*, 25 (1984), 61–72; Cynthia Lewis, ' "Wise Men, Folly-Fall'n": Characters named Antonio in English Renaissance Drama', *Renaissance Drama*, 20 (1989), 196–236. Corballis interprets both roles as over-fond father figures (62), while Lewis points to a tradition of associating Antonios with wise folly. She also notes that in Christian iconography St Anthony the hermit represents temptation resisted. I would add that St Anthony of Padua might be another appropriate figure in the imaginative hinterland of *The Merchant of Venice*, since one of his miracles concerns the discovery of a miser's heart in his money-chest.

> And such a want-wit sadnes makes of mee,
> That I have much adoe to know my selfe.[110]

The *aposiopesis* in line 5 is a gesture of demurral: the question cannot be answered, the line cannot be completed. The answer lies in the inaccessible space created by Antonio's silence—a space inaccessible to himself as well as to others. His companions Salerio and Solanio suggest that he is anxious about his trading ventures, but Antonio denies this. Then Solanio suggests:

> Why then you are in love.
> *Ant.*   Fie, fie.[111]

Editors have noted that Antonio fails to complete Solanio's line metrically: the missing two syllables are another significant silence, the pause being in effect an admission that Solanio is right, for 'Fie, fie' is a reproach rather than a denial.[112] Salerio and Solanio diplomatically drop the questioning, and leave the stage when Bassanio arrives, recognizing that the two men should be left alone.

But the space shared by Antonio and Bassanio is tense, and Shakespeare shows this by giving them different idioms. Here are friends who do not quite speak the same language. Bassanio tells Antonio in a careful (but perhaps wounding) rhetorical pairing of love and money, 'to you *Anthonio* | I owe the most in money and in love',[113] but Antonio's reply transforms the terms, as he suggests a willingness to offer more than money:

> My purse, my person, my extreamest meanes
> Lie all unlockt to your occasions.[114]

The purse is Elizabethan slang for the genitals,[115] and the grammar of the speech states that Antonio's person lies all unlocked to Bassanio's needs; the offer is at once financial and sexual. (Contrast the phrasing of Philautus' comparable offer to his friend Euphues: 'heere is my hand, my heart, my lands and my lyfe at thy commaundement'.[116]) But

---

[110] *The Merchant of Venice*, 1. 1. 1–7.

[111] Ibid., 1. 1. 46.

[112] *The Merchant of Venice*, ed. John Russell Brown (London, 1955), 7.

[113] *The Merchant of Venice*, 1. 1. 130–1.

[114] Ibid., 1. 1. 138–9.

[115] Williams, *s.v.* Cf. the innuendo in 'to gueld a Cod-peece of a Purse' (*The Winter's Tale*, 4. 4. 611–12); Partridge, *Shakespeare's Bawdy*, 160, *s.v.* pinch; and Antonio's loan of his purse to Sebastian (*Twelfth Night*, 3. 3. 38–47).

[116] *The Complete Works of John Lyly*, ed. R. Warwick Bond, 3 vols. (Oxford, 1902), i. 199.

Bassanio does not respond directly, embarking instead on a long analogy to justify borrowing more money in order to clear his original debt. Antonio is prepared to hazard and venture his person sexually with Bassanio, but Bassanio will take only his money—his literal but not his metaphorical purse.

On other occasions, too, Shakespeare delineates a special kind of space for Antonio and Bassanio, while differentiating them linguistically. The parting of Antonio and Bassanio is not staged, but rather reported by the sympathetic Salerio to Solanio, framing the pair—but particularly Antonio—in an inset space within the homosocial world of Venetian masculinity:

> A kinder gentleman treades not the earth,
> I saw *Bassanio* and *Anthonio* part,
> *Bassanio* told him he would make some speede
> Of his returne: he aunswerd, doe not so,
> Sluber not business for my sake *Bassanio*,
> But stay the very riping of the time,
> And for the Jewes bond which he hath of me
> Let it not enter in your minde of love:
> Be merry, and imploy your cheefest thoughts
> To courtship, and such faire ostents of love
> As shall conveniently become you there,
> And even there his eye being big with teares,
> Turning his face, he put his hand behind him,
> And with affection wondrous sencible
> He wrung *Bassanios* hand, and so they parted.
> *Solanio.*   I thinke hee onely loves the world for him.[117]

Antonio initially speaks with a merchant's perception about Bassanio's voyage to Belmont with his 'Sluber not business', but then redescribes Bassanio's interest in Portia as 'love', its repetition at two line endings gently emphasizing the choice of word, perhaps ironically, perhaps in pain. (One wonders whether 'ostents' and 'conveniently' also subtly characterize Bassanio's expedition as a financial venture rather than an affair of the heart. This may be wishful thinking on Antonio's part.) When Salerio describes Antonio's emotion as 'affection', he is using a word which was much stronger in Elizabethan English than it is today. As well as 'kind feeling, fondness'[118] it also meant 'passion', especially sexual passion, and the disturbance of the mind's equanimity by

    [117] *The Merchant of Venice*, 2. 8. 35–50.   [118] *OED* 6.

violent feelings which it cannot control.[119] And 'wondrous sencible' underlines the intensity of the emotion, since 'sencible' is 'acutely felt; markedly painful'.[120] While Salerio emphasizes Antonio's emotion, and reports Antonio's speech and action, there is no such account of Bassanio: once again there is a disparity of language (verbal and gestural) between the two men.

In the court scene, when Antonio prepares to die, Portia asks him whether he has anything to say. She and the other onlookers are perhaps expecting a last-minute plea for mercy, or some general leave-taking, but his apparently final speech is directed entirely to Bassanio, using a public language to define—as far as he is able—their relationship:

> Commend me to your honourable wife,
> Tell her the processe of *Anthonios* end,
> Say how I lov'd you, speake me faire in death:
> And when the tale is told, bid her be judge
> Whether *Bassanio* had not once a love:
> Repent but you that you shall loose your friend
> And he repents not that he payes your debt.
> For if the Jew doe cut but deepe enough,
> Ile pay it instantly with all my hart.[121]

Though the first line is coolly courteous, 'Say how I lov'd you' grows more intimate, and leads up to the poignant 'Whether *Bassanio* had not once a love'. What exactly 'friend' means here, and whether 'love' means 'experience of love' or 'sexual partner' is impossible to determine.[122] One editor glosses 'love' as 'friend', with a cross-reference to Sonnet 13, thus neatly saving both texts from any suspicion of impropriety.[123] Lorenzo had described Antonio to Portia as 'How true a gentleman ... I How deere a lover of my Lord your husband', to which

[119] *OED* 3; cf. the examples collected in *The Winter's Tale*, ed. J. H. Pafford (London, 1963), 166–7; the title of Barnfield's poem 'The Teares of an Affectionate Shepheard Sicke for Love'; and 'Affection and rapture' in the description of Edward II, quoted on p. 119 below.

[120] *OED* 6.

[121] *The Merchant of Venice*, 4. 1. 270–8.

[122] Pequigney, 211, noting these two possible readings, says that 'love' in the sense of a man's male sexual lover does not occur in Shakespeare outside the *Sonnets*, or elsewhere in the period: but for an example see Barnes, quoted above, p. 40. And Marlowe's 'Come live with me and be my love' could be addressed by one male shepherd to another.

[123] Russell Brown, 115.

Portia replies that she knows Antonio to be 'the bosome lover of my Lord'.[124] All the characters recognize Antonio's special love for Bassanio, but what exactly it amounts to, no one says. Once again, the public language of male friendship contains within it the possibility of a more private and sexual relation.[125]

If in *The Merchant of Venice* Shakespeare added homoerotic possibilities to his source story, in the case of *Twelfth Night* he has both added and removed them. The basic plot of *Twelfth Night* exists in several different versions, and scholars have been unable to say precisely which form or forms Shakespeare knew, and in which language. Probably he was assisted by his half-Italian friend John Marston.[126] But it is clear that he must have worked at least in part from the Sienese play *Gl'Ingannati* (1537).[127] Here one finds several moments of explicitly homosexual comedy. Lelia when dressed as the boy Fabio in the service of her beloved Flamminio says: 'Oh come mi starebbe bene che qualcun di questi giovani scapestrati mi pigliasse per forza e, tirandomi in qualche casa, volesse chiarirsi s'io son maschio o femina'.[128] The nurse asks Fabio/Lelia what would happen if one night Flamminio, 'tentato dalla maladetta tentazione',[129] were to call his page into bed

[124] *The Merchant of Venice*, 3. 4. 6–7, 17. For the sexual significance of 'bosom' see Williams *s.v.*; cf. Sonnet 31, l. 1 (and Duncan-Jones's note, 172); and 'K. James, who could not live without a bosom Favourite cast his Eye upon George Villiers, a young Gentleman of a fine shape . . . And now lying in the King's Bosom, every man paid Tribute to his Smiles, and he managed all affairs' (R. B., *The Unfortunate Court-Favourites of England* (London, 1695), 168).

[125] One contemporary reader of the play annotated his copy of the First Folio with comments on Antonio and Bassanio's exemplary friendship: 'brotherlie offer to a distressed friend', 'Courteous and kind friend', 'perfite friendship' (*The First Folio of Shakespeare: A Transcript of Contemporary Marginalia in a Copy of the Kodama Memorial Library of Meisei University*, ed. Akihiro Yamada (Tokyo, 1998), 52, 54).

[126] Katherine Duncan-Jones, *Ungentle Shakespeare* (London, 2001), 155.

[127] *Gl'Ingannati degli Accademici Intronati di Siena*, ed. J. P. (Edinburgh, 1943); abridged and bowdlerized trans. by Bullough, ii. 286–339; fuller trans. by Bruce Penman in *Five Italian Renaissance Comedies*, ed. Bruce Penman (Harmondsworth, 1978), 193–278. From *Gl'Ingannati* the story spread across Europe, and is extant in English, French, Spanish, and neo-Latin adaptations. For a summary see *Laelia: A Comedy Acted at Queens' College, Cambridge Probably on March 1st, 1595*, ed. G. C. Moore Smith (Cambridge, 1910), p. xxiv. Shakespeare probably used more than one version of the story.

[128] *Gl'Ingannati*, 20: 'It would serve me right if one of those reckless young idiots grabbed hold of me and dragged me into a house somewhere to find out whether I'm really a boy or a girl!' (tr. Penman, 202).

[129] Ibid., 25: 'tempted by a wicked temptation'. Penman calls it 'a wicked, unnatural

with him. Evidently this festive version of Italy is imagined to be a
society where young men experiment with sex with other men. And
when Fabio/Lelia tells Pasquella that he has to serve his own master,
Pasquella wonders what sort of service that entails:

> *Lelia.*   A me bisogna servire il padrone; intendi, Pasquella?
> *Pasquella...*   Dormi forse con lui?
> *Lelia.*   Dio il volesse ch'io fusse tanto in grazia sua![130]

We the audience know that the disguised Lelia is expressing her desire
for her master, but the comment is heard on stage as undisguised
desire of the page Fabio for his master—an interesting indication that
homosexual desire is imagined to attract the young lad to the older
man, and not only the older man to the younger, *à la grecque.* The idea
that men may be moved by both homosexual and heterosexual desire
is evident again when we are told that Isabella's father Gherardo had
found Fabio in his house a couple of times, 'ed hagli fatto mille carezze,
presolo per la mano, toccato sotto 'l mento, come se fusse suo
figliuolo'. But Giglio, a Spanish soldier, suspects that this is hardly a
paternal caress: 'Ah, reniego del putto, vieio puerco, vellacco! Ya, ya. Sé
io lo que quiere.'[131] Gherardo is also interested in Fabrizzio. Gherardo
is under the mistaken impression that Fabrizzio is not a boy but a girl
in male disguise, and offers to marry him. Fabrizzio, unaware of
Gherardo's misapprehension, thinks that he is the object of a homosexual seduction. But Fabrizzio is not entirely mistaken in this
assumption, for it is clear that Fabrizzio's masculine attire adds
significantly to his appeal in Gherardo's eyes: 'L'abito 'l mostra'.[132]
Meanwhile, Master Piero the schoolmaster is enticed into an inn by
being told that the landlord's son is as beautiful as an angel, and his
servant calls Piero a sodomite, ushering in a dialogue full of abusive
homosexual bawdy.[133] In the world of *Gl'Ingannati*, some men may be

---

temptation' (208), and Bullough 'the accursed temptation' (297). The neo-Latin play
staged in Cambridge omits the moralizing: *Quid si imperaret aliquando tibi vt secum
cubes?* ('What if he were to command you some time to sleep with him?': *Laelia*, 16).

[130] Ibid., 35: 'I have to serve my master. You understand what I mean, Pasquella? I . . .
Do you sleep with him? I Would to God I were so much in his favour' (tr. Bullough, 304;
cf. Penman, 218).

[131] Ibid., 39: 'he has given him a thousand caresses ['made a great fuss of him':
Penman, 222], taken him by the hand, tickled him under the chin, as if he were his son'
. . . 'Ah, bloody queer, old pig. Yes, yes. I know what he's after.'

[132] Ibid., 63: 'her [boy's] clothes show her off well' (cf. Penman, 248).

[133] Ibid., 54, 65–6; tr. Penman, 238, 249–50.

ridiculed for their exclusively homosexual interests, while others are recognized as potentially interested in bedding other men, or attracted by the ambiguities of an androgynous appearance.

Some of this material survives into *Twelfth Night*, but transmuted into subtler forms. Shakespeare was evidently not interested in the comedy of homosexual lust, in provoking laughter at sexually omnivorous masters or pederastic pedants. But the idea that a man might with equal enthusiasm bed a pretty boy or a pretty girl does surface in *Twelfth Night*, as the homosexual elements in *Gl'Ingannati* are reconstructed as something much more inward and difficult to articulate, thus developing a line of thought already essayed theatrically in *The Merchant of Venice*. In place of easily identifiable types, and easily satisfied lust, observed from a comfortable distance, Shakespeare imagines characters puzzled by their feelings, rather at sea emotionally, and finding that their sense of self is bound up with their love for an unreadable and unattainable other. In a reprise of the opening of *The Merchant of Venice*, Shakespeare begins *Twelfth Night* with another melancholy lover, Orsino. (By contrast, the equivalent figure in *Gl'Ingannati*, Flamminio, displays no such temperament.) Orsino, of course, is in love with Olivia; but the play makes it clear that he is also attracted to Viola in her disguise as Cesario. This may be an adaptation of Gherardo's interest in Fabrizzio in male clothing, for no such attraction exists in the case of Flamminio; the most he says to Fabio/Lelia is that he loves him like a brother ('ch'io t'amo come fratello').[134] As early as Act 1 scene 4 we find the words 'love' and 'favours' used for Orsino's disposition towards Cesario;[135] and while both words in Renaissance English can refer to a master's dutiful care for his servant, both can also refer to a sexual relationship. The semantic field here is productively ambiguous. Orsino draws Cesario aside, away from his other servants, creating a semi-private space for the two of them. Orsino is fascinated by Cesario's physicality, unsure whether to read him as a man or a woman,[136] but by the end of the play he has become passionately attached to Cesario qua young man,[137] perhaps more enraged at the prospect of losing Cesario to Olivia than losing Olivia to Cesario. It is a mark of Shakespeare's move inwards that he makes Orsino inadvertently show the intensity of his love for Cesario by citing the example of the robber captain in Heliodorus' *Ethiopica* who determines to kill a beloved captive when his own life is in danger:

---

[134] *Gl'Ingannati*, 32; tr. Penman, 215. [135] *Twelfth Night*, 1. 4. 1, 6–7.
[136] Ibid., 1. 4. 30–4. [137] Ibid., 5. 1. 115–29.

> Why should I not, (had I the heart to do it)
> Like to th'Egyptian theefe, at point of death
> Kill what I love:[138]

By contrast, when Flamminio wonders whether to kill Fabio for (as he thinks) having sex with Isabella, he only says, 'Parti ch'io amazzi questo traditore o no? Egli è pure un buon servitore.'[139] In Orsino's outburst we touch unexpectedly deep feeling; in Flamminio's question, only comic role-play. At the end of *Twelfth Night* Viola's true identity has been revealed, but she is still dressed as Cesario, thus making the closing tableau a visual marriage between two men; indeed, Orsino continues to call her 'Boy' and '*Cesario*'.[140] In *Gl'Ingannati*, however, Lelia changes back into female costume for the equivalent scene. Shakespeare prefers the pleasurable simulacrum of a homosexual union.

The character who in *Twelfth Night* most clearly manifests love for another man is the sea-captain Antonio, deeply attached to Viola's twin brother Sebastian. In plot terms, Antonio is the equivalent of *Gl'Ingannati*'s tutor, who arrives with his young charge in a strange city and sets about finding a suitable inn. But Shakespeare has completely reimagined this character's circumstances and history. No danger threatens the tutor, but Antonio is at risk because he has fought against Orsino's men in a sea battle. This detail has been added by Shakespeare as he imagines what it would be like for an older man to feel self-sacrificial love for a younger man who is unattainable—which is the story of *The Merchant of Venice*, and perhaps of the *Sonnets*.

The initial scene between the two men is tense, and quite different in tone from the equivalent scene between tutor and pupil in *Gl'Ingannati*, where the tutor quickly becomes embroiled in a comic rivalry between two innkeepers eager for their custom.[141] It seems that Sebastian recognizes Antonio's feelings, and is seeking some gentle way of indicating that he cannot (or perhaps dare not) reciprocate.[142] As with Antonio and Bassanio, Shakespeare gives the two men different idioms, so marking out the asymmetrical relationship

[138] Ibid., 5. 1. 115–17.
[139] *Gl'Ingannati*, 86: 'Do you think I should kill that traitor or not? He *is* a good servant' (tr. Penman, 272; cf. Bullough, 336).
[140] *Twelfth Night*, 5. 1. 265, 381.
[141] Ibid., 2. 1. 1–42; *Gl'Ingannati*, 3. 2.
[142] There is a thoughtful discussion of this scene in *Twelfth Night*, ed. Roger Warren and Stanley Wells (Oxford, 1994), 39–40.

between them, the lack of mutuality. Sebastian's syntax is cumbersome, no doubt embarrassed; and his language is full of words with
potential sexual charge which are deflected into other meanings. 'I
perceive in you so excellent a touch of modestie, that you will not
extort from me, what I am willing to keepe in', he says. This appears to
be a way of warding off a sexual advance, but the next sentence gives it
another meaning: 'therefore it charges me in manners, the rather to
expresse my selfe'. But what he goes on to express is not his feelings but
merely his family history. Antonio is more outspoken: 'If you will not
murther me for my love, let mee be your servant.' This is a blunt form
of Petrarchan language, the sea-captain's straightforwardness putting
its stamp on the Italianate courtly imagery of the lover serving his
mistress and dying for unrequited love. Sebastian's reply points to a
depth of emotional response which he cannot trust himself to explore:
'If you will not undo what you have done, that is kill him, whom you
have recover'd, desire it not. Fare ye well at once, my bosome is full of
kindnesse.' He is on the point of tears. Why would it kill Sebastian to
accept what Antonio offers, unless this were to entail something more
than friendly services? 'Kindnesse' is glossed 'tenderness' by the Arden
and Oxford editors, but this is only one possible meaning selected
from the semantic field defined by *OED* sense 5: 'Kind feeling; a feeling
of tenderness or fondness; affection, love. Also, Good will, favour,
friendship.' Not only do editors eliminate the meanings 'affection,
love', they also ignore the meaning 'reciprocated sexual desire, sexual
availability'. This is not recognized by the *OED*, but is common in the
early modern period.[143] Again, Sebastian's language reveals homosexual possibilities which the speaker is trying to keep at bay. And
again, Antonio is more explicit, saying in his parting soliloquy, 'I do
adore thee so.'

   Much of the comedy of *Gl'Ingannati* and similar plays stems from
misrecognition, the misreading of appearances, motives, emotions,
and gender. But for Shakespeare, misrecognition, and in particular the
misreading of other people's feelings towards one, also generates
uncomfortable and near-tragic moments. Two characters in this play
go out on a limb and expose their feelings for someone else, only to be

---

[143] Williams, *s.v.* Cf. '*Bawd*: ... she should ... doe mee the kindnesse of our profession
... will you use him kindly?' (*Pericles*, 19. 14–16, 62–3). In *Troilus and Cressida*, 4. 6. 21,
Ulysses comments on Cressida being kissed by Agamemnon: 'Yet is the kindnesse but
perticular, | Twere better shee were kist in general', where the kissing is a sign that she is
regarded as sexually available: in effect the kiss is a synecdoche for sexual intercourse.

very publicly hurt by the revelation of their misapprehension. One is Antonio, the other Malvolio, who is likewise Shakespeare's addition to his source. Malvolio is tricked into voicing his desire for his mistress Olivia, and is humiliated when it is revealed that she does not love him.[144] Antonio, encountering Viola dressed as Cesario, takes her for Sebastian, and is mortified when she will not acknowledge any obligations to him. As a plot motif, this goes back to Plautus' *Menaechmi* and Shakespeare's own *Comedy of Errors*, but the mistake brings forth a declaration of Antonio's love for this apparently worthless boy:

> This youth that you see heere,
> I snatch'd one halfe out of the jawes of death,
> Releev'd him with such sanctitie of love;
> And to his image, which me thought did promise
> Most venerable worth, did I devotion.
>
> . . . .
>
> But oh, how vild an idoll proves this God:
>
> . . . .
>
> None can be call'd deform'd, but the unkinde.
> Vertue is beauty, but the beauteous evill
> Are empty trunkes, ore-flourish'd by the devill.[145]

The religious language of adoration stems from the Petrarchan tradition, and has parallels in the *Sonnets*,[146] but more remarkable is the strong sense of betrayal, of misreading, which Antonio voices. Like the speaker of the *Sonnets*, he has taken the beautiful exterior to be a sign of inner worth, and has been proved wrong:

> They that have powre to hurt, and will doe none,
> That doe not do the thing, they most do showe,
> Who moving others, are themselves as stone,
>
> . . . .
>
> Lillies that fester, smell far worse then weeds.[147]

---

[144] If Shakespeare himself played Malvolio (as Katherine Duncan-Jones suggests in *Ungentle Shakespeare*, 158) there is a bitter self-directed irony in the writer of the *Sonnets* enacting on the public stage a version of the pain which he traces in the privacy of the poems: 'Alas 'tis true, I have gone here and there, | And made my selfe a motley to the view' (Sonnet 110, ll. 1–2).

[145] *Twelfth Night*, 3. 4. 350–61. Similarly, Viola had voiced anxiety about reading the sea-captain's moral character from his appearance: 'though that nature, with a beauteous wall | Doth oft close in pollution: yet of thee | I will beleeve thou hast a minde that suites | With this thy faire and outward character' (ibid., 1. 2. 48–51); 'character' here = outward appearance.   [146] *Twelfth Night*, ed. Warren and Wells, 40.

[147] Sonnet 94, ll. 1–3, 14.

In the final scene, this hurt is repeated, as Antonio recalls bitterly that

> His life I gave him, and did thereto adde
> My love without retention, or restraint,
> All his in dedication.

Moreover,

> for three months before,
> No *intrim*, not a minutes vacancie,
> Both day and night did we keepe companie.[148]

This revelation that Antonio and Sebastian had lived together for three months might suggest a private space of homosexual intimacy, as Joseph Pequigney argues,[149] but it is one which Shakespeare never actually shows us. It is a scene for the space of Antonio's memory, and the audience's imagination, not for the stage.[150]

The opening of Barnaby Riche's *Apolonius and Silla*, an offspring of *Gl'Ingannati* and another source for *Twelfth Night*, points up a moral about love affairs which could almost be used as an abstract for the *Sonnets*, and poignantly summarizes Antonio's plight:

If a question might be asked, what is the ground indeede of reasonable love, whereby the knot is knit of true and perfect freendship, I thinke those that be wise would answere—deserte: that is, where the partie beloved dooeth requite us with the like; for otherwise, if the bare shewe of beautie, or the comelinesse of personage might bee sufficient to confirme us in our love, those that bee accustomed to goe to faires and markettes might sometymes fall in love with twentie in a daie; desert must then bee (of force) the grounde of reasonable love; for to love them that hate us, to followe them that flie from us, to faune on them that froune on us, to currie favour with them that disdaine us, to bee glad to please them that care not how they offende us, who will not confesse this to be an erroneous love, neither grounded uppon witte nor reason?[151]

Perhaps it was the opportunity inherent in the plot of *Gl'Ingannati* for pondering this uncomfortable truth which led the author of the *Sonnets* to seek in his imagined Italy a space where homosexual desire might be given voice, if not satisfaction.

---

[148] *Twelfth Night*, 5. 1. 74–76, 89–91.

[149] Pequigney, 'The Two Antonios', 203–4, 206.

[150] It was a faux pas in the RSC's 2001 production when Act 2 scene 1 opened with Sebastian getting out of their shared bed, and dressing.

[151] Barnaby Riche, *Riche his Farewell to Militarie Profession* (1581), from Bullough, ii. 345.

THE ERASURE OF HOMOEROTICISM FROM
SHAKESPEARE'S TEXTS

During the course of the seventeenth century, new editions and adaptations of Shakespeare's work introduced textual changes which removed the productive ambiguities through which Shakespeare had allowed homosexual desire to be made visible. Through these interventions the nature of male relationships is clarified, and friendship is purged of homoeroticism. An early sign of anxiety about homoeroticism in Shakespeare's work is the reshaping of the *Sonnets* in the generation after Shakespeare's death. First published in 1609, the *Sonnets* were reissued by the bookseller John Benson in 1640.[152] His preface stresses the purity both of the poems and of their author, and reassures prospective purchasers that there is nothing difficult or ambiguous about them: 'some excellent and sweetely composed Poems, of Master *William Shakespeare*, Which in themselves appeare of the same purity, the Authour himselfe then living avouched ... you shall finde them *Seren*, cleere and eligantly plaine, such gentle straines as shall recreate and not perplexe your braine.'[153] Would Benson have stressed their purity if there had not been some doubt about that, or their clarity, if some readers had not thought them full of multiple meanings? And would Shakespeare himself have (supposedly) 'avouched' their 'purity' if no one had questioned it? Whether or not we give any credence to Benson's testimony,[154] his preface seems to imply that Shakespeare had been forced to defend his poems after some scandal resulted from their publication in 1609. Benson himself made sure that no such scandal would attach to his own publication. It is well known that Benson rearranged the poems, ran several sonnets together to form new poems, gave them titles which referred to the

---

[152] Benson's edn. of the *Sonnets* appeared as *Poems: Written by Wil. Shake-speare. Gent* (London, 1640); cited hereafter as *1640*. Benson's changes are described in *The Sonnets*, ed. Hyder Edward Rollins, 2 vols. (Philadelphia, 1944), ii. 18–28. Recent discussions of *1640* include Arthur F. Marotti, 'Shakespeare's *Sonnets* as Literary Property' in Elizabeth D. Harvey and Katharine Eisaman Maus (eds.), *Soliciting Interpretation: Literary Theory and Seventeenth-Century English Poetry* (Chicago, 1990), 143–73; Margareta de Grazia, 'The Scandal of Shakespeare's Sonnets', *Shakespeare Survey*, 46 (1994), 35–49; and David Baker, 'Cavalier Shakespeare: The 1640 *Poems* of John Benson', *Studies in Philology*, 95 (1998), 152–73.

[153] *1640*, sigs. *2^{r–v}.

[154] For a debate over this, see *Sonnets*, ed. Rollins, ii. 23–5.

poet's mistress, and altered the wording in several places to make the poems address a female lover.

In so doing, he was adapting Shakespeare for a new readership attuned to a Cavalier ethos,[155] but he was also extending a tradition of appropriating the *Sonnets* which had begun earlier, since some of the poems which had previously been anthologized in print or in manuscript were precisely those which were either addressed to a woman or, when detached from their context, could be made to seem so, especially when given new titles such as 'On his Mistris Beauty', which one manuscript attached to Sonnet 106.[156] Some of Benson's new titles, such as 'Love-sicke',[157] or 'A bashfull Lover',[158] or 'A good construction of his Loves unkindnesse',[159] or 'An intreatie for her acceptance',[160] implicitly create miniature narratives from among the recognizable scenarios of heterosexual love and courtship, whereas in their original form the *Sonnets* had largely eschewed a legible narrative sequence, and had instead presented readers with various forms of discontinuity and obsessive return. Textual alterations also rewrite the relationships. In Sonnet 101 Benson prints:

> Excuse not silence so, for't lies in thee,
> To make her much out-live a gilded tombe:
> And to be prais'd of ages yet to be.
>> Then doe thy office muse, I teach thee how,
>> To make her seeme long hence, as she showes now.[161]

Benson has 'her' and 'she' where the original *Shakes-speares Sonnets* had printed 'him' and 'he'. In another case, where the 1609 edition had referred to the addressee as 'sweet boy' the 1640 edition changes this to 'sweet-love'.[162]

Other of Benson's titles present the sonnets as poems of unambiguous friendship, as in 'Two faithfull friends' (Sonnets 46–7) or 'The benefit of Friendship' (Sonnets 30–2).[163] Such explicit references to friendship serve to define and contain the otherwise fluid meanings of the words 'friend', 'love', and 'lover' which occur in Sonnets 30–2:

> Then can I drowne an eye (un-us'd to flow)
> For precious friends hid in deaths dateles night,

---

[155] As Baker argues.

[157] Added to Sonnets 80–1; *1640*, sigs. D3[r–v].

[159] Over Sonnet 120; ibid., sig. E5[v].

[161] Ibid., sig. E1[v].

[162] Sonnet 108, l. 5, *1609*; *1640*, sig. F6[v].

[156] Duncan-Jones, 114, 453–66.

[158] Over Sonnet 23; ibid., sig. B5[r].

[160] Over Sonnet 125; ibid., sig. E7[r].

[163] *1640*, sigs. C5[v], B6[r–v].

And weepe a fresh loves long since canceld woe

. . . .

But if the while I thinke on thee (deare friend)
All losses are restord, and sorrowes end.[164]

Thou art the grave where buried love doth live,
Hung with the trophies of my lovers gon.[165]

By labelling these poems as articulating 'The benefit of Friendship', Benson ensures that their usages of 'love' are understood to refer not to passionate erotic feelings but to that Ciceronian exchange of benefits between male friends which is not merely acceptable and profitable, but necessary for the smooth running of the social order. And when in Sonnet 104 the male 'faire friend' of 1609 becomes the implicitly female 'faire love' of 1640,[166] Benson seems to be marking out a distinction between male friends and female lovers, delineating where Shakespeare did not. Shakespeare addresses the youth both as 'friend' and 'love', each word slightly changing its semantic field and emotional charge with each new context. In Sonnet 144 (which Benson omits) Shakespeare had written that his 'two loves', the boy and the woman, are 'both to each friend', when he suspects that they are having sex together.

Renaissance ideals of male friendship drew upon the classical model which expected these bonds to be between men who were roughly equal in social standing, who would share their goods, and would enjoy a relationship of reciprocity and trust. But it is remarkable that in all the areas where this ideal would require stability, the *Sonnets* register instability. There is a difference of age between poet and friend, and probably a difference of social status; the feelings are not reciprocal, or at least not reciprocated consistently or in their intensity; the exchanges of gifts between the two (far from being signs of equality and security in friendship) are occasions of anxiety and signs of an uncertainty which is not only emotional but even existential: the friend's apparent theft of the poet's mistress is rewritten as an exchange of gifts between the three, but this triangular relationship throws up searing anxieties about the stability of the poet's self, a self which in turn becomes part of the traffic between the two men (Sonnets 133–6). *Pace* the extraordinary claim by John Kerrigan that 'the sonnets to the youth grow out of comradely affection in the

---

[164] Sonnet 30, ll. 5–7, 13–14, *1609*.   [165] Sonnet 31, ll. 9–10, *1609*.
[166] *1640*, sig. E1ᵛ.

literature of friendship',[167] the *Sonnets* are almost an extended definition of what classic Renaissance friendship was not.

The anxiety over the vocabulary of friendship and love which Benson displayed in his textual alterations to the *Sonnets* may signal a new need for the kind of social assurance which craves secure definition, foreshadowing a move away from a world in which masculine friendship and desire formed a continuum, towards one where the admission of sexual attraction between men was taboo, or confined to a special subculture, so requiring that expressions of ordinary male friendship be purged of any over-intense emotion or gesture which might imply a sexual motivation, and requiring that 'love' be confined safely to heterosexual relations.

There are also manifest tensions and anxieties around the friendship between Antonio and Bassanio in the adaptation of *The Merchant of Venice* which was made in 1701 by George Granville under the title of *The Jew of Venice*, and this reworking of the story may help to bring into focus the differing sensitivities about male relationships which prevailed at the beginning of the seventeenth century and at the end.

The prologue to *The Jew of Venice*, contributed by Bevill Higgons, is spoken by the ghosts of Shakespeare and Dryden, who rise crowned with laurel. After the two playwrights have lamented the debased judgement of audiences who are unmoved by passion, and are 'deaf indeed to Nature and to Love', deserting true drama for French farce, 'Dryden' complains:

> Thro' Perspectives revers'd they Nature view,
> Which give the Passions Images, not true.
> *Strephon* for *Strephon* sighs; and *Sapho* dies,
> Shot to the Soul by brighter *Sapho's* Eyes:
> No Wonder then their wand'ring Passions roam,
> And feel not Nature, whom th' have overcome.
> For shame let genal[168] Love prevail agen,
> You Beaux Love Ladies, and you Ladies Men.
>   *Shakes.*   These Crimes unknown, in our less polisht Age,
> Now seem above Correction of the Stage;
> Less Heinous Faults, our Justice does pursue.[169]

---

[167] Kerrigan, 55.
[168] Genial, procreative.
[169] [George Granville], *The Jew of Venice. A Comedy* (London, 1701), sig. [A]4[r].

So in 1701—at a time when the molly houses have made homosexual relations visible as a special form of male bonding—English society is thought to be deserting the natural in pursuit of the unnatural, and not only when it comes to theatrical preferences: men are now in love with other men, and women with other women. The ghost of Shakespeare says that such behaviour was unknown in his day, admitting to a lack of refinement, but exculpating himself, his plays, and his contemporaries from any imputations of unnatural behaviour. Although the prologue says that Granville's play is not concerned to punish these deviations from nature and from procreative love, it is striking that Higgons should think it appropriate to raise this issue in relation to an adaptation of *The Merchant of Venice*. One commentator on this adaptation claims that 'the suspicion that constant companions of the same sex who continually show signs of affection may well be homo-erotically involved never appears to have crossed Granville's mind'.[170] On the contrary, this is exactly the possibility that Granville understands and is at pains to avoid, as his play drives home a clear and emphatic distinction between friendship and love, and consistently excises lines which might suggest an exclusive and possibly physical union between the two men. As he stresses in his preface, 'the judicious Reader will observe . . . many Manly and Moral Graces in the Characters and Sentiments', and it is into the extended definition of moral manliness that Granville's play puts much of its energy.[171]

The adaptation opens without any trace of Antonio's melancholy: there is no secret here to be read or guessed. Whereas in Shakespeare's play Antonio had defined his role in life as a sad one, in Granville's version it is merely 'serious'. When he offers to help Bassanio, he does not say:

> My purse, my person, my extreamest meanes
> Lie all unlockt to your occasions.[172]

but:

> My Purse, my Person, my extreamest Means,
> Are all my Friend's.[173]

---

[170] Ben Ross Schneider, 'Granville's *Jew of Venice* (1701): A Close Reading of Shakespeare's *Merchant*', *Restoration*, 17 (1993), 111–34, at 119.

[171] Granville, *The Jew of Venice*, sig. [A]3ʳ. A small sign of Granville's concern to avoid homoerotic suggestions is his excision of Jessica's disguise as a boy, and the pleasure which this gives Lorenzo.   [172] *The Merchant of Venice*, 1. 1. 138–9.

[173] *The Jew of Venice*, 2.

In Shakespeare, what is locked away from others lies all unlocked to Bassanio. Granville's erasure of these implications of a shared secrecy may reflect unease about the new connotations which secrecy shared between men was acquiring with the arrival of the clandestine molly houses, while the idea that Antonio's person might 'lie all unlockt' to Bassanio's needs may now have seemed too clear a sexual invitation. To avoid any doubt, Granville makes his Antonio define friendship:

> Is this to be a Friend? With blushing Cheek,
> With down-cast Eyes, and with a faltring Tongue,
> We sue to those we doubt: Friendship is plain,
> Artless, familiar, confident and free.[174]

Friendship is open, unblushing; to be a man of silence and secrecy, or to hesitate about putting one's desires into words, would run the risk of being interpreted as a man with something unmanly to hide, like the new kind of Strephon.

Friendship involves openness in asking and in granting, but Granville carefully stresses that, although Antonio may give his body for his friend, this gift has no erotic significance; instead it is an example of that generosity and benevolence which is characteristic of manly and moral virtue:

> what is a Pound of Flesh,
> What my whole Body, every Drop of Blood,
> To purchase my Friend's Quiet! Heav'n still is good
> To those who seek the Good of others:
>
> .   .   .   .
>
> Of all the Joys that generous Minds receive,
> The noblest is, the God-like Power to give.[175]

If Antonio's offering of his body for (rather than to) Bassanio is pure benevolence, Shylock's obsession with Antonio's flesh is perhaps motivated by something more than the stereotypical malevolence of the Jewish usurer. Shylock himself protests that his proposals can 'bear no wrong | Construction',[176] thus alerting the audience to the possibility that more than one construction might indeed be placed on them. Whereas Shakespeare's Shylock simply says:

> let the forfaite
> Be nominated for an equall pound

---

[174] *The Jew of Venice*, 2.   [175] Ibid., 9.   [176] Ibid.

> Of your faire flesh, to be cut off and taken
> In what part of your bodie pleaseth me.[177]

Granville's Shylock takes pleasure in contemplating which part of Antonio's body he will cut off:

> Let me see, What think you of your Nose,
> Or of an Eye—or of—a Pound of Flesh
> To be cut off, and taken from what Part
> Of your Body—I shall think fit to name.[178]

The play pauses over the possibility that the as yet unnameable part of Antonio's body represented here only by dashes is an object of Shylock's perverse sexual interest.[179] In any case, he clearly represents the opposite of Antonio and Bassanio's form of manliness.

Manliness, in Granville's view, does not require that displays of affection and emotion be suppressed, but it does require that these be carefully defined and not left open to misconstruction. When Antonio and Bassanio part for the latter to go to Belmont, Granville stages the scene (unlike Shakespeare) and Bassanio exclaims:

> One more Embrace: To those who know not Friendship
> This may appear unmanly Tenderness;
> But 'tis the frailty of the bravest Minds.[180]

For Granville there is no blurring of friendship and love, nor is there any conflict of interest between the friendship of Antonio and Bassanio on the one hand, and the love of Bassanio and Portia on the other; indeed, he is careful to stress that friendship and love are at once distinct and allied. Antonio urges Bassanio not to give 'your Heart so far away, | As to forget your Friend'[181] when courting Portia, but at the same time he urges Bassanio to make haste to Belmont. Bassanio is eager to board ship, but at the same time reluctant to leave Antonio. The friendship is entirely reciprocal and unselfish. When Antonio at a banquet proposes a toast to 'immortal Friendship', Bassanio responds with 'Let Love be next, what else should | Follow Friendship?'[182] Antonio's image of their friendship being like the marriage of Venice

---

[177] *The Merchant of Venice*, 1. 3. 147–50.

[178] *The Jew of Venice*, 8.

[179] It is also possible that Granville is drawing upon the common association of the Jewish rite of circumcision with castration: for a suggestion that this fear is already implicit in Shakespeare's play see Lorna Hutson, *The Usurer's Daughter: Male Friendship and Fictions of Women in Sixteenth-Century England* (London, 1994), 226–7.

[180] *The Jew of Venice*, 20.   [181] Ibid.   [182] Ibid., 12.

and the sea requires some careful definition to ensure that the marital
simile and the language of love are not misconstrued; Antonio says:

> Be thou to me, and I to my *Bassanio,*
> Like *Venice* and her *Adriatick* Bride,
> For ever link'd in Love.
>   *Bass.*   Thou joyn'st us well: And rightly hast compar'd;
> Like *Venice* on a Rock, my Friendship stands
> Constant and fix'd; but 'tis a barren Spot;
> Whilst like the liberal *Adriatick,* thou
> With Plenty bath'st my Shoars—
> My Fortunes are the Bounty of my Friend.
>   *Anto.*   My Friend's the noblest Bounty of my Fortune.[183]

Portia for her part sees Bassanio's concern to rescue Antonio from the
consequences of the bond as a sign of those very qualities which will
make him a good husband: 'as you prove, | Your Faith in Friendship, I
shall trust your Love'.[184]

Granville will not allow us to think that the male association
between Antonio and Bassanio might have priority over the marriage
of Portia and Bassanio. In Shakespeare's play, Portia and Lorenzo
discuss the deep bond between the two men: Lorenzo tells Portia that
she would be proud of Bassanio's prompt desertion of her in order to
rescue Antonio if she knew 'How deere a lover of my Lord your
husband' Antonio is: the implication seems to be that this is a man's
world, understood by Lorenzo but not shared by Portia. She replies
that she realizes how the two 'beare an egall yoke of love' and that
Antonio is 'the bosome lover of my Lord'.[185] But this scene in which
Lorenzo and Portia discuss the primacy of the male bond is trimmed
by Granville; 'bosome lover' becomes 'how true a Lover', and Portia
now remarks that 'I never did repent of doing good',[186] showing that
she shares that overriding concern for beneficence which Antonio and
Bassanio have stressed in their speeches to each other: thus she is
linked to them, instead of being excluded from their world.

In Shakespeare's court scene Antonio describes himself as 'a tainted
weather of the flocke',[187] but Granville cuts this, for he will admit
nothing which suggests that Antonio is anything other than the perfect
gentleman. In the adaptation, Antonio's speech of farewell to Bassanio

---

[183] *The Jew of Venice,* 12.   [184] Ibid., 28.
[185] *The Merchant of Venice,* 3. 4. 13, 17.   [186] *The Jew of Venice,* 28.
[187] *The Merchant of Venice,* 4. 1. 113.

when Shylock is about to cut out his heart omits the lines in which Shakespeare's character asks Bassanio to tell Portia how much Antonio loved him:

> Say how I lov'd you, speake me faire in death:
> And when the tale is told, bid her be judge
> Whether Bassanio had not once a love:
> Repent but you that you shall loose your friend.[188]

Is there an asymmetry in Antonio's phrasing, implying that he has loved Bassanio, while Bassanio has only thought of him as a friend? If so, it is not present in Granville's equivalent speech, where Antonio says 'Grieve not my Friend, that you thus lose a Friend':[189] here the balanced phrasing marks out an entirely mutual friendship, in which there is no place for the word 'love', at least, not as a noun meaning 'lover'. This moment of self-sacrifice is made into a moment of total openness, for Antonio says:

> Now, do your Office,
> Cut deep enough be sure, and whet thy Knife
> With keenest Malice; for I would have my Heart
> Seen by my Friend.[190]

His heart is to be disclosed to his friend, but this happens in a public arena for all to see. Antonio's heart evidently harbours no secrets: there is nothing suspect, embarrassing, or dangerous in this male bond.

In Shakespeare, Bassanio and Gratiano both say that they would willingly sacrifice their wives so as to redeem Antonio's life. Granville cannot permit such an assertion of the male bond over the obligations of love and marriage, and cuts out these speeches, replacing them with an offer from Bassanio to die in Antonio's place. There then follows a contest between Antonio and Bassanio as to which of them is to die for the other, so that the focus is not on the primacy of male friendship over marriage, but on which of the two men is to have the opportunity to make the ultimate demonstration of friendship. Then Bassanio draws his sword to kill Shylock, and although the Duke is outraged at this violation of the court, he does admit that he admires Bassanio's virtue more than he blames his passion: thus the passion is clearly virtuous, not excessive or suspect.

At the end of the court scene Bassanio embraces Antonio, but at the same time celebrates his love for Portia; these are the twin guarantors of his existence:

---

[188] Ibid., 4. 1. 272–5.   [189] *The Jew of Venice*, 35.   [190] Ibid.

> Once more, let me embrace my Friend, welcom to Life,
> And welcome to my Arms, thou best of Men:
> Thus of my Love and of my Friend possess'd,
> With such a double Shield upon my Breast,
> Fate cannot peirce me now, securely Blest.[191]

The play's conclusion seems to be that love and friendship are comple-mentary, but also that successful marital love needs that solidity of trust, benevolence, and reciprocity which one finds in friendship:

> Love, like a Meteor, shows a short-liv'd Blaze,
> Or treads thro' various Skies, a wond'ring Maze;
> Begot by Fancy, and by Fancy led,
> Here in a Moment, in a Moment fled:
> But fixt by Obligations, it will last;
> For Gratitude's the Charm that binds it fast.[192]

This seems to be the voice of companionable marriage, founded on sentiment, reason, and interest, in which the relationship of husband and wife has some of the qualities provided by male friendship. The two bonds are not merely compatible, but mutually reinforcing, and understood through reciprocal definition.

Granville's play, written at the very point when a homosexual sub-culture emerges in London, takes considerable pains to define the relationship between Antonio and Bassanio as friendship, and to define the meaning of friendship as mutual benevolence; it makes the relationship open to the view, avoids places of secrecy, and calls atten-tion to how any displays of emotion or offerings of the body are sure tokens of moral manliness. In the light of the anxieties voiced so clearly in the prologue, it is hard to avoid concluding that Granville is taking great pains to remove from Shakespeare's text any emotion which in the new climate could be construed as suggesting covert homosexual bonding.[193]

One particular kind of friendship which often entails close emotional

---

[191] *The Jew of Venice*, 38.

[192] Ibid., 46.

[193] Similarly, performance versions of *Twelfth Night* in the 18th and 19th cents. display considerable unease over the relationship between Antonio and Sebastian, often shifting or cutting their scenes; e.g. the Inchbald version makes Orsino carefully explain the terms of Antonio's proximity to Sebastian in a closing speech: 'Thou hast a noble spirit, | And, as Sebastian's friend, be ever near him'. See Laurie E. Osborne, 'The Texts of *Twelfth Night*', *ELH* 57 (1990), 37–61, esp. 52–3.

bonds is that between soldiers, and whereas Shakespeare seems to have permitted a vein of homoeroticism to colour his depiction of military comradeship, his Restoration adaptors sought to purge comradeship from any sexual implication. The principal example here is *Coriolanus* and the adaptation of it by Nahum Tate in 1682 as *The Ingratitude of a Commonwealth.* Tate's handling of the meeting between Coriolanus and Aufidius alters or removes some of the lines which most suggest that there is an erotic charge to the martial bond between the two men, at least on Aufidius' side. Shakespeare's Aufidius greets Coriolanus with a speech heady with emotion and excitement, a speech which has no precedent in his source in Plutarch:

> Let me twine
> Mine armes about that body, where against
> My grained Ash an hundred times hath broke,
> And scarr'd the Moone with splinters:
> *He embraces Coriolanus*
>
>   heere I cleep
> The Anvile of my Sword, and do contest
> As hotly, and as Nobly with thy Love,
> As ever in Ambitious strength, I did
> Contend against thy Valour. Know thou first,
> I lov'd the Maid I married: never man
> Sigh'd truer breath. But that I see thee heere
> Thou Noble thing, more dances my rapt heart,
> Then when I first my wedded Mistris saw
> Bestride my Threshold. Why, thou Mars I tell thee,
> We have a Power on foote: and I had purpose
> Once more to hew thy Target from thy Brawne,
> Or loose mine Arme for't: Thou hast beate mee out
> Twelve severall times, and I have nightly since
> Dreamt of encounters 'twixt thy selfe and me:
> We have beene downe together in my sleepe,
> Unbuckling Helmes, fisting each others Throat,
> And wak'd halfe dead with nothing.[194]

Here Shakespeare makes the feeling of Aufudius for Coriolanus an ecstatic fusion of enmity, rivalry, comradeship, and sexual desire,[195]

---

[194] *Coriolanus*, 4. 5. 107–27.

[195] See *LBM* 62–4; for a discussion of masculinity generally in the play see Janet Adelman, *Suffocating Mothers: Fantasies of Maternal Origin in Shakespeare's Plays, 'Hamlet' to 'The Tempest'* (New York, 1992), 146–64.

but Tate removes some of the more extravagant expressions and the suggestions of erotic interest. In Tate's version the words 'Let me twine | Mine armes about that body' become, more soberly, 'Let me embrace that Body'.[196] The lines in which Aufidius compares his excitement at meeting Coriolanus with his rapture on his wedding night (running from 'Know thou first . . .' to 'Bestride my Threshold') are removed altogether. In Shakespeare, Aufidius has repeatedly dreamt of encounters with Coriolanus, but in Tate's adaptation this obsession is played down: 'nightly' becomes 'might'ly', and 'fisting' becomes 'grasping'. When the servants are discussing Aufidius' reception of Coriolanus at the banquet, one of them comments in Shakespeare: 'Our Generall himselfe makes a Mistris of him, Sanctifies himselfe with's hand, and turnes up the white o'th'eye to his Discourse.'[197] Tate's servant simply says, 'My Lord himself makes a very Mistress of him',[198] and Tate cuts out the description which suggests that Aufidius is hanging on Coriolanus' person and words like a besotted lover. Tate implies that Aufidius has been unmanned by his over-ready reception of Coriolanus, but this is envisaged not as a sexual effeminization of Aufidius, rather as a loss of political status and individual selfhood: Nigridius tells him that he has reduced himself 'To Less, than Man, the Shaddow of your self',[199] while Aufidius himself realizes that his standing has been diminished by Coriolanus' arrival.

Tate steers away from any suggestion that Aufidius' revenge may be motivated in part by a spurned homoerotic desire for Coriolanus: instead, Tate's scenario is that Aufidius had previously been in love with Coriolanus' wife Virgilia, and when he sees her again in the scene where the women plead for Rome, his desire for her is rekindled. He plans to kill Coriolanus, and then rape Virgilia:

> For soon as I've secur'd my Rivals Life,
> All stain'd i'th' Husbands Blood, I'll Force the Wife.[200]

Aufidius and Coriolanus fatally wound each other, but Tate omits the stage direction which in Shakespeare's text calls for Aufidius to stand on the body of Coriolanus (another of Shakespeare's additions to Plutarch), a gesture of military triumph which (given Aufidius' earlier speeches) cannot be without some erotic overtones, and which is

---

[196] Nahum Tate, *The Ingratitude of a Common-Wealth: or, The Fall of Caius Martius Coriolanus* (London, 1682), 39.   [197] *Coriolanus*, 4. 5. 199–202.
[198] Tate, *Ingratitude*, 41.   [199] Ibid., 42.   [200] Ibid., 57.

evidently alien to Tate's purposes. When Virgilia arrives on stage she is seen to be wounded by an attempt which she has made to commit suicide in order to avoid rape. Aufidius is overcome with remorse, and dies. One could construe Aufidius' grotesque plan to rape Virgilia before the eyes of her dying husband as in part a displaced manifestation of a desire to possess Coriolanus himself, yet Tate's plot provides ample motivation for Aufidius in his renewed passion for Virgilia and his resentment at being overshadowed by Coriolanus. The homosocial bond between the two soldiers has been purged of homosexual implications, and the rivalry of Aufidius and Coriolanus has become the classic paradigmatic plot of Restoration tragedy.

So too in Thomas Otway's adaptation of *Romeo and Juliet* as *The History and Fall of Caius Marius* (1680),[201] much of the possibly homoerotic bawdy in which Mercutio teases Romeo about his sexual activities has been removed. Mercutio has been transformed into a military leader who fears that the Romeo figure has turned effeminate, in the seventeenth-century sense that his passion for women has led him to neglect his manly public duty. In Otway's adaptation the relationship between the equivalents of Mercutio and Romeo is rewritten so that the problem of manliness can be represented in its familiar Restoration form as a need to reconcile the demands of marital passion and martial responsibilities. The Restoration counterparts of Aufidius and Mercutio can be acceptable examples of soldierly masculinity only if they show no erotic interest in the bodies of other soldiers.

A comparable sensitivity can be seen at work in Dryden's *Troilus and Cressida* (1679). In the second scene of Shakespeare's play, Pandarus appraises the military and sexual prowess of the Trojan warriors as they pass over the stage, and, although he is doing this for the benefit of Cressida, there is a homoerotic undertow to this sexually aware gaze of male on male. Dryden does not remove this scene, but he does modify it in some details: Aeneas is no longer 'one of the flowers of Troy' but, more robustly, 'a swinger'.[202] Pandarus no longer vows that he could 'live and die i'th'eyes of *Troylus*', like the protagonist of an Elizabethan sonnet sequence pining for a glance from his mistress; instead, in Dryden's version he claims that he 'cou'd live and dye with *Troilus*' like a comrade in battle.[203]

[201] Thomas Otway, *The History and Fall of Caius Marius. A Tragedy* (London, 1680).

[202] Shakespeare, *Troilus and Cressida*, 1. 2. 183; Dryden, *Troilus and Cressida*, 1. 2. 176.

[203] Shakespeare, 1. 2. 239–40; Dryden, 1. 2. 225.

There is also a marked difference in the way that Shakespeare and Dryden imagine the relationship of Achilles and Patroclus. In Shakespeare, Thersites explicitly accuses Patroclus of being Achilles' sexual partner:

> *Thersites.*   . . . thou art thought to be *Achilles* male varlot.
> *Patroclus.*   Male varlot you rogue whats that.
> *Thersites.*   Why his masculine whore.[204]

It is remarkable that Shakespeare's play neither confirms nor refutes this suggestion, leaving it as a possibility, an imaginable element in the comradely association of Achilles and Patroclus. But it is not imaginable to Dryden, who removes this exchange altogether. When Patroclus reminds Achilles that his refusal to participate in the war is damaging his reputation, the speech runs thus in Shakespeare:

> To this effect *Achilles* have I moov'd you,
> A woman impudent and mannish growne,
> Is not more loath'd then an effeminate man
> In time of action: I stand condemnd for this
> They thinke my little stomack to the warre,
> And your great love to me, restraines you thus,
> Sweete, rouse your selfe.

In Dryden's adaptation the speech becomes:

> 'Tis known you are in love with *Hector*'s Sister,
> And therefore will not fight: and your not fighting
> Draws on you this contempt: I oft have told you
> A woman impudent and mannish grown
> Is not more loath'd than an effeminate man,
> In time of action: I'm condemn'd for this:
> They think my little appetite to warr
> Deads all the fire in you: but rowse your self.[205]

At the beginning of the speech Dryden carefully establishes Achilles' love for Polyxena rather than Patroclus' influence as the reason for Achilles' withdrawal from the war; and while Achilles is 'an effeminate man' in the eyes of Shakespeare's Greeks because of his love for Patroclus, in Dryden he is 'effeminate' in the Restoration sense of one who (like Charles II) is so strongly devoted to the pleasures of women that he neglects his masculine social responsibilities. The

---

[204] Shakespeare, 5. 1. 15–17.
[205] Shakespeare, 3. 3. 209–15; Dryden, 4. 2. 35–42.

importance of Patroclus is also lessened by the excision of the phrase 'your great love to me' and of the epithet 'sweete'. Similarly, Dryden's Achilles calls his companion 'My dear *Patroclus*' instead of 'My sweet *Patroclus*'.[206] It is not that Dryden recoils altogether from using the word 'sweet' for a male comrade, for he introduces it later in a new speech which he writes for Achilles lamenting the death of Patroclus and swearing revenge, but here it is used as part of a careful definition of the friendship between the two men:

> O thou art gone! thou sweetest, best of friends;
> Why did I let thee tempt the shock of war
> Ere yet thy tender nerves had strung thy limbs,
> And knotted into strength! Yet, though too late,
> I will, I will revenge thee, my *Patroclus*![207]

Here the attention to the male body focuses on the youth's physical unreadiness for the strains of combat, and the feeling in these lines seems more like pity than desire. Similarly John Bankes in his play *The Destruction of Troy* (1679) explains Achilles' emotion as that of one friend towards another, and his kiss as a sign of sacred friendship. Achilles addresses the Myrmidons who are carrying the body of Patroclus:

> Down with your Sacred Burthen of my Friend—
> Let me receive this Kiss from his pale Lips,
> And catch the dear remainder of his Soul.
>
> .   .   .   .
>
> Tell me of Laws, when Sacred Friendship here
> Lies bleeding so.[208]

In such examples from Restoration drama, the intense feelings which arise between men have no erotic colouration.

In adaptations of Shakespeare during the late seventeenth century we can see a shift in the way that passionate male relationships are conceptualized. To Shakespeare, homoerotic desire could form part of male friendship: the intimate bond between men is threatened not by homosexual feelings but by heterosexual ones, as *Othello* or *The Two Noble Kinsmen* demonstrate in tragic mode. His comedies often promise marriage rather than deliver it, ending just on the brink of

---

[206] Dryden, 4. 2. 205; Shakespeare, 5. 1. 34.

[207] Dryden, 5. 2. 142–6.

[208] John Bankes, *The Destruction of Troy* (London, 1679), 39–40.

making an irrevocable exit from the comfortable all-male milieu; and in the occasional reminders (for instance in *Twelfth Night*) that the 'women' to whom the men are joined are actually boy actors there may even be an element of reassurance, a translation of women back into boys which permits a final lingering in that imaginative world where homosocial and homoerotic possibilities coexist. Restoration comedy, on the other hand, is more interested in the sexual arrangements which adult men and women fashion: several plays end with explicit negotiations about the terms on which marriage will be conducted. In such a world there is no room for the ambiguities of Shakespeare's erotic imagination, his pursuit of multiplicity, and his desire to blur definitions, to postpone the moment at which choices have to be made. One could not claim that all of the changes which have been described here in Restoration versions of Shakespeare were motivated consciously or exclusively by a fear of homosexual implications: some of the highly charged language between Shakespeare's male characters may have offended Restoration adapters by its poetic rather than its emotional excess, and the removal or curtailment of speeches might result from other dramaturgical considerations. But there is a sufficiently coherent pattern here to suggest that these Restoration adaptations were motivated partly by a concern to protect male friendship from the suspicion of homosexual desire and, by removing the productive ambiguities of Shakespeare's language, to preserve the clarity and stability of the definition of masculinity in the face of a new world of homosexual self-definition.

3

Politics and 'Sodomy'

Chapters 1 and 2 have explored the repertoire of literary tropes and rhetorical figures through which sex between men was imagined in plays and poems which primarily explored private desire in private spaces. We have seen various strategies for imagining kinds of private space and for voicing individual subjectivity within the conventions which governed the production of a literature which would be acceptable in the public sphere. And we have seen how expressions which were deemed acceptable in one time or place were thought unacceptable in another. The present chapter turns to a group of texts which present sex between men as a public matter, in that they focus on figures who wielded political power. Labelling prominent people as 'sodomites' is a way of discrediting them and making them as alien to the English establishment as Turks and Jesuits. Here the 'sodomite' who supposedly undoes the social fabric is found at the apex of the social order, as a politician, a courtier, or even as the sovereign. How, then, were rulers with homosexual inclinations presented by contemporary historians, poets, and dramatists? What conceptual and linguistic problems were generated by such anomalies in the symbolic order?

If the way in which sex between men is conceptualized in this period depended at least in part on political motives, the story of Edward II and his infatuation with Piers Gaveston was particularly liable to be told with some contemporary political inflection.[1] In

---

[1] For a discussion of various Renaissance treatments of the story, including those by Marlowe, Holinshed, and Drayton, see *LBM* 47–57. I have not included any discussion of Marlowe's *Edward II* here because it has been well treated by various scholars, notably by Normand, ' "What Passions Call You These?": *Edward II* and James VI', in Darryll Grantley and Peter Roberts (eds.), *Christopher Marlowe and English Renaissance*

France the precedent of Edward II was used to attack Henri III,[2] while the influence of Robert Cecil on Elizabeth I was likened to that of Gaveston on Edward II,[3] and the behaviour of favourites and barons in the reign of Edward II was cited as a warning to Charles I.[4] In a culture where the perception of historical parallels was commonplace, and the writing of history often served as a scarcely veiled reflection on contemporary affairs, the arrival on the throne of James I, a king who, like Edward, was known to be susceptible to the attractions of handsome male favourites, made the story of Edward II topical and sensitive.[5]

The historians who chronicled Edward's reign often had problems in finding the right words for the relationship of the King and Gaveston. As early as the medieval *Vita Edwardi Secundi* we see that the historian has difficulty in thinking of a precedent: *Sane non memini me audisse unum alterum ita dilexisse. Jonathas dilexit Dauid, Achilles Patroclum amauit, sed illi modum excessisse non leguntur. Modum autem dilectionis rex noster habere non potuit, et propter eum sui oblitus esse diceretur, et ob hoc Petrus malificus putaretur esse.*[6] For this medieval chronicler there is no precedent which can explain Edward's passion, and to go beyond the bounds established by biblical and classical example leads a man to forget himself: by departing from the collectively established memory of past behaviour between men, Edward risks being set down in the memory of future generations as an anomaly, something without a name. The holding back from naming may hint that this is the crime not to be named among Christians, but

---

Culture (Aldershot, 1996), 172–97, by Smith, 209–23, and in the edn. by Charles R. Forker (Manchester, 1994).

  [2] David Potter, 'Marlowe's *Massacre at Paris* and the Reputation of Henri III of France', in *Christopher Marlowe and English Renaissance Culture*, 70–95, at 70.

  [3] Robert Persons in 1592, cited in *The Works of Michael Drayton*, ed. J. William Hebel, 5 vols. (Oxford, 1931–41), v. 24.

  [4] Alexander Leighton, *An Appeal to the Parliament; or Sions Plea against the Prelacie* [London, 1628], 60, 65.

  [5] Lawrence Normand argues that James's early relationship with the Duke of Lennox may have influenced Marlowe's treatment of Edward II: ' "What Passions Call You These?" ', 172–97.

  [6] 'Certainly I do not remember that I have heard of any man who loved another like this. Jonathan loved David, Achilles loved Patroclus, but they are not said to have gone beyond the bounds. Our King, however, could not set any bound to his love, and on account of him he was said to have forgotten himself, and so Piers was thought to be a sorcerer.' (*The Life of Edward the Second by the So-called Monk of Malmesbury*, ed. N. Denholm-Young (London, 1957), 14, my trans.)

this is only a possible inference, not an inevitable one. There is a tension of uncertainty in the chronicler's prose. The confident *Sane* immediately becomes the subjective and fallible *non memini me audisse*, and the chronicler continues to stress what others say: Jonathan and David, Achilles and Patroclus, are not said to have gone beyond the bounds (the negative is carefully placed, for he does not write: 'they are said not to have gone beyond the bounds'). These figures for comparison with Edward and Gaveston are themselves uncertain, not altogether legible (*non leguntur*), the tradition about them being only a matter of report—indeed, a matter of there being no report. And because the King could not set any limit to his love, Gaveston was accounted a sorcerer, and so placed beyond the limits of human society for using powers which are not available to ordinary mortals.

Similarly, in the account of Edward II published in 1680 but possibly composed in the 1620s by a member of the Carey family, we are told:

Such a masculine Affection and rapture was in those times without president, where Love went in the natural strain, fully as firm, yet far less violent. If the circumstances of this passionate Humour, so predominant in this unfortunate King, be maturely considered, we shall finde them as far short of possibility as reason; which have made many believe, that they had a supernatural operation and working, enforc'd by Art or Witchcraft.[7]

This passage momentarily offers an explanation in terms of contemporary psychology or physiology in referring to a 'passionate Humour', yet that explanation is quickly withdrawn because the writer cannot find such behaviour either rational or precedented: precedent determines here what is rationally possible, and beyond that the only explanation can be witchcraft. But another phrase in that paragraph makes one pause: 'in those times' such affection was without precedent; perhaps, by implication, in the writer's times King James I provides another example of the passions which Edward II displayed.

---

[7] *The History of the Life, Reign, and Death of Edward II . . . Written by E. F. in the year 1627* (London, 1680), 28. A shorter version was published in the same year, attributed to Henry Carey, Viscount Falkland: *The History of the most Unfortunate Prince King Edward II* (London, 1680). The two texts have been published in facsimile in *Works by and Attributed to Elizabeth Cary*, ed. Margaret W. Ferguson (Aldershot, 1996). The authorship and status of the two versions have been much contested, but there is no actual evidence for the attribution to Elizabeth Carey, and a cogent argument that both texts belong to the 1680s (at least in their present form) has been mounted by D. R. Woolf, 'The True Date and Authorship of Henry, Viscount Falkland's *History of the Life, Reign, and Death of King Edward II'*, *Bodleian Library Record*, 12 (1985-8), 440–55.

To the author of the 1680 history, 'their hearts ... seem'd to beat with one and the self-same motion; so that the one seem'd without the other, like a Body without a Soul, or a Shadow without a Substance'. This is not a romantic but a sinister image, continuing the notion of diabolical possession as the body loses its soul. It also has political implications, for Edward is 'a Royal Shadow without a Real Substance' and a mere 'Pageant'. Gaveston too lacks 'a deep and solid Knowledge', but has 'a winning Behaviour, which he could at all times fashion and vary according to the condition of time and circumstance, for the most advantage'. For 'this inchanting Mountebank had in the Cabinet of his Masters heart, too dear a room and being'. Images of emptiness and unreality inform this presentation. From Gaveston Edward takes 'those tainted humours of his Leprosie', and leprosy in this period was regarded as a punishment for sexual misbehaviour (as in Henryson's *Testament of Cresseid*) or as a sexually transmitted disease.[8] Gaveston is a Ganymede, a Siren, and not a Gascon but an Italian. His beauty is imagined as excessive, and so unmanly and unnatural:

Nature in his outward parts had curiously exprest her workmanship, giving him in shape and Beauty so perfect an excellence, that the most curious eye could not discover any manifest errour, unless it were in his Sex alone, since he had too much for a man, and Perfection enough to have equal'd the fairest Female splendour that breath'd within the Confines of this Kingdom.[9]

Here there seems to be no idea that male and female beauty differ in kind, but only in degree, and the only error which can be discerned in Gaveston's appearance is a beauty which is too perfect for a man.

Here we have several ways of approaching the story: the historians offer explanations and precedents and then withdraw them, suggesting parallels and ways of understanding without committing themselves, and implying that there is something here which escapes definition. This may be construed as a way of gesturing towards the terrible category of 'sodomy' without invoking the name and its attendant consequences, but the effect for the reader is to suggest not one stable category but rather the absence of a tradition, the lack of a discourse, and instead multiple possibilities, various and discontinuous

[8] Williams, *s.v.* leprosy.

[9] *History of the Life*, 4–5, 20. These observations adapt several of the topoi with which Raphael Holinshed had conceptualized the relationship: see *LBM* 47–8.

ways of seeing. Sex between men confuses the observer's understanding of soul and body, of beauty, of the natural, the unnatural, and the supernatural.[10]

The treatment of the passion of Edward and Gaveston by Michael Drayton in his poem *Piers Gaveston Earle of Cornwall* (1593–4)[11] offers a complex picture of an erotic attachment between men which often speaks the same language as heterosexual love. Indeed, one of the most significant influences upon Drayton as he designed and composed this poem was Samuel Daniel's *The Complaint of Rosamund*, and when Drayton wrote the stanzas in which Gaveston describes his beauty and its effect he evidently had Daniel's poem open on his table.[12] Drayton sees no difficulty in using the account of Rosamund's beauty as an aid to imagining Gaveston's, though Daniel's description is not sufficiently detailed for us to be able to say that Drayton saw male and female beauty in the same terms. Indeed, Gaveston's 'lyons heart' and 'courage never daunted'[13] clearly mark out his masculinity. Drayton, then, is not suggesting that there is anything effeminate about Gaveston's attractions. And Marston in his defence of Drayton speaks without difficulty of the two characters in a single line:

> What, shall not *Rosamond*, or *Gaveston*,
> Ope their sweet lips without detraction?[14]

The poem is spoken by the ghost of Gaveston, released from hell with a 'tormented heart', and so a first-person narrator is used at once to voice desire and to offer moral reflections on his tragic story. Drayton also introduces first-person speeches by Edward. The poem therefore adds up to a complex drama in which Gaveston is at once protagonist, narrator, and moralist, an anthology of voices which may not coalesce

[10] Cf. Normand on Marlowe's play: 'while characters in the play recognize sexuality in the relationship of the King and Gaveston, they do not have one single discourse in which to represent it . . . same-sex eroticism appears in several discourses which are not necessarily tabooed nor specifically marked as sexual: marriage, sodomy, neo-platonism, friendship, patronage. Marlowe dramatizes his characters attempting various ways adequately to represent the Edward–Gaveston relationship' (188).

[11] For a discussion of Drayton, esp. his contacts with other writers in what seems to have been a homoerotic literary milieu, see Mary Bly, *Queer Virgins and Virgin Queans on the Early Modern Stage* (Oxford, 2000), 96–103.

[12] Drayton, ed. Hebel, v. 23. Drayton also studied Shakespeare's *Venus and Adonis*, as Hebel shows.

[13] Drayton, *Piers Gaveston*, l. 142.

[14] John Marston, *Reactio* (1598), cited in Drayton, ed. Hebel, v. 25.

to create an imaginable subjectivity for Gaveston, but do offer the reader alternative ways of understanding the story.

But this poem caused Drayton considerable difficulties, for he revised it frequently, first tinkering with the phrasing, and then in 1605—two years into the new reign of James I—producing a drastically revised and shortened version which reimagines the relationship between Edward and Gaveston in significantly different terms, influenced no doubt by the arrival on the throne of England of a king with embarrassingly similar sexual inclinations:

The emphasis is now solely on Gaveston; almost all the passages describing Edward's feelings are cut. Thus the poem is simplified, and . . . considerably sobered emotionally . . . The eroticism of the poem is reduced and the influence of Marlowe's play much less apparent . . . The history of the poem from 1596 is a systematic progress of de-intoxication . . . It has gained coherence but lost enchantment.[15]

Several revisions indicate Drayton's sensitivity to the possibility that the poem might be read as a critique of James and his entourage. He slims down the passage which extols the uncorrupt court of Edward I, and omits the explicit parallel between Edward I and Elizabeth I which could imply a parallel between their successors.[16] The revision also omits the criticism of venal courtiers and favourites,[17] the suggestion that Gaveston was used by Edward II as the instrument of his tyranny,[18] the idea that in making Gaveston Lord Protector in his absence Edward was yielding up his sceptre and paving the way for Gaveston to succeed him,[19] and the violent reaction against Gaveston by the nobles and their supporters.[20] Thus the material on the way in which kingly government is swayed by an unpopular favourite is reduced, and as a politic addition Drayton pens a new stanza which is advertised in a marginal note as 'An admiration of the Majesty of Kings'.[21] Drayton also diverts attention away from Edward, and thus from the embarrassing precedent of a king's homosexual desire. In doing so, he suppresses virtually all of Edward's own emotional part in the story:

[15] Hebel in Drayton, ed. Hebel, v. 161–2.
[16] *1593–4*, ll. 43–60; cf. *1619*, ll. 25–36. The most drastic revision of the poem took place in the 1605 edn.; the 1619 text makes a few further minor changes. Hebel takes *1619* as his copy-text for the revised version, and this is the text which I follow to represent the poem as reconceived in the reign of James.
[17] *1593–4*, ll. 361–4.   [18] *1593–4*, l. 1281.
[19] *1593–4*, ll. 787–92.   [20] *1593–4*, ll. 1429–76.
[21] *1619*, ll. 469–74.

his being an 'aprentice' to Gaveston's pleasure, and his 'thrall',[22] his dilemma over sending Gaveston away and his desolation at his repeated banishments,[23] his ecstatic joy at his return,[24] and his grief at his death.[25] This removes almost completely the language in which a king expresses passionate erotic attachment to a male courtier.

Gaveston's own physical attractiveness is likewise played down.[26] In the original version Gaveston wonders how to account for the attraction which he held for Edward:

> Whether it were my beauties excellence,
> Or rare perfections that so pleasd his eye,
> Or some divine and heavenly influence,
> Or naturall attracting *Sympathie*:
>> My pleasing youth became his senses object,
>> Where all his passions wrought upon this subject.[27]

In the revised version, the stanza runs thus:

> But whether it my rare Perfections were,
> That wonne my youth such Favour in His Eye,
> Or it pleas'd Heaven (to shew it held Me deare)
> To showre on Me this Blessing from the Skye,
>> I know not, but it rightly could direct,
>> That could produce so powerfull an effect.[28]

The vocabulary of the original indicates that it was physical desire which attracted Edward to Gaveston ('beauties . . . eye . . . senses . . . passions'), and also that this union of the two men was something wrought by the heavens or by the natural order of the universe: it was the reverse of unnatural—at least in Gaveston's eyes, and in the Elizabethan text he is a fairly sympathetic figure. The Jacobean recension excises the language of physical attraction and heavenly union; now Gaveston's youth merely finds favour, rather than being the object of Edward's senses and passions, and heaven is credited with favouring Gaveston, not with bringing about their union.

Such revisions have the effect of destroying that mutuality which was so strong a feature of the original poem, and in the later text Drayton represents the bond between Edward and Gaveston quite

---

[22] *1593–4*, ll. 656, 767: 'By byrth my Soveraigne, but by love my thrall' is a dangerously epigrammatic line.

[23] *1593–4*, ll. 439–528, 913–18, 1297–320. [24] *1593–4*, ll. 847–64.

[25] *1593–4*, ll. 1663–1704. [26] *1593–4*, ll. 109–62; cf. *1619*, ll. 61–78.

[27] *1593–4*, ll. 193–8. [28] *1619*, ll. 97–102.

differently. The Jacobean revision introduces the word 'Friendship' to describe their relationship, and at the same point inserts an encomium of love which is described as the means 'Whereby we hold Intelligence with Heaven'.[29] This idealizing view may be suggesting that a Platonic love is all that links the King with his favourite, and in any case contrasts with the equivalent point in the original poem which had described the perfect concord between the two men, an achieved rather than an ideal union, and one which was both spiritual and sensual.[30] The physical embraces of Edward and Gaveston are no longer described so ecstatically; here is the *1593–4* text:

> My youth the glasse where he his youth beheld,
> Roses his lipps, my breath sweete *Nectar* showers,
> For in my face was natures fayrest field,
> Richly adornd with Beauties rarest flowers.
>> My breast his pillow, where he laide his head,
>> Mine eyes his booke, my bosome was his bed.
>
> My smiles were life, and Heaven unto his sight,
> All his delight concluding my desier,
> From my sweete sunne, he borrowed all his light,
> And as a flie play'd with my beauties fier,
>> His love-sick lippes at every kissing qualme,
>> Cling to my lippes, to cure their griefe with balme.
>
> Like as the wanton Yvie with his twyne,
> Whenas the Oake his rootlesse bodie warmes,
> The straightest saplings strictly doth combyne,
> Clipping the woodes with his lascivious armes:
>> Such our imbraces when our sporte begins,
>> Lapt in our armes, like *Ledas* lovely Twins.[31]

And here is the equivalent passage in the *1619* text:

> My Smiles His life, so joy'd He in my sight,
> That His Delight was led by my Desire,
> From my cleere Eyes, so borrowing all His Light,
> As pale-fac'd CYNTHIA, from her brothers fire.
>> He made my Cheeke, the Pillow for His Head,
>> My Brow His Booke, my Bosome was His Bed.[32]

---

[29] *1619*, ll. 84, 86.   [30] *1593–4*, ll. 169–80.   [31] *1593–4*, ll. 223–40.
[32] *1619*, ll. 127–32.

The physical contact between the two men is still signalled in the couplet of the *1619* text, but the heady eroticism of the *1593–4* version has gone. Overall, there is a shift from Gaveston as the object of Edward's sexual desire to Gaveston as the chief corrupting influence on his King. There is a subtle shift even in the significance of the gifts which Edward sends him: in the original poem they are a lover's tokens ('Letters enterlynd with love, | . . . His Ring, his Bracelet, Garter, or his Glove', all intimate gifts) but these are pared down in revision to only a rich robe and jewels, items which suggest that the realm's regalia are being misused: they signal an abuse of power rather than the fashioning of a private relationship through the idiom of love-tokens.[33] Not surprisingly, the allegation that their relationship was said by some to be sodomy is also excised.[34]

Consistent with these revisions is the alteration or omission of those allusions which had associated Edward and Gaveston with the heterosexual lovers of classical history and legend. The comparisons with Antony and Cleopatra and with Hero and Leander disappear.[35] A reference to Ganymede is carefully altered: the name disappears from the text into a new marginal note which defines the boy simply as Jove's 'Cup-bearer'; and Edward now feeds Gaveston with 'Ambrosiall Delicacies' rather than living a 'lustie life' with him.[36] Also altered is an allusion to Venus and Adonis, which is pruned of its eroticism. Here is the excited Elizabethan simile:

> Or as Love-nursing *Venus* when she sportes,
> With cherry-lipt *Adonis* in the shade,
> Figuring her passions in a thousand sortes,
> With sighes, and teares, or what else might perswade,
>   Her deere, her sweete, her joy, her life, her love,
>   Kissing his browe, his cheeke, his hand, his glove.[37]

And here is the cooler Jacobean version:

> Like faire IDALIA, bent to amorous sport,
> With young ADONIS, in the pleasant shade,
> Expressing their affections in that sort,
> As though her utmost passion should perswade

---

[33] *1593–4*, ll. 1070–2; cf. *1619*, ll. 435–6. The robe and jewel feature in both texts, but in *1593–4* it is a jewel 'that my fancie might content', and in *1619* a jewel 'that him infinitely cost': the focus has shifted from Edward contenting his lover to Edward spending unwisely.   [34] *1593–4*, l. 1268.   [35] *1593–4*, ll. 1153–8, 1417–22.   [36] *1593–4*, ll. 211–14; cf. *1619*, ll. 117–18.   [37] *1593–4*, ll. 241–6.

> The one of us, the other still to move,
> To all the tender Dalliances of Love.[38]

Altogether, Drayton's revised poem represents a drastic simplification not only of the narrative structure and voice, but of the conceptual framework within which the relationship is imagined.

Another poem on the same subject was Sir Francis Hubert's *The Historie of Edward the Second* (1629). Hubert himself records that the poem was '*conceived and borne in Queene* Elizabeths *time, but grew to more maturitie in King* JAMES's'. Written in 1598–9, it was prohibited from being printed by Elizabeth's censors, and subsequently received a limited circulation in manuscript. In 1628—the year of the assassination of the Duke of Buckingham—two pirated editions of the poem appeared, prompting Hubert to publish a corrected edition in 1629.[39] There were two impressions issued that year, and a further edition in 1631, so this was evidently a poem which spoke to public interest in the behaviour of princes and their favourites. The opening of the poem overtly invites the reader to construe parallels between the past and the present, for, says Hubert,

> Onely I would have those same errours knowne
> By which the State did then to ruine runne,
> That (warn'd by theirs) Our Age like sins might shunne.[40]

And Hubert carefully indicates that he intends no criticism of the current King, Charles I:

> O let it not be thought to derogate
> From thy perfections (admirably rare)
> If I some errours of these Times declare.[41]

Hubert has no interest in the homoeroticism articulated by Drayton, and instead focuses on the dangers of kings led astray by evil counsel. Most of the poem is spoken by Edward reflecting on the way in which

---

[38] *1619*, ll. 133–8.

[39] *The Poems of Sir Francis Hubert*, ed. Bernard Mellor (Hong Kong, 1961), 2. Mellor (xli) says that Hubert hurriedly revised the poem after the appearance of the pirated edn., but this revision was probably in addition to the revisions which Hubert himself says were made under James. Various MSS survive (Mellor, 280–3) with substantial variants which may derive from a sporadic process of revision over some thirty years.

[40] Hubert, *Edward the Second*, st. 8.

[41] Ibid., st. 10.

he allowed himself to be corrupted by Gaveston. Gaveston is accorded a fair exterior, but his gifts are, with hindsight, superficial:

> Hee was in face a *Cupid* or more faire,
> A *Mercurie* in speech or else as much.
> In active vigor hee was *Mars* his heire,
> In wit *Jove*-bred *Minerva* was not such.
> But (O) these guifts will not abide the touch
>   Except with Inward vertues of the mind.
>   Both beautie, speech, strength, wit are all refin'd.[42]

Gaveston is thoroughly demonized—as 'This highest Scholler in the Schoole of Sinne, | This Centaure, halfe a man and halfe a Best'; as a reincarnation of Sardanapalus, an 'Angell-Div'll', a 'loathsome witch'.[43] He promises Edward pleasures which are an inversion of the natural order, for over against God's daylight Gaveston sets, in a striking phrase, 'Night-Sunnes', for he stages 'Maskes, Revels, Banquets, mirthfull Comedies, | Night-Sunnes (kind Natures dearest Prodigies)'. Like Milton's Comus,[44] Hubert's Gaveston argues that God has 'wisely fitted every thing to pleasure', and that these gifts should be used without restraint. His speech of seduction appropriates the language of Platonic love ('Pure love, that sublimates our Earthly parts | And makes them ayerie by Ingenious Arts'), while also deploying an Epicurean summons to exquisite pleasure, promising 'The quintissence of pure essentiall sweet, | The point where all the lines of Pleasures meet', and assuring Edward that 'With one sweet night thou wilt be so delighted | That thou wilt wish the world were still benighted.'[45] Edward is deluded by the specious wit of this seducer whose false and, indeed, impious arguments he ought to be able to see through. What chiefly offends Hubert is not so much the sexuality of the relationship as the way that Gaveston insinuates himself into Edward's affection and trust, for this favourite was

> One that Indeed was second unto none
> In winding in himselfe to great mens favour,
> That by their hazards he might be the Saver.[46]

The moral is that princes should learn insight, learn self-control, and

[42] Hubert, *Edward the Second*, st. 46.
[43] Ibid., sts. 52, 51, 53, 80.
[44] John Milton, 'A Masque Presented at Ludlow Castle, 1634', ll. 709–43.
[45] Hubert, *Edward the Second*, sts. 73–9.
[46] Ibid., st. 39.

learn to spurn advisers who say that 'There is no law I Can bind a King but onely his desire.'[47] Kings should have plain counsellors, 'Jewels of the heart not of the eare', who will not turn the court into 'a pompous Theater . . . I Pester'd with Panders, Players, and with Pages'.[48] Ultimately, the responsibility lies with the King, for, as Edward admits, 'The witch that wrought on mee was in my brest'.[49] For Hubert, the lessons to be drawn from this story concern less the wickedness of sodomy, and more the danger of a king being ruled by favourites.

JAMES I AND HIS FAVOURITES

On 1 January 1604, the first New Year's Day of the new reign, a masque was performed in front of King James. Each of the masquers presented the King with an impresa on a shield, accompanied by a set of verses to explain it. The lords

in theyr order delivered theyr scutchins with letters and there was no great stay at any of them save only at one who was putt to the interpretacion of his devise. It was a faire horse colt in a faire greene field which he meant to be a colt of Busephalus race and had this virtu of his sire that none could mount him but one as great at lest as Alexander. The King made himself merry with threatening to send this colt to the stable and he could not breake loose till he promised to dance as well as Bankes his horse.[50]

The young colt who invited James to mount him was the 16-year-old Philip Herbert, handsome younger brother of William Herbert, Earl of Pembroke. Of course, the compliment to the King could be taken simply to signify that this headstrong youth could only be controlled by a firm ruler such as James or Alexander the Great; but given the sexual connotations of 'mount',[51] and the reputation of Alexander for homosexual devotion to Hephaestion,[52] Herbert's invitation was cheekily sexual. James seems to have enjoyed the joke, and responded with an invitation of his own ('threatening to send this colt to the

---

[47] Hubert, *Edward the Second*, st. 57.

[48] Ibid., sts. 94, 177.

[49] Ibid., st. 225.

[50] Letter from Dudley Carleton to John Chamberlain, quoted in E. K. Chambers, *The Elizabethan Stage*, 4 vols. (Oxford, 1923), iii. 279.

[51] Williams, *s.v.*

[52] Cited as a precedent for the relationship between Edward II and Gaveston by Marlowe (1. 4. 391) and Hubert (st. 156).

stable') and perhaps a tight embrace from which Philip 'could not breake loose'. Four years later, when Herbert married, the King joined the couple in bed: 'They were lodged in the councill chamber, where the King, in his shirt and night-gown, gave them a *revileé matin* before they were up, and spent a good time in or upon the bed, chuse which you will believe.'[53]

James's predilection for handsome young men—notably James Hay, Robert Carr, Philip and William Herbert, and most of all George Villiers, Duke of Buckingham—was well known at the time,[54] and his habit of embracing and kissing them in public occasioned some observers to conjecture about what happened in private. Francis Osborne wrote:

these went under the appellation of his favourites or minions, who, like burning-glasses, were daily interposed between him and the subject, multiplying the heat of oppressions in the generall opinion, though in his own he thought they screened them from reflecting upon the crowne . . . Now, as no other reason appeared in favour of their choyce but handsom-nesse, so the love the king shewed was as amorously convayed, as if he had mistaken their sex, and thought them ladies; which I have seene Sommerset and Buckingham labour to resemble, in the effeminateness of their dressings; though in w— [whorish] lookes and wanton gestures, they exceeded any part of woman kind my conversation did ever cope withall. Nor was his love, or what else posterity will please to call it, (who must be the judges of all that history shall informe,) carried on with a discretion sufficient to cover a lesse scandalous behaviour; for the kings kissing them after so lascivious a mode in publick, and upon the theatre, as it were, of the world, prompted many to imagine some things done in the tyring-house, that exceed my expressions no lesse then they do my experience: And therefore left floting upon the waves of conjecture, which hath in my hearing tossed them from one side to another.[55]

This account convicts James of effeminizing his favourites, and his favourites of interposing themselves between the King and his subjects. Osborne's imagery suggests that these relationships both wrongly erected and wrongly traversed boundaries between public

[53] Letter from Dudley Carleton to Ralph Winwood, quoted in *Secret History of the Court of James the First*, 2 vols. (Edinburgh, 1811), ii. 349.

[54] For James's erotic relationships with his male favourites see David M. Bergeron, *King James and Letters of Homoerotic Desire* (Iowa City, 1999), which reprints the extant letters between James and Lennox, Somerset, and Buckingham.

[55] Francis Osborne, 'Some Traditional Memorialls on the Reign of King James the First', in *Secret History*, i. 274–5; 1st publ. 1658.

and private. Instead of the 'minions' being a screen to shield James from critical subjects, they acted as a burning glass which intensified those subjects' disaffection. And while the favourites created an improper boundary between the King and his subjects in matters which affected the state, the King himself crossed the proper boundary between private and public behaviour, acting lasciviously 'upon the theatre, as it were, of the world', neither comporting himself regally nor confining his kisses to the bedroom. In part, the offence is that observers are being made to see what they would wish not to see. Osborne is in no doubt that James's relationships with his young men were erotic, and his sarcastic hesitation over using the word 'love' to describe them plainly invites the reader to redescribe them in coarser terms.

Another retrospective account offered by Sir Anthony Weldon in 1651 may not be the *ne plus ultra* of impartial reporting, but it does provide an indication of how James's conduct was perceived; and it is the literary record rather than the historical facts which concerns us here. James was partial to favourites 'with young Faces, and smooth Chins', and 'purchased, built, and repaired [hunting lodges] at *New-Market*, and *Royston*, and this pleased the Kings humour well, rather that he might enjoy his Favourite with more privacy, then that he loved the sports'.[56] When the young Scot Robert Carr, James's former page, reappeared on the scene, 'the *English* Lords, who formerly coveted an *English* Favourite (and to that end the Countess of *Suffolke* did looke out choyce young men, whom she daily curled, and perfuming their breaths) left all hope, and she her curling and perfuming, all adoring this rising Sun, every man striving to invest himselfe into this mans favour'.[57] And so too when Villiers was perceived to have caught the King's eye, 'one gave him his place of Cup-bearer, that he might be in the King's eye; another sent to his Mercer and Taylor to put good Cloathes on him; a third, to his Sempster for curious Linnen, and all as prefacive[58] insinuations to obtain Offices upon his future Rise'.[59] James's own person is described with distaste: 'His Legs were very

---

[56] Sir A[nthony] W[eldon], *The Court and Character of King James. Whereunto is now added the Court of King Charles: Continued unto the Beginning of these Unhappy Times . . . Qui nescit dissimulare, nescit regnare* ['Who does not know how to dissemble, does not know how to rule'] (London, 1651), 7, 47. As the full title and epigraph suggest, this Commonwealth tract is one of several which cite James's behaviour as a way of disparaging the Stuarts generally.   [57] Ibid., 59.

[58] Prefacing, looking forward.

[59] Ibid., 84.

weake . . . that weaknesse made him ever leaning on other mens shoulders, his walke was ever circular, his fingers ever in that walke fidling about his Cod-piece.'[60] But what chiefly concerns Weldon is not so much the gender as the power of these favourites, and the advancement into positions of power and influence of those who had no merit.

Published in the same year as Weldon's book is the anonymous tract *The None-such Charles His Character*. The writer introduces his diatribe against the Stuarts by offering to acquaint the reader with 'the crying Sins which have brought downe so signall a wrath from God upon that Family.'[61] James's sins are summarized in an epigram said 'to have been left on his Cupboard':

> Aula Prophana, Religione Vana,
> Spreta Uxore, Ganymedis amore,
> Lege sublata, Prerogativa inflata.
> Tolle libertatem, incende Civitatem,
> Ducas Spadonem
> &
> Superasti Neronem.[62]

The writer builds upon Weldon's description of James to deplore his public behaviour:

How could that blasphemous man doe any thing that might amend his language? and how could he deceive the eares of men, who did discover himselfe so openly to the eyes of all the World? Who could not contract his horrid filthinesse within his Bed, his Ganimedes Pallet, or his Closets . . . But hee could not contract it there; He must have the Publique to be witnesse of his lascivious tongue licking of his Favourites lips, and his hands must (as his Court and Character mentions) bee seen in a continual lascivious action. Those hands, which by the publique, should have been ever seene clinging to the Scepter, Reigning in Equity, and open to give, or to receive the Petitions of his people.[63]

James has confounded public and private, using his hands to betoken 'horrid filthinesse' rather than kingly rule. From these Commonwealth attacks on James, it was a short step to the Restoration versifier

---

[60] Ibid., 165.

[61] *The None-such Charles His Character* (London, 1651), 2.

[62] Ibid., 17: 'The temple profaned with an empty religion; a wife scorned with a Ganymede's love; the law subverted with an inflated prerogative: take away liberty, fire the city, marry your eunuch, and you will have surpassed Nero.'

[63] Ibid., 20–1.

who, in an attack on the whole Stuart line, tersely dismissed him as 'A Coward Scott, a Sodamite of Hell'.[64]

These are retrospective accounts, but it was quite early in James's reign that writers started to express anxiety about or disapproval of the new King's behaviour. John Day's play *The Isle of Guls* (1606) was a thinly veiled critique of the new court in which 'from the highest to the lowest, all men's parts were acted of two divers nations'.[65] It seems, then, that James's English and Scottish courtiers were impersonated on stage. The prologue gives a broad hint that an attentive audience will hear sexually suggestive material:

2   ... Give me a sceane of venery, that will make a mans spirrits stand on theyr typ-toes, and die his bloode in deepe scarlet, like your *Ovids Ars Amandi*...
Prol.   Chast eares would never endure it sir.
2   Chast eares, now deafnes light uppon em, what should chast eares doe at a play.[66]

Unchaste ears probably recognized that a conversation between two captains reflected directly upon the behaviour of the new King:

1 *Cap.*   Now Captaine Observation, times bawde, thou that hast kept the Ages doore, whilst up-start basenes crept into the bedde of greatnesse, what doost thou thinke of this change?
2 *Cap.*   That it pleasd the Duke, and becomes not subjects to examine his actions.[67]

But subjects did examine the actions of their rulers, and many in the audience would know that this miniature allegory of baseness creeping into the bed of greatness was true literally as well as metaphorically. The Duke's favourite in this play is Dametas (a name from the pastoral poetry of Theocritus and Virgil) who is almost certainly intended for Sir Robert Carr (later Earl of Somerset). We are told that the Duke 'having one day lost his way, wandring in the woods'—the moral allegory here is elementary—'found this *Dametas*, affected his

---

[64] 'The Lord Lucas' Ghost' (*c.* 1673), BC MS Lt 55, fols. 30ʳ–31ᵛ; Crum F 755. In *Mundus Foppensis: or, The Fop Display'd* (London, 1691), 13, the new habit of men kissing other men 'renews the shame | Of *J.* the first, and *Buckingham*: | He, true it is, his Wives Embraces fled | To slabber his lov'd *Ganimede*.'

[65] Letter from Sir Edward Hoby to Sir Thomas Edmondes, quoted in Chambers, *Elizabethan Stage*, iii. 286.

[66] John Day, *The Ile of Guls* (London, 1606), sig. A2ᵛ; 'spirit' = erect penis, or (pl.) the bodily humours which produce an erection (Williams, *s.v.*).   [67] Ibid., sig. A4ᵛ.

discourse, tooke him along to the Court, and like great men in love with their owne dooings, countenanct his defects, gave him offices, titles, and all the additions that goe to the making up of a man worshipfull'.[68] Dametas himself says that 'though it please the Duke for some fewe good parts that he sees in me, to make me his familiar, I scorne to be publique, or every Courtiers companion'.[69] 'Parts' has sexual innuendo to unchaste ears, while the implications of 'familiar' range from 'member of a person's family or household' (*OED* 1) to 'intimate friend' (*OED* 2) to 'evil spirit supposed to attend at a call' (*OED* 3). It also means 'sexual partner'.[70] The plot of *The Ile of Guls* has a twist which allows some mockery of James's pursuit of young men, in that both the Duke and the Duchess are courting Lisander, a man who is dressed as a woman. The Duke is taken in by the disguise, but the Duchess is not, and she observes that while she will enjoy parodying his ogling of Lisander, 'the cheefe sports this | To see an old man with a young man kisse'.[71] We do not know, of course, what happened on stage, but one can imagine not only the Duke kissing Lisander, but the actor playing the Duke mimicking James's rolling gait and lascivious hand-movements—if the company wanted to take the risk.

There is some evidence to suggest that censors occasionally intervened to remove material which might be thought to reflect upon the King's behaviour with his favourites. It was suggested in Chapter 2 that Shakespeare may have misread the conventions of the homoerotically charged homosocial culture around James when he published the *Sonnets*. Another Shakespearian text which may have offended was *King Lear*, which was already politically sensitive in that its interest in the division and unity of the kingdoms had an obvious relevance to James's project to unite the crowns of England and Scotland. One of the most puzzling differences between the Quarto and Folio texts of *King Lear* is the absence of the mock trial of Goneril from the Folio text of Act III.[72] The cut begins a little before the start of the mock trial itself. In the Quarto text the Fool has started a new topic by asking Lear:

Foole. Prithe Nunckle tell me, whether a mad man be a Gentleman or a Yeoman.

---

[68] Ibid., sig. B1^r. [69] Ibid., sig. B1^{r-v}.

[70] Williams, *s.v.* [71] Day, *Ile of Guls*, sig. D2^r.

[72] This argument is adapted from my 'James I's Homosexuality and the Revision of the Folio Text of *King Lear*', *Notes and Queries*, 242 (1997), 62–4.

Lear. A King, a King, to have a thousand with red burning spits come
hiszing in upon them.
[*The Folio cut begins at this point.*]
Edg. The foule fiend bites my backe,
Foole. He's mad, that trusts in the tamenes of a Wolfe, a horses health, a
boyes love, or a whores oath.
Lear. It shalbe done, I wil arraigne them straight.[73]

A careful reviser concerned solely to remove the mock trial—whether
for artistic or political reasons—would probably have begun the cut
not with Edgar's speech but with Lear's line 'It shalbe done . . .'. He
would not have cut the preceding speeches by Edgar and the Fool, since
they are necessary to complete the discussion of madness, and do not
include any material relating to the trial. So perhaps the offence lay
not in the mock trial (or not only in the mock trial) but in the Fool's
answer to his own question: 'He's mad, that trusts in . . . a boyes love'
might well have struck a government censor or a cautious printer as
uncomfortably like an allusion to the sexual preferences of King James,
particularly when it comes so soon after Lear's vehement answer, 'A
King, a King'.[74] The Fool's reference to 'a boyes love' does not necessarily have to carry a sexual implication: 'love' could evoke, for example, the kind of attachment which Fidele forms for Lucius in
Cymbeline, and it was proverbial to comment on the fickleness of boys'
affections.[75] We cannot know whether the reference passed inoffen-
sively when the play was staged before the King on 26 December 1606
and was printed in 1608, or quite why or when someone intervened;
but since the King's reliance upon favourites was an issue which had
the potential to offend both moral sensibilities and political interests,
all manner of incidents or rumours could have made a censor or
printer specially sensitive to the Fool's words.

Among the examples of politically motivated censorship of Jacobean drama there is one other piece of evidence which suggests that a
censor might have been nervous about possible allusions to James's
patronage of beautiful young men. In a prompt book for *The Faithful
Friends* (probably from the early 1620s) someone has excised a

[73] *King Lear: 1608 (Pied Bull Quarto),* Shakespeare Quarto Facsimiles, 1 (London,
1939), sig. G3ᵛ.
[74] In such a context the reference to 'red burning spits' could be construed as an
allusion to the method of Edward II's murder. Janet Clare suggests that passages may
have been cut from *Richard III* because of sensitivity about allusions to a Duke of
Buckingham (*'Art Made Tongue-Tied by Authority': Elizabethan and Jacobean Dramatic
Censorship* (Manchester, 1990), 108, 200).   [75] Tilley, L 526.

reference to rulers' homosexual love affairs along with other sensitive political material, in this case a discussion of the royal prerogative which is also a discussion of the King's prerogative of choosing his own pleasures without being criticized, which makes for an exceptionally sensitive combination of topics:

> pardon mee
> if I make question of your loyalties
> that dare disparrage thus my soveraigns choyce
> of his respected subject, it infers,
> a doubt made of his wisdome, why should wee
> tax the prerogative pleasures of our Prince
> whome he shall grace, or where bestowe his favors[?]
> that Law's allowed to every private man,
> then to confine or disallowe a king
> were most in[j]urious and preposterous,.
> {for as   as their gods
> there subject to their passions as theire men
> Alexander the great had his Ephestion
> Phillip of Spaine his Lerma, not to offend.
> I could produce from Courts that I have seene
> more royall presidents, but ile not give
> such satisfaction to detractive toungs
> that publish such fowle noyse gainst aman
> I know for truly Vertuous.}[76]

The whole passage is marked for deletion, with the particularly offensive lines additionally enclosed within brackets and underlined. But the scarcity of parallel examples may suggest that dramatists tended to avoid the issue, or that censorship was unsystematic, or that it left few traces in the written record. Indeed, the revisions made to Marston's *The Malcontent* as it was going through the press in 1604 took out sensitive remarks about religion and government, yet left in the depiction of the Duke's 'Ganymede'.[77] In the same year, a remark in *Measure for Measure*—'I never heard the absent Duke much detected for Women, he was not enclin'd that way'—may allude to James, who has often been thought a partial model for the Duke's role.[78]

---

[76] *The Faithful Friends*, Malone Society Reprint (Oxford, 1975), 6.

[77] John Marston, *The Malcontent*, ed. George K. Hunter (London, 1975), pp. xxvii–xxx, 21.

[78] *Measure for Measure*, 3. 1. 385–6. I owe this idea to a suggestion by Professor Andrew Hadfield. The play was performed at court on 26 Dec. 1604.

Concern seems to have affected the representation of kingly authority, and its usurpation by favourites, more than any reference to sex between men *per se*. Some plays at Whitefriars even seem to have been designed for an audience with homoerotic interests.[79] By contrast with the priorities of Jacobean censorship, there is the case of John Fletcher's *Honest Mans Fortune*, where the 1647 folio appears to restore material staged in 1613 but cut in 1625, at the outset of the new, chaster regime of Charles I. Gordon Williams has noted that the 1625 prompt book heavily deletes a passage in which an unemployed servant contemplates setting up a male brothel, and replaces the ending of the play, where 'in performance a page-boy evidently had his breeches taken down to remove doubts about his sex . . . it would seem that such business could pass in 1613, but not in a 1625 revival'.[80]

One topical play which could never have been staged was Francis Osborne's *The True Tragicomedy*, an account of life in the Jacobean court which was composed *circa* 1655–8 but not printed in the period, and remained in manuscript until 1983.[81] Here the characters are named courtiers. In the dramatis personae the Earl of Somerset is described as being 'of a fair complexion, equally sharing the beauty of both sexes (therefore thought by his recommenders the fittest subject for the humour of King James)'.[82] In the play itself, Somerset complains to Sir Thomas Overbury: 'I am so stifled with the unnatural heats of the old King—that I would exchange it for any fire on this side Hell.'[83] And in another scene Overbury remarks that the King is anxious 'to rid his fingers of Carr which have long itch'd to be— Villiers'.[84] In a particularly intriguing conversation between the Earl of Northampton and a Jesuit, the former confides that William Herbert Earl of Pembroke has given a hostage to fortune by writing compromising letters to the King: 'he hath drawn his own process[85] by writing letters and bawdy verses to one the law makes it treason to solicit— though connived at in his age, where the distaff appeared more prevalent than the scepter'.[86] Even in the semi–privacy of manuscript this is

---

[79] Bly, *Queer Virgins*, 103–11.

[80] Gordon Williams, *Shakespeare, Sex and the Print Revolution* (London, 1996), 33.

[81] Francis Osborne, *The True Tragicomedy Formerly Acted at Court*, ed. John Pitcher and Lois Potter (New York, 1983).

[82] Ibid., 6.

[83] Ibid., 114.

[84] Ibid., 110.

[85] i.e. written his own indictment.

[86] Ibid., 95.

somewhat enigmatically phrased, but the reference to bawdy verses implies that the letters are also sexual in their content, and that 'solicit' here has its sexual meaning too; and 'treason' must refer to the King. If it is true that Pembroke made sexual advances to the King in letters and verses, and was subsequently blackmailed for it,[87] this would make any public association of Shakespeare's *Sonnets* with Pembroke even more of a faux pas.[88]

James himself appears in a scene with Villiers, and begins by praising the superiority of love for a man over love for a woman:

Love to men is seasoned with stronger delights than that to silly women because pricked on by the sharp spurs of restraint and rarity.[89] Which the vulgar affections, wanting, grows flat and distasteful, like over-oiled herbs without vinegar, maiming rational satisfaction for want of confidence and discourse. The most elegant ladies carrying no wittier arguments (in the apprehension of an imagination unsuborned by fond formalities) than a dairy maid, yet strong enow in both to confute desire before it is able to consider the best way and means to resolve itself.[90]

James goes on to argue that Nature's concern for the propagation of the species has resulted in over-population, and the consequent need for sex to be confined within legal restraints, 'which this barren desire would soon accomplish, were it more epidemical'.[91] Villiers professes that 'your Majesty hath convinced my reason, though my sense stands stiffest for feminine embraces', showing that Villiers himself has no homosexual desire. James then offers Villiers an arrangement whereby 'if I may enjoy my humor without impeachment of waste, you are left free to employ your talent either in the phlegmatic trade of Holland and other congealed climates or on the less dilated banks of warm Italy'.[92] Here, the woman's body is figured as cold and sluggish, and intercourse with her a form of 'trade'; by contrast, homosexual or

---

[87] In his *Advice to a Son* (1655) Osborne refers to an unnamed earl 'led by the Nose all King James his Reign, for fear of being questioned about Letters writ to so high a Person as is Treason by the Law, to Sollicite' (quoted in *True Tragicomedy*, p. iii).

[88] See pp. 84–6 above.

[89] James is almost quoting Shakespeare's Sonnet 52 (see p. 71 above).

[90] Osborne, *True Tragicomedy*, 116.

[91] Ibid., 116–17: i.e. homosexual sex, not resulting in children, would limit the population more quickly than legally enforced chastity, if it were more widely practised.

[92] Ibid., 117. 'Phlegmatic' means cold, dull, and sluggish, which were characteristics commonly associated with Holland and its inhabitants; 'congealed' means 'frozen'; and for the genital connotations of 'talent' and 'Holland' see Williams, *s.vv.* talent, Low Countries.

Italian sex is not only warmer but 'less dilated'—arguing that anal intercourse is tighter and so provides a more acute pleasure than vaginal intercourse. In a later scene between James and Somerset, the dramatist delineates the sexual contact between the two men as a form of political gamesmanship, confirming Overbury's earlier suspicion of James's intentions:

Somerset.   Sire, I have only this to add: that since this feminine love hath not rebated any desire in me to satisfy yours, my enemies might not be gratified with a hope of making your favors so much shine upon Villiers, as wholly to eclipse them towards me.

King.   By G—, Villiers is no more to me than the dry bones of my grand-father. 'Tis thou alone, dear Ganymede (*the King embraceth and kisseth Somerset*), shall quench the thirst of my—

Somerset.   I am assured.

King.   Thou mayest, that I will—(*the King makes a mouth another way.*)[93]

Despite his revulsion, Somerset is prepared to satisfy James in order to retain power and ward off the threat from Villiers; while James is prepared to display love for Somerset in order to hide his true desire for Villiers and his determination to abandon Somerset. Neither of the King's lovers is shown to display any actual affection or desire for him.

This critique stayed in manuscript, and can only ever have had the most limited circulation among trusted friends. By contrast, a work critical of James's sexual behaviour was actually printed in James's reign, and was written in Latin in order to reach a wide European readership—and perhaps to exclude literate but uneducated English readers from the lower orders. Isaac Casaubon's *Corona Regia* (1615) offers itself as a panegyric, but its ironies are cutting, and its lacunae mischievously placed:

In te quidem si vlla vitia sunt (hominem enim te esse fatemur, non tantum Regem, non tantum Pontificem;) si vitia inquam vlla sunt, elegantiae sunt, quae etsi secreto clausae, & silentio obumbratae, tamen velut per rimas in publicum erumpunt, & se populo insinuant: quam non mala specie, hinc maxime discimus, quod imitari plerique malunt quam reprehendere; quod nihil a Pontifice suo nisi sanctum, nihil a Rege suo nisi imitatione dignum putent proficisci. Idcirco oblectari meliori forma, suauitas est:

---

[93] Osborne, *True Tragicomedy*, 120–1; the last phrase means that he has been dissembling all along (thus Potter). For another account of James's dissimulation in professing his love and support for Somerset at the very moment when he was abandoning him, see Weldon, *Court and Character*, 94–6.

indulgere genio, hilaritas est: agere quae in tali fortuna animus dictet, remissio est. Noctes clandestinae quantum voluptatis * * Vterque sexus; quod quum mirandum in frigidis his plagis, in te virile regium est. * * *[94]

The asterisks which ostensibly denote lacunae in a fragmentary text draw the reader's attention to what is left unsaid and unsayable, so inviting us to imagine the off-stage scenes for ourselves. Playing on James's image of himself as a godly and philosophical ruler, Casaubon remarks acidly that Christ said, 'suffer the little children to come unto me', whereas James says, 'suffer the pretty boys to come unto me'.[95] This philosopher-king is a Socrates only in that he loves his Alcibiades.[96] In another passage Casaubon charts the rise of a succession of pretty boys in James's favour, young lads to whom the King gave preferment not for their virtue but their appearance: there was the Scot John Ramsey, *non minus pulchrum quam fortem arbitratus;*[97] then there was Philip Herbert, *adolescentem venustate gratiosum, a cubiculo tibi esse voluisti, quo in gradu beneficio obsequium reddi potuit;*[98] then there was Robert Carr, who *praemiisque mox dignus habitus, non lentis gradibus ad summas dignitates ascendit;*[99] and finally *hos secutus est*

---

[94] *Is. Casauboni Corona Regia. Id est Panegyricus Cuiusdam vere Aurei, Quem Iacobo I. Magnae Britanniae, &c. Regi, Fidei Defensori delinearat, Fragmenta* (London, 1615), 67–8: 'If there are indeed any imperfections in you (for we acknowledge you to be a man, not only a king, not only head of the church); if, I say, there are any imperfections, they are refined ones—and yet, though they are hidden away in secret and shrouded in silence, they break out as if through cracks into the public sphere, and make themselves known to the people [or 'insinuate themselves into (i.e. corrupt) the people']: and we learn particularly from such things as appear in a fair guise, which many would rather imitate than condemn. For they imagine that nothing proceeds from the head of their church which is not holy, nothing from their king which is not worthy of imitation. For that reason to be delighted by an unusually pretty face is charming; to indulge one's bent is pleasurable; to act in such circumstances as your mind dictates, is a weakness. Clandestine nights so much pleasure * * and each sex; which while marvellous in this frozen clime, in you is virile and regal.***'

[95] *Christi vox erat*: Sinite paruulos venire ad me: *tu pueros, eosq; formosissimos vocas*: 'Christ said: *suffer the little children to come unto me*; you call the boys—and of those the prettiest ones' (ibid., 105).

[96] *Alcibiades habes, & philosophari potes; Rex es, & Socratem agis; amas, & pius es.* * *: 'you have your Alcibiades, and you can philosophize; you are a king, and you act the Socrates; you love and are holy * *' (ibid., 105).

[97] Ibid., 91: 'whom you thought both good-looking and strong'.

[98] Ibid.: 'a young lad of charming appearance, whom you wanted in your bed-chamber, in which position he could render thankful service'.

[99] Ibid.: 'soon thought worthy of reward, rose to the highest honours by no slow steps.'

incomparabili forma adolescens, Georgius Villiers, à regina ipsa in cubiculum tuum introductus, vbi eodem die & Eques, & à Cubiculo factus est.[100] It is remarkable that such comments could be printed in 1615, and that the apostolic succession of boyfriends in the bed of the Fidei Defensor was so clearly visible to a European observer.[101]

But it was principally through manuscript verse that criticism of James and his sexual behaviour was voiced.[102] One set of verses begins with praise of Henry VIII, whose heroic acts contrasted with the sorry performance of the present monarch, for Henry 'would swive while he was alive | ffrom the Queene unto the begger.'[103] The poem then goes on to comment on James's devotion to sports of various kinds:

> Att Royston and newmarkett he'll hunt till he be leane
> But he hath menny boys that with masks and toyes
> Can make him fatt againe.

Though there are some indications that the writer disapproves of the all-male world of James's entertainments—

> 'Tis a lovely grace to dance with a lasse
> When a man may kisse, and court[;]
> But to dance with A man like a puritan
> . Tis a drie and ugly sport.

—the poem says little about James's sexual proclivities.

[100] *Corona Regia*, 92: 'these were followed by a young man of incomparable beauty, George Villiers, introduced by the Queen herself into your bedchamber, where on the same day he was knighted and appointed to the bedchamber'.

[101] Given the sensitivity of these comments on the royal favourites, it may be no accident that one of the BL copies (292. a. 42) lacks 91–2.

[102] For the prevalence of topical satirical poems in the Jacobean period see Alastair Bellany, ' "Raylinge Rymes and Vaunting Verse": Libellous Politics in Early Stuart England, 1603–1628', in Kevin Sharpe and Peter Lake (eds.), *Culture and Politics in Early Stuart England* (Basingstoke, 1994), 285–310; Thomas Cogswell, 'Underground Verse and the Transformation of Early Stuart Political Culture', in Susan D. Amussen and Mark A. Kishlansky (eds.), *Political Culture and Cultural Politics in Early Modern England* (Manchester, 1995), 277–300; James Knowles, 'To "scourge the arse | Jove's marrow so had wasted": Scurrility and the Subversion of Sodomy', in Dermot Cavanagh and Tim Kirk (eds.), *Subversion and Scurrility: Popular Discourse in Europe from 1500 to the Present* (Aldershot, 2000), 74–92; Andrew McRae, 'The Literary Culture of Early Stuart Libeling', *Modern Philology*, 97 (2000), 364–92, and his *Unauthorized Texts: Satire and the Early Stuart State* (forthcoming). I am grateful to Dr McRae for the use of a first-line index of manuscript and printed poems on James which he has compiled.

[103] Bodl. MS Malone 23, pp. 19–22; Crum L 429.

More direct and more far-reaching is the following poem on the King's five senses, which seems to have been fairly widely distributed in manuscript:

The Senses

Seeing From such a face whose excellence
     May captivate my soveraynes sense
     And make him Phoebus-like his throne
     Resigne to some yong Phaeton:
     Whose skillesse and unsteadie hand
     May prove the ruine of our land
     Unlesse greate Jove downe from the skie
     Beholding earths calamitie
     Strike with his hand that cannot erre
     That proud usurping charioteer
     And cure, though Phoebus greive, our woe[:]
     From such a face that can doe so
     Wheresoere it have a being
     Blesse my soveraigne and his seeing.

Hearing From jests profane and flattring tongs
     From baudie tales from beastly songs
     From after-supper suites that feare
     A parliament or counsels eare
     From Spanish treaties that may wound
     Our countries peace or Gospels sound
     From Jobs false friends that would entice
     My sov'rayne from heavens Paradice
     From Prophets such as Ahabs were
     That flattering would abuse his eare
     His frowne more then their makers fearing
     Blesse my soveraigne and his hearing.

Tasting From all fruit that is forbidden
     Such for which old Eve was chidden
     From bread of labourers' sweat and toile
     From the poore widdowes meale and oile
     From blood of innocents oft wrangled
     From their estates and for that strangled
     From the candid[104] poyson'd baites
     Of Jesuits and their deceits
     Italian salletts[105] Romish drugs

---

[104] Candied, sweet. [105] Salads.

The milke of Babells proud whores dugs
From wine that can destroy the braine
And from the dangerous figs[106] of Spaine
At all banquets and all feastings
Blesse my soveraigne and his tastings[.]

Fealing   From prick of conscience[,] such a sting
As slayes the soule[,] Heaven blesse my King[;]
From such a bribe as may withdraw
His thoughts from equitie and law
From such a smooth and beardlesse chinne
As may provoke or tempt to sinne
From such a hand whose moist palme[107] may
My soveraigne lead out of the way
From things polluted and uncleane
From all thats bestiall or obscene
From what may set his soule a reeling
Blesse my soveraine and his feeling[.]

Smelling   Where Myrrhe and Frankincense is throwne
And altars built to Gods unknowne
Oh let my soveraigne never smell[:]
Such damn'd perfumes are fit for hell[;]
Let no such sent his nostrils staine[.]
From smels that poyson can the braine
Heaven still preserve him, next I crave
Thou wilt be pleasd great God to save
My soveraigne from a Ganymed
Whose whorish breath hath powre to lead
His excellence which way it list[:]
O let such lips be never kist[.]
From a breth so farre excelling
Blesse my soveraigne and his smelling.

Seeing   And now just God I humbly pray
That thou wilt take that filme away
That keepes my soveraignes eyes from viewing
The things that will be our undoeing
Hearing   Then let him heare good God the sounds
As well of men as of his hounds
Tasting   Give him a tast and timely too
Of what his subjects undergoe

---

[106] Poisoned figs.   [107] A moist palm was a sign of lechery.

Feeling	Give him a feeling of their woes
Smelling	And then no doubt his roiall nose
	Will quickly smell those rascalls forth
	Whose black deeds have eclipsd his worth[.]
	They found and scourgd for their offences
	Heaven blesse my King and all his senses.[108]

Several fears dominate this poem: that James may be seduced into false religion through foreign influence; that the people's real needs may never reach the King's ear because of what is whispered to him in private; that the sovereign will be sexually corrupted, surrendering control of the state to an upstart and forfeiting the love of his people. Indeed, one manuscript[109] changes 'sovereign' to 'lover', which indicates the power of the trope that love is the bond which unites subjects and sovereigns. In effect, the love between James and Buckingham displaces the love between James and his people. The medieval and Tudor doctrine of the King's Two Bodies[110] made the ordinary, mortal body of the king the bearer of heavy symbolic significance, for in an almost incarnational theology the divinity of kingship was twinned with the human flesh of the ruler. The present poem focuses on the King's five senses to emphasize that the body not only carries kingship but—if corrupted through one of its senses—may bring about the loss of kingship. The senses are particularly vulnerable to the sexual attractions of a Ganymede: captivated visually by his beauty; aurally by bawdy songs and stories; in taste by the forbidden fruit; through touch by the pleasure of a boy's smooth chin and the sweating palm which betokens sexual excitement; and through smell by the perfumed breath which comes from the lips as they are kissed. James's sexual body is betraying not only his kingly body but also his immortal soul, which risks being sent reeling to hell.

Another poem even envisages that James's sexual behaviour may

---

[108] Crum F 751; edited from the facsimile in 'Poems from a Seventeenth-Century Manuscript with the Hand of Robert Herrick', ed. Norman K. Farmer, Jr., *Texas Quarterly*, 16 (1973), 121–85. I differ repeatedly from Farmer's transcript, and introduce two emendations from BL MS Add. 23229, fols. 99ʳ–100ʳ: l. 29, *labourers'* for *labours*; l. 47 *such* added; editorial punctuation added in square brackets. Amongst the MSS which I have seen, the Herrick MS provides the best text, but the poem deserves to be properly edited from a complete collation of surviving MSS. The poem is sometimes attributed to William Drummond, but the attribution is insecure.

[109] BL MS Egerton 923.

[110] Ernst H. Kantorowicz, *The King's Two Bodies: A Study in Medieval Political Theology* (Princeton, 1957).

lead to him being deposed. Here it is not the reckless young Phaethon who is bound for a fall, but Jove himself:

The Warres of the Gods.

Arme, arme, in heaven there is a faction
　　And the Demy-Gods
Now are bent for Action;
　　They are att Odds
With him that rules the Thunder,
　　And will destroy
　　His white fac't Boy
Or rend the heavens asunder.

2.
Great Jove that swayes the emperiall Scepter
　　With's upstart Love
That makes him drunke with Nectar[111]
　　They will remove;
Harke how the Cyclops labour,
　　See Vulcan sweates
　　That gives the heates
And forges Mars his Armour.

3.
Marke how the glorious starry Border
　　That the heavens hath worne
Till of late in Order
　　See how they turne
Each Planets course doth alter,
　　The sun and moone
　　Are out of Tune
The spheares begin to faulter.

4.
See how each pretty starre stands gazinge
　　And would fayne provoke
By theyr often blazinge
　　Flame to this smoke:
The dogge: starre burnes with ire,
　　And Charles his Wayne
　　Would wondrous fayne
Bringe fuell to his fire.

---

[111] 'Nectar' = semen (Williams *s.v.*).

5.

Loves Queene stood disaffected
    To what shee had seene
Or to what suspected
    As shee in spleene
To Juno hath protested
    Hir servant Mars
    Should scourge the Arse
Jove's marrow[112] so had wasted.

6.

The chast Diana by her Quiver
    And ten thousand maydes
Have sworne, that they will never
    Sporte in the shades,
Untill the heavens Creator
    Be quite displac't
    Or els disgrac't
For lovinge so 'gainst nature.

7.

The fayre Proserpine next whurryes[113]
    In fiery Coach
Drawne by twelve blacke furies;
    As they approach
They threaten without mercy
    To have him burn'd
    That thus hath turn'd
Love's pleasures Arse Verse.

8.

Slow pac'd Saturne he doth follow
    Hermes will make one
So will bright Apollo,
    Thetis hath wonne
Rough Neptune to this action,
    Æolus huffes
    And Boreas puffes
To see the ffates probaction.[114]

---

[112] 'Marrow' = semen, or sexual capacity generally (Williams, *s.v.*).
[113] Hurries.
[114] Examination.

[9.]
Still Jove with Ganymed lyes playinge,
  Here's[115] not Tritans sound
Nor yet horses neighinge
  His Eares are bound,
The fidlinge God doth lull him
  Bacchus quaffes
  And Momus laughes
To see how they can gull him.[116]

A faction amongst the gods is seeking to remove Jove along with
his 'white fac'd Boy'. The emphasis on martial preparations in the
second stanza implicitly contrasts with James's reluctance to become
embroiled in war, and since the peace which Jove enjoys is devoted
only to drink and sex, his masculinity is suspect. As the heavenly order
(in the third stanza) is affected by Jove's inattention to everything
except his Ganymede, so the nation's social order too goes awry.
Stanzas 4 and 5 imply that Prince Charles and Queen Anne are both
discountenanced by James's sexual behaviour and are part of this
oppositional group, though there appears to be no surviving historical
evidence for this. The message of the poem is clear enough: the King is
neglecting his duties, and instead of the old aristocracy listens only to
those upstarts who provide him with his pleasures, Ganymede and
Bacchus, while Momus, god of ridicule and the satirist's alter ego,
laughs at the scene. At one point the poem strikes a note which one
sometimes forgets in reading the homoerotic literature of this period:
in stanza 7 the gods threaten to burn Ganymede, a reminder that being
burnt at the stake as a sodomite was a real—if remote—possibility
for James, Buckingham, and the rest of the white-faced boys with
perfumed breath.

    There may be an allusion to this poem in Thomas Carew's masque
Coelum Britannicum, which was staged before Charles I in 1634. There
has been a purge of the constellations which symbolize various kinds of
'impiety . . . and lustfull influences', and the conduct of heaven is being
reformed. As the scoffer Momus remarks:

Heaven is no more the place it was; a cloister of Carthusians, a Monastery
of converted gods, *Jove* is growne old and fearefull, apprehends a subversion of his Empire . . . Wee have had new orders read in the Presence

---

  [115] Hears.
  [116] BL MS Add 22603, fols. 33ʳ–34ᵛ; Crum A 1403; also in Herrick MS; emended at l. 57
(*Saturne* for *Diana*) from Herrick MS.

Chamber... *Cupid* must goe no more scandalously naked, but is enjoyned to make him breeches though of his mothers petticotes. *Ganimede* is forbidden the Bedchamber, and must onely minister in publique. The gods must keep no Pages, nor Groomes of their Chamber under the age of 25. and those provided of a competent stocke of beard.[117]

Perhaps, nearly ten years into the reign of James's successor, this could pass as an unthreatening joke, licensed by its speaker's privileged status, and reflecting creditably on the reformed court and the different personal conduct of James's son.[118]

The poem on James as Jove is probably directed particularly at his relationship with the Duke of Buckingham, which attracted much attention in manuscript verses.[119] Buckingham's acquisition of power made him increasingly unpopular, and some writers would greet his assassination in 1628 with delight. In a Restoration ballad on the first and second Dukes of Buckingham, the reasons for the first Duke's advancement are clear enough:

> I sing the praise of a worthy Wight
> Whose Father King *Jemmy,* that never would fight
> For his Face, but more for his Arse made a Knight.[120]

But already in the reign of James himself satirical verses began to circulate in manuscript, such as these lines with their suggestive references to the game which the two bucks enjoy, and their invitation to the reader to expect an alternative rhyme for 'Buck':

[117] *The Poems of Thomas Carew, with his masque Coelum Britannicum,* ed. Rhodes Dunlap (Oxford, 1949), 159. For Carew's source in Giordano Bruno, ibid., 279.

[118] Even the republican Lucy Hutchinson recognized that Charles I's court was an improvement in this respect on that of his father: whereas Buckingham's advancement was due to 'no merit but that of his beauty and his prostitution . . . the face of the court was much changed in the change of the king, for . . . the fools and bawds, mimics and catamites of the former court grew out of fashion' (Lucy Hutchinson, *Memoirs of the Life of Colonel Hutchinson,* ed. N. H. Keeble (London, 1995), 67).

[119] For a sympathetic reading of the James–Buckingham relationship see (besides Bergeron) Roger Lockyer, *Buckingham: The Life and Political Career of George Villiers, First Duke of Buckingham 1592–1628* (London, 1981). Selected poems on Buckingham are printed in *Poems and Songs relating to George Villiers, Duke of Buckingham; and his Assassination by John Felton, August 23, 1628,* ed. Frederick W. Fairholt (London, 1850).

[120] BL MS Harley 7315, fols. 46ᵛ–49ʳ; Crum I 479.

To the Duke of Buckingham
The King loves you, you him; both love the same,
You love the King, he you, both *Buck-in-game*[;]
Of sport the King loves game, of game the *Buck*[,]
Of all men you, why you? Why see your luck.[121]

Another poem on Buckingham as a buck makes him into an overtly
sexual object, with 'His horne exalted'.[122] Perhaps this may be a public
version of language actually used between the two lovers, for the hunting trope carries a sexual innuendo in this letter from James to
Buckingham:

I can take no pleasure in Theobalds Park till thou come, and yet the thistle
is here. If thy health permit thee to be here tomorrow night, it will be a
great comfort unto me that thou and thy cunts may see me hunt the buck
in the park upon Friday next. And if thou show me not all the devices in
this park before I go from hence, I shall never have comfort in it.[123]

When Buckingham and Prince Charles embarked on their hare-
brained journey to Spain in 1623, one poet reflected on the plight of
James, left alone in England:

For Buckingham, his spouse, is gone,
And left the widdow'd king alone,
With lacke and greife upp blowne.[124]

Though sarcastic in its tone, this is no more than the imagery which
James himself used when writing to Buckingham:

I cannot content myself without sending you this present, praying God
that I may have a joyful and comfortable meeting with you and that we
may make at this Christmas a new marriage ever to be kept hereafter; for,
God so love me, as I desire only to live in this world for your sake, and that
I had rather live banished in any part of the earth with you than live a

---

[121] *Wit Restor'd in Severall Select Poems not formerly Publish't* (London, 1658), 58;
Crum T 849. A variant text in Fairholt, *Poems and Songs*, 5 ends: 'of games the duke; | Of
all men you; and you | Solely, for your looke.' 'Buck' = sexually active male (Williams,
s.v.). For hunting deer as a metaphor for sex, see Williams, *s.v.* doe, and cf. Shakespeare,
Venus and Adonis: 'since I have hemd thee here | Within the circuit of this ivorie pale, |
Ile be a parke, and thou shalt be my deare' (ll. 229–31). John Hepwith in his beast-fable
The Calidonian Forrest (London, 1641), 4–5, casts Buckingham as a hart and James as a
lion.

[122] Fairholt, *Poems and Songs*, 5. 'Horn' = erect penis (Williams, *s.v.*).

[123] Bergeron, *King James*, 175.

[124] Herrick MS ed. Farmer, 145; Crum S 506.

sorrowful widow's life without you. And so God bless you, my sweet child and wife, and grant that ye may ever be a comfort to your dear dad and husband.[125]

In 1627 Buckingham on his return from the ill-fated military expedition to the Ile de Rhé is accused of effeminacy: 'a manly heart disdaines I This female follie'; stay at court and play tennis instead, the poet advises, for 'Venus pavilions doe befit thee best I Perriwigs with helmets are not to be prest.'[126] A poem on Buckingham's death derides him for 'his courting lady-hand', and his 'Ganimedian lookes', but is more concerned to lament the overturning of the social hierarchy which Buckingham's rise exemplifies and effects.[127] Another poem spoken in the persona of the Duke after his assassination reflects on his success as 'a monarch's minion' and the ways in which he gained possession of the King's heart; like Gaveston in some accounts, Buckingham is seen as excercising a kind of witchcraft over James:

> Nature her forces did combine with art
> To gett possession of my soveraignes heart
>
> .   .   .   .
>
> For fates, or philters, worse direction,
> Wonne my disposers deare affection:
> That I was entertain'd with great applause,
> And though, on my part, shape was all the cause,
> Yet was I lodged like some oracle
> In's royall heart.[128]

In such cases the notion of sexual influence as a kind of witchcraft goes beyond the romantic image of enchantment, and begins to associate witch and sodomite as threats to a godly society. It is one thing for Henry V to compliment the French princess by saying, 'You have Witch-craft in your Lippes, *Kate*',[129] but the trope begins to lose its metaphorical status when onlookers trying to figure out the mysteries of sexual attraction turn to witchcraft as an explanation: it is typically the outsider whose sexual power is thus construed, whether it is Othello drawing Desdemona away from her father,[130] or Cleopatra

---

[125] Bergeron, *King James*, 175.
[126] BL MS Sloane 826, fols. 33[r-v]; Fairholt, *Poems and Songs*, 19; Crum A 1240. For the sexual connotations of tennis see p. 42 above.
[127] Fairholt, *Poems and Songs*, 49.
[128] Ibid., 37–9.
[129] Shakespeare, *Henry V*, 5. 2. 274.
[130] *Othello*, 1. 3. 64, 92, 168.

seducing Antony from his Roman duties,[131] or Perdita transgressing social boundaries by presuming as a mere shepherdess to think of marriage with Prince Florizel.[132] In all these cases the notion of witchcraft is used by those who resent the outsider's possession of a loved one, one over whom they think they have rights. So it is not only the sodomite who is a kind of witch: any threat to the social order which comes about as a result of someone being sexually attracted outside its parameters is liable to be thus construed. What prompts observers to reach for the terminology of witchcraft or sodomy is, it seems, a transgression of boundaries—between private and public signs of affection, between ruler and subject, or between aristocrat and parvenu. In the cases of Gaveston and Buckingham it was perhaps the latter offence— the power of the *arriviste*—which most rankled.

SODOMY AND CIVIL WAR

During the Civil War and Commonwealth, with the breaking down of both the social and the symbolic order, one might have expected allegations of sodomy to have proliferated, figuring an overturning of the traditional ways, and exemplifying the sexual liberty of the age.[133] In fact, there are few such references in the polemical literature of the period, though charges of sodomy were occasionally made to signal the wickedness of political opponents. Cavalier drinking clubs employed homosocial male bawdy,[134] and were said by one observer to 'live upon the Sin of Sodom'.[135] Parliamentarian newsbooks occasionally turned their attention to instances of sodomy which were discovered and reported by the godly, and one can sometimes glimpse biographical fragments, shards of past lives whose real texture and emotion now elude us:

There are two Youths; the one called *Holgate*, and the other *Harlow* brought up prisoners from the fleet, to be tryed at the Goal delivery for most horrid Buggery with each other, who were first discovered to five

[131] *Antony and Cleopatra*, 2. 1. 22.
[132] *The Winter's Tale*, 4. 4. 423.
[133] Maria McCann's novel *As Meat Loves Salt* (London, 2001), set in the Civil War, plausibly suggests how a sexual relationship between two men might have been conducted and conceptualized in this period.
[134] See p. 28 above.
[135] John Tatham, *The Scotch Figgaries* (London, 1735), 15; written 1652.

young godly Youths of the ships, that had several consultations about it, and upon their discovery revealed it to the officers, and two more were sent up for that filthy Crime a while before, that are to be tryed the next Sessions.

Severall Letters from other parts of *England* speak much of that horrible sin, being committed by many in *England,* which may endanger its destruction, if the Lords great mercy prevent it not. But among others there was the last Assizes at *Lincoln* a Schoolmaster hanged for Buggering one of his Schollars; he was a man that did often preach, and held forth strange Notions; but when he was to die, confest that he was a Papist.[136]

Here buggery is discovered and denounced by the 'godly', confessed by a papist, and may attract God's retribution upon the nation at large; so its recognition becomes a small element in the work of defining and establishing the puritan order.

Amongst those on the Royalist side who were singled out by name was John Wilson, vicar of Arlington in Sussex, who was sequestered

for that he in most beastly manner, divers times attempted to commit buggery with *Nathaniel Browne, Samuel Andrewes* and *Robert Williams* his Parishioners, and by perswasions and violence, laboured to draw them to that abhominable sinne, *that* (as he shamed not to professe) *they might make up his number eighteene*; and hath professed, *that he made choice to commit that act with man-kind rather then with women, to avoide the shame and danger that oft ensueth in begetting Bastards.*[137]

According to this account, Wilson's penchant for buggery was pragmatic, a wish to avoid the embarrassment and expense of illegitimate children; but the description of Wilson's activities continues in a vein which makes him an anthology of socially unacceptable attitudes and practices; for he

hath also attempted to commit Buggery with a Mare, and at Baptizing of a Bastard child, blasphemously said, openly in the Church, *That our Saviour as he was in the flesh, was a Bastard*; and usually preacheth, *That Baptisme utterly taketh away originall sinne, and that the sinnes committed after Baptisme, are only by imitation, and not by naturall corruption*; and hath in his Sermons, much commended Images in Churches, as good for edification, and that *men should pray with Beades,* and hath openly said,

---

[136] *Severall Proceedings of State Affaires,* 255 (10–17 Aug. 1655), from *Making the News: An Anthology of the Newsbooks of Revolutionary England 1641–1660,* ed. Joad Raymond (Moreton-in-Marsh, 1993), 317.

[137] John White, *The First Century of Scandalous, Malignant Priests* (London, 1643), 1.

that the Parliament were Rebels, and endeavoured to starve the King, and that whatsoever the King commands, we are all bound to obey, whether it be good or evill; and hath openly affirmed, *that Buggery is no sinne,* and is a usuall frequenter of Ale-houses, and a great drinker.[138]

The purpose of this particular tract, published just a year into the Civil War, is to mobilize opinion against abuses in the Anglican Church: hence the rhetorical strategy which begins the account of Wilson with his alleged buggery with his male parishioners, and proceeds to accuse him also of blasphemy, Roman Catholic practices in worship, contempt for the principles of legitimacy and inheritance, and an absolutist view of kingship. That the passage concludes by mentioning that Wilson frequented ale-houses also makes a social and ideological point: since ale-houses were lower-class drinking establishments which were associated with prostitution and free-thinking radicalism,[139] Wilson has betrayed his class as well as his calling.

Also in 1643, the Parliamentarian newsbook *Mercurius Britanicus* accused royalist lords and clergy of '*prodigious fornication*' in a variety of manifestations. Rebutting an allegation that a Parliamentarian prisoner had committed buggery on a mare (evidently a common recreation in the 1640s) the newsbook writer claims that Cavaliers themselves were susceptible to bestiality, amongst other offences:

now they have bethought them of this kind of impiety, you shall have them *sinning* with the very beasts of the field shortly, and keeping Mares for *breeding* Cavaliers on, and they may do it as lawfully as the Ladies of honour may keep Stallions and Monkies, and their Bishops Shee-goates and Ganimedes, for they make nothing of such *prodigious fornication,* they make nothing of Sodomy and Gomorrahisme, especially your Italianated Lords, and your hot privy Counsellors, that have seen fashions abroad, as *Dorset* the Earle, that hath travelled to Venice for his sins . . . But of all sinners, your *Cathedrall men* are the worst, some of your Prebends makes nothing of sinning with the little singing boyes after an Anthem; Oh! this is prodigious lust, which rages after *Organ pipes,* and *Surplisses;* I could tell you a strange story of a reverend *Prelate* that you all know, you would little imagine what doings he hath had in his vestry.[140]

So Royalist lords who have had the opportunity to travel to Italy are

---

[138] John White, *The First Century of Scandalous, Malignant Priests,* 1–2.
[139] Peter Clark, *The English Alehouse: A Social History* (London, 1983).
[140] *Mercurius Britanicus,* 19 (28 Dec.–4 Jan. 1643 [i.e. 1643/4]), from Raymond, *Making the News,* 107.

suspect. As for the clergy, seducing choirboys goes along with a papist penchant for ritual, and an unhealthy interest in organ pipes—in both senses. But while the rhetoric plays merrily with various forms of transgression, the principal interest of the writer seems to be in religious rather than sexual corruption: the latter stands as a sign of the former, and is of mimimal interest *per se*.

But republicans were also victims of this form of propaganda. The Parliamentarian preacher Hugh Peters was accused of sodomy, and appeared as the character Sodome in Cosmo Manuche's play *The Loyal Lovers* (1652).[141] Henry Marten was called 'that *pockifi'd Cattamite*' by *Mercurius Dogmaticus*.[142] Henry Neville was said to have brought back two of the local vices from a trip to Italy:

> *I prethee be not too rash,*
> *With Atheism to court the Devil,*
> *You'r too bold to be his Bardash.*[143]

And the Members of Parliament who passively submitted to Cromwell's will are called '*State-Catamites*, upon whom any *Votes* whatsoever may be begotten.'[144]

Newsbooks and pamphlets often parade examples of horrid sexual excesses, and antinomian attitudes certainly encouraged sexual freedom amongst the radical sects.[145] Ranters in particular were notorious for allegedly indulging in free sex.[146] But it is very rare to find homosexual behaviour associated with these groups. One exception is the story of the Wiltshire minister Thomas Webbe, recounted by his enemy Edward Stokes. Webbe's story is intricate and murky, and includes him committing adultery, and then encouraging his wife to do the same, so that she cannot reproach him when he is with his mistress. Articles detailing Webbe's offences also included preaching false doctrine, abusing his parishioners, and cutting down the timber on the glebe lands. But Webbe also had a male partner:

[141] Cosmo Manuche, *The Loyal Lovers: A Tragi-Comedy* (London, 1652).

[142] *Mercurius Dogmaticus*, 4 (27 Jan.–3 Feb. 1648), 30.

[143] 'A New Ballad on the Old Parliament', quoted in Williams, *s.v.* bardash.

[144] *Mercurius Pragmaticus*, 19 (19–25 Jan. 1648), sig. T^v, quoted in Williams, *s.v.* catamite.

[145] Christopher Hill, *The World Turned Upside Down: Radical Ideas during the English Revolution* (London, 1972; 2nd edn. Harmondsworth, 1975), 306–23.

[146] Several woodcuts from contemporary pamphlets showing Ranters dancing naked are reproduced in J. C. Davis, *Fear, Myth and History: The Ranters and the Historians* (Cambridge, 1986).

Webbs most principall favourite, and greatest choicest associate in the whole Country;[147] for one of his own Sex, was one J. O. a comely young man, and a man of a seeming sober behaviour, even as *Webbe* himself, of whom a stranger cannot but say, or at least think, that butter would not melt in his mouth (as we use to say) yet here you will perceive, as the Proverb is, *The still Sow eats all the draught*.[148] This man with his Cob-webb seeming sobriety, and unclean inside, is taken by *Tho. Webbe*, as men use to take their wives, For better for worse: So I say, this man is honoured with the title of *Webbs* wife, for so he calls him, My wife *O*; and *O* owns *Webb* for a husband; and now where ever they come, 'tis my wife *O*, and my husband *Webb*. True it is, *Webb* is become a great lover of Musick, which to prophane hearts is an in-let to lust: but whether ever he plaied any hellish tune with his Organ or Church musick yea or no, is not yet discovered: But this is discovered, that both the man and the man-wife were in other things brethren in iniquity, and have brought more shame upon the professors of the Gospel, then all the hypocrites and whoremongers of this later age.

This *J. O.* is of an honest Stock and Parentage and lived in his Country in good esteem, and with good repute, till such time as he was all wooed and Married to this holy unholy Parish-Parson, *Tho. Webb*. But now Cat after kinde,[149] he soon becomes Ranting ripe, and enters with the first upon the Stage, publickly to act what he had privatly learnt from husband *Webb*: Whereupon he shakes hands with, and bids farwell to his naturall affection (the first step towards the perfection of Ranters) he forsakes his own lawfull wife, dwelling, and children, and Country to boot; and takes to himself as a Companion and Traveller, a light Maid forsooth, being his neighbours daughter, which he takes without parents consent, as his fellow creature; and away he goeth: and as *Webbe* before, so M^r *O*. now travels into other Countries, to gain credit and esteem, which in his own Country was totally extinct. And the better to do this, *Webbe* makes him a Preacher before he goeth; for *Webbe* is most eminent this way, to teach men how to use the tongue; so as it may not prejudice the principle or the practice of their purely impure sect, or hinder the building of their R[anters'] Babel.[150]

At least in Stokes's account, Webbe and J. O. seem to have called each

---

[147] County.

[148] Meaning to pretend one thing and do another: Tilley S 681.

[149] Meaning that one behaves according to one's true nature ('kind'): 'that cat is out of kind that sweet milk will not lap': Tilley C 167.

[150] Edward Stokes, *The Wiltshire Rant; or a Narrative wherein the most unparallel'd Prophane Actings, Counterfeit Repentings, and Evil Speakings of Thomas Webbe Late Pretended Minister of Langley Buriall, are Discovered* (London, 1652), 7–8.

other husband and wife, but there is no suggestion that either of them is exclusively or even primarily interested in men sexually. And while Stokes is keen to assemble all the allegations that he can against Webbe, he can only speculate about 'whether ever he plaied any hellish tune with his Organ'. When Webbe has corrupted J. O., the latter leaves his wife and family, but with a young girl, not with Webbe or another man; and he sets off on his career as a Ranter preacher. What we glimpse here is less a homosexual love affair than an upheaval in the social order which allows all manner of mobility—mobility of desire, of domestic arrangements, of religious belief and practice.

TITUS OATES

His marks are as followeth; The off Leg behind something shorter than the other, and cloven Foot on the nether side; His Face Rain-bow-colour, and the rest of his Body black: Two slouching Ears, ready to be cropp'd the next Spring, if they do not drop off before; His Mouth is in the middle of his Face, exactly between the upper part of his Forehead and the lower part of his Chin; He hath a short Neck, which makes him defie the Pillory; A thin Chin, and somewhat sharp, bending up almost to his Nose; He hath few or no Teeth on the upper Jaw, but bites with his *Tongue*; His voice something resembles that of the *Guinney*-Pigs . . . His eyes are very small, and sunk, and is suppos'd to be either thick-ey'd, or Moon-blind . . . He has a natural Bob-tail, because he never was dock'd nor gelded; He seldom frequents the Company of Women, but keeps private Communication with four *Bums*, to make good the old Proverb, *Lying together makes Swine to love*; His Food is the Intrals and Bloud of *Loyalists*; His Drink the Tears of Widows and Orphans . . . His usual haunts are *Dick's Coffee-House*, Aldersgate-street, *B—'s* Conventicle, and St. *Lobb's* Convent in *Swallow-street*; He is one that preached *B—y* before the Weavers, in respect to his Father being one of the same Trade and Tribe . . . He is one that brought nothing but Rags and Lice into *White-hall*, but carried away Cartloads of Goods, whereof part was his Famous Library, (*viz.*) *That Famous History of Tom Thumb, Guzman, The Spanish-Rogue, French-Rogue, Don Thomazo Dangerfieldo, English-Rogue, All the Famous Histories of Robin Hood and Little-John, The History of* Wat Tyler *and* Jack Straw, *All the Infamous Works of* Smith, Janeway, Curtis, *and* Care; *As also the great Works of that Unreverend Divine* R. B—r, *and another brave Book, much admired by the Doctor, called,* Hobbs's Leviathan; *also two brace of* Bums, *with a Masculine Chamber-maid, which he keeps to scour his* Yard: All

which, and a great deal more, he hath purchased by *the price of Bloud and Damnation*, since he creep'd into *White-hall*, and created himself *Saviour of the Nation* . . .
    These are some part of the Marks of the Beast . . .[151]

This quotation is part of a satirical description of Titus Oates which was published as a single sheet (and therefore suitable for posting up on a wall) under the title *A Hue and Cry after Dr. T. O.* It appeared in 1681, the year when the fortunes of Oates and his Whig associates were on the turn.[152] Since the autumn of 1678, when Oates had alleged that there existed a Popish Plot to assassinate Charles II, overthrow the government, impose Catholicism, and massacre Protestants, the nation had been amazed by successive revelations, trials, and executions, all of which were chronicled and debated in a plethora of newspapers and pamphlets whose publication was facilitated by the lapse of the Licensing Act in 1679. As in the Civil War, the almost unrestricted circulation of printed material extended the social and ideological range of voices which could take part in political debate, fashioning a new textual space and enabling the creation of a discourse through the medium of print which used scurrilous and satirical rhetoric of a kind which had previously existed principally in manuscript.[153] By 1681 the tide of public opinion, or at least the balance of power, was turning against Oates and the Whigs, and it was becoming more common and less dangerous to voice scepticism about his veracity and alarm at the ease with which his words were taking away men's lives. This revulsion is evident in Dryden's portrait of Oates as Corah in *Absalom and Achitophel*, published in November 1681, which represents Oates not as 'the Saviour of the Nation', as his supporters styled him, but as a monster and a liar—which is what he was.

[151] *A Hue and Cry after Dr. T.O.* (London, 1681), single sheet. For a complete modernized text see *Restoration Literature: An Anthology*, ed. Paul Hammond (Oxford, 2002), 67–9.

[152] For Oates's life and career the best account is still Jane Lane (Elaine Dakers), *Titus Oates* (London, 1949). For quotations from the pamphlet attacks on him see *The Poems of John Dryden*, ed. Paul Hammond and David Hopkins, in progress (London, 1995–), i. 503–10. For the Popish Plot see John Kenyon, *The Popish Plot* (London, 1972; Harmondsworth, 1974), and for the wider context John Miller, *Popery and Politics in England 1660–1688* (Cambridge, 1973).

[153] For the manuscript circulation of politically controversial material see *POAS*, esp. the introduction to vol. i; Harold Love, *Scribal Publication in Seventeenth-Century England* (Oxford, 1993); Paul Hammond, 'Censorship in the Manuscript Transmission of Restoration Poetry', in Nigel Smith (ed.), *Literature and Censorship* (Cambridge, 1993), 39–62.

Dryden's lines invite us to read Oates's body as a collection of signs:

> Yet Corah, thou shalt from oblivion pass:
> Erect thyself, thou monumental brass.
>   .   .   .   .
> Sunk were his eyes, his voice was harsh and loud,
> Sure signs he neither choleric was, nor proud:
> His long chin proved his wit, his saintlike grace
> A church vermilion and a Moses' face.[154]

Contemporary accounts of Oates describe him as repulsive to the point of deformity, so the satirical representations of his physical appearance in *Absalom and Achitophel* or *A Hue and Cry* are not wholly invented. But primarily Oates's body is being redescribed in order to suggest that he and his cause are a perverted parody of, and threat to, the body politic, a grotesque antithesis to the sacred body of the King.[155] Sexuality is part of this political discourse. The Exclusion Crisis had been generated partly because Charles II had no legitimate child who could be a Protestant heir, and because his illegitimate son the Duke of Monmouth was available to be cast in that role by the Whigs. Charles's prolific sexual activity is made part of the subject-matter of *Absalom and Achitophel*, and contrasted with the crippled Shaftesbury's fathering of a son who is 'born a shapeless lump, like anarchy'.[156] The only sexual innuendo in Dryden's passage on Oates is the phrase 'erect thyself', but no doubt Dryden knew that such a brief hint would remind his readers of what was being said about Oates in other texts. Dryden's phrase signals that, by contrast with Charles's behaviour, Oates's sexuality is solipsistic, and his creativity is the murderous textual creativity of the lying witness. Beyond this innuendo, the wider discourse about Oates which this deft but still decorous innuendo brings into play is the persistent allegation of sodomy.

The historical moment of Titus Oates is also the moment of an important transition in the cultural possibilities for the expression of desire between men in English society. Towards the end of the seventeenth century the specialized meeting places called 'molly houses' grew up in London, enabling men to meet in relative safety to enjoy sex with other men: thus arose a self-contained, self-defining culture

---

[154] John Dryden, *Absalom and Achitophel*, ll. 632–49; quoted from *The Poems of John Dryden*, ed. Hammond and Hopkins.

[155] See Paul Hammond, 'The King's Two Bodies: Representations of Charles II', in Jeremy Black and Jeremy Gregory (eds.), *Culture, Politics and Society in Britain, 1660–1800* (Manchester, 1991), 13–48.   [156] Dryden, *Absalom and Achitophel*, l. 172.

within the metropolitan social world, and the emergence of such men as a recognizable group prompted (or at least coincided with, for the relations of cause and effect here are unclear) a more sharply defined and targeted hostility to homoerotic desire, its subjects and its objects, in the public press. Definitions were becoming crucial; the scope for possible interpretations of individuals and of relationships was changing, as close social relations between men (particularly if they involved some element of secrecy, or association across classes) began to be seen to permit a sexual construction. But the Oates of the pamphlets only intermittently inhabits the recognizable social geography of London, for he is also placed within a grotesque, Rabelaisian world of sexual and social inversion.

That Titus Oates was sexually interested in other men is as securely established a biographical fact as one could expect for such a question in this period. In some cases the archive is admittedly no more than suggestive: it may not have been sexual misbehaviour which was responsible for his expulsion from Merchant Taylors' School, or his expulsion from Caius College Cambridge, or his expulsion from St John's College Cambridge; but his rapid exit from his post as chaplain on the naval ship *Adventure* was certainly due to his having embarked on homosexual adventures. There was another scandal when Oates alleged that he had seen the local schoolmaster having sex with a boy in the church porch, a charge which was proved in court to be a total fabrication. It would not be difficult to speculate on the psychological motivation for such an accusation. Later in his career, one of his servants claimed that Oates had repeatedly sodomized him, which resulted in the unfortunate lad being tried and convicted of attempting to impede the discovery of the Popish Plot by discrediting Oates.[157] Other direct testimony about Oates's sexual behaviour is lacking, but John Kenyon makes the intriguing but unverifiable suggestion that it was Oates's homosexuality that gave him access to Catholic circles, which one would otherwise expect to have been firmly closed to him.[158] In any case, in a small city like Restoration London tales would

[157] Lane, *Titus Oates*, 21–31, 224–6; see also *The Tryal and Conviction of Thomas Knox and John Lane, for a Conspiracy, to Defame and Scandalize Dr. Oates and Mr. Bedloe* (London, 1680). John Lane's mother testified that her son left Oates's employ because he objected to being sodomized, but she had persuaded the boy to return to Oates because times were hard and jobs scarce (*The Tryal*, 59).

[158] Kenyon, *Popish Plot*, 55. Kenyon also says that Oates 'was often in the company of Matthew Medburne, "actor and comedian", who "picked him up in the Earl of

have travelled fast, and much more gossip about Oates must have been in circulation than we can now document. The allegations of sodomy which appear in the propaganda against Oates assume that readers will have heard about such behaviour. The question is what such allegations mean when they appear in the public sphere.

A Hue and Cry makes Oates's sodomy into an important feature of his character—using 'character' in the seventeenth-century sense of a recognizable social type rather than with the later meaning of 'personality', for Oates's sexual behaviour is being read as one sign amongst many which delineate and make legible his social role, rather than as an aspect of his individuality which has a psychological cause and contributes to fashioning his subjectivity. The 'marks' by which he may be recognized identify him as a devil with a cloven foot, and a criminal who is ripe for corporal punishment, though it is literally and symbolically difficult to fit him into the scheme of criminal justice, as 'He hath a short neck, which makes him defie the Pillory'. He also has 'a natural Bob-tail, because he never was dock'd nor gelded', which means that he is a eunuch.[159] This is clearly a suggestion that Oates is

---

Suffolk's cellar at Whitehall" . . . With Medburne he frequented a low club in Fullers' Rents, Holborn, which was the haunt of many Catholics, and may have had other specialized attractions' (55). Kenyon does not give the source of that quotation containing the phrase 'picked him up', which in modern English would certainly suggest a sexual rendezvous. The quotation actually comes from William Smith, *Intrigues of the Popish Plot Laid Open* (London, 1685), 4, where in context it does not seem to require any sexual inferences. Smith says that the club which met at the Pheasant in Fuller's Rents, Holborn, consisted of both Protestants and Catholics. He gives no indication that it was a homosexual club, but since he attended it himself that is not surprising. He does feel the need to explain his presence there, however, assuring his readers that he frequented it purely out of charity to the landlord, who was poor and had many children, whom Smith had taught (8). Smith also says that during a raid which Oates led on a supposed convent in Hammersmith, a scourge was confiscated, 'Which Relique Oates kept afterwards in his pocket still, and I have seen him flaug his menial Ganymedes with it' (22). But one might well wonder in what circumstances Smith had been watching Oates flogging his Ganymedes. Moreover, there is evidence that Holborn was a part of London where sex—and perhaps particularly homosexual sex—was readily available. In *Troia Rediviva, or, the Glories of London Surveyed in an Heroick Poem* (London, 1674), 9, Gray's Inn in Holborn is described as a place of justice in an area of villainy: 'So *Lot* amongst the Sodomites did dwell, | And in the greatest plagues was alway's well, | And if that theere a few Such now had bin, | They had attonement made for *Sodoms* sin'. The problem is that we do not know that '*Sodoms* sin' here is being used to refer to sodomy, since Sodom was often used as an example of wickedness in general.

159 Williams, *s.v.* bob.

politically impotent (a piece of wishful thinking), and echoes the representation of that other Protestant champion Andrew Marvell, who was similarly described both as a eunuch and a sodomite in pamphlets from the early 1670s.[160] This is a way of denying the political potency of the Whig champions, and is therefore analogous to the Tory treatment of Shaftesbury's physical weakness,[161] but it goes further: the idea that the sodomite is less than a man enables him to be represented as womanly, or bestial, or diabolical: better still, as womanly and bestial and diabolical, so that he is moved from being a defective example of the normative category to being an impossible amalgam of different categories; thus moved out of the range of possible sexual or political behaviour into a realm where words fail.

Like this allegation of impotence, other details in *A Hue and Cry* are also overdetermined, packing multiple implications into a single word. When Oates 'preached B—y before the Weavers', did he preach blasphemy or buggery? The two kinds of transgression seem interchangeable, fitting neatly into the same textual space. Is St Lobb's Convent an appropriate haunt for Oates because he is a lout (*OED* lob *sb.*[2] 2) or because he is impotent (*OED* lob *v.* 2: 'to droop')? As for the male servant who scours his yard, that double entendre would have been obvious.[162] Oates's sexual interest in men is a sign of deviance which is assumed to fit rhetorically alongside the references to his religious Nonconformity, association with Catholicism, working-class origins, lack of personal hygiene, and ownership of that supposedly atheistical defence of absolutist government, *Leviathan*. His library consists principally of chap-books which retail fairy-stories and the exploits of rebels, rogues, and cheats, and these appropriately belong alongside his volumes of Whig propaganda and Nonconformist theology. Grammatically the two brace of bums and the masculine chambermaid are made part of this collection of goods which are being bundled out of Whitehall, and so Oates's sexual partners are placed in the same confused category as his infantile and seditious books.

Indeed, the very incoherence of this portrait is itself significant.[163] Oates's body is both realistically deformed ('His Mouth is in the

---

[160]   See pp. 190–9 below.

[161]   Dryden, *Absalom and Achitophel*, ll. 156–8 and notes in *Poems*, ed. Hammond and Hopkins, i. 468.

[162]   'Yard' = penis (Williams, *s.v.*).

[163]   There is similarly a stress on the incoherence (physiological, sexual, political, and religious) of Marvell in the pamphlets attacking him: see pp. 195–8 below.

middle of his Face', a detail confirmed by portraits) and fantastically allegorized ('His Food is the Intrals and Bloud of *Loyalists*'), with most of the details functioning indeterminably somewhere between these two extremes. His library is a generically and ideologically confused collection which is apparently heaped in a cart along with his five sexual partners. He is displaced from Whitehall—the space of authority, in which he has only ever been an intruder—and haunts a strange collection of incompatible meeting places, a gentlemen's coffee-house, a Nonconformist conventicle, and a Roman Catholic convent. An impossible body, an improbable library, an uninhabitable geography. And Oates's sexual behaviour contributes to this confusion. Not only is sodomy itself a confused category, as Foucault observed,[164] it is used in political propaganda to help construct a confused category—or more precisely to construct one's opponent as a thoroughly incoherent figure who sows confusion in the state, and whose own multiple confusion signals to rational readers the impossibility of thinking or acting in such a way. Oates is made unthinkable, a picture which it would puzzle even Archimboldo to paint.

This pamphlet is appropriately called *A Hue and Cry* because it would rally the community to hunt down and cast out this monster, and the broadside on Oates belongs in the same genre as this item from the collapse of the Commonwealth ('the Good Old Cause') in 1659:

Whereas information hath been given, that a certain sturdy Vagabond, under a new name and notion, hath committed many Treasons, Felonies, faults, and misdemeanours, against the Publicke Welfare of the Nation . . . you are to take notice, that it is called the *Good Old Cause*, meanly clad in a party-coloured Coat of *Atheism, Anabaptism, Quakerism*, lately scoured in Bow River, and now trimmed with the sequestration of the *Cheshire* and *Lancashire* Gentry, lately grown poor, and like the Eagle with her beak renewing her age, yet for want of strength, forced to walk upon the crutches of a decayed free State; its hands being like lime-twigs, holding fast all that comes into them, and whose feet, though lame, yet are swift to shed blood, beetle-brow'd, and squint-ey'd, looking on the people, as the Devil looked over *Lincoln*, or like the statue of *Richard* the 3*d.* in the old *Exchange*, looking awry upon his Nephew *Edward* the 5*th.*[165]

As in Spenserian allegory, error is multiple, truth single, and the convoluted corruptions of error serve only to define the purity and unity

[164] Michel Foucault, *Histoire de la sexualité*, i. *La Volonté de savoir* (Paris, 1976), 134.
[165] *A Hue & Crie after the Good Old Cause* [London, 1659], 3.

of truth: so in recognizing this beast from its many marks, readers recognize the coherence and interdependence of their own community's values. Oates's multiplicity signals by contrast the singleness and clarity of the social norms, implicitly reassuring readers *inter alia* of the simple and unproblematic nature of male sexuality.

The idea that Oates enjoyed sex with men and boys is a recurring topos in the literature about him, though it figures principally in brief satirical pamphlets and in scurrilous verses rather than in the serious controversial tracts, and it is also notable that (in so far as this material can be dated) it only occurs after the political tide has turned against him. The limited range of variations on this topic is exemplified in a broadside ballad called *Cupid turn'd Musqueteer*.[166] It is decorated with a crude woodcut of Oates gazing salaciously at a boy who is crouched on a bed displaying his bare buttocks, while Cupid fires a gun in the direction of Oates. Oates is exclaiming 'Boccone di Cardinal', which might be translated as 'the cardinal's bribe' (probably with a pun on *bocca*, 'opening'). The ballad describes how Cupid makes Oates enamoured of 'a young Fellow as brawny as *Mars*', and he is attracted particularly by a feature which conveniently happens to rhyme with that god's name. Apart from an initial reference to the demise of the Plot, the verses have little overt political content, being primarily a piece of satirical pornography, but they manage to associate Oates with cardinals and Turks, and by describing the brawny soldier as one of Oates's 'Saints Tutelars' they neatly imply that there is little difference between Catholicism with its devotion to guardian saints and Nonconformity with its élite of self-proclaimed saints.

Other texts play variations on these themes. In a prose pamphlet called *The Auricular Confession*[167] Oates is made to admit sodomy but deny rape and incest: 'of all the Catalogue of Crimes, I am of this only Innocent, having the strongest aversion imaginable for the use of Women the right way'. It is clear that, for the author of this pamphlet, sodomy is much less serious than the other crimes of atheism and treason of which Oates is also accused. In *A New Ballad*[168] Oates is

---

[166] *Cupid turn'd Musqueteer* [London, 1683?]. The apparently unique copy in the library of Trinity College, Cambridge (RW. 6. 1[122]) is cropped at the foot, removing any date or printer's name, but an allusion to the death of Shaftesbury provides a *terminus a quo* of Jan. 1683.

[167] *The Auricular Confession of Titus Oates to the Salamanca-Doctor, His Confessor* (London, 1683), 1–2.

[168] *A New Ballad upon Dr. Oates his Retreat from White-Hall, Into the City* (London, 1681), 2.

thought likely to sodomize women, who are warned, 'Keep close your Fore-Doors; but be sure, | Guard well your *Posterne-Gates*'. But the pamphleteers are generally in agreement that Oates's interests are in men and boys. J. Dean's verses on *Oates's Bug- Bug- Boarding School*[169] make him say:

> For my own spending I will keep
> Of Boys Three Hundred more,
> They are to my *Appetite*, more sweet
> Then Bawd or Bucksome Whore.

In *The Melancholy Complaint*[170] Oates reminisces sadly about the days when 'I liv'd in Palaces of Ease | Sporting with my pritty Gammedes [*sic*]'. An 'Advice to Dr. Oates not to be Melancholly'[171] concludes bluntly: 'Instead of fulsome Ar— use wholsom C—'. In *Dr Oats's last Legacy's*[172] he bequeaths to his followers all his goods except for 'ready money, and my necessary Bums'.

The use of accusations of sodomy to defame the political and religious opposition is evident in several texts. The association between Oates and Shaftesbury is imagined sexually in *Sh— Ghost to Doctor Oats*,[173] where the ghost of Shaftesbury appears to Oates while the Saviour of the Nation is in bed recovering from 'a strong Debauch of *French*-Wine, and *Itallian*-Love'. In an ironic echo of the episode in Marvell's *Last Instructions to a Painter* (where the allegorical figure of England appears naked in Charles II's bedroom, only for the King to mistake her intentions) the sad appearance of Shaftesbury's ghost makes Oates, as he says,

take compassion of the trembling shade, offering him share of my Bed, which (methought) he willingly accepted, laying himself in such a posture as was most suitable for my present Fancy to work upon. He had no sooner

---

[169] J. Dean, *Oates's Bug- Bug- Boarding School, at Camberwell* (London, 1684), single sheet.

[170] *The Melancholy Complaint of D. Otes, of the Black Ingratitude of this present Age Towards Him* (London, 1684), 7.

[171] 'Advice to Dr. Oates not to be Melancholly. 1685' in Bodl., Oxford, MS Firth c. 15, pp. 182–4; quotation from 184.

[172] *Dr Oats's last Legacy's and his Farewel Sermon. He being sent for to be high Priest to the Grand Turk* (London, 1683), 1.

[173] *Sh— Ghost to Doctor Oats. In a Vision, Concerning the Jesuits and Lords in the Tower* (London, 1683), 1, 4. John Dunton alleges a '*Catamitish* Flame' between Oates and the Earl of Danby (*Athenianism* (London, 1707), ii. 94; quoted from Williams, *s.v.* catamite).

laid down, but imagining it had been my old Familiar, whom I had often made use of on that occasion[,] I fell in close Embraces, like *Æneas*, in Combat with a Shadow, but with the violent strugling I awaked, which troubled me when I found it was but a Dream.

This is, of course, wildly improbable: Oates would have been incapable of such a classical allusion.[174] The connection between sodomy and radical Protestantism is made in a second work with the title of *A New Ballad*, where it is said to have been from Calvin that Oates learned how to find 'a way in at Boy's Back-gate'.[175] The association is made at greater length in *The Salamanca Doctor's Farewel*, where Oates, speaking from the pillory where he is being punished after the accession of James II, laments:

> A curse on the day, when the *Papists* to run down,
> I left buggering at *Omers*, to swear Plots at *London*;
>
>   .   .   .   .   .
>
> Had the Parliament sate till they'd once more but put
> Three Kingdoms into the *Geneva old Cut*,
> With what Homage and Duty to Titus in Glory,
> Had the worshipping Saints turn'd their Bums up before me
>   But oh the poor Stallion
>   *Alamode de Italian*,
> To be futured at last like an *English Rascallion*.[176]

And *Raree Show* comments:

> Her's the *Synod of Saints* that will sometimes refresh
>   The failings of nature with means of their own.
> They'l preach you the *mortification* of flesh
>   With eyes up to *Heaven* and *Breeches* let *down*.[177]

In a letter to Oates from 'Timothy Trimmer', the Protestant champion is warned that the public revelation of his sexual conduct would damage the reputation of the godly:

[174] Sir Roger L'Estrange slyly insinuates an innuendo about Oates's sexual preferences into an attack on his ignorance of Latin: Oates's blunder '*meus culpa*' is due to his 'Affection, I suppose, to the Masculine, because it is more Worthy than the Feminine' (*The Observator*, 25 Oct. 1682; quoted from Lane, *Titus Oates*, 24).

[175] *A New Ballad, or, The True-Blew-Protestant Dissenter* (London, 1682), single sheet.

[176] *The Salamanca Doctor's Farewel* [London, 1685?], single sheet. The same verses appear as *Titus' Exaltation to the Pillory, upon his Conviction of Perjury* (London, 1685), single sheet.

[177] *Raree Show Or the True Protestant Procession* ([London], 1681), 2.

It is very Hot Weather, and the Rebellions of the Flesh are many and often ... you indeed have a double Advantage over your Neighbours, for Man and Woman both Administer to your Occasions. But of this no more, till I see you, least it should come to a Discovery of the Worlds Eye; and who knows what advantage may be made thereof amongst the Wicked, who consider not the *Spiritual License* which is taken by the *Brethren*, in relation to these Matters; whilst the same is used for the inward Comfort and Refreshment of the *Righteous*, and in a *True-Protestant* Privacy.[178]

But the association between Rome and sodomy is also strong, and *A Letany for St. Omers* prays for deliverance

> From *All* who cannot Sleep with *Homers*,
> Unless they *Sin* to *serve* the *Romers*:
> From all the beardless Boys at Omers.[179]

Some of the strategies in *A Hue and Cry* presenting Oates as a grotesque amalgam of monstrous features are also deployed in other pamphlets. *Bob. Ferguson or the Raree-Shew of Mamamouchee Mirsty*[180] presents a double image of Oates, dressed on one side as a sober Protestant Englishman and on the other as a Turk, the whole amounting to a freak, a raree show. The theme of Oates's doubleness is pursued in the verses under the picture. He is '*skill'd in* Turkish *and* Italic Fashion', and not only in matters of dress. He is '*An* Odd Amphibious Animal'[181] who combines incompatible religions, '*QUAKER, PRESBYTER | MUSULMAN IESUITE and for HIM not HER*'. The idea that Oates is both physically and morally a monster is taken up in *The Petition of Themis*, which hopes that 'his beastly Buggeries may be proved upon him, and that the foul Monster may appear in its own shape, which is no other than a prodigious lump of Deformity'.[182] His offspring, the Popish Plot, is also deformed, and has been created not by intercourse and birth but by sodomy: according to

---

[178] *A Letter to the True Protestant Doctor, the Reverend Titus Oates* (London, 1684), 2. 'True Protestant' was a designation adopted by the Whigs.

[179] *A Letany for St. Omers* (London, 1682), single sheet. I have been unable to trace 'Homers'; perhaps it means friends of the same sex with whom one shares a bed at home.

[180] *Bob. Ferguson or the Raree-Shew of Mamamouchee Mirsty* (n.p., n.d.), single sheet. I have been unable to trace a copy, so have quoted from the reproduction in Lane, *Titus Oates*, opposite 240.

[181] For the sexual implications of 'amphibious' cf. the pamphlet attacks on Marvell: see pp. 195–6 below.

[182] *The Petition of Themis against the Salamanca Fiend* (London, 1684), 2.

The last Memorial, Oates has 'bugger'd out your ill favour'd and imperfect Embryo'.[183] He is accompanied by a troop of 'Beardless Buggeroons',[184] and in a possibly punning spelling the Plot is called a 'Farse'. The bizarre association of Oates with Hobbes which we observed in *A Hue and Cry* gives extra force to the stream of abuse in *A Dialogue,* where he is called a 'Buggering, Brazen-fac'd, Lanthorn-jaw'd, Tallow-chap't Leviathan'.[185] Oates's end is imagined to be a close embrace with the gallows at Tyburn, which in *Tyburn's Courteous Invitation* welcomes him with extended arms:

> My dearest, hopeful, that long-wish'd-for One . . .
> Hast! hast! my choicest Darling, whom I love,
> And thy long-promis'd kindness let me prove . . .
> Oh, how I love thee! 'cause I've heard thou'st been
> So well acquainted with all kinds of Sin . . .
> With *Buggery* methinks I am well pleased.[186]

They would have made a well-matched couple.

Oates's fictions resulted in scores of judicial murders and inflicted a state of terror on the nation at large. Against such fictions, bolstered by bribed witnesses, packed juries, and bullying judges, protestations of innocence were ineffectual, and it may be that a certain despair at the prospect of truth winning through by means of reasoned argument and factual evidence encouraged some writers to think that the most effective response to Oates's fictions would be other forms of fiction. Oates had suggested that people's everyday appearances and roles concealed other more sinister identities as priests and plotters who were bent on implementing a seditious narrative which had been scripted in Rome. In Oates's stories the familiar geography of London became an unfamiliar warren of clandestine meeting houses where plots were hatched and weapons concealed, while public spaces became potential sites for assassinations. Moreover, the streets were periodically transformed by Whig sympathizers into theatrical spaces where crowds played out emblematic narratives of the Popish Plot, the dastardly murder of Sir Edmund Berry Godfrey, and the longed-for overthrow

---

[183] *The last Memorial of the Agent from the K. of Poland, to the Salamanca Dr.* (London, 1683), 1–2; wrongly dated 1673 in the BL catalogue.

[184] For *buggeroon* see *OED s.v.* bougeron.

[185] *A Dialogue Between a Yorkshire-Alderman and Salamanca-Doctor* (London, 1683), 1.

[186] *Tyburn's Courteous Invitation to Titus Oates* ([London], 1684), single sheet.

of the Pope.[187] While space was transformed, so too was time: the present was a fearful interlude between what might have been plotted and what might yet unfold. Normal suppositions about the plausibility of narrative scenarios ceased to apply in the interpretations of people's words and actions. One way to counter this grotesque fictionalizing of the public sphere was to make Oates himself into the protagonist of a grotesque fiction.

Strange and Wonderful News from South-wark does just that.[188] It recounts 'how a Sham Doctor got two Aldermen Students of the same University with Child. How they long'd for Venison, and what Ensued upon it.' The story begins with the narrator acknowledging that 'there have been so many *Garragantua* Stories of this *Pantagruel* Doctor, and himself found in so many Lies, that if I writ Gospel, I shou'd not be believ'd'. Straight away Oates is displaced into the world of tall stories, where he evidently belongs, and the allusion to Pantagruel not only provides an indication that this is to be a narrative of grotesque exploits (and grotesque bodies), but also makes an ironic reflection on Oates's prodigious strength, omniscience, and judgement. Various signals early in the narrative place this in the tradition of chap-book tales of adolescent exploits, for the characters include 'two Aldermen students' and the narrative takes place in the romance space of a forest, though since this is 'the Forrest of new *Troy*' it is an appropriately paradoxical space, the city made wild. Here there are 'several Famous Colleges for Correction of Vice and Instruction of good Manners and Discipline, as St. *Bridewell*, St. *Newgate*, and that beyond the River which for its Eminency before the rest is call'd Kings Colledge'. Two aldermen have been sent here for slandering the government, and Oates comes to join them, 'after a great many unparralleld Villanous Actions, Murders, Perjuries Blasphemies and bitter Revelings to Learn to Govern that unruly Member'.

---

[187] For the transformation of the London streets into sites of political debate and theatre see Tim Harris, *London Crowds in the Reign of Charles II* (Cambridge, 1987), and Sheila Williams, 'The Pope-Burning Processions of 1679–81', *Journal of the Warburg and Courtauld Institutes*, 21 (1958), 104–18.

[188] *Strange and Wonderful News from South-wark, Declaring how a Sham Doctor got two Aldermen Students of the same University with Child. How they long'd for Venison, and what Ensued upon it* (London, 1684). For a complete modernized text see *Restoration Literature*, ed. Hammond, 69–71. The story also appears in ballad form as *The Sodomite, or the Venison Doctor, With his Brace of Aldermen-Stags* (London, [1684]); the apparently unique copy in the William Andrews Clark Library, Los Angeles, carries the manuscript date '13 Sept. 1684'.

We soon learn that Oates's tongue is not his only unruly member. Oates is greeted joyfully by the aldermen, and is 'soon made free of their Boord, and Bed; which he liked as well as the other, being as great a Sodomite as an Epicure', and so is 'excercis'd by turns as the Spirit moved him'. Since 'spirit' was seventeenth-century slang for 'erect penis',[189] a blasphemous pun here punctures the Nonconformists' claims to divine inspiration. In the idiom of the novella we are told that 'This Piece of *Itallian* Gallantry was manag'd with such Art, and Secresy, that though they were mutual Rivalls to each other, yet neither of the Aldermen suspected, or was Jealous of the other' until eventually 'this Loving Intrigue is Discover'd, and the Amour that was carried on to every ones Thought in Secret is now come to Light'. Then the style changes as the pamphlet deploys the familiar satirical tropes of physical deformity, and relates that the aldermen 'began to concieve the Monstrous Effects of this unhumane Conjunction . . . their Bellies and Mouths began to meet and were in as close Copulation as the Doctors Nose and Chin'. This image of Oates's body engaged in self-copulation is a bizarre fusion of the tropes of physical deformity and sexual deviance which we have already encountered. Oates laments that, having already palmed off one bastard on the people (the Popish Plot), he will be unable to find anyone to rear his offspring. In a miniature beast-fable he says: 'The Loyal City has crush'd the Cockatrice head that was thrown out of Court, what Woolf shall I find to Cherrish my *Orsons*?'[190] Both the expectant father and the pregnant aldermen become ravenous: 'The Aldermen long'd for a Change, so did the Doctor. The Aldermen long'd for change of Government, the Doctor for change of Bedfellows . . . The Aldermen long for a new hash of Anarchy, The Doctor for a Frigacy[191] of Democracy.' In default of anarchy and democracy, they order a venison pasty and a chest of burgundy, but these are devoured before they can get their hands on them by 'a Crew of *Hungarian* sharpers' (an allusion to the Whig hero the Hungarian Count Teckely). The aldermen are about to give birth, but their pangs are prolonged by the goddess of childbirth, Latona, because the Observator (Sir Roger L'Estrange) has informed her 'what a Monstrous Production it wou'd prove, begot in Conjunction of *Capricorn* on a *Gemini* of Citts'. Eventually the monstrous children are born from the aldermen's heads in a parody of the birth of Minerva,

---

[189] Williams, *s.v.*

[190] '*Orsons*' means 'bear cubs', no doubt with a pun on 'whoresons', and perhaps even on 'arse-sons'.   [191] 'Fricassee'; with a pun on 'frig'?

goddess of wisdom, from the head of Jove, and gnaw their way into the world like a viper's brood.[192]

This pamphlet places Oates in a fictional world which does not even have a stylistic or generic coherence, as it moves between different registers of language and brings in fragmentary versions of incompatible kinds of narrative, chap-book exploits, chivalric adventures, amorous intrigue, and beast-fable. Oates's sodomy is now not simply one trait among many which we read as signs of his deviance, but has been made an element in a narrative. To counter Oates's grotesque and improbable narratives we are offered a grotesque and impossible narrative which imagines the consequence of sodomy as a monstrous birth, signalling the likely consequence of Oates's politics. We have moved even further away from 'sodomy' as an aspect of desire, further away from the possibility of it being a constituent of an individual's subjectivity.

It is instructive to compare this fantastic narrative from 1684 with one which dates from 1693, well after the Popish Plot had receded into history, and after Oates had first been punished under James II and then pensioned by William III. Tom Brown's pamphlet *The Salamanca Wedding* makes fun with Oates's marriage in 1693 to a Muggletonian widow.[193] This is said to be 'as unnatural and unexpected a Change as for an Old Miser to turn Prodigal', but Oates is apparently marrying in order to father more witnesses to the Plot, and also to make amends 'for some Juvenile Gambols that shall be Nameless'; for although 'he had quitted the other Corruptions of Popery, yet he still fancied *Cardinalism*'. It is now high time for him 'to sow his Wild *Oats*, and not to hide the Talent which God had plentifully given him, in an *Italian* Napkin'. When Oates seeks a licence, he is asked whether he requires it to marry a boy or a girl, and whether 'he would have a License for Behind or Before'. The articles of the marriage agreement prevent him from keeping in the house any male servant under the age of 60, and insist that he hang a picture of the destruction of Sodom in his bed chamber as a warning to himself. He also has to promise not to 'attack' his new wife '*à parte post*, but to comfort, refresh and relieve

---

[192] For the image cf. Dryden, *Absalom and Achitophel*, l. 1013, and note in *Poems*, ed. Hammond and Hopkins, i. 531.

[193] [Tom Brown], *The Salamanca Wedding: Or, A True Account of a Swearing Doctor's Marriage with a Muggletonian Widow in Breadstreet. London, August 18th 1693* (London, 1693), 1–4.

her *à parte ante*.[194] After the wedding, a spiritual jig is danced by a group of Fifth Monarchy Men and Ranters.

Brown's pamphlet is jocular in tone, and lacks the polemical urgency of the texts from the early 1680s. Though the marriage licence and marriage contract are parodic, they are close enough to normal legal arrangements to contain Oates within a recognizable world of comic, genially degrading domesticity. Husband and wife agree terms for a tolerable life, as happens at the end of several Restoration comedies. Oates has been thoroughly displaced both from the public domain and from the fantasy milieu invented for him in *Strange and Wonderful News*. But Brown's pamphlet still reveals some politicized ways of thinking about sodomy. He makes the predictable connections both with Catholicism and with radical Protestantism, so that the marriage of the ex-Catholic sodomite to the Muggletonian widow symbolically unites the two religious extremes which were equally repugnant to the ordinary Anglican. Other elements in the narrative reveal Brown's rather confused, and perhaps overdetermined, assumptions about sodomy. He imagines that Oates would wish to sodomize his wife, which might be read as a comment about sexual behaviour, defining sodomy specifically as a particular sexual act which pleases irrespective of the gender of the partner; or it might be read as another ideologically motivated marker of deviance, as convenient for this purpose as any other departure from ostensibly normal sexual behaviour. More curiously, Brown sees sodomy as a predilection which may even be hereditary, for Oates 'always expressed, and perhaps inherited an aversion to the Fair Sex'. Actually, Oates's father had been notorious for the over-enthusiastic way he had baptized his female followers naked in rivers and ponds,[195] but if we refer back to *A Hue and Cry* and its claim that Oates's preaching to the weavers was influenced by his father's example, we perhaps touch upon an assumption about the ineradicability of class bonds and identities, an idea exemplified in other texts by the mocking of Oates's attempt to get the College of Arms to establish a noble pedigree for him.[196] This erstwhile opponent of the ancient laws of succession is imagined as a hereditary sodomite, and is now paired off with a Muggletonian widow in a virtual parody of legal marriage and in an

---

[194] '*à parte post*' is 'by the back way' and '*à parte ante*' is 'by the front way'.

[195] Lane, *Titus Oates*, 12–16.

[196] Dryden, *Absalom and Achitophel*, ll. 639–41 and note in *Poems*, ed. Hammond and Hopkins, i. 506.

arrangement which removes him from the public sphere, and removes sodomy from the story.

But this safe placing and disempowering of Oates is effected by a writer who was sympathetic to the post-Revolution settlement, and a very different use of Oates is made in verses from a Jacobite source. Here Oates is placed in dangerous proximity to William III, who was himself being accused of sodomy in many contemporary manuscript satires. Oates presents the King with a copy of a book which he has dedicated to him, and kisses his hands:

> When Williams hands, Oates with his Lipps Approach't[,]
> Lipps which the Gosspell had so oft debauch't[,]
> From the Smooth Surface of his beardless Chin
> He did this Shameless Complemt begin[:]
>> Great Sir
> Tho' I can't nor dont pretend to Court
> Or Rivall *Benting* in your Joviall Sport[,]
> Yet, since by Perjury what I've begun
> By your undaunted Armes att Last is done[,]
> No Lipp shou'd kiss these hands, but only mine
> No hand should grace these Lipps but only thyne[:]
>> Since you and I both act the selfe same thing
>> What difference, twixt Sham Doctor, and Sham King[?][197]

This meeting of Oates and William is the meeting of two equivalents, both sodomites, both shams. Oates humbly refuses to contemplate displacing Bentinck in the King's bed, but to this Jacobite author Oates and William nevertheless share the same symbolic space. By bringing Oates into contact with William, making the two men share the same space, and uniting them by a kiss, the writer reveals William too as a travesty. They 'act the selfe same thing', and what they act is sodomy—that is to say, subversion, parody, the displacement both of a supposedly normative heterosexuality and of the political order which is built upon patrilineal succession. As he is brought into contact with Oates, that unthinkable body, William becomes an unthinkable King.

[197] 'On Oates his delivering his 3d part of his Gross Baz: dedicated to King Wm. thereupon Kissing his hands', Bodl. MS Rawl. poet. 169, fol. 13^r. The lines also occur in MS Rawl. D. 361, fol. 47^v, where they are accompanied by a Latin version (fol. 47^r). The Latin is rather more explicit, for Oates says: 'Non Ego me dignor Battavi Ganimedis honore' ('I am not worthy of the honour of being the Dutch Ganymede'). The two men are also associated in 'The Shash' (*POAS* v. 154), where they are both false deliverers of the nation.

WILLIAM III

The upheaval in the political and symbolic order brought about in 1688–9 by the deposing (or 'abdication') of James II and his replacement by William III was unwelcome to many, and the trope of sodomy is deployed in manuscript verses which attack the new King and his new court. Many of the satirical poems about William III which circulated in the 1690s alleged that he was engaged in homosexual relations with some of his close Dutch advisers. The sexual allegations are no doubt motivated in part by a resentment at foreigners monopolizing places of power and influence, so there is in some respects a reprise of the criticisms of James I and his (initially Scottish) favourites. Indeed, one set of verses comments that William III 'renews the shame | Of J. the first, and *Buckingham*: | He ... his Wives Embraces fled | To slabber his lov'd *Ganimede*'.[198] But it would be naïve to believe that these comments on William's sexual behaviour can simply be ascribed to 'xenophobia' and 'William's baffling refusal to trust any but a few chosen men with his political or private opinions, and ... his statesmanlike care to see that young men of promise were preferred rather than old men rewarded'.[199] Such allegations do not arise *ex nihilo*: in the case of Charles II there were dozens of poems which commented on his addiction to his mistresses, and suggested that the government of the country suffered through his inattention to business due to his pursuit of pleasure. This was no invention by the poets. As disaffection with Charles grew in the late 1670s and early 1680s, poems figured his pursuit of sexual pleasure as a form of tyranny. The King's sacred body had been thoroughly desacralized, first by the King, then by the poets.[200] It was as if Charles's openly promiscuous sexuality had made it increasingly difficult to regard the monarchy as a sacred institution, and this coincided with the development of Whig political theory which regarded the king as being entrusted with power by the people, to be exercised for their benefit, or withdrawn from him. The Revolution of 1688–9, and the installation of a king who owed the throne to election (if not to conquest) confirmed the new theory of monarchy—divine right 'dwindled to a Poor Elective *Crown*', as one Jacobite poet phrased it.[201]

---

[198] *Mundus Foppensis* (1691), 13.

[199] William J. Cameron in *POAS* v. 38.

[200] Hammond, 'The King's Two Bodies'.

[201] 'King James's Sufferings Describ'd by himself': Beinecke Library, Yale University,

When William's body is derided in Jacobite poems, he is deformed and a monstrous perversion of the symbolic body politic; in this poem the writer uses the idiom of the hue and cry after a criminal which was also used for Titus Oates:

> His Head is large; his Neck awry,
> His Ears are long, and squints with Eye,
> A Sparrow Mouth, a *dumb Jack*'s Chin,
> A crooked Snout which denteth in;
> *His* Back and Breast do both combine
> To make his beastly Parts more fine;
> For like a Dove he pouts his Breast,
> *His* Back the same I do protest;
> *His* Body's round, if you regard,
> *His* A— — sticks out almost a Yard:
> 'Tis mighty handy for a Kick,
> But very limber is his — — —
> Which will I doubt breed some Disgust
> With those who search the Monster first.[202]

He is not only a monster, but a kind of player-king, a mere 'bundle of clouts':

> He has gotten in part the shape of a man
> But more of a monkey deny it who can;
> He has the tread of a goose and the legs of a swan.
>
> . . . . . .
>
> Have you not seen on a stage, come tell ho,
> A strutting thing called a Punchinello?
> Of all things I know 'tis the likest this fellow.
> A dainty fine King indeed.
>
> A carcass supported by a rotten stump
> Plastered about the back and the rump.
>
> . . . . . .

MS Osborn b. 111, p. 12. There may be an echo here of 'dwindled to a Farce' in Dryden's *Mac Flecknoe*, l. 182.

[202] *The Disappointed Marriage, or an Hue and Cry after an Outlandish Monster* (London, 1733). Although the colophon is clear, the date looks too late, and the typography suggests the 1690s. The BL copy (C. 20 f. 2 (184)) is endorsed in MS 'Libel on ['K. W^m.' deleted] the Pr: of Orange'. The marriage in question seems to be the political marriage of William to England. For other verses on William as a monster see 'The Five Monsters' in Beinecke MS Osborn b. 111, p. 439.

> He is not qualified for his wife,
> Because of the cruel midwife's knife,
> Yet buggering of Benting doth please to the life.[203]

The idea that William was impotent was perhaps wishful thinking,[204] for an impotent king could not father an heir who might exclude the Stuart line from the throne, but it is also a sign of William's disruption of the hereditary principle. Even if William is more animal than human, that does not preclude him from responsibility and punishment:

> If a willy Dutch Boar for a rape on a Girle
> Was hang'd by the Laws approbation
> Then what does he merit that Buggers an Earl
> And ravish's the whole nation[?][205]

And William is also likened to Tiberius, by turns indolent and tyrannical, whose catamite 'rules alone the state, | Whilst monarch dozes'.[206] Not only a second Tiberius, William is a second Cromwell too, but he even displaces Cromwell from his pre-eminent position in hell, where his spokesman tells Cromwell triumphantly:

> What shall I tell you of his Treacheries?
> His Hellish Lust and brutish Buggeries?
> Which was so horrid and so black a Sin,
> That you durst nere so much as Think upon.[207]

As these examples have already shown, one of the principal allegations about William was that he had a sexual relationship with his confidant Hans Willem Bentinck, Earl of Portland.[208] The historical facts about William's private life are probably beyond our reach,[209] but it is clear that Englishmen in the 1690s thought that he was having sexual relations with one or more of his male courtiers; and, true or not, this provided a thread of imagery which expressed Jacobite disgust at the deposition of James II and the violation of the hereditary principle. Bentinck's elevation to high office and honour certainly rankled:

---

[203] 'The Coronation Ballad', *POAS* v. 41–2.
[204] Thus Cameron, *POAS* v. 41; for another poem on William's impotence, ibid., 298.   [205] Untitled, BL MS Sloane 2717, fol. 98ʳ.
[206] [Arthur Mainwaring], 'Suum Cuique'; *POAS* v. 121–2.
[207] 'The Rivalls': Beinecke MS Osborn b. 111, p. 350.
[208] Bentinck was not a young man at the Revolution in 1689: *DNB* gives his date of birth as 1649, but records a suggestion that the correct date may be 1645.
[209] For a sober biography see Stephen B. Baxter, *William III* (London, 1966).

When King William rul'd this Land
A Monarch of great fame
For Mercy, Justice and a thing
Which here I dare not name

2

He had a Knight of high Renown
Of Garter eke was he
Who for his Birth, and you know what
He rais'd to that degree.[210]

Few poets were so coy about why William rewarded Bentinck. The King is called 'Bugg'ring *Will*';[211] for 'Billy with Benting does play the Italian'.[212] The hereditary principle will be reinstated in a grotesque new way if 'pregnant Mynheer spawn a true Prince of Wales'.[213] Bentinck is the King's 'he-bedfellow',[214] 'the *Dutch-Man* who serves instead of a whore'.[215] Sometimes Bentinck is called William's 'Bardasha',[216] his passive sexual partner; at other times the power relationship between them is differently figured, and Bentinck is resented for exercising undue influence over the King, keeping him away from others: 'Then Benting uplocks | His King in a box'.[217] While his soldiers are away fighting the French, 'William enjoys his Bentinck and his whore.'[218] And William turns to Bentinck for both sexual satisfaction and military advice in this dramatic fragment:

Actus Quintus
Enter K. Phys.[219] *in his Night-Gown, and* Benting *with his Breeches down.*
K. Phys.   Come here my *Benting* and Indulge thy charms,
            More dear than Untoucht virgins to my Arms,
            For thee I have Abandon'd Woman-kind,
            And all my Wishes to that Arse confin'd:

---

[210] 'An Excellent New Ballad', BL MS Harley 7315, fol. 294ᵛ; also in BC MS Lt q 38, dated 1700.
[211] 'Old Jemmy': Beinecke MS Osborn b. 111, p. 61.
[212] 'A Litany', *POAS* v. 221.
[213] Ibid.
[214] 'The Shash', *POAS* v. 153.
[215] 'A Litany. 1689', BL MS Harley 7317, fol. 96ᵛ.
[216] 'The Reflection', *POAS* v. 60; 'bardash' = passive sexual partner (Williams, *s.v.*).
[217] 'A Description of Hampton Court Life', *POAS* v. 56.
[218] *POAS* v. 386.
[219] 'Phys.' is probably derived from φῦσα, wind, bubble, bladder; so an empty form rather than a real king.

My Consort in her Bed neglected lyes,
Whilst I am rev'lling in thy whiter Thighs[.]
Assist me with thy Councill, if thou can,
How to o'ercome this most Prodigious man,
This LUXEMBURGH, whose name my Genius awes,
And Conquest still attends the sword he draws.[220]

The way in which various resentments against Bentinck coalesce can be seen in this passage from 'Advice to a Painter' (1697), which weaves together his lowly social origin and his sexual favours to his King:

Next cringing *Benting* place, whose Earth-born Race
The Coronet and Garter does disgrace;
Of undescended Parentage, made great
By Chance, his Vertues not discover'd yet.

.   .   .   .

To black Designs and Lust let him remain
A servile Favorite, and Grants obtain:
While antient Honours sacred to the Crown
Are lavish'd to support the Minion.

.   .   .   .

Artist retire, 'twere Insolence too great
T' expose the Secrets of the Cabinet;
Or tell how they their looser Moments spend;
That Hellish Scene would all chast Ears offend.
For should you pry into the close Alcove,
And draw the Exercise of Royal Love,
Keppell and He are *Ganymede* and *Jove*.[221]

The very title 'Advice to a Painter' links this piece into the Restoration tradition of satirical attacks on the government, but in the reign of Charles II it had been oppositional writers pursuing a generally Whig and Protestant agenda who used the genre to expose the financial and sexual corruption of the Stuart court. Now the Protestant champion himself is being depicted in a 'Hellish Scene' which offends more than anything that Charles contrived.

[220] 'Actus Quintus': Beinecke MS Osborn b. 111, p. 373. The duc de Luxemburg was marshal of France.

[221] 'Advice to a Painter', *POAS* vi. 16–18. 'Keppell' is the King's younger favourite Arnold Joost van Kepell (1670–1718), described in one poem as 'that royal dainty' whom William tastes before passing him over to Mary (*POAS* v. 366). Mary herself is compared with the sacred river Jordan 'lost in the Sodom Sea' ('On the Two Sisters', *POAS* v. 156).

Although William does not find himself translated into the grotesque prose fiction which Oates inhabited, there is one prose satire which neatly brings together the topoi of tyranny and sodomy by turning him into a Turkish Sultan:

> The Peticion of Hassan a Turk, condemn'd for sodomy, as it was translated by Sir William Hedges.
>
> To the most High & Mighty Hunkyar {or manslayer, a Title of Honour given to the Grand Seigneur} William, Sultan of England and Holland, whose end as his begining be prosperous.

> The sound of thy Renown being born on the wings of an Angel of Victory into the Dominions of the Lord {The Grand Seigneur} of the Earth, and thy mighty contest with the Padishaw {The French King} of the Franks having reacht the Ears of True Beleivers {The Turks}, hath caused me to turn the steps of my Pilgrimage to the setting of the Sun, to behold the face of him so much favour'd by our Prophet, for such ar't thou O Sultan, and so esteemed by the Osmantys {subjects of Osman of Ottoman} for thy Orthodox opinion of the Determination of days,[222] inscribed in the front of Mortals, and for the manner of obtaining the Kingdom of thy Mansould {deposed or dispossest} Father, which by the Event I find destyned for thee, and written down from former Ages in the world of Similitudes, {The Mahometans have a notion, that all things here have a resemblance in a distinct world of Ideas, which some think to be a kind of local paradise, others a part of Heaven.} This O Hunkyar hath caused me to bring my Scimeter, sanctifyed by the Blood of Idolaters to thy assistance, in hopes the Messenger {Mahomet} of the disposer of Kingdoms may inspire thee to search out the truth of the Book of Flowers {The Alcoran}; But behold O Sultan, passing through the brighter Beiship {Lordship or Government} of Holland, and finding there some resemblance of the Recreation of the East, practised by those thy Infidells, and at my Arrival here not having mony to buy a slave, nor opportunity to Ut Kavin {To contract a temporary mariage so call'd among the orientals}, but according to the noble use of soldiers, as thou knowest, confining my satisfaction to my own sex, Thy Cadyes {Judges} here for this small Crime have condemned me to dye, notwithstanding my alledging it was against the Laws of the Successor of the Prophets, {Grand Seigneur} and an ill requital thy slaves enjoy in the Imperial City {Constantinople} and Ports of my Padishaw; I need not repeat to thee, O thou Favourite of the Holy Envoy {In Arab Resoul Messenger Envoy, Ambassador. Prophet} that such things are not imputed as death to the Predestinated, {So the Turks

---

[222] Calvinist doctrine of predestination.

call themselves & all whom they favour by that Godly name.} Therefore I kiss thy noble stirrup {phrases always used by them to their Princes}, and wipe the dust of Affliction[223] from my Brow with the Tayle of thy Horse, {The horse of their Prince so called always in Courtly Language} the Throne of Victory, beseeching thee to Answer this my Arz {supplication} with mercy for the sake of thy Mosaip the Basha {Favourite or beloved} of Portland, and thy Solictar {Sword bearer attendant of the Bedchamber} Aga Keppel, whose intercession I hope will prevail at thy Footstool, {another usual phrase} so may thy Sofa {Bed or rather Couch} never want delights, and mayst thou go on to possess all the Dominions of thy mis-beleiving Kinred, and may the Dawning of true beleif in thee be enlightned into perfect day of our sacred Law by the influence of our holy Prophet.

From my prison the 26. of the Moon Shaban.[224]

And in a further appeal to Sir William Hedges, the petitioner claims that he is 'made a sacrifice of formal Justice for that, which the favoured of thy Court comitt'.[225] As in the attacks on Oates, this satire associates Calvinism with sodomy, alleging that the elect regard them-selves as beyond the moral law; for if William is predestined to depose James, then there can be nothing reprehensible about his action. As Calvinism was no longer now the dominant strain in Anglicanism, William's extreme Protestantism makes him as foreign to England as his tyrannical Turkish rule and his Turkish sexual preferences.

Other writers maintain that the reign of William has seen a wide-spread change in the nation's sexual behaviour—not the puritanical revolution promoted by the Societies for the Reformation of Manners, which persecuted prostitutes and sodomites, but a general addiction to sodomy, which has spread beyond the court. 'Jenny Cromwell's Complaint against Sodomy' laments the demise of heterosexual inter-course, which is part of a loss of traditional English values. The speaker of the poem, Jenny Cromwell, was a well-known bawd or procuress,[226] and she shows particular anger at the plight of prostitutes facing a decline in their trade. The first line echoes the opening of *Absalom and Achitophel* ('In pious times, e'r Priest-craft did begin'), so evoking the

---

[223] Affection *MS.*

[224] BC MS Lt q 38, pp. 161–3; also in BL MS Harley 7315. Marginal notes have been incorporated into the text inside curled brackets. The piece can be dated *c.*1694. Sir William Hedges (1632–1701) was a Turkey merchant and head of the factory at Constantinople; in 1693 he was chosen as sheriff and alderman in London. It is not clear whether this text is entirely fictional, or has some basis in the plight of an actual Turkish prisoner.   [225] Ibid., 165.

[226] *POAS* iv. 201.

reign of Charles II as a lost golden age of heterosexual sex and female influence:

> In pious times e're Bugg'ry did begin,
> When women only rul'd at In and In,
> When Brittains did encounter fface to fface,
> And thought a Back stroke treacherous & base,
> Then Punk reign'd uncontroll'd, but now she plys
> In Hackny Coach
>
> .   .   .   .
>
> Crys, Damns and Curses Bardash K— and all,
> That e're were instrumental in her fall.

Then the prostitute who has been deprived of her customers rails against the King's bad influence on the country. The appropriate kingdom for this 'Arsy Versy' ruler is not England but Italy:

> With the respect that's due to Majesty,
> Why were your Arms not turn'd towards Italy?
> And since your Business was a Fathers throne,
> Why not your Father Antichrist at Rome.
> There you had fix'd your Peacefull Goverment,
> And plac'd your Throne on Downy Fund——
> There had each Sodomite his Brother Beast
> And with Lascivious Lust his joy exprest.
> For the great Change to find old Popery
> Turn'd out, and truckl'd t' Almighty Sodomy.
> But here content with our own homely Joys,
> We had no Relish of the fair fac'd Boys,
> Till you came in, and with your Reformation
> Turn'd all things Arsy Versy in the Nation.

While women have lost out under this new dispensation, male courtiers have made their fortune, among them Thomas Wentworth, third Earl of Strafford, groom of the bedchamber to the King:

> *Wentworth* the new Ephestion[227] of our Age
> Wentworth the fortunate was once a Page,
> But now he thinks that all to him must yeild,
> Because he sometimes does the scepter wield,
> Yet well I knew the Boy about the Town,
> Flat foot and trudging, glad of half a Crown.[228]

---

[227] Hephaestion.   [228] Half a crown was the price of a prostitute.

Seeing that sodomy is a guaranteed route to preferment, other would-be courtiers,

> Thinking they must be Mimicks to the Crown,
> They to each other put their breeches down,
> If *Wentworth* one of these with Bum will bless,
> He's not a little proud of his Success.[229]

Another writer concurred that there is now only one way to acquire influence at court:

> Declining *Venus* has no Force o'er Love,
> The tender *Ganymede* now rules above:
> By Influence we die for amorous Boys,
> Changing to Godlike Pleasures from vain Toys:
> Besides, 'tis Interest, and by that we steer,
> To love with Princes is to gain their Ear
> He's an ill Courtier who can have a Passion
> For nauseous Petticoat when out of fashion,
> B—s are still the stamp of Revolution.[230]

Several of these poems are spoken (if not actually written) by women,[231] and resent a change in the way that the structure of power operates, excluding women from influence and confining access to the King to a group of young male courtiers:

> The Ladys complaint

> since Ladys were Ladys, I dare boldly say,
> they ne're had more reason to fast & to pray,
> for our Holland Reformer to perfect the work
> makes love like Italians, as He rules like a Turk;
>   when in closett shutt close
>   deep in thought You'd suppose
> free from Loving his pages, & picking his nose,
> Ah who wou'd have thought a low country Stallion
> and a protestant Prince shou'd prove an Italian.

---

[229] BC MS Lt q 38, pp. 139–40; also Crum I 1440, BL MS Harley 7315.

[230] 'Satyr', in *Poems on Affairs of State, From 1640. to the Present Year 1704*, iii (London, 1704), 370; also in BC MS Lt q 38, BL MS Harley 7315. The BC MS completes 'B—s' as 'Breeches'. The poem is attributed to John Howe, for whom see p. 234 below.

[231] See also p. 235 below.

> In love to his Minions, He partiall, & rash is
> makes Statesmen of blockheads, & Earls of Bardashes
> his bed chamber service, He fills with young fellows,
> as Essex & Windsor, who makes Capall jealous
> > Young Capall take heed
> > least Windsor succeed
> for his face, & his A— are fitt for the deed

After saying that the King also sodomizes his mistress and the Queen (which is why 'she has a great A— instead of great belly'), the poem concludes:

> Butt the loss of our auncient & laudable fasshion
> has lost our good King one halfe of the Nation
> letts pray for the good of our State, & his soule
> that He'd putt his finger into the right hole,
> > for the case Sir is such
> > the people think much
> that your love is Italian, & Goverment Dutch.[232]

In several respects this poem epitomizes the resentments voiced against William: that he has betrayed English Protestant liberties, which he originally landed in order to protect, by governing through a small cabal of young men who monopolize his attention politically and sexually. In the more overtly Jacobite poems, the trope of sodomy as a parodic form of sex helps to enforce the idea that William is a mere travesty of a king.

These poems circulated in manuscript through the system of scriptoria which had developed since the 1660s for the circulation of politically or sexually outspoken material. Some manuscripts were entirely devoted to Jacobite works, evidently produced for a specialist market.[233] Authorship was generally anonymous, implying that the poem was the product of a collective, communal voice rather than one man's grievance.[234] Williamite poems may have celebrated his military prowess, but seem to have had no way of countering the comments on his sexuality.[235]

[232] BL MS Add 29497, fols. 101^r–v; also in BL MS Lansdowne 852.

[233] e.g. Beinecke MS Osborn b. 111, which was probably produced for the Stuart court in exile at St Germain.

[234] Paul Hammond, 'Anonymity in Restoration Poetry', *The Seventeenth Century*, 8 (1993), 123–42.

[235] However, one MS of Dryden's Jacobite poem 'The Lady's Song' alters the text not only to make it a Williamite poem but to ward off criticisms of William's

In more public media, oppositional writers had to be more cautious, and generally proceeded by allusion and innuendo. Dryden, for example, introduces some glances at William's sexuality in his translations,[236] and in his plays. In *Don Sebastian* (1690) Dorax greets Benducar thus:

> *Dorax.*   Well, *Benducar!*
> *Bend.*   Bare *Benducar!*
> *Dor.*   Thou wouldst have Titles, take 'em then, Chief Minister,
> First Hangman of the State.
> *Bend.*   Some call me Favourite.
> *Dorax.*   What's that, his Minion?
> Thou art too old to be a Catamite![237]

The barbed *paradiastole* in 'Chief Minister . . . First Hangman . . . Favourite . . . Minion . . . Catamite' dramatizes the resentment at William's conferring of honours on Bentinck and others while his own title is, in Dryden's eyes, a sham. The former Poet Laureate looks with derision on those who have acquired titles under the new dispensation, for the titles do not conceal the nature of the services which bought them. Later in the play Dorax accuses Sebastian of having been susceptible to flattery from parasites and 'hungry Minions'. Dorax's requests for reward were answered by the King's minister Enriquez, 'That Woman, but more dawb'd; or if a man, | Corrupted to a Woman: thy Man Mistress'.[238] In *Cleomenes* (1692), Coenus brings spirited horses to sell to the King, and Cleomenes says:

> Mistaken Man:
> Thou shouldst have brought him Whores and Catamites;
> Such Merchandize is fit for such a Monarch.[239]

This comment is quickly reported to the King, so we see the dangers of speaking out. Dryden in his Preface to the play is careful to say that he

---

homosexuality and effeminacy (see Dryden, *Poems*, ed. Hammond and Hopkins, iii. 246).

[236] Paul Hammond, *Dryden and the Traces of Classical Rome* (Oxford, 1999), 184–8; Rachel Miller, 'Physic for the Great: Dryden's Satiric Translations of Juvenal, Persius, and Boccaccio', *Philological Quarterly*, 68 (1989), 53–75.

[237] John Dryden, *Don Sebastian*, 1. 1. 65–9. See James Anderson Winn, *John Dryden and his World* (New Haven, 1987), 441.   [238] *Don Sebastian*, 4. 3. 449, 458–9.

[239] John Dryden, *Cleomenes, The Spartan Heroe*, 2. 1. 60–2; the comment is reported to the King at 4. 1. 2–19.

is following the ancient historians in making the King 'a Lazy, Effeminate, Cowardly, Cruel, and Luxurious Prince, manag'd by his Favourite, and impos'd on by his Mistress'.[240] Against this image of an 'Effeminate Tyrant'[241] is set strong, martial male friendship, as when Cleanthes promises to share Cleomenes' fate in Greece: 'So I shall have thee wholly to my self, | And be thy Wife, thy Mother, and thy Son, | As thou art all to me.'[242] This, it seems, is how true masculine valour speaks.

To what discourse do these texts belong? Is there a discourse of sodomy? Perhaps it would be a mistake to imagine that anything as coherent as a discourse is formulated in the 1680s and 1690s, either around sexual relations between men or around the rather different idea of sodomy. In the early eighteenth century the growth of the molly houses in London would make society at large much more aware of sexual relations between men, and would provoke responses (ranging from mockery to murder) from the guardians of public morality. But this only happens once an imaginable social life with its own idiolect, fashions, and geography has begun to coalesce around the practice of men enjoying sex with one another. In the texts about Titus Oates and William of Orange, sex between men is not imagined as part of a possible subjectivity or community: it is a sign of something other. (If there is a community of bardashes around William, it is one to which no ordinary Englishman has access.) Sodomy in these texts is an overdetermined trope, a signifier with multiple signifieds. It hardly refers to realizable sexual experiences and desires, but instead reassures readers that all alternatives to their norms are incoherent, monstrous, or impossible. Because sexual nonconformity is linked to religious nonconformity—both Puritan and Catholic—the alternatives to Anglicanism are placed beyond the pale. Englishness is confirmed by linking such deviant figures with Italians and Turks. Social stability is strengthened by warning of the danger of mobility across boundaries of class and religious denomination. Oates has crossed the dividing line between Protestantism and Catholicism, and back again; and crossed from the weavers to Whitehall, and back again. Buckingham and Bentinck have risen beyond their station, often in the process excluding those whose right to power and influence was

---

[240] Dryden, *Works*, xvi. 80–1.
[241] *Cleomenes*, 2. 2. 77
[242] Ibid., 3. 3. 28–30.

hereditary—hence, perhaps, the attraction of sodomy as an image for such an alternative order. William has upset the hereditary principle, displaced his own father-in-law, and sired no heir.

But this interpretation almost empties the representation of sodomy of its sexual significance, locating it in a politically motivated discourse. Does this material, then, have a place in the history of the figuring of sexual relations between men, or is it always a metaphor for political transgression? In the earlier texts, those which present Edward II and James I, there is a strong element of homoeroticism, even if Drayton tries to write this out of his poem when revising it. Even when reading about the improper hold which Gaveston has over Edward, we are aware of the sexual attraction between them; and the poems which satirize James acknowledge the sensual pleasures of sex with young men. The poem on the King's five senses is aware of this physical delight in a way which does not happen in any of the later poems on William, where the sex which he supposedly had with Bentinck is described in the crudest terms. Writers in the earlier part of the period seem to acknowledge that homoeroticism can colour, indeed, strengthen, homosocial bonds. But some elements in these later texts suggest an anxiety, specific to the Restoration period, about the prevalence of sexual relations between men as a threat to homosociality. The molly houses may not have arrived until the 1700s, but the concern to read Oates, to interpret his 'marks', may be fuelled partly by an anxiety about whether men who enjoyed sex with other men could be identified from outward signs. Then the anxiety about where to place Oates, about the kind of space which he could be imagined to inhabit, and the kinds of connections which there might be between his world and the reader's world, may also betoken a nervousness about the sexual geography of London. If it was indeed Oates's homosexual contacts which enabled him to cross geographical, social, and religious boundaries in London, no wonder readers became anxious about the security of definitions.

The trope of the political sodomite translates individuals into mythic figures who exemplify the community's fears—about the status of the monarchy, the coherence of Englishness, the safety of the Protestant religion—and running through these texts there is a sense that the proper boundaries of the public and the private have been disregarded. Perhaps the sodomite has made his private desires embarrassingly public, or more generally has placed his own self-interest above that of the society which he is supposed to serve. In response, the satirist stages private sexual scenes in a public medium. And in a period of plots and revolutions, what men choose to conceal becomes the object of paranoid interest and inventive reading—as the case of Andrew Marvell will illustrate.

4

Marvell's Ambiguities

Much of Marvell's poetry is prized for its enigmatic character; much of his biography is equally enigmatic. Scholars have argued about his political allegiances, and about how to interpret his public poetry, wondering whether it is possible to identify a political stance which is either coherent at any one moment or consistent across his career. The present chapter explores another aspect of Marvell which raises problems about coherence and consistency—his sexuality. However, this is not (and because of the lack of surviving evidence cannot be) a biographical inquiry into the private sexual desires and practices of a historical individual, even though there are some texts which look tantalizingly like biographical evidence;[1] rather, the Marvell of this chapter is a Marvell who is created through two quite different groups of texts, whose relations to each other, and to the historical Andrew Marvell, are difficult to interpret. First come the contemporary pamphlet attacks on Marvell, which are full of sexual innuendo. Here 'Marvell' is a set of politically motivated caricatures of one who was a spokesman for a Whiggish and Nonconformist[2] form of Protestantism. Reading these tracts one can trace the conceptual structures and rhetorical strategies which associate various forms of sexuality with political and religious positions. Secondly, certain motifs which are prominent in these pamphlets can be seen as parodic

[1] William Empson has explored Marvell's biography provocatively in *Using Biography* (London, 1984). Empson made an important contribution in identifying a homoerotic sensibility in some of Marvell's poems, even if one is unconvinced by some of the biographical hypotheses which he elaborates around them. For another reading of Marvell and masculinity see Derek Hirst and Steven Zwicker, 'Andrew Marvell and the Toils of Patriarchy: Fatherhood, Longing, and the Body Politic', *ELH* 66 (1999), 629–54.

[2] Neither term fits Marvell exactly: he died before the formation of the Whig party, and is not known to have belonged to a particular Nonconformist sect. But he espoused a politics which was suspicious of the court and the clerical establishment.

versions of sexual interests which inform Marvell's own poetry, so that to read the poems in the light of the pamphlets may reveal sexual nuances—particularly homoerotic subtexts—in the verse which critics have ignored or suppressed. And here 'Marvell' is the variety of voices and personae which are found in his poetry, often with characteristic erotic sensibilities which persist across the canon.

THE PAMPHLET ATTACKS ON MARVELL

To begin with the pamphlets: these belong to the controversy generated by Marvell's book *The Rehearsal Transpros'd* (1672), which was an attack on the Anglican divine Samuel Parker. Marvell had objected to Parker's argument that the ruler should have absolute power in matters of religion, and be able to punish dissent. He had mixed thoughtful argument with boisterous personalized satire which included sexual innuendo: Marvell pretended, for example, to infer that when Parker said that he had been occupied with '*matters of a closer and more comfortable importance to himself*' he had meant a woman.[3] Parker, he said, had written in an extravagant and indecent way: 'Thus it must be, and no better, when a man's Phancy is up, and his Breeches are down; when the Mind and the Body make contrary Assignations, and he hath both a Bookseller at once and a Mistris to satisfie: Like Archimedes, into the Street he runs out naked with his Invention.'[4] Parker's admiration for Bishop Bramhall has led him to write about him in too warm a language, 'part Play-book and part-Romance', and so 'our Author speaks the language of a Lover' and has made 'a dead Bishop his Mistress'.[5] Marvell also presents a sketch of the young cleric consumed with self-esteem and soliciting the admiration of his female congregation:

For being of an amorous Complexion, and finding himself (as I told you) the *Cock-Divine* and the *Cock Wit* of the Family, he took the priviledge to walk among the Hens: and thought it was not impolitick to establish his new-acquired Reputation upon the Gentlewomens side. And they that perceived he was a Rising-Man, and of pleasant Conversation, dividing his Day among them into Canonical hours, of reading now the Common-

---

[3] Andrew Marvell, *The Rehearsal Transpros'd and The Rehearsal Transpros'd The Second Part*, ed. D. I. B. Smith (Oxford, 1971), 5–6.

[4] Ibid., 7.

[5] Ibid., 12–13.

prayer, and now the Romances; were very much taken with him. The Sympathy of Silk began to stir and attract the Tippet to the Pettycoat and the Petticoat toward the Tippet. The innocent Ladies found a strange unquietness in their minds, and could not distinguish whether it were Love or Devotion. Neither was he wanting on his part to carry on the Work; but shifted himself every day with a clean Surplice, and, as oft as he had occasion to bow, he directed his Reverence towards the Gentle-womens Pew. Till, having before had enough of the Libertine, and under-taken his Calling only for Preferment; he was transported now with the Sanctity of his Office, even to extasy ... I do not hear for all this that he had ever practised upon the Honour of the Ladies, but that he preserved alwayes the Civility of a *Platonick Knight-Errant*. For all this Courtship had no other operation than to make him stil more in love with himself . . . being thus, without Competitor or Rival, the Darling of both Sexes in the Family and his own Minion.[6]

Marvell never alleges any actual sexual impropriety in Parker's behaviour with these women, and the passage becomes increasingly concerned with his self-love. At this point a curious element enters Marvell's text. Into this account of Parker's relations with women there suddenly intrudes the suggestion that Parker is sexually attrac-tive to other men, 'the Darling of both Sexes'; moreover, Parker becomes 'his own Minion', in other words not only his own favourite but also his own catamite.[7] Marvell's flight of fancy has started with the vision of Parker as a cockerel parading in front of his admiring hens, but has arrived at an image of Parker as an object of homoerotic interest to other men, and of autoerotic interest to himself. Just why Marvell's imagination should have travelled this path is unclear, but if he had foreseen the attacks on his own sexual conduct and interests which this pamphlet provoked, he might have avoided the use of such satirical strategies.

Parker himself, in his reply called *A Reproof to the Rehearsal Transprosed* (1673), resisted the temptation to respond in kind to Marvell's sexual innuendo, and suggested that this passage bore no relation to him personally and was merely a satirical piece of character-writing recycled from Marvell's bottom drawer: 'And so we arrive at

---

[6] Andrew Marvell, *The Rehearsal Transpros'd and The Rehearsal Transpros'd The Second Part*, 30–1.

[7] 'Minion' is 'a beloved object, darling, favourite: a lover or lady-love' (*OED* 1a); 'a dearest friend ... [or] servant' (*OED* 1b); a sexual partner, esp. of subordinate status (Williams, *s.v.*). The specific sense 'homosexual partner' is common, as in 'The king is lovesick for his minion' (Marlowe, *Edward II*, 1. 4. 87).

the Character of a Noble-man's Chaplain; for having heretofore (among other your juvenile Essays of Ballads, Poesies, Anagrams and Acrosticks) laid out your self upon this subject also, and your Papers lying useless by you at this time when your Muse began to tire.'[8] Even in his posthumously published autobiography, Parker made no specific allegations about Marvell's sexual behaviour, contenting himself with the vague slur that 'he had liv'd in all manner of wickedness from his youth' and had turned into 'a vagabond, ragged, hungry Poetaster' and a 'drunken buffoon'.[9] But by the time Parker's *Reproof* appeared, other pamphleteers had already entered the fray, and in the course of their polemic had made free with Marvell's sexual interests and abilities.

The first of these rejoinders to Marvell was written by Henry Stubbe and published under the title of *Rosemary & Bayes* (1672). 'Bayes' was the name which Marvell had used for Parker, and Stubbe now applied 'Rosemary' to Marvell, referring to him in the text as 'Mr. *Rosemary*'.[10] Rosemary and bays were commonly linked, for they were used together as a decoration,[11] but were also gendered in their symbolism, so that the phrase 'rosemary and bays' alludes to a proverbial contrast between masculine and feminine characteristics. The bay is the laurel, the tree of Apollo, signifying masculine strength, military conquest, and poetic excellence. Rosemary is associated with women, and not only as a girl's name: Gerard says that its Latin name is 'Rosmarinus Coronaria' because 'women have been accustomed to make crownes and garlands thereof'.[12] Rosemary was entwined in a bride's wreath. It also came to symbolize the dominance of the woman, for it was said that where rosemary flourished in a garden, the woman ruled the household.[13] Marvell himself, the poet of gardens and of

---

[8] [Samuel Parker], *A Reproof to the Rehearsal Transprosed* (London, 1673), 269.

[9] *Bishop Parker's History of his own Time*, tr. Thomas Newlin (London, 1727), 332, 348. The original Latin text says of Marvell's youthful wickedness: *Hic ut inhonestius ab adolescentia vixerat*, but the translation actually seems closer to the variant version of the passage added in manuscript (perhaps from Parker's papers) in one of the Bodl. copies (4° Rawl 325): *Hic ut omni Vitae Turpitudine ab Adolescentia vixerat* (*Reverendi Admodum in Christo Patris, Samuelis Parkeri . . . De Rebus sui Temporis Commentariorum Libri Quatuor* (London, 1726), 274).

[10] [Henry Stubbe], *Rosemary & Bayes* (London, 1672), 8.

[11] They were used together to decorate churches (*OED* bay[1] 3) and the boar's head (*OED* rosemary 2d).

[12] John Gerard, *The Herball or Generall Historie of Plantes . . . very much enlarged and amended* by Thomas Johnson (London, 1633), 1293.

[13] M. Grieve, *A Modern Herbal* (Harmondsworth, 1976), 681–2; *OED* rosemary 2c.

wreaths, would have understood this allusion well enough. Apart from this satirical renaming of Marvell, however, Stubbe's pamphlet avoids commenting on his sexuality, except for a reference to his having put on a '*perruke* and *Visor-mask*',[14] the former a male fashion, the latter a female accessory which at this date was coming to be associated with prostitutes.[15] So this phrase implies an androgynous appearance, and calls attention to some riddle which needs to be solved, some mask to be removed.

The second contribution to the controversy is less restrained. The anonymous *A Common-place-Book out of the Rehearsal Transpros'd* (1673) suggests in several ways that Marvell is a eunuch. First he is said to be 'as tough and lasting as a Stone-horse in a race; yet I have heard those who use the *Newmarket*-Course say that the *Colingwood-Gelding* would hold it out to the end as the best'.[16] 'Colingwood' probably puns on 'coll' meaning 'to cut close'.[17] So this writer who appears to have a stallion's strength and stamina may actually be a gelding. Then there is a snide reference to a fictitious bookseller operating at 'the sign of the *Counter-Tenor-Voice*'.[18] The pamphlet also invites us to make a comparison between Marvell and the historian Eutropius, suggesting that the parallel between the two men extends beyond their opposition to ecclesiastical power: 'Eutropius the Eunuch was a busie Solicitor with the Civil Magistracy, to have a Law made against the Priviledges and Power of the Church, not long after it happen'd that he was utterly ruin'd by the very same contrivance, which his malice against Ecclesiastical Politie had framed.'[19] With these allegations of castration and impotence so clearly established, one hears insinuations in other comments. The writer says to Marvell: 'Do you plead with the *Casuists*, that any man may dispense with his own Promise, where the *Non-performance* prejudices no one?' And commenting on Marvell's remark that he was on the horns of a dilemma, the writer replies: 'Now a *Dilemma* is otherwise call'd, *A two-horned Argument*; whereas most men would have believed that he could have made neither two horns nor one, since he left the *Colledge*'.[20] This is to say that Marvell was

[14] Stubbe, *Rosemary & Bayes*, 11.

[15] *The Poems of John Dryden*, ed. Paul Hammond and David Hopkins (London, 1995–), i. 241.

[16] *A Common-place-Book out of the Rehearsal Transpros'd* (London, 1673), 22.

[17] *OED* coll v.².

[18] *A Common-place-Book*, 4.

[19] Ibid., 56.

[20] Ibid., 10–11.

incapable of making another man a cuckold (by giving him two horns), and incapable of having an erection.[21] The innuendo is given a homosexual colouring when Geneva (the home of Calvin, and thus implicitly the spiritual home of Marvell the militant Protestant) is imagined to share the same fate as Sodom.[22]

The third pamphlet in this series is Richard Leigh's *The Transproser Rehears'd* (1673), which is the most sustained, detailed, and vituperative of all the pamphlets in the allegations which it makes about Marvell's sexuality.[23] One passage imagines Marvell as a lover, but only to mock him with the improbability of this scenario. He is cast in the role of 'Prince *Pretty-man*' who is

passionately in Love (you may allow him to be an *Allegorical Lover* at least) with old *Joan* (not the *Chandlers*, but Mr. *Calvins* Widow) walks discontentedly by the side of the Lake *Lemane*, sighing to the Winds and calling upon the Woods; not forgetting to report his Mistresses name so often, till he teach all the *Eccho's* to repeat nothing but *Joan*; now entertaining himself in his Solitude, with such *little Sports*, as *loving his Love with an I*, and then *loving his Love with an O*, and the like for the other Letters[24] . . . To be short, after he has carv'd his Mistresses Name with many *Love-knots* and *flourishes* in all the *Bushes* and *Brambles*; and interwoven those sacred Characters with many an *Enigmatical* Devise in *Posies* and *Garlands* of *Flowers*, lolling sometimes upon the Bank and sunning himself, and then on a sudden (varying his Postures with his Passion) raising himself up, and speaking all the fine things which Lovers us'd to do. His Spirits at last exhal'd with the heat of his Passion, swop, he falls asleep, and snores out the rest.[25]

Perhaps the type of the melancholy lover is too much of a contemporary commonplace for this passage to be making sarcastic, disbelieving allusions to the echoing song and the complaining lover in 'To his Coy Mistress', or to the conceit about names carved on trees in 'The Garden'.[26] But Leigh clearly regards Marvell as an improbable lover in

[21] 'Horn' = erect penis (Williams, *s.v.*).

[22] *Common-place-Book*, 10. In other contexts this might simply betoken a corrupt and ungodly city ripe for destruction, without any implications of sexual misconduct; but in the context of the other sexual references the homosexual nature of the allusion is surely brought into play.

[23] This tract has also been attributed to Samuel Butler: see Nicholas von Maltzhan, 'Samuel Butler's Milton', *Studies in Philology*, 92 (1995), 482–95.

[24] See Williams, *s.v.* lovers' alphabet.

[25] Richard Leigh, *The Transproser Rehears'd* (Oxford, 1673), 137–8.

[26] Neither poem was printed until 1681, so any allusion would presuppose MS

any but an allegorical context, and interprets any love-rhetoric from him as mere imitative posturing to occupy his solitude, and leading only to masturbation.[27]

Once again Marvell is presented as a eunuch. In a scene set in a coffee-house, Marvell 'the Man of Observations draws out his Table-book ('tis his most dangerous Tool)'. Marvell the observer makes notes on the conversation which could prove dangerous to the participants if they were talking sedition. But clearly the notebook is the only really dangerous weapon which Marvell has, and any other 'tool' of his, whether sword or penis, would be ineffectual.[28] He is god-father to other people's children, but has no offspring of his own.[29] He may bristle with ruffled pride like a turkeycock, though that would be 'too Masculine an Emblem for a *Capon-wit*',[30] a pointed variation on Marvell's description of Parker as a '*Cock Wit*'. Slyly adapting the mode of Marvell's own *Last Instructions to a Painter*, Leigh offers advice to any painter who undertakes Marvell's portrait:

if ever he draws him below the Wast, to follow the example of that Artist, who having compleated the Picture of a Woman, could at any time, with two strokes of his Pencil upon her Face, two upon her Breast, and two betwixt her Thighs;[31] change her in an instant into Man: but after our Authors Female Figure is compleated, the change of Sex is far easier; for Nature, or *Sinister Accident* has rendered some of the Alteration-strokes useless and unnecessary. This expression of mine may be somewhat uncouth, and the fitter therefore (instead of *Fig-leaves*, or *White Linnen*) to obscure what ought to be conceal'd in Shadow. Neither would I trumpet the Truth too loudly in your ears, because ('tis said) you are of a delicate Hearing, and a great enemy to noise; insomuch that you are disturb'd with the tooting of a Sow-gelders Horn.[32]

The passage continues to play with the idea of castration, and then turns to overt allegations of sodomy:

circulation, but there are no extant 17c MSS of 'The Garden' and only one of 'To his Coy Mistress' (see n. 164 below).

[27] Implied in 'His Spirits at last exhal'd with the heat of his Passion', since 'spirits' = semen (Williams, *s.v.*; *Poems of John Dryden*, ii. 334).

[28] Leigh, *Transproser Rehears'd*, 36–7; 'tool' = penis (Williams, *s.v.*).

[29] Leigh, *Transproser Rehears'd*, 8.   [30] Ibid., 128.

[31] Is this rapid sketch of the woman's face, breast, and thighs another sly allusion to 'To his Coy Mistress', ll. 14–17, especially if Leigh knew the version which referred to her 'thighs' rather than 'the rest'? (For that version, see p. 223 below.)   [32] Ibid., 134–5.

Some busie People there are, that would be forward enough it may be to pluck the Vizor off this *Sinister Accident*, not without an evil Eye at your Distich on *Un Accident Sinistre*, to which they imagine some officious Poet might easily frame a Repartee to the like purpose as this Tetrastich.

> *O marvellous Fate. O Fate full of marvel;*
> *That* Nol's Latin *Pay two* Clerks *should deserve ill!*
> *Hiring a* Gelding *and* Milton *the* Stallion;
> *His* Latin *was gelt, and turn'd pure* Italian.

Certainly to see a *Stallion* leap a *Gelding*, (and this *leap't* fair, for he *leapt* over the *Geldings* head) was a more preposterous sight, or at least more *Italian*, then what you fancy of *Father Patrick's bestriding Doctor Patrick*.[33]

Leigh is alluding to a passage in *The Rehearsal Transpros'd* where Marvell referred to an occasion when the French King Henri IV challenged his courtiers to rhyme extempore on a given subject:

The Subject was, *Un Accident sinistre*. Straight answers, I know not whether 'twas *Bassompierre or Aubignè*:

> *Un sinistre Accident & un Accident sinistre;*
> *De veoir un Pere Capuchin chevaucher un Ministre.*[34]

For when I said, to see Popery return here, would be a very sinister accident; I was just thinking upon that story; the Verses, to humour them in translation, being only this,

> *O what a trick unlucky, and how unlucky a trick,*
> *To see friend Doctor Patrick, bestrid by Father Patrick!*[35]

Marvell's reference is to the Anglican divine Simon Patrick and the Roman Catholic priest Father Patrick MaGinn, so that for the latter to bestride the former symbolizes the triumph of Catholicism over the Church of England. The image is primarily equestrian, fashioning the kind of emblem of inverted authority familiar from Renaissance representations of Aristotle being ridden by Phyllis;[36] and yet the sexual implications of riding[37] cannot be excluded from Marvell's lines, which thus present sodomy as an appropriate image of political

---

[33] Leigh, *Transproser Rehears'd*, 135; for 'preposterous' cf. p. 24 above.

[34] 'A terrible accident and a sinister occurrence, to see a Capuchin Father bestride a Minister'.

[35] Marvell, *The Rehearsal Transpros'd*, 121.

[36] Two of these illustrations are reproduced in *Saints and She-devils*, ed. Lène Dresen-Coenders (London, 1987), 51.

[37] Williams, *s.v.*

subversion. The sexual possibilities of the image are exploited by Leigh when he adapts the lines to suggest that the relationship between Marvell and Milton in their time as Cromwell's Latin Secretaries was that of catamite and sodomite: Marvell the gelding played the passive role to Milton the stallion. Earlier Leigh had anticipated this slur in his play on the word 'conjunction': 'among other Calamities of late, there has happen'd a prodigious Conjunction of a *Latin Secretary* and an *English School-Master*, the appearance of which, none of our Astrologers foretold, nor no Comet portended'.[38]

There is a further example of Leigh drawing out a sexual meaning from Marvell's own text when a remark in *The Rehearsal Transpros'd* is interpreted as revealing Marvell's own sexual interests. Marvell had written that, in Parker's scheme of things, Nonconformists 'must still be subjected to the *Wand* of a *Verger*, or to the wanton lash of every *Pedant*; that they must run the *Ganteloop*, or down with their breeches as oft as he wants the prospect of a more pleasing *Nudity*'.[39] To run the ganteloop (now generally called 'run the gauntlet') is a military punishment which requires an offender to be stripped to the waist, or stripped naked, and run between two lines of soldiers who rain blows on him as he passes. It is not surprising that Leigh's attention was caught by these lines, for Marvell's sentence gathers in sexual content as it moves from the Nonconformists being subject to a verger's wand of office, to them being beaten by a schoolmaster, to the homoerotic sadism of the military punishment, and finally to the bare buttocks which provide 'the prospect of a more pleasing *Nudity*'. What starts as a purely symbolic subjection to the verger's wand of office has by the end of the sentence become a literal (and explicitly visualized) physical punishment. It is not clear why such male nudity would please Parker, whom Marvell has already accused of being too interested in elegantly dressed women. Perhaps Marvell simply meant that the prospect of Nonconformists being punished would please Parker more than any sexual pleasure could. In any case, to Leigh this flight of fancy seemed evidence of Marvell's personal predilections, and he remarked that '*Nol's Latin Clerks* were somewhat *Italianiz'd* in point of Art as well as Language'.[40] These overt suggestions of homosexual interests may invite us to hear an innuendo in Leigh's remark that the boy who waits

---

[38] Leigh, *Transproser Rehears'd*, 128. For other examples of the play on the astro-logical and sexual senses of 'conjunction' see Williams, *s.v.*

[39] Marvell, *The Rehearsal Transpros'd*, 36.

[40] Leigh, *Transproser Rehears'd*, 136.

on the customers in the coffee-house is Marvell's 'principal Camerade
. . . and no less then our Authors Library-Keeper'.[41] Why should
Marvell prefer the boy's company to that of other adults? What might
be the duties of such a library-keeper?

Other pamphlets took their cue from these earlier attacks. *S'too him
Bayes* (1673) also questions Marvell's interest in removing breeches:
'*Britches* again: So often *fumbling* with them? What, ar't a *Taylor*?
Marry pray—He ben't *worse*'.[42] The eunuch topos recurs too: an argument which is too sophisticated for Marvell to grasp will have to be
'*Castrated* into *Conformity* with your understanding'.[43] Moreover,
'thou debauchest the very *Age* too, for thou bringest *Love* it self, which
should be a Divine thing, and the noblest passion of an *Heroick* mind
to meer—*Boar beckons Pig-hog wilt thou be mine?*'[44] Marvell is accused
of having reduced the noble passion of love to the physical union of
two male pigs, one a boar, the other a castrated hog.[45] This, says the
writer, is no more love's sweet variety than boiled capon would be a
varied diet.[46]

Edmund Hickeringill's *Gregory, Father Greybeard* (1673) deploys the
familiar pun in referring to Marvell as a marvel, but now he is seen as a
sinister kind of marvel, a '*monstrous* beast', 'desperately disingenuous
and *unnatural*' and an 'Amphibious' creature.[47] 'Amphibious' was
applied not only to a creature which lived both on land and in water,
but also to something which occupied two positions or combined two
classes; and so, for example, to a creature of indeterminate gender,
or one which combined both genders.[48] The pamphlet refers to
Marvell as 'it' rather than 'he', saying that 'the thing should be female
by the *Billings-gate* Oratory of scolding' which Marvell employs.[49]
Hickeringill also refers to the 'unmanlike . . . and effeminate Practices'

[41] Ibid., 35.

[42] *S'too him Bayes* (Oxford, 1673), 42.

[43] Ibid., 126.

[44] Ibid., 126.

[45] This gives a homosexual twist to the proverb 'pigs love that lie together' (Tilley,
P 313). For the same proverb similarly applied to Titus Oates see p. 155 above.

[46] *S'too him Bayes*, 125.

[47] [Edmund Hickeringill], *Gregory, Father Greybeard* (London, 1673), 6–7.

[48] *OED* 1–3. Titus Oates is similarly described as '*An* Odd Amphibious Animal': see
p. 165 above. This usage is also seen clearly in Alexander Pope's description of Sporus
(Lord Hervey): 'now Master up, now Miss, | And he himself one vile Antithesis. |
Amphibious Thing! that acting either Part, | . . . Now trips a Lady, and now struts a
Lord.' (*Epistle to Dr Arbuthnot* (1735), ll. 324–9).

[49] *Gregory, Father Greybeard*, 37.

of the Nonconformists, remarking that their 'soft and unmanly Rules of Government and Policy, may perhaps agree with your own effeminate temper'.[50]

Sober Reflections, or, a Solid Confutation of Mr. Andrew Marvel's Works, in a Letter Ab Ignoto ad Ignotum (1673), signals in its title that Marvell presents a problem of interpretation: it is addressed '*ad Ignotum*' ('to the unknown one' or 'to the unknown thing'), and in the context of the strategies deployed in these pamphlets the phrase does not simply allude to the anonymity of *The Rehearsal Transpros'd*, but implies that its author is also unknown in the sense of eluding or transgressing one's conceptual categories. *Sober Reflections* also puns on 'marvel', and writes of his 'Amphibious valour'.[51] His ambiguous state is described through an adaptation of Falstaff's innuendo-laden conversation with Mistress Quickly in *1 Henry IV*: 'What though you are neither Flesh nor Fish, nor good Red-herring, your Adversary is not us'd to Otter-hunting, never fear him Man, let him come if he dare: Oh happy if he come not, he shall soon be taught what it is to meddle with any of the Race of *Dametus* hereafter.'[52] The otter is amphibious, feeding on land and in the water; it is also, in seventeenth-century beast lore, a symbol of those who seek a life of retirement from the world, as well as a symbol of those who dislike their rulers, but obey them out of fear.[53] As for Marvell being one of 'the Race of Dametus', at one level

[50] *Gregory, Father Greybeard*, 222, 318. In this period the word 'effeminate' slides between meaning 'too fond of the company of women and so neglecting masculine responsibilities' (applied, for example, to Charles II preferring his mistresses to state business) and 'too womanly in manner and interests (including sexual interests) to be a real man'. For examples see *OED* and Williams, *s.v.*

[51] *Sober Reflections, or, a Solid Confutation of Mr. Andrew Marvel's Works, in a Letter Ab Ignoto ad Ignotum* (London, 1674), 1, 5. The work is signed Theophilus Thorowthistle.

[52] Ibid., 5; Shakespeare, *1 Henry IV*, 3. 3. 125–30.

[53] 'Although it live in the waters, yet it doth not suck in water, but; that is, it doth not breath like fishes through the benefit of water' (Edward Topsel, *The History of Four-footed Beasts and Serpents* (London, 1658), 445). It was a suitable image for a satirist, for as Topsel says, 'it is a sharp biting Beast, hurtful both to men and dogs . . . Otters are most accomplished biters. It is a very crafty and subtil Beast, yet it is sometimes tamed' (ibid.). Wolfgang Franzius supplies several symbolic meanings for the otter which are useful in suggesting how Marvell's contemporaries saw him. First, he says that the otter is to be included amongst the 'doleful creatures' mentioned in Isaiah 13. 21, 'by all which, is represented unto us the lives of those who live privately, and solitarily in the World, only looking after what concerneth themselves, meat and drink . . . holding this for a Maxime, *Bene qui latuit bene vixit*, He liveth the best that liveth the privatest life' (*The History of Brutes; or, A Description of Living Creatures*, tr. N. W. (London, 1670),

this simply means one of the race of poets, since Dametas is the teacher of music who passes his pipes over to the shepherd Corydon; and yet because this is an allusion to Virgil's *Eclogue* 2, there is the further implication that Marvell is a second Corydon nursing a sexual longing for some Alexis. The double allusion neatly associates oppositional verse with unorthodox sexual interests.

Marvell is also imagined in the unedifying position of being 'set Doctor-*Cathedraticus* in a Cucking-stool, Lording it over your Female-Auditory, the Water-*Nymphs* of Wapping, Magisterially maintaining your polemical Arguments and Debates'.[54] His female audience greet him with this 'chearful *Antyphon*',

> *Welcome* Cloris *to the Shore,*
> *Thou shalt go to Sea no more.*[55]

But although Cloris/Marvell is surrounded by women and has his head well rubbed with their shifts, he is unable to oblige them sexually: 'what think you now of a comfortable importance? I am afraid in this critical minute you would be found *minus habens*, and when once a man pleads *non solvent*, it is high time to put up his Pipes and go to sleep'.[56] ('Minus habens' means 'having too little', and 'non solvent' means 'they are unable to fulfil their obligations'.) Moreover, his arguments are equally impotent:

Marvel of *Marvels*, for that is the *Character* given you by a certain sort of Impertinent People who love mischief; Mischief your Minion Medium, which like a rich vein runs through the heart of all your Syllogismes, to the utter impoverishing of their Consequences; for, from a vicious medium (as unfledg'd a Logician as you are) you may Cock-sure, inferr, there must necessarily follow a vile consequence.

But, how defective soever you are in your *Syllogismes*, you make ample satisfaction; nay, you supererrogate in your *Dilemma's*.[57]

This rather intricate insult draws parallels between styles of writing and forms of sexual behaviour, and starts from the assumption that

---

224). Franzius adds: 'Some are of opinion, that they can fore-see a storm long before it cometh, and defend themselves against it', and otters are also emblems of 'those people, who although they have no love for their rulers, yet are forced to obey them out of fear' (ibid., 225).

[54] *Sober Reflections*, 3. [55] Ibid., 6.
[56] Ibid., 6; 'pipe' = penis (Williams, *s.v.*).
[57] *Sober Reflections*, 1–2.

Marvell's sexual impotence is reflected in his impotence as a writer and a logician, for he is defective in his syllogisms which do not arrive at any consequence—or, we might say, come to a climax. This is because he prefers another form of writing, mischief-making, which is his 'Minion Medium'. As a logician Marvell is unfledged, so a virgin (or perhaps a '*Capon-wit*'). He knows that from a vicious medium (use of mischief/use of catamites) there must follow vile consequences (subversion/sodomy). Though inadequate in syllogisms, Marvell excels in the field of dilemmas (the state of being caught between two paths, so an ambiguous or amphibious condition), and here he can indeed give ample satisfaction. The mischief-making of his writing is therefore the appropriate public medium for one who makes mischief with his minions in private.

A final example of an attack on Marvell is a manuscript satire entitled 'A Love-Letter to the Author of the Rehearsall Transpros'd'.[58] This also alleges that Marvell has been castrated, echoing Leigh's jibe about the turkeycock and the capon-wit:

> You bristle, like a Turkey-cock,
> But have not half so fine a Dock,
> 'Tis as in vain to attempt to spread
> Your tail, as it would be to tread;
> You dare not walk among the Hens,
> Lest they find out your impotence:[59]

Later in the poem a Nonconformist conventicle is discussing how to reward Marvell for his services to their cause, and how to relieve his want, since he has apparently been left destitute and 'naked, without one Ragg on him'. One brother says:

---

[58] Royal Society, London, MS 32 (the commonplace book of George Ent). The poem is mentioned by Pierre Legouis in his *André Marvell, poète, puritain, patriote 1621–1678* (Paris, 1928), 459–60, as existing solely in a manuscript owned by H. M. Margoliouth. The whereabouts of that manuscript are now unknown. Legouis dates the 'Love-Letter' to 1673 on the basis that there is no mention in it of *The Rehearsall Transpros'd: The Second Part* which appeared in Nov. 1673. However, the Royal Society text concludes with a paragraph in which the writer says that he has just heard of the publication of Part II, though he has not yet read it, and the satire is dated 30 Jan. 1674. (Normally one might suppose such a dating to be old style, and so to be 30 Jan. 1675 new style, but this seems unlikely in this case.) It is possible that the poem was composed earlier in 1673, and the final lines added when Part II appeared.

[59] Royal Society, MS 32, p. 45; 'dock' = tail, esp. one which has been cut to a stump (*OED* 1, 6); 'tail' = either penis or buttocks; 'tread' = have intercourse with (Williams, *s.vv.*).

> But let us call to mind his Crosses,
> His person's, & his purs's Losses,
> For the first, you may conceive what pain,
> What anguish, he must needs sustein,
> When he, so sadly, underwent
> The Barber's cutting Instrument:[60]

This reference to the 'Barber' (i.e. the surgeon) is the most explicit indication so far that the impotence which these pamphlets allude to is the result of surgical castration. A 'malicious Sister' opposes the proposal for a collection, and objects to giving

> money, rings, & plate
> To one, who could not propagate;
> To one, of wonderfull abilities,
> When the Barber hangs up his Virilities
> On an old musty Pack-thread, with
> Dry'd Orang-peel, & rotten pith.
> What's more apparent than his lewdness?
> And since where's his reformed goodness?[61]

The satire goes on to recommend that Marvell hang himself, since this is what all decent men are expecting of him, and suggests that he could pass this off as the act of a jilted lover thrown into despair by the unkindness of this Nonconformist sister. Linked with these references to his castration are suggestions of effeminacy, for he is renamed 'Tom Thimble' the prick-louse tailor, and the satirist helpfully suggests that if all else fails he could sell his services to the Turk. The Turks' disposition to sodomy was proverbial.[62]

How did Marvell respond to these attacks? After all the printed rejoinders had appeared, he published *The Rehearsall Transpros'd: The Second Part*, and the chastened tone of much of *The Second Part* suggests that he had been unprepared for the personalized abuse which he had received.[63] Anxiety for his reputation seems actually to have

---

[60] Royal Society, MS 32, p. 46. For the phrase 'person and purse' cf. Antonio in *The Merchant of Venice*, p. 91 above.

[61] Royal Society, MS 32, pp. 47–8.

[62] See pp. 24–8 above.

[63] Robert Ferguson, while unsympathetic to Marvell, objected to the 'unhandsome terms' in which Parker had handled Marvell in his *Reproof* (R[obert] F[erguson], *A Sober Enquiry into the Nature, Measure, and Principle of Moral Virtue* (London, 1673), sig. A6ᵛ).

preceded the publication of the attacks, for he relates how he had con-
tacted Parker to warn him that 'any unjust and personal reflections' in
Parker's reply would result in severe retaliation on him and his friends.
But while Parker assured him that 'my private reputation nor no mans
else should ever be injur'd in publick by his consent', others did the job
on Parker's behalf.[64] Some of Marvell's reflections in *The Second Part*
on his own previous handling of Parker have an apologetic tone,
suggesting that he regretted his tactics now that he saw their consequences, and was reconsidering the ethics of such rough discourse.
He recognizes that people's reputation can be damaged not only by
lies but also 'by a truth too officious'.[65] In his own polemic he had
mixed fact and fantasy, and 'as is in that stile usual, intermixed things
apparently fabulous, with others probably true, and that partly out of
my uncertainty of the Author'.[66] But although one might expect a
controversialist to mount a vigorous defence of himself, or to reply in
kind, Marvell does not take issue with the pamphleteers' fabulous
accounts of his own sexuality and bodily condition. He reflects that it
had taken the extraordinary provocation of Parker's treatise to 'tempt
me from that modest retiredness to which I had all my life time hitherto been addicted',[67] and the sombre tone of these pages bespeaks a man
who has been badly hurt by having his private life caricatured before
the public. But more than his reputation was at stake: since sodomy
was a capital offence, Marvell was wise not to become embroiled in
arguments about what was true and what was fabulous.

These various allegations about Marvell make him not so much a
marvel as a monster, an amphibian of indeterminate or double gender;
he is a solitary figure whose mistresses are fictitious; he is impotent,
perhaps surgically castrated, but in any case incapable of performing
sexually with a woman; he is effeminate, womanly, and belongs with
other women; he has sexual desire for other men, and is interested in
male nudity; he engages in sodomy, particularly as the partner who is
penetrated. There are several ways in which one might attempt to
make sense of this farrago: as a description of a particular individual; as
a reading of his texts; as the fashioning of a sexual stereotype; and as a
trope within the discourse of Restoration politics. Let us first consider
the political dynamic which is motivating these caricatures.

As the previous chapter showed, when allegations of homosexual
behaviour are made in political poems and pamphlets they tend to be

---

[64] Marvell, *The Rehearsal Transpros'd*, 171.   [65] Ibid., 161.
[66] Ibid., 170.   [67] Ibid., 169.

motivated by an ideological agenda which has seized upon a polemically convenient personal trait. Explicitly in the pamphlets against Oates, and implicitly in the pamphlets against Marvell, sodomy is a sign of religious and political nonconformity. And in their emphasis on sexual ambiguity, on Marvell as an amphibian, the pamphleteers seem uneasy about his political and cultural allegiance. There were good reasons for regarding him as amphibious politically: a respectable Restoration MP, but also a sometime republican; a sharp political and theological writer, but within the same text also a purveyor of personalized abuse and almost frenzied comedy; a denizen of coffee-house society, but more as an observer than a participant—as it were the eunuch who can watch but not act. But who could know that the role of impotent observer was not just assumed for some ulterior motive, as would happen with Horner in Wycherley's *The Country Wife* (written 1672–4; performed and printed 1675)? In a society which was paranoid about spies and plots, any ambiguity, inscrutability, or secrecy could be dangerous. Marvell himself told Aubrey that 'he would not play the good-fellow in any man's company in whose hands he would not trust his life'. 'He had not a generall acquaintance' comments Aubrey, and adds that he preferred to drink alone in his room.[68] Evidently he was a difficult man to know.

One can also see why readers might have doubts about whether the attitudes expressed in *The Rehearsal Transpros'd* were those in which Marvell actually believed. He was known to have served Cromwell's government and to have written in his praise, and yet in *The Rehearsal Transpros'd* he deplored Parliament's resort to arms and in *The Second Part* wrote that when taking office under Cromwell he had chosen an employment which seemed to him at the time to be doing the least harm to the interests of the exiled King.[69] An otter indeed. Moreover, Marvell was known to be a current friend and erstwhile political colleague of Milton, and yet in *The Second Part* Marvell represented Milton not as a man of principle but as one who had been passively 'toss'd' onto the wrong side by war and fortune, and whose errors were now being 'expiated' by his silence and retirement.[70] It is unlikely that Milton would have appreciated this account of his life. Marvell's readers might well wonder whether these rewritings of history were masking a very different story.

---

[68] *Aubrey's Brief Lives*, ed. Oliver Lawson Dick (Harmondsworth, 1972), 356.
[69] Marvell, *The Rehearsal Transpros'd*, 135, 203.
[70] Ibid., 312.

Another way of understanding this anxiety about Marvell's ambiguity might relate it not to political paranoia but to an increasing
awareness of male homosexuality, with a consequent unsettling of
commonplace assumptions about other men's probable sexual
behaviour. The development of molly houses and cruising grounds in
London is generally dated roughly to the end of the century, but some
evidence from Restoration poetry and drama suggests that a recognition of an alternative male sexuality as a present social reality rather
than just as a mythological or poetic fiction was already spreading in
the 1670s.[71] Outsiders might well be anxious about how to locate this
culture within a culture, and how to interpret its signs. Secrecy might
now betoken sodomy; a man's inscrutability or marginality in the
masculine milieux of the coffee-houses and ale-houses might suggest a
secret sexual life. Some confusion about what homosexual interests
entailed can be seen in the very multiplicity and incoherence of the
allegations.[72] The Marvell who is being produced by these pamphlets is
a figure of incoherence and excess. This is itself significant, for he is
principally being thought of as the opposite of a certain kind of
masculinity and male sexual behaviour which is implicitly assumed to
constitute a norm: this norm is supposedly single, recognizable, and
unproblematic, the man who has intercourse with women. As with
Titus Oates, the opposite to this is multiform and difficult to read, with
multiplicity itself used as a sign of confusion, a sexual confusion which
both threatens and symbolizes a moral and ideological confusion in
society. It was perhaps in response to these destructive configurations
of Marvell that his friends inserted at the front of the posthumous
Miscellaneous Poems of 1681 a prominent notice signed 'Mary Marvell',
authenticating the poems as 'Printed according to the exact Copies of
my late dear Husband, under his own Hand-Writing'.[73] Maybe it was
not only his textual but also his sexual integrity to which the supposed
Mrs Marvell was witnessing.

We need hardly consider as a biographical possibility the suggestion
that Milton sodomized Marvell in the office of the Latin Secretary,
because their 'conjunction' is obviously presented as a sign of their
political alliance, and the representation of Milton as a stallion

---

[71] See Ch. 5, and *LBM* 88–101.

[72] Cf. the aptly named character Sir Jolly Jumble in Otway's play *The Souldiers
Fortune* (1681), who takes a strong sexual interest in men (*LBM* 101–2).

[73] *Miscellaneous Poems. By Andrew Marvell, Esq;* (London, 1681), sig. A2ʳ. Many
scholars have doubted that Mary Marvell was indeed Marvell's wife.

reminds readers that he had been an advocate of divorce, and thus supposedly of freer sex. In Milton's case sodomy is being used simply as a marker of moral turpitude and political deviance, without any implication about his personal sexual preferences.[74] But the caricatures of Milton as a stallion and Marvell as a gelding are not performing quite the same functions. In Marvell's case the story has an obvious polemical purpose in making him the junior partner politically, and so attempting to diminish his status as a spokesman for a version of the Good Old Cause in the 1670s. But unlike the depiction of Milton, the presentation of Marvell is part of a series of such persistent allegations that biographers should not brush aside this material as casually as they have done. These caricatures are not hard evidence of Marvell's sexual behaviour or medical history, but they are certainly evidence of how some contemporaries read his behaviour, his speech, his writing, and his silences. However tendentiously, the pamphleteers were skilled and well-informed readers of his work. Their interpretations of his prose suggest that his poetry (most of which was still unpublished in the 1670s) might also bear reconsideration, and in particular that the poetic ambiguity so prized by modernist critics might be reread in the light of these contemporary perceptions of Marvell's sexual ambiguity. The difficulties of such a reading are considerable, since the personae of the poems are never uncomplicatedly autobiographical. What one can do, however, is to trace certain recurring motifs in the verse, to scrutinize its ambiguities, to examine the disturbances created by homoerotic subtexts within apparently heterosexual or homosocial narratives, and so to chart the kinds of textual spaces which Marvell created for and through his exploration of a complex—and strongly homoerotic—sexuality.

But first there may be one autobiographical text to be considered. In the 1681 *Miscellaneous Poems* we find this:

> Upon an Eunuch; a Poet
> Fragment
> *Nec sterilem te crede; licet, mulieribus exul,*
> *Falcem virginiae nequeas immitere messi,*
> *Et nostro peccare modo. Tibi Fama perennè*

---

[74] Salmasius had indeed alleged that Milton 'sold his buttocks to Italians' during his stay in Italy (William Riley Parker, *Milton: A Biography*, 2 vols. (Oxford, 1968), ii. 1027), but this seems to be an isolated polemical fiction, rather than part of a network of allegations such as one finds in the pamphlets against Marvell. But see p. 28 above.

Praegnabit; rapiesque novem de monte Sorores;
Et pariet modulos Echo *repetita Nepotes.*[75]

Pierre Legouis noted the connection between these verses and the
allegations made by the pamphleteers, but dismissed any element of
self-reflection on Marvell's part, saying that 'such aspersions were
flung about in seventeenth-century controversies too readily to
deserve any credit; and Marvell, if he had suffered that disability,
would probably have abstained from adding one more specimen to the
epigrams on that well-worn theme'.[76] But it is not common for such
aspersions to be so specific, or to be repeated by so many writers.
Moreover, Marvell did not print the poem, and it could have been a
purely private reflection left among his papers at his death.[77] We
cannot at this distance either substantiate or refute the idea that the
epigram was addressed by Marvell to himself. But in any case this
poem adds an important element to the topic of the eunuch, for this
eunuch-poet is promised offspring by means of Echo, an allusion to
the story from Ovid's *Metamorphoses* which thus implicitly casts the
poet in the role of Narcissus.[78] And this is actually a principal myth—
perhaps the principal myth—through which sexuality is imagined in
Marvell's poetry.

MARVELL'S POETRY

Readers of Marvell's poetry have remarked upon his recurrent use of
figures of reflection, enclosure, and self-resemblance.[79] Repeatedly

---

[75] 'Don't believe yourself sterile, although, an exile from women, | You cannot thrust
a sickle at the virgin harvest, | And sin in our fashion. Fame will be continually pregnant
by you, | And you will snatch the nine sisters from the mountain; | Echo too, often
struck, will bring forth musical offspring' (tr. in Andrew Marvell, *The Complete Poems*,
ed. Elizabeth Story Donno (Harmondsworth, 1972), 137). Marvell's poetry is quoted
from *The Poems and Letters of Andrew Marvell*, ed. H. M. Margoliouth, 3rd edn. rev.
Pierre Legouis and E. E. Duncan-Jones (Oxford, 1971).

[76] Marvell, *Poems and Letters*, i. 274.

[77] There is also a reference to a eunuch in 'The Mower against Gardens', ll. 27–30.

[78] The idea of the poet as Narcissus also appears in Thomas Edwards's *Narcissus*
(1595): see Louise Vinge, *The Narcissus Theme in Western European Literature up to the
Early Nineteenth Century* (Lund, 1967), 174–8. For Marvell and the Narcissus myth see
also Lynn Enterline, *The Tears of Narcissus: Melancholia and Masculinity in Early
Modern Writing* (Stanford, Calif., 1995), 146–88.

[79] See Christopher Ricks, ' "Its own resemblance" ' in C. A. Patrides (ed.), *Approaches*

Marvell imagines something seeing or seeking its own reflection, being like itself, being satisfied only with its own reflection. In part this is a philosophical issue, and Marvell seems fascinated by the epistemological problem of how we identify something, how we recognize similarity and difference, and how a recognition of the other may serve to produce self-knowledge in the observer. But this process of self-observation, self-knowledge, and, ultimately, self-pursuit, also has sexual implications: such a turn of mind is potentially narcissistic.

The story of Narcissus, which Marvell would have found most readily in book 3 of the *Metamorphoses*, includes the image of the boy gazing at his own reflection in the water while Echo is helplessly reduced to articulating her unrequited love through repetitions of another's voice. Narcissus stands for self-love, for autoeroticism, for one so enraptured with himself that desire travels in a circle, and is reflected back on its origin. Narcissus also, therefore, exemplifies a form of homoerotic love, since the male gaze is enraptured by a male image, heedless of the charms of the female represented by Echo. To say this is not to imply that homoerotic desire *per se* is necessarily autoerotic or misogynistic, nor to endorse Freud's delineation of a narcissistic character to homosexuality;[80] rather it is to point out how strongly (and with what a finely Freudian condensation) the story of Narcissus and Echo brings together for Marvell a group of profoundly resonant topics: the homoerotic gaze, self-absorption, the natural setting as the mediator of desire, and the disempowered voice. There were other interpretations of Narcissus which Marvell might well have pondered. In Neoplatonic writers (including Plotinus and Ficino) his story was taken as an allegory of man failing to distinguish material from spiritual beauty, mistaking the transitory world for the true world and so condemning the soul to confinement in the body.[81] Others, notably Francis Bacon in *De Sapientia Veterum*, saw Narcissus as an emblem of irresponsible retirement from public life.[82] George Sandys in his notes to his translation of the *Metamorphoses* followed Bacon's line, writing that Narcissus signifies those 'who likely sequester themselves from publique converse and civill affaires, as subject to neglects and disgraces, which might too much trouble and deject

to Marvell: The York Tercentenary Lectures (London, 1978), 108–35; John Carey, 'Reversals Transposed: An Aspect of Marvell's Imagination', ibid., 136–54, esp. 140–2.

[80] *LBM* 16–23.   [81] Vinge, *Narcissus Theme*, 36–40, 125–6.
[82] Ibid., 182.

them'.[83] It was a multivalent myth. So in composing 'A Dialogue between the Soul and Body', or the lines which contemplate the soul's flight in 'The Garden', Marvell is revisiting the Narcissus myth, as he is when writing of the forward youth at the beginning of 'An Horatian Ode', or Fairfax in 'Upon Appleton House', or his own solitary pleasures in 'The Garden'.

The only explicit reference to Narcissus in Marvell's poetry occurs in 'Upon Appleton House' where the river snakes through the meadows:

> See in what wanton harmless folds
> It ev'ry where the Meadow holds;
> And its yet muddy back doth lick,
> Till as a *Chrystal Mirrour* slick;
> Where all things gaze themselves, and doubt
> If they be in it or without.
> And for his shade which therein shines,
> *Narcissus* like, the *Sun* too pines.[84]

Sexual allusions had coloured the previous stanza, for the couplet 'No *Serpent* new nor *Crocodile* | Remains behind our little *Nile*' recalls the serpent in the Garden of Eden, and Cleopatra, that 'serpent of old Nile'.[85] By contrast with these reminders of a dangerous heterosexual world, the 'wanton . . . folds' with which the river embraces the meadows are entirely 'harmless'. The muddy riverbank becomes a shining mirror in which the sun (explicitly male here) sees his own reflection ('shade' means 'reflected image'[86]) and pines for it. This is overtly a moment of homoerotic and autoerotic rapture.

However, the figures of reflexivity and self-regard in Marvell's poetry do not always have a homoerotic element, even though they never quite escape from having some form of sexual implication. In the lines 'On a Drop of Dew' the water 'round in its self encloses',[87] and tries to shun the impurity which would result from its contact with the world. Towards the end of 'Upon Appleton House' Mary Fairfax is

[83] G[eorge] S[andys], *Ovid's Metamorphosis Englished, Mythologiz'd, and Represented in Figures* (Oxford, 1632), 106. Bacon's interpretation was also available in 17th-cent. edns. of Ovid (e.g. *Pub. Ovidii Nasonis Operum Tom. 2. Metamorphoseon Libri XV. Cum notis selectiss. Varior: studio B. Cnippingii* (Leiden, 1670), 140).

[84] 'Upon Appleton House', ll. 633–40.

[85] Ibid., ll. 629–30; Shakespeare, *Antony and Cleopatra*, 1. 5. 25.

[86] As the Oxford editors note.

[87] 'On a Drop of Dew', l. 6.

said to have given the gardens and meadows their beauty, and in return the brook becomes a mirror 'Where *She* may all *her* Beautyes look'.[88] This image of gazing at one's own beauty in the water is a version of the Narcissus story, though its sexual element is immediately translated from autoeroticism to a Diana-like modesty when 'the Wood about *her* draws a Skreen'.[89] Here again, as in 'On a Drop of Dew', self-enclosure is thought of as virginal. In 'Mourning', Chlora 'courts her self in am'rous Rain; | Her self both *Danae* and the Showr',[90] so in this instance the self-courting narcissist is a female who turns androgynous, simultaneously both Danae and Zeus. When composing 'Mourning', Marvell had been attracted to a poem in Cowley's collection 'The Mistress' for the conceit that the woman's tears are like babies; Cowley's version of the idea had included a further twist to the comparison:

> As *stars* reflect on *waters*, so I spy
> In every drop (methinks) her Eye.
> The *Baby*, which lives there, and alwayes plays
> In that illustrious *sphaere*,
> Like a *Narcissus* does appear,
> Whilst in his *flood* the lovely *Boy* did gaze.[91]

Marvell has altered the tenor of this conceit, but was it the Narcissus reference in the original which caught his attention, and prompted his idea of the woman's self-courtship?

A possible version of the Narcissus motif occurs in 'The Definition of Love', where

> My Love is of a birth as rare
> As 'tis for object strange and high:
> It was begotten by despair
> Upon Impossibility.[92]

The loves are 'so truly *Paralel*' that they can never meet. The lovers in this poem are not given any gender, though one might suppose that a precise parallel would require two lovers of the same gender, or, even more precisely, a lover and his own parallel reflection in the water

[88] 'Upon Appleton House', l. 702.
[89] Ibid., l. 704.
[90] 'Mourning', ll. 19–20.
[91] Abraham Cowley, *Poems*, ed. A. R. Waller (Cambridge, 1905), 136. The borrowing from Cowley is noted in the Oxford edn. of Marvell.
[92] 'The Definition of Love', ll. 1–4.

which he can never meet without destroying. Although critics have routinely assumed that the poem describes love for a woman, perhaps one of an impossibly elevated social position, nowhere in this poem does Marvell suggest that the object of this impossible love is female, and it makes very good sense as a definition of the impossible love of one man for another, or of one man for himself.[93] Like 'Mourning', this poem too has a curious relationship to one of its sources, which is another poem from 'The Mistress'. This one is called 'Impossibilities', and suggested some of Marvell's imagery:

> As *stars* (not powerful else) when they *conjoin*,
>   Change, as they please, the Worlds estate;
> So thy *Heart* in *Conjunction* with mine,
>   Shall our own fortunes regulate;
> And to our *Stars themselves* prescribe a *Fate*.[94]

Whereas Marvell's lovers are for ever held apart, Cowley's lovers make their own destiny, and refuse to tolerate impossibilities. But this is not the most striking contrast with Marvell's poem. Cowley explicitly makes his beloved female: she is a 'gentle maid' and is compared to Hero. Marvell, in adapting some of Cowley's conceits, has erased all trace of their heterosexual context.

In the 'Dialogue between the Resolved Soul and Created Pleasure' the Soul is presented with various sensuous temptations. When Pleasure has to select one temptation which epitomizes the seductiveness of sight, it is this:

> Every thing does seem to vie
> Which should first attract thine Eye:
> But since none deserves that grace,
> In this Crystal view *thy* face.[95]

---

[93] A curious example of Marvell's interest in the impossibility of love occurs also in his quotation of lines from Guarini's *Il Pastor Fido* at the beginning of *The Rehearsal Transpros'd* (3): 'S'il peccar è si dolce e'l non peccar si necessario, | O troppo imperfetta Natura che ripugni a la Legge. | O troppo dura Legge che Natura offendi.' Marvell's trans. of these lines adapts them to apply to Parker's compulsion to write, but their original meaning is: 'If to sin is so sweet, and not to sin so necessary, O too imperfect nature which offends against the law, O too hard law which offends against nature.' Why might Marvell have been particularly struck by this cry of a desire prompted by nature but thwarted by law?

[94] Cowley, *Poems*, 130. This borrowing is also noted by the Oxford editors.

[95] 'Dialogue between the Resolved Soul and Created Pleasure', ll. 31–4.

Marvell can imagine no visual pleasure more seductive than that of gazing upon one's own reflection.

The Narcissus motif may be only occasionally or potentially homo-erotic, but there are several texts in which a gaze of erotic appraisal is directed at another man. The most striking and extended example is the passage on Archibald Douglas in the *Last Instructions*, reworked later for *The Loyal Scot*. Here is the opening of this passage:

> brave *Douglas*; on whose lovely chin
> The early Down but newly did begin;
> And modest Beauty yet his Sex did Veil,
> While envious Virgins hope he is a Male.
> His yellow Locks curl back themselves to seek,
> Nor other Courtship knew but to his Cheek.
> Oft has he in chill *Eske* or *Seine*, by night,
> Harden'd and cool'd his Limbs, so soft, so white,
> Among the Reeds, to be espy'd by him,
> The *Nymphs* would rustle; he would forward swim.[96]

Politically, the function of this episode in the *Last Instructions* is primarily to foster admiration for the heroism of the young man, and a sense of the tragic waste of potential caused by the government's incompetent management of the Dutch War. One would expect the writer of a political satire to interest himself in Douglas's youthful heroism, but instead the poem relishes his youthful sexuality, making the young man's body an object of erotic interest rather than of heroic admiration. In one respect this does have a political purpose, in that it produces an icon of pure and self-contained masculinity which contrasts with the seedy and rapacious heterosexual behaviour of the court, which the poem has been presenting as a sign of the regime's political and moral degeneracy. But Marvell's image of Douglas is eroticized beyond what would be necessary for this contrast to be established. Douglas's chin is 'lovely', and is only just showing signs of a beard; this hint of a still-ambiguous gender is continued in the allusion to the modest virgins' hope (rather than certainty) that he is a male. The descriptions of his hair and cheek contribute nothing to any martial image, but present a doubly narcissistic movement as the

---

[96] *Last Instructions to a Painter*, ll. 649–58. Empson (*Using Biography*, 78–80) calls attention to the oddity of the passage on Douglas, though I disagree that the lines exhibit a 'craving to gloat over the torturing of a tender innocent'. See also Barbara Riebling, 'England Deflowered and Unmanned: The Sexual Image of Politics in Marvell's "Last Instructions"', *Studies in English Literature 1500–1900*, 35 (1995), 137–57.

'yellow locks'[97] seek themselves, and also court his own cheek. Except in order to facilitate a conceit around the tragic contrast of fire and water, there is no political reason to include the account of Douglas swimming in rivers; nor, within that digression, is there any political reason to add the detail that his soft, white limbs are hardened and cooled by his swimming. The poetry is clearly offering him to the reader as an object of erotic pleasure, as happens in the description of Leander in Marlowe's poem.[98] Douglas swimming in the river is observed by nymphs who wish in turn to be observed by him, but he swims away from them: the poem thus inserts voyeurs into this scene, introducing observers who can act as surrogates for us, while at the same time reassuring us (the implicitly male readers) that these nymphs are not our rivals, since Douglas shuns their gaze. Characteristically Marvellian interests inform this passage: the narcissistic motif; the delight in an immature body (Douglas is twice called 'boy'[99]); the apprehensive concern for one on the verge of sexual maturity who is liable to be hurt by the flames of passion.[100] (This is entirely Marvell's fiction: in reality, Douglas was a married man.[101]) Moreover, Douglas is made an amphibian, first through his androgynous appearance and uncertain gender, and secondly as a creature of both land and water, prior to becoming a creature of both water and fire.

The account of Douglas's death continues this eroticism. Once again he is observed, though this time by another man. Monck's gaze is the homosocial gaze of soldier on soldier (*'Monck* looks on to see how *Douglas* dies'[102]), though because the poem has so strongly eroticized the way the nymphs and the reader look at Douglas it is difficult to find this new act of looking to be wholly free from a homoerotic purpose, particularly since 'dies' is a ubiquitous term for reaching orgasm, and the death which Monck observes is described as a sexual encounter:

---

[97] In revising the passage for inclusion in *The Loyal Scot* Marvell changed this to 'shady locks' (l. 19). Had he been told that Douglas's hair was dark rather than fair? And had the original 'yellow locks' (an inessential detail) owed more to Marvell's own erotic ideal than to Douglas's actual appearance?

[98] Christopher Marlowe, *Hero and Leander*, ii. 153–226.

[99] *Last Instructions*, ll. 659, 693.

[100] For similar interest in an immature body, and apprehensiveness about the onset of sexual maturity, cf. 'The Nymph Complaining for the Death of her Fawn'; 'Young Love'; 'The Unfortunate Lover', st. 1; 'The Picture of Little T.C.'; and 'The Mower's Song', st. 1.

[101] *Poems*, ed. Margoliouth *et al.*, i. 368.

[102] *Last Instructions*, l. 676.

Like a glad Lover, the fierce Flames he meets,
And tries his first embraces in their Sheets.
His shape exact, which the bright flames infold,
Like the Sun's Statue stands of burnish'd Gold.
Round the transparent Fire about him glows,
As the clear Amber on the Bee does close:
And, as on Angels Heads their Glories shine,
His burning Locks adorn his Face Divine.
But, when in his immortal Mind he felt
His alt'ring Form, and soder'd Limbs to melt;
Down on the Deck he laid himself, and dy'd,
With his dear Sword reposing by his Side.
And, on the flaming Plank, so rests his Head,
As one that's warm'd himself and gone to bed.[103]

Douglas is imagined as a lover, but there is no partner provided for him, male or female: the first line implies that he encounters the flames as if they were his partner, but that idea disappears as the next line makes the flames into sheets. Marvell avoids envisaging a lover for Douglas, keeping the beautiful boy single, and concentrates instead on imagining how the beauty of Douglas's body is transfigured as he loses his virginity in a consummation which is enacted with himself alone. His shape is 'exact',[104] and he becomes like a statue of the sun; his hair as it burns is like an angel's halo around his divine face. Besides this emphasis on his beauty (rather than, say, his courage), there are several details which invite us to read Douglas with homo-erotic pleasure. The allusion to the statue of the sun is implicitly to the sun-god Apollo, icon of male beauty but also lover of the boys Hyacinthus and Cyparissus; at the end of the passage there is a com-parison with Hercules, icon of male strength but also lover of the boy Hylas.[105] And we cannot help noticing that the description con-cludes with the image of Douglas in bed 'with his dear Sword reposing by his Side', this quintessentially phallic symbol sharing his bed like a lover.[106]

Marvell concludes the account of Douglas with this promise of immortality:

---

[103] Ibid., ll. 677–90.
[104] 'Perfect': *OED* 1.
[105] Ibid., l. 695.
[106] In *The Loyal Scot* (l. 56) the line becomes: 'As one that Huggs himself in a Warm bed', which is also implicitly autoerotic.

> Fortunate Boy! if either Pencil's Fame,
> Or if my Verse can propagate thy Name.[107]

This is an echo of the lines in the *Aeneid* where Virgil assures Nisus and Euryalus of eternal fame at the end of the episode in which he has recounted their heroic death.[108] But it is a curious echo. Nisus and Euryalus were passionate friends, and the episode was used by Restoration writers to exemplify devoted friendship or to mourn the loss of a much-loved friend.[109] For Marvell to work this echo into his text goes beyond the deployment of a classical promise of immortality, and signals an emotional commitment to Douglas—at least as a type of the beautiful youth if not as an individual. It may be poignantly typical of Marvell that the story which in other writers is used to celebrate or lament a reciprocated love is used here to lament a lost, unattainable ideal of male beauty and singleness.

This is not the only occasion on which Marvell introduces an erotic element into an elegy for a soldier. The much earlier poem 'An Elegy upon the death of my Lord Francis Villiers' has extended praise of the 19-year-old's beauty:

> Never was any humane plant that grew
> More faire than this and acceptably new.
> 'Tis truth that beauty doth most men dispraise:
> Prudence and valour their esteeme do raise.
> But he that hath already these in store,
> Can not be poorer sure for having more.
> And his unimitable handsomenesse
> Made him indeed be more then man, not lesse.[110]

As in the case of the lines on Douglas, this discussion of Villiers's beauty seems superfluous to the occasion: indeed, the poet has to excuse this beauty as a trait which makes him more than manly (i.e. godlike) rather than less (i.e. womanly). Marvell's approach contrasts interestingly with that in another anonymous elegy on Villiers. The

---

[107] *Last Instructions*, ll. 693–4.

[108] *Aeneid*, 9. 446–7; noted by the Oxford editors.

[109] *Poems of John Dryden*, ii. 258; and Ch. 1 n. 92 above.

[110] 'An Elegy upon the death of my Lord Francis Villiers', ll. 39–46. The attribution to Marvell is based solely upon the testimony of George Clarke, but I agree with the Oxford editors and Donno that the poem is probably by Marvell. It has been related to Marvell's political thinking by James Loxley in 'Prepar'd at Last to Strike in with the Tyde? Andrew Marvell and Royalist Verse', *The Seventeenth Century*, 10 (1995), 39–62, esp. 44–50.

author of 'Obsequies On the untimely Death, of the never to bee too much praised and pitied Francis Lord Villiers'[111] reads Villiers's face as a sign of his valour:

> Th' indented Face
> (Though no great Volume) was the *Common-Place*,
> And *Index* of Thy Valour: everie scar
> Seeming at least som mistick *Character*;

And when he does refer to Villiers's beauty, it is to make it signal the tragedy of a youth cut down before his time in the loyal service of his King:

> But why do I revolv the short-writ-storie
> Of fading Youth; or recollect the Glorie
> Of thy blest Beautie (which though once the Throne
> Oth' Lillie and Rose) was blasted before blown?
> Prepo'strous Fate! t' anticipate and bring
> On Winter e're Thou did'st enjoie Thy Spring!

By contrast, Marvell's fascination with Villiers's beauty has a characteristic train of thought:

> Lovely and admirable as he was,
> Yet was his Sword or Armour all his Glasse.
> Nor in his Mistris eyes that joy he tooke,
> As in an Enemies himselfe to looke.[112]

One might have expected the poem to say that Villiers took no interest in his own beauty and concentrated on martial prowess, but instead it elaborates the idea of self-observation. Villiers looks at himself not in an ordinary mirror but in the polished surface of his sword or armour—implicitly, therefore, in objects which are signs of masculinity and tokens of an all-male world. There is a narcissistic, self-enclosing movement about the gaze which is directed at himself, and which finds other masculine objects—even the eyes of an enemy soldier—to reflect it back, rather than the eyes of his mistress. Marvell's conceit labours to preserve the all-male circuit of vision.

Moreover, when describing Villiers's death, Marvell allows an erotic sensibility to colour his lines:

---

[111] *Vaticinium Votivum: or, Palaemon's Prophetick Prayer* (n.p., 'Anno Caroli Martyris Primo' [i.e. 1649]), 63–7; quotations are from 65–6.
[112] 'An Elegy upon . . . Villiers', ll. 51–4.

> Such fell young *Villiers* in the chearfull heat
> Of youth: his locks intangled all with sweat
> And those eyes which the Sentinell did keep
> Of love closed up in an eternal sleep.
> While *Venus* of *Adonis* thinks no more
> Slaine by the harsh tuske of the Savage Boare.
> Hither she runns and hath him hurried farre
> Out of the noise and blood, and killing warre:
> Where in her Gardens of Sweet myrtle laid
> Shee kisses him in the immortall shade.[113]

The poem dwells upon Villiers's hair entangled with sweat, and his eyes, the guardians of love. The interest in masculine sweat anticipates the poet's emphasis on the mowers' 'wholesome heat' which 'Smells like an *Alexanders sweat*' in 'Upon Appleton House'.[114] The dead body is read as a lover's rather than a soldier's body, and is mourned as Venus had mourned Adonis. The introduction of the story of Venus and Adonis eroticizes the poem's gaze at Villiers even more strongly, for it not only makes him an icon of male beauty, it makes him an unattainable object of sexual desire. Shakespeare's handling of the story had emphasized the attractiveness of the male body, and through his shaping of the narrative had allowed a male reader to gaze with longing on this form, and align himself with Venus and her desire rather than with Adonis and his chastity. The Venus and Adonis story is not an overtly homoerotic tale, but it does permit the male body to be appreciated as the object of another man's sexual longing.

There are also some briefer instances of a homoerotic sensibility in Marvell's poetry. In 'Young Love' the 'Infant' addressed by the poet is ungendered, but in stanza 4 the objects which Love (here explicitly made masculine) is said to prize include 'the lusty Bull or Ram', two obvious emblems of masculine sexuality: this implies that the 'snowy Lamb | Or the wanton Kid' with which the child is compared are also male, but even without that assumption the stanza clearly imagines a male god of Love delighting in symbols of male sexuality. Stanzas 7–8 also imply that the addressee is male, since the poet crowns the child

---

[113] 'An Elegy upon . . . Villiers', ll. 105–14.

[114] 'Upon Appleton House', l. 428. Marvell puns on sweat/sweet, alluding to the story that the sweat of Alexander the Great was naturally perfumed. Alexander's love for the boy Hephaestion was well known, so this is a doubly homoerotic moment. For another example of an erotic interest in male sweat, see 'Damon the Mower', l. 46, discussed below, pp. 217–19.

with his love in order to ward off Fate just as kingdoms crown their king when he is still a child in order to avoid dissension. If Marvell had wanted us to see the child as a girl, he could easily have made the comparison refer to a queen. Critical commentary on this poem has assumed that the child is female,[115] but there is no evidence for this, and the logic of Marvell's similes clearly points the other way. At the very least critics need to consider why Marvell was so carefully unspecific about the child's gender. Similarly, it is worth remarking that 'Beauty, aiming at the Heart' in 'Upon Appleton House' is carefully ungendered, for Marvell refers to 'its useless Dart' whereas one might have expected '<u>her</u> useless Dart'.[116] Why such diplomatic evasion, unless 'its' conceals a wish to write 'his' instead, or at least signals a preference for androgynous beauty over the unambiguously female form?

Different kinds of ambiguity beset those notoriously enigmatic and contentious poems 'The Unfortunate Lover' and 'The Nymph Complaining for the Death of Her Fawn'. First, 'The Unfortunate Lover', while it may indeed be a political allegory, is also at one level explicitly a poem about a male lover; more specifically, it is about '<u>my</u> poor Lover', not, for example, '<u>this</u> poor Lover'.[117] (Indeed, one might expect '<u>our</u> poor Lover' if this were a poem about the young Prince Charles addressed to other Royalist sympathizers.) The lover is 'nak'd',[118] and although 'naked' can simply mean unarmed it primarily means nude. The opening stanza laments the loss of that state of innocence in which 'Infant Love' still plays, or plays with one, in a green shade, and thus echoes other poems which contemplate innocence threatened by sexual maturity. The connection between this vision and the remainder of the poem is obscure, but this evocation of a lost pre-sexual innocence was evidently a necessary prelude to the depiction of the passionate and ill-fated lover. The poem's stress on the impossibility of the unfortunate lover's plight might be thought to recall 'The Definition of Love' and its (possibly homosexual) concerns. Finally, the lover is an '*Amphibium* of Life and Death',[119] and we have already seen how important the idea of the amphibium is, not only in the pamphlet attacks on Marvell, but also in his own sexual

[115] Donno, 245; Margoliouth in the Oxford edn., 252; J. B. Leishman, *The Art of Marvell's Poetry*, 2nd edn. (London, 1968), 166.

[116] 'Upon Appleton House', ll. 604–5; emphasis added.

[117] 'The Unfortunate Lover', l. 11; emphasis added.

[118] Ibid., l. 49.

[119] Ibid., l. 40.

imagination.[120] No doubt 'The Unfortunate Lover' carries some political significance for those able to read its allegory, but critics have been too reluctant to ponder the sexuality of the poem before proceeding to allegorize it. And yet, even its political hinterland is not without sexual ambiguity, for it has been suggested that Marvell may be drawing upon an epigram in which the young Prince James is described as 'armata Venus', an armed Venus.[121] Perhaps the blurring of gender in this description of the lad might have been one feature which caught Marvell's attention.

As for 'The Nymph Complaining', it is possible that Marvell adopts the female persona as a way of exploring the experience of being seduced and jilted by a male lover. Such a reading would not thereby make the poem a coded autobiographical statement, but Marvell's interest in imagining how the sexual awakening of a youngster may be brought about by an adult male, and his obsession with the dangers of innocence confronted by mature male sexuality, need more discussion than critics have been willing to accord. The speaker delights in the androgynous beauty of the fawn, which is described throughout by the ungendering pronoun 'it'.[122] This is also one of a number of poems which, while they ostensibly describe heterosexual passion, include details which suggest a homoerotic subtext. In this case there is a possible allusion to the story of Cyparissus, whose beloved stag is accidentally killed.[123] This is one of the stories which Ovid associates with Orpheus' turn to love for boys after his final loss of Eurydice.[124]

Finally in this collection of poems with homoerotic subtexts, there is 'The Garden'. Lovers who carve their mistresses' names in the bark of trees are rebuked because the trees are more beautiful than any

---

[120] It is also, curiously, the final image in 'Upon Appleton House' (ll. 773–6).

[121] P. R. K. Davidson and A. K. Jones, 'New Light on Marvell's "The Unfortunate Lover"?', *Notes and Queries*, 230 (1985), 170–2.

[122] Lyndy Abraham, in *Marvell and Alchemy* (Aldershot, 1990), 248–54, associates the fawn with the hermaphroditic figure of Mercury.

[123] Ovid, *Metamorphoses*, 10. 106–42. Abraham notes this parallel. See also Sarah Annes Brown, 'Ovid and Marvell's *The Nymph Complaining for the Death of her Faun*', *Translation and Literature*, 6 (1997), 167–85.

[124] In addition to the thematic parallel, two details suggest that this fable contributed to Marvell's poem. The nymph's fawn has a 'silver Chain and Bell' (l. 28), and Cyparissus' stag has a silver boss (*bulla argentea*) on its forehead (l. 114), tr. by Sandys as a 'silver bell' (340; noted by Abraham). Secondly, the curious allusion in l. 99 to the 'brotherless *Heliades*' could have been suggested to Marvell by Ovid's reference to the Heliades in the passage preceding the story of Cyparissus (l. 91).

woman could be; moreover, Eden was only truly paradisal before the creation of Eve:

> Two Paradises 'twere in one
> To live in Paradise alone.[125]

This pose of suave misogyny and masculine self-sufficiency does not necessarily imply any positive homoerotic interests, but there are some lines whose sexual implications seem to have been overlooked:

> *Apollo* hunted *Daphne* so,
> Only that She might Laurel grow.
> And *Pan* did after *Syrinx* speed,
> Not as a Nymph, but for a Reed.[126]

These lines are usually taken to be a version of the earlier conceit about carving women's names on trees: the gods did not pursue Daphne or Syrinx because they wanted them as women, but because they wanted them as plants. But what these women actually turn into are symbols of masculinity: the laurel of Apollo and the phallic reed of Pan.[127] This is not to deny that the overt purpose of the lines is the witty praise of trees and plants, but one ought to register that Marvell's choice of examples and phrasing has metamorphosed the gods' objects of desire from feminine into masculine.

In the lyrics discussed so far, occasional homoerotic motifs have complicated the poems' apparent presentation of heterosexual desire. But in the case of 'Damon the Mower' there is so much material which Marvell has taken from a classic poem of homosexual love that one needs to reconsider the ostensible subject-matter of his poem. The editors of the Oxford edition of Marvell have noted that 'Damon the Mower' has echoes of Virgil's *Eclogue* 2, but without exploring the implications of this. *Eclogue* 2 is the poem in which Corydon expresses his unrequited love for Alexis, and it had become a *locus classicus* of homosexual love in the Renaissance.[128] It is also a

---

[125] 'The Garden', ll. 63–4.
[126] Ibid., ll. 29–32.
[127] For Pan's pipe being used as a phallic symbol cf. 'Clorinda and Damon', l. 23, where Pan causes Damon's 'slender Oate' to swell. In Barnfield's *The Affectionate Shepheard* Daphnis promises Ganymede that 'To Pans owne Pipe Ile helpe my lovely Lad, | (Pans golden Pype) which he of Syrinx had' (ll. 143–4). See also n. 56 above. For the masculinity of Apollo's laurel see the discussion of bays on p. 189 above, and for the possible homosexual implications of references to Apollo see the discussion of *Last Instructions* on p. 211 above.   [128] Smith, 80–1, 89–92.

poem which was thought in antiquity to have an autobiographical element, so Marvell could have found his own homosexual desires reflected in Virgil's, and written his poem as a conscious reflection on Virgil's text.[129] 'Damon the Mower' relates how Damon[130] is overcome by his love for Juliana. Details which occur in both Virgil's poem and Marvell's are that the weather is unbearably hot; the lover proposes to bring various rustic gifts to his loved one; he boasts of his rural wealth; and he denies that he is ugly.[131] There is a further parallel between Marvell's green frog and grasshoppers and Virgil's green lizards and cicada.[132] But what needs to be stressed is that to provide himself with suitable material for this poem about the devastating power of sexual desire, Marvell turned to one of the few great poems of homosexual passion, instead of one of the myriad poems of heterosexual passion. Nor is this the only homosexual trace in 'Damon the Mower'. The 'gelid Fountain' is a literal translation (only transposed into the singular) of Virgil's *gellidi fontes*, a phrase which occurs in *Eclogue* 10.[133] In that poem Virgil is writing about his beloved Gallus, and Gallus' unrequited love for the girl Lychoris, and so a structural parallel suggests itself between Virgil/Gallus/Lychoris and Marvell/Damon/Juliana.[134]

Besides these intertextual references there are also other homoerotic touches. 'The Sun himself licks off my Sweat', says Damon,[135] and the personification, together with the explicit reminder in 'himself' that the sun is traditionally male, makes this a homoerotic gesture. Later Damon uses his scythe as a mirror.[136] This is a Narcissistic moment in

[129] Virgil's homosexual interests were noted in antiquity by Donatus, Servius, and Martial: see *Vergil: Eclogues*, ed. Robert Coleman (Cambridge, 1977), 108–9.

[130] The name 'Damon' is found in Virgil's *Eclogues* 3 and 8, but may have appealed to Marvell because of the celebrated classical friends Damon and Pythias.

[131] For heat, cf. *Eclogue* 2. 8–9, 12–13; gifts, 36–51; wealth, 20–2; ugliness 25–7; these parallels are noted in the Oxford edn.

[132] 'Damon the Mower', ll. 13–14; cf. *virides lacertos* and *cicadis* (*Eclogue* 2. 9, 13). The importance of *Eclogue* 2 as a pre-text for Marvell is not confined to this poem: one of the characters in *Eclogue* 2 is Thestylis, who occurs in 'Upon Appleton House' (l. 401) when she brings refreshments to the mowers, and again in 'Ametas and Thestylis'. There is another possible echo of *Eclogue* 2 in 'The Mower against Gardens', where the line 'The Gods themselves with us do dwell' (l. 40) may be an echo of *habitarunt di quoque siluas* and *nobis placeant ante omnia siluae* (ll. 60, 62).

[133] 'Damon the Mower', l. 28; *Eclogue* 10. 42.

[134] For Virgil's love for Gallus see *Vergil: Eclogues*, ed. Coleman, 294, 297.

[135] 'Damon the Mower', l. 46.

[136] Ibid., l. 58.

which Damon gazes at his own reflection, but it also has a homoerotic overtone since the scythe was a phallic symbol.[137] There is an echo here of the poem on Villiers. When Damon is mown by his own scythe, the accident could be seen as the consequence of an autoerotic or homo-erotic passion—and as an act of castration. But what of Juliana, who ostensibly inspired Damon's desire? Empson, who thinks that Marvell fell in love with the mower at Appleton House, comments: 'Damon keeps saying he is in despair for love of a woman, and this allows love to be talked about, but he would not have accepted the situation so passively. It is the poet who is in love with Damon; Freud calls the device "displacement", when interpreting dreams.'[138] Putting aside the biographical speculation, Empson is surely right that some form of displacement is at work here. Juliana may be no more than a name suggested by Herrick's Julia, or by the month of July (which was named after the homosexual Julius Caesar), and thus an elegant way of permitting Marvell to write about the 'unusual Heats' (l. 9) of homo-sexual desire. The poem does not necessarily need an object of desire in the world outside the text.

But, rather surprisingly, the poem in which Marvell's imagination turned aside most insistently to seek help from homoerotic pre-texts was 'To his Coy Mistress'. The pre-text which lies behind this poem is, once again, the passage from the *Metamorphoses* recounting the story of Narcissus and Echo. It has been suggested that certain phrases in Marvell's poem were influenced by Sandys's translation of this episode,[139] but Arthur Golding's translation is another possible source.[140] Several striking verbal echoes, stronger than those from Sandys, suggest that Marvell had been reading this version of the story attentively when composing 'To his Coy Mistress'. First, in Golding's translation we find the phrases 'morning dew' and 'lively hue' in close proximity.[141] Other words which might have caught Marvell's

---

[137] Cf. *falcem* in 'Upon an Eunuch; a Poet', l. 2, which could be translated as knife, sickle, or scythe. For the sexual implications of sickles see Williams, *s.v.*

[138] Empson, *Using Biography*, 15.

[139] Robert H. Ray, 'Marvell's "To his Coy Mistress" and Sandys's Translation of Ovid's *Metamorphoses*', *Review of English Studies*, 44 (1993), 386–8.

[140] *Shakespeare's Ovid, Being Arthur Golding's Translation of the Metamorphoses*, ed. W. H. D. Rouse (London, 1904), 72–5.

[141] Ovid, tr. Golding, ll. 614, 617; cf. 'To his Coy Mistress', ll. 33–4. There is, however, a notorious crux at this point in Marvell's poem: see Paul Hammond, 'Marvell's Coy Mistresses', in Maureen Bell *et al.* (eds.), *Re-constructing the Book: Literary Texts in Transmission* (Aldershot, n.d. [2001]), 22–33, at 28–30.

attention in Golding's passage include 'marble',[142] 'gazing',[143] 'embrace' as a rhyme word,[144] the rhyme of 'rest' and 'brest',[145] and of 'sound' and 'found'.[146] The fate of the coy mistress, reduced to a body in a vault, could have been suggested by the fate of Echo, whose 'body pines to skin and bone'.[147] Cumulatively these verbal echoes point to Golding's translation as a source for this poem.

But as a classically trained poet, Marvell would hardly have been content with translations, and the Latin text, together with the commentary found in Renaissance editions, also lodged in his memory.[148] Details which might have contributed to Marvell's poem include Ovid's *marmore*,[149] *amor crescit*,[150] and *non tamen invenio*[151] which, aided by the repetition of *inveniunt*,[152] may have suggested the unusual verb in 'Thy Beauty shall no more be found'.[153] The lines which compare the mistress's 'youthful glew' to 'morning dew' may have taken a hint from Ovid's account of the delicate glow on Narcissus' bare chest as he pines away with love, just as hoar frost melts away.[154] Some phrases from the editorial commentaries may have played their part too: *scelestam* suggesting 'crime',[155] *quandocunque igitur* suggesting 'Now therefore',[156] *currum* suggesting 'Charriot',[157] *vastae . . . tenebrae* and *aeternam . . . noctem* suggesting 'vast Eternity'.[158]

---

[142] Golding, l. 523; cf. 'marble Vault' in Marvell, l. 26.

[143] Golding, l. 524; cf. 'gaze' in Marvell, l. 14.

[144] Golding, l. 523; cf. 'embrace' as an emphatic rhyme word in Marvell, l. 32.

[145] Golding, ll. 548–9; cf. the same rhyme in Marvell, ll. 15–16.

[146] Golding, ll. 637–8; cf. the same rhyme in Marvell, ll. 25–6.

[147] Golding, l. 494.

[148] Quotations from Ovid and his commentators are taken from the edn. by Cnipping cited in n. 83.

[149] 'Marble': Ovid, l. 419; cf. Marvell's 'marble Vault', l. 26.

[150] 'Love grows': Ovid, l. 395; cf. Marvell's 'Love should grow', l. 11.

[151] 'However I do not find': Ovid, l. 447.   [152] 'They find': Ovid, l. 510.

[153] 'To his Coy Mistress', l. 25.

[154] Ibid., ll. 33–4 (emending the 1681 folio text from Bodl. MS Eng. poet. d. 49); Ovid, ll. 481–9. For the textual crux see n. 141 above.

[155] 'Criminal', Ovid, l. 463 n.; Marvell, l. 2.

[156] 'Whenever therefore', Ovid, l. 503 n.; Marvell, l. 33.

[157] 'Chariot', Ovid, l. 504 n.; Marvell, l. 22.

[158] 'Vast darknesses' and 'eternal night', both together in Ovid, l. 503 n.; Marvell, l. 24. Perhaps Marvell's attention was also caught by Ovid's repeated use of the Latin for 'marvel' (*miratur . . . mirabilis . . . mirantia*; ll. 424, 503). The commentators also refer three times to Terence's play called the *Eunuch* (ll. 395 n., 447 n., 463 n.). This is not the only passage from Ovid which contributed to this poem, for Marvell's lines 'Rather at once our Time devour, | Than languish in his slow-chapt pow'r' (ll. 39–40) echo the

Some of these parallels are stronger than others, and some may be thought insignificant coincidences, but there are sufficient traces of the Narcissus story in Marvell's text to suggest that when he composed this poem about desire for a woman, Marvell's imagination was dwelling on other forms of desire. Moreover, there is a homosocial pre-text for this poem in a poem by John Hall. Here is Marvell's concluding invitation to the mistress:

> Let us roll all our Strength, and all
> Our sweetness, up into one Ball:
> And tear our Pleasures with rough strife,
> Thorough the Iron gates of Life.
> Thus, though we cannot make our Sun
> Stand still, yet we will make him run.[159]

And here are lines from John Hall's poem, 'To his Tutor, Master Pawson. An Ode':

> Come, let us run
> And give the world a girdle with the sun;
> For so we shall
> Take a full view of this enamelled ball . . .
>
> O let us tear
> A passage through
> That fleeting vault above;[160]

It is remarkable that the very lines in which Marvell is imagining vigorous intercourse with a woman should carry echoes of a poem— addressed by one man to another—which evokes ecstatic intellectual and social pleasure between men. There are different ways in which we

---

celebrated apostrophe to Time in *Metamorphoses*, 15. 234–6, which Sandys translates thus: 'Still-eating Time, and thou ô envious Age, | All ruinate: diminisht by the rage | Of your devouring teeth, All that have breath | Consume, and languish by a lingring death' (496). With 'devouring' (and 'devoures' shortly before these lines) and 'languish', Sandys is Marvell's source here rather than Golding, who translates: 'Thou tyme, the eater up of things, and age of spyghtfull teene, | Destroy all things. And when that long continuance hath them bit, | You leysurely by lingring death consume them every whit' (300).

[159] 'To his Coy Mistress', ll. 41–6.

[160] John Hall, 'To his Tutor, Master Pawson. An Ode', ll. 13–16, 50–2, in *Minor Poets of the Caroline Period*, ed. George Saintsbury, 3 vols. (Oxford, 1905–21), ii. 208–9. The parallel is noted by Nigel Smith, ' "Courtesie is fatal": The Civil and Visionary Poetics of Andrew Marvell', *Proceedings of the British Academy*, 101 (1999), 173–89.

might read this intertextual connection. At one level it illustrates the degree to which the languages of love and friendship overlap in this period, making it possible for a man to write to a male friend in passionate language without sexual suggestiveness. It also reminds us how Marvell's contemporaries were often ravished with excitement as they contemplated the expansion of their knowledge of the natural world. But at the level of the workings of Marvell's imagination, if we are tracing his characteristic habits of thought and the kinds of connections which he repeatedly made between texts, it unsettles the ostensibly confident, bravura conclusion to this poem of heterosexual seduction. Why, at the very climax of his poem to the coy mistress, did Marvell's imagination turn aside to the well-known, secure excitements of the all-male world?

There are further echoes from other texts which raise questions about the process of composition. The Oxford editors note a precedent for this poem in verses by Thomas Randolph called 'A Complaint against Cupid that he never made him in love!'. Is it significant that a poem with this title came into his mind when composing 'To his Coy Mistress'? Cowley's poem 'My Diet' also contributed hints, as, perhaps, did lines by Francis Wyrley.[161] Perhaps Marvell had also been studying his Herrick. If he had turned to Herrick's poem 'To the Virgins, to make much of Time', he might have noted some useful ideas: the *carpe diem* motif, the allusion to virginity, the idea of time flying, the rhyme of 'sun' and 'run', the word 'coy', and the phrase 'while we may'. Leafing on through his copy of Herrick, Marvell might have noted the comparison of Julia's nipples with rubies ('Upon the Nipples of *Julia*'s Breast'), and decided that, although he was not capable of writing convincingly about a woman's nipples, he could find a use for rubies.[162] Perhaps even Herrick's innuendo 'the rest' in the same poem suggested Marvell's identical euphemism and rhyme.

---

[161] The use of Cowley is noted by the Oxford editors. For Wyrley's poem see Arthur F. Marotti, *Manuscript, Print, and the English Renaissance Lyric* (Ithaca, NY, 1995), 81. Professor Marotti suggests only a 'stylistic resemblance' between the two poems, but I would propose that the reference to worms in both is so similar that either Wyrley's lines are a source for Marvell's poem, or they share a common ancestry as yet undiscovered; in any case, the parallel suggests that Marvell's startling conceit is not original. Marotti was working from a MS in which the poem was anonymous; the attribution to Wyrley is made by Jeremy Maule, 'A New Poem by John Ford', *English Manuscript Studies 1100–1700*, 8 (2000), 137–59, at 150, but without citing Marotti. Wyrley's poem probably dates from before the late 1630s (Maule's date for the transcription of the MS).

[162] 'To his Coy Mistress', l. 6.

The suspicion that Marvell turned for help to a clutch of heterosexual love poems because his imagination was more deeply engaged elsewhere can only be speculation, but if we compare Donne's excited blazon of the woman in 'To his Mistress Going to Bed', or Herrick's sensual delight in Julia's nipples, with Marvell's attempt to blazon the attractions of the coy mistress, there does seem to be in Marvell's poem a lack of passionate and focused sensuality.

It might be appropriate to think of this as essentially a homosocial poem, an exercise which Marvell wrote to impress a male audience, possibly in an attempt to demonstrate his heterosexual credentials— or even as an ironic piece of self-mockery for an audience which knew how unlikely this scenario was in Marvell's case. It relies heavily on other poems; it is set out as a logical argument whose structure would appeal to an educated audience; and its style invites declamation in front of a company. J. B. Leishman called attention to the poem's 'essentially dramatic tone ... the way it makes us feel that we are overhearing one of the speakers in a dialogue',[163] but what we overhear is surely not one lover speaking to another, but a wit performing in front of an audience who are connoisseurs of such poetry. The poem is aimed at a male readership, in spite of being formally addressed to this (nameless) woman, since it hardly has the tone and rhetoric appropriate to courtship. There is evidence that 'To his Coy Mistress' was known in court circles around 1672, for that is when it was copied by Sir William Haward into his manuscript anthology, where it keeps company with poems by Rochester and Dryden.[164] The year 1672 is exactly the time at which Marvell's heterosexual masculinity was being questioned in the satirical pamphlets. Moreover, in Haward's manuscript it has been given a more blatantly raunchy tone:

> Two hundred to adore your eyes,
> But thirty thousand to your Thighes.

And in the manuscript line 'Your beauty will stand need of salt' we hear the coarse tone of the coffee-house wits. Whoever was responsible for the readings in this manuscript text, it seems likely that 'To his Coy Mistress' was being made more salacious in order to suit the fashionable masculine taste of the 1670s.

---

[163] Leishman, *Art of Marvell's Poetry*, 70.

[164] Now Bodl. MS Don. b. 8. For a facsimile of the text of Marvell's poem, and a brief discussion, see Hilton Kelliher, *Andrew Marvell: Poet and Politician* (London, 1978), 53; and for a discussion of the two texts see Hammond, 'Marvell's Coy Mistresses'.

To return to the implications of the intertextual relationship between this poem and the story of Echo and Narcissus, the story which one might even call Marvell's private myth: in this 'ecchoing Song' Marvell is casting himself as Echo in pursuit of Narcissus, the poet in pursuit of the unresponsive and unattainable boy. One implication of this is that Marvell could only write about courting a woman if he imagined himself courting a boy. Another is that Marvell thought of his own song as 'ecchoing', not simply in the sense that it reverberates in the vault, but because, like Echo's cries, it can only imitate the fragments of other men's speech. Marvell's song, and this poem in particular, echoes intertextually, and the pre-texts which it echoes are frequently homoerotic.

This chapter has described how Marvell's opponents called him effeminate, impotent, and a sodomite, and how his own poetry repeatedly figures unrequited homoerotic desire and the self-sufficient, even self-loving, observer. Perhaps the pamphlets reflect in a grotesquely distorting mirror that sensibility which was given finer form in the poems; and whereas the satires on Marvell present a threateningly paradoxical and illegible amphibian, his own poetry is living out ambiguities, and thinking through the strangenesses of self-understanding. Like Shakespeare, Marvell may have found that his sexuality (or at least the sexuality and emotional sensibilities which he wished to explore poetically) prevented him from locating himself easily in traditional narratives of desire, and set him at a tangent to contemporary idioms. He is typically an observer. He writes a poetry not of relationship but of self-relationship. His verse is enamoured of masculine prowess—admired in Villiers, in Douglas, in the heroic nude Unfortunate Lover, in the Mower with his scythe, even Cromwell with his erect sword—but is also fascinated particularly by liminal states: innocence caught at play just before the fires of sexual desire begin to make themselves felt; mature manhood dying when still virginal; the male whose beauty invites us to read him as a female; the forward youth just before he decides whether the time has come to leave his books; the amphibian poised between two worlds. Marvell's characters are still unravished, whether by Time or anyone else.

The spaces which Marvell's poetry creates are singularities, places of solitude and self-reflection. And yet his textual spaces echo with other men's voices. Virgil's second *Eclogue* and Ovid's tale of Narcissus insinuate themselves into those poems where Marvell says that he is writing about heterosexual love. These poems acknowledge that homoerotic desire cannot at this period inhabit a coherent textual space—even one as contrived as Barnfield's or as dislocated as Shakespeare's. Because his poems have teasing gaps, ambiguities of gender, and suggestive traces of classic homosexual texts, their textual fabric allows the reader to enter this imagined world and adjust it. Marvell wrote that the mind is

> that ocean where each kind
> Does streight its own resemblance find;[165]

and the same might be said of his poetry, in which readers may find their own resemblance. Critics who have seen the poems as uniformly heterosexual have simplified them to suit their own interests; but the poems' complexities invite us to imagine a more complex sexuality, and to recognize the fashioning of textual spaces in which homosexual desire can find its own resemblance, albeit only intermittently.

What 'kind' was Marvell? His enemies might laugh at him as an amphibian, but it is precisely its amphibious quality which gives his poetry its exceptional power. The poems seem to exist in some liminal state themselves, always on the edge of turning into something else, the tone elusive, the text teasingly suggesting subtexts and remaking pre-texts, fashioning worlds which we almost recognize but whose intensity we cannot quite account for, and whose boundaries and conjunctions we cannot quite trace. And crucial to this was Marvell's sexuality, for whatever may, or may not, have happened in his own private life, he took English poetry into new territory by finding a language for the ambiguities of sexuality—including homoerotic desire, but including also the desire to be rid of desire and its complexities and to retreat to the green shade of impossible innocence. That amphibious understanding was the real marvel.

[165] 'The Garden', ll. 43–4.

5

Rochester and Restoration Homoeroticism

Restoration literature brought sex into the public domain with unprecedented freedom. Manuscript satires on the King, on courtiers and their ladies, and on writers and actors, often made explicit remarks about their sexual behaviour and their sexual bodies. In the public theatre, comedy presented both men and women in the pursuit of sex, as a game but also as a way of asserting their autonomy, their capacity to make adult decisions about how to use their own bodies. The world in which this takes place is recognizably Restoration London, albeit a city whose geography has been transformed. In *The Country Wife* Mrs Pinchwife soon learns from her sister where to find men—Mulberry Garden, St James's Park, the Exchange, and above all, the playhouse.[1] But in the reign of Charles II there is as yet no sense that men who enjoy sex with other men can be placed on this map as a group, as what we would now call a subculture with its own haunts, styles, and idioms. This, with the development of the molly houses, would come in the late 1690s and early 1700s.[2] Instead, in the reign of Charles II the figuring of sex between men can be seen principally in two areas: first on the stage, chiefly between men and boys rather than two adults, and mostly in cases of mistaken identity;[3] secondly as an aspect of

---

[1] William Wycherley, *The Country Wife*, 2. 1. 1–54.

[2] See Rictor Norton, *Mother Clap's Molly House: The Gay Subculture in England 1700–1830* (London, 1992). However, in 'Another Epilogue' to Dryden's *The Duke of Guise* (written summer 1682), sex between men is described as 'a damn'd Love-trick new brought o'er from *France*' for which men 'club for Love' (Dryden, *Works*, xiv. 214–15), the latter phrase suggesting recognized meeting places.

[3] For a thorough survey of homosexual desire in Restoration drama see John

libertine culture, a role or pose which typifies an excess of debauchery (as in the play *Sodom*).[4]

When Charles II allowed actresses to take female roles in place of boy players, one of the principal sources of homoerotic pleasure was removed from the theatre.[5] The King's patent recognized that some had taken offence at the playing of women's roles by men in the pre-war theatres,[6] but of course the new arrangements merely permitted a different form of sexual opportunity. One theatrical epilogue reminded the audience of what used to happen in an earlier generation:

> When boys play'd women's parts, you'd think the Stage,
> Was innocent in that untempting Age.
> No: for your amorous Fathers then, like you,
> Amongst those Boys had Play-house Misses too:
> They set those bearded Beauties on their laps,
> Men gave 'em Kisses, and the Ladies Claps.[7]

Franceschina, *Homosexualities in the English Theatre: From Lyly to Wilde* (Westport, Conn., 1997), 111–66.

[4] There is also the question of the sexuality of beaux or fops, and the connection between beaux and mollies, for which see Susan Staves, 'A Few Kind Words for the Fop', *Studies in English Literature 1500–1900*, 22 (1982) 413–28, and Laurence Senelick, 'Mollies or Men of Mode?', *Journal of the History of Sexuality*, 1 (1990), 33–67. Furthermore, a number of Lee's plays, mainly set in classical or Renaissance Europe, explore versions of masculinity in ways which sometimes distinguish passionate friendship from (*a*) sexual interest in men or boys and (*b*) 'effeminate' devotion to women: e.g. *The Tragedy of Nero* (1675); *The Massacre of Paris* (written *c.*1679, printed 1690), esp. Anjou; *Theodosius* (1680), for the friendship of Theodosius and Varanes; *Caesar Borgia* (1680), for the Cardinal and Ascanio; *The Princess of Cleve* (staged 1680, printed 1689) for Nemours and his eunuch; *Lucius Junius Brutus* (1681), figuring civic masculinity through frequent uses of the male body.

[5] See Elizabeth Howe, *The First English Actresses: Women and Drama 1660–1700* (Cambridge, 1992), 19–26. However, Howe is mistaken in saying that the King 'decreed that henceforth women should play women's parts' and her edited quotation from the royal patent wrongly makes Charles 'strictly command and enjoin' this (25). In fact, the full text of the patent clearly states: 'we do likewise <u>permit</u> and <u>give leave</u> that all the women's parts to be acted in either of the said two companies for the time to come <u>may</u> be performed by women': the patent is permissive, not compulsive (quoted from David Thomas and Arnold Hare, *Restoration and Georgian England, 1660–1788*, Theatre in Europe: A Documentary History (Cambridge, 1989), 18; emphasis added).

[6] Ibid., 17.

[7] Epilogue to Thomas Killigrew's *The Parson's Wedding* (1672?), in *The Prologues and Epilogues of the Restoration 1660–1700*, ed. Pierre Danchin, 7 vols. (Nancy, 1981–8), ii. 498.

In another epilogue, this attraction of men to boy players is seen as un-English; the actress speaking the lines resents criticism of the women who have given Restoration playgoers so much pleasure, and reminds these ungrateful patrons:

> Did not the Boys Act Women's Parts Last Age?
> Till We in pitty to the Barren Stage
> Came to Reform your Eyes that went astray,
> And taught you Passion the true *English* Way.[8]

But if boy actors were no longer available as objects of homosexual pleasure,[9] some of the adult male actors acquired a reputation for having sex with men.[10] The following lines on the comedian James Nokes would not number amongst the more sophisticated satires of the period:

> You smooth facd lads secure your gentle bums
> For full of lust and fury see he comes
> Tis Buggering Nokes whose damnd unweildy Tarse
> Weeps to be buried in his foremans Arse.
> Unnaturall sinner letcher without sence
> To leave kind C—t to dive in excrements.[11]

Nokes began his acting career in 1659 playing young female roles during the brief revival of the Renaissance tradition of boy actors before the arrival of actresses, and later on he would play elderly women, 'nurse' roles for which his comic talents specially suited him.[12] Whether the satire (if it merits that term) is a biographical comment or

---

[8] Epilogue to Elkanah Settle's *The Conquest of China* (1675), ibid., 665–6.

[9] However, an epilogue to a school performance of Samuel Shaw's *Poikilophronesis* (1692) ends: 'the Eagle that carries away the Child is our best Emblem, she will mount all the pretty Lads into the Skies upon the Wings of Fame, and so every Boy shall be a *Ganymedes*. And I assure you to be a Butler to *Jupiter* is no small preferment' (ibid., v. 45–6).

[10] See Kristina Straub, 'Actors and Homophobia', in J. Douglas Canfield and Deborah C. Payne (eds.), *Cultural Readings of Restoration and Eighteenth-century English Theatre* (Athens, Ga., 1995), 258–80. For homosexual allegations about the actor William Mountfort see the verses quoted in *POAS* iv. 72.

[11] 'Satyr on the Players', Bodl. MS Rawl. poet. 159, fol. 121ᵛ; dated 1683. Another text in BL MS Harley 7319 fol. 145ʳ calls them 'smock fac'd Lads', with which cf. the quotation from Mountfort below, p. 229 ('smock' = women's underwear (*OED* 1)).

[12] For biographical details of Nokes and other actors see Philip H. Highfill *et al.*, *A Biographical Dictionary of Actors . . . in London, 1660–1800*, 16 vols. (Carbondale, Ill., 1973–93), *s.vv.*

an extrapolation from his stage roles is at this distance impossible to say.

But it is clear that some actors specialized in roles for which the playwrights created occasional homoerotic possibilities.[13] Anthony Leigh played some characters who manifest homosexual interests:[14] as Sir Jolly Jumble in Thomas Otway's *The Souldiers Fortune* (1681),[15] as a Catholic priest in Nathaniel Lee's *Caesar Borgia* (1680),[16] as the Abbé in Thomas Southerne's *Sir Anthony Love* (1691), and as Sir Thomas in William Mountfort's *Greenwich-Park* (1691), who greets a boy with: 'Why, How now, you little Smock-fac'd Dog, a pretty Boy faith; Sirrah, Sirrah, if you were in *Italy*—.'[17] In Thomas Durfey's *The Marriage-Hater Match'd* (1692), Leigh as Van Grin kisses Sir Philip, saying that he reminds him of a Dutch prostitute of his acquaintance.[18] The expression of sexual interest in a boy is generally licensed by the boy's role being played by a woman, so that the audience is not presented with the spectacle of two male actors kissing or caressing, and the older man's interest in the younger can be explained by him being unconsciously attracted to the boy's feminine qualities. This happens in Durfey's *The Royalist* (1682), when Sir Charles Kinglove is being followed by Philipa dressed as a boy. Attracted to the youth, Sir Charles calls him 'my little *Ganymed*', and his friend Heartall suspects that the attraction is explicable by the boy actually being Sir Charles's illegitimate son: 'I fancy he's like you.—He looks as if he were begot in the Riot of Appetite. The Youth may come to preferment in time; for to my knowledg there's many a *Noble Peer* in this Country would give 100 Guineys for such a Page.'[19] Sir Charles duly takes the boy as his servant, explaining that he is struck by his likeness to a lady he once loved. But when Sir Charles and the page prepare to share a bed, and Philipa as the page is reluctant to undress, Sir Charles exclaims:

Leave blushing ye shamefac'd Fool, and let me embrace thee: Gad I shall fancy thee some fine Woman or other, and have a pleasant time on't.

---

[13] I am indebted here to correspondence from Professor Derek Hughes. For a further example, see n. 80 below.

[14] One satire recorded Leigh himself as 'Fooling with the Boys' (Highfill, *Biographical Dictionary, s.v.*).

[15] See *LBM* 101–2.

[16] Nathaniel Lee, *Caesar Borgia*, 1. 1. 38–41.

[17] William Mountfort, *Greenwich-Park* (London, 1691), 56.

[18] Thomas Durfey, *The Marriage-Hater Match'd* (London, 1692), 22.

[19] Thomas Durfey, *The Royalist* (London, 1682), 5.

> The Drowsie God will heighten my Delight,
> In pleasing Fancies I shall waste the Night:
> Think tho' a Youth, thou hast soft Female Charms,
> And dream I have my Mistress in my Arms.[20]

Here the Act ends, and the curtain falls. Sir Charles's explanation is that he desires the boy as a substitute for his lost mistress, and the audience knows that the boy is really a girl; yet the prospect which is entertained here is that Sir Charles will enjoy sex with the lad, even if the latter is being valued for his feminine qualities.[21]

In these plays, male interest in a youth is often framed by some displacement to a foreign setting, or explained as being a misapprehension about the beloved's true gender. But in other texts it is seen as—or, indeed, flaunted as—a libertine trait. On 1 July 1663 Pepys recorded an exploit by Sir Charles Sedley:

after dinner we fell in talking, Sir J. Mennes and Mr. Batten and I—Mr. Batten telling us of a late triall of Sir Charles Sydly the other day, before my Lord Chief Justice Foster and the whole Bench—for his debauchery a little while since at Oxford Kates; coming in open day into the Balcone and showed his nakedness—acting all the postures of lust and buggery that could be imagined, and abusing of scripture and, as it were, from thence preaching a Mountebanke sermon from that pulpitt, saying that there he hath to sell such a pouder as should make all the cunts in town run after him—a thousand people standing underneath to see and hear him . . .

Upon this discourse, Sir J. Mennes and Mr. Batten both say that buggery is now almost grown as common among our gallants as in Italy, and that the very pages of the town begin to complain of their masters for it. But blessed be God, I do not to this day know what is the meaning of this sin, nor which is the agent nor which the patient.[22]

'Buggery' is common, apparently, amongst 'our gallants' like Sedley—not gentlemen like Pepys and his friends, who may not even know quite what the word means—and it is a quintessentially Italian habit. Here we see the staging of a libertine role by Sedley, a self-conscious performance in which 'buggery' is little more than

---

[20] Thomas Durfey, *The Royalist*, 20.

[21] Another example of a travesty role being used to facilitate a homoerotic encounter is in Aphra Behn's *The Amorous Prince* (1671), set in the court of Florence, where Lorenzo attempts to seduce Cloris who is dressed as Phillibert (4. 2. 82–8, 5. 1. 97–154).

[22] *The Diary of Samuel Pepys*, ed. Robert Latham and William Matthews, 11 vols. (London, 1970–83), iv. 209–10.

a side-show, an addendum to the rake's repertoire of outrageous poses.

One anonymous song which begins by voicing a preference for boys over women, celebrates Sedley's achievements in this field:

> *Dear* friends you know I keep two pages
> More for my pleasure than my pride
>
> .   .   .   .
>
> *Some* formal fops are apt to censure
> This my plain & honest design
>
> .   .   .   .
>
> But I'm resolved to use good Nature
> And Bugger every living creature.
>
> *Sidley* has fuck't a thousand Arses
> And so has Vaughan as well as he.[23]

But the 'I' of this poem, as well as being anonymous, is striking a pose, in that the song replies to another poem in which a woman says, '*Dear* Friends you know I keep two Chairmen', which is her response to the inadequacy of husbands.[24] The second song makes an asymmetrical reply, since the crude misogyny of some of its lines does not match any comparable misandry in the first song, which simply rehearses the common Restoration topos of the sexual boredom of marriage.

Another anonymous poem, the 'Mock Song', strikes much the same attitude, and similarly disparages women in the course of celebrating an alternative:

> Methinks my poor P—ck has been troubled to[o] long
> With *Phillis's* Cunt and my mouth with her tongue
> At once sheel dispise it and ask againe for it
> And never leve calling it limber and short
> Which justly provok's one from C—t to divorce
> And in Rymes sing the praise of *Corridon*['s] arse
> This boy is soe fair, and charming heed make
> A *Jove* both his sky, and *Gannimede* forsake
> He has *Buchurst*['s] red lips and *Rochesters* eye
> *Harry Sidneys* fine shape, and his Mistresses thigh

---

[23] '*A Song*, the second', BL MS Harley 7317, fols. 69ᵛ–70ʳ.

[24] '*A Song. The First*', BL MS Harley 7317, fols. 69ʳ⁻ᵛ. A chairman is the porter of a sedan chair, strong and sexually satisfying according to several Restoration poems: Rochester's Duchess of Cleveland says, 'I had rather be fuckt by *Porters*, and *Car-men*' (*The Works of John Wilmot Earl of Rochester*, ed. Harold Love (Oxford, 1999), 90).

> His buttocks are hard I no farther dare peep
> But I know what I think, when I spend in my sleep.[25]

This is perhaps the most explicit Restoration acknowledgement of the sexual pleasure provided by a young male body, and while the youth is given a pastoral name, there is no other attempt to veil desire in classical dress. Indeed, where other texts assume that what is attractive about a boy is his femininity—as seen in the homosexual approaches made to actresses in travesty roles, or in the description of youths as 'smock faced'—here the writer explicitly reads Corydon's body as an amalgam of attractive features in adult male rakes, Rochester, Sidney, and Buckhurst.

But, like the previous poem, this too is a rejoinder, in this case a reply to a song written by Buckhurst himself:

> Methinks the Poor Town has been troubled too long
> With *Phillis* and *Cloris* in every Song;
> By fools, who at once can both love and despair,
> And will never leave calling them cruel and fair;
> Which justly provokes me, in Rhime, to express
> The truth that I know of bonny *Black Bess.*
>
> This *Bess* of my Heart, this *Bess* of my Soul,
> Has a Skin white as milk, and Hair black as Cole;
> She's plump, yet with ease you may span round her waste,
> But her round swelling thighs can scarce be embraste:
> Her Belly is soft, not a word of the rest,
> But I know what I think when I drink to the Best.[26]

Buckhurst's song rejects pastoral convention in praise of the unconventional but real attractions of Betty; the 'Mock Song' in turn parodies Buckhurst's poem with a more radical departure from convention. It also moves away from the lyrical and almost decorous idiom of Buckhurst's song (which could be performed in mixed company) to an overtly libertine idiom which in the last line of the quotation plays against the coy phrasing inherited from Buckhurst in its reference to ejaculation. This is another performance, another posture.

On a similar theme is a poem by John Chatwin, and once again an element of role-play affects the expression of homosexual interests.

---

[25] 'Mock Song', Nottingham University Library MS Portland PwV 40, p. 155.
[26] Charles Sackville (Lord Buckhurst), Earl of Dorset, 'A Song', from *The Penguin Book of Restoration Verse*, ed. Harold Love, 2nd edn. (Harmondsworth, 1997), 121.

Chatwin experimented with different voices, writing 'A Satyr against Sobriety', followed by 'A Counter-Satyr to the Foregoing against Sobriety', and then 'A Counter-counter-Satyr to both the Foregoing', so it is hardly *in propria persona* that he expresses the following sentiments:

> The Sober Sot, whose greatest care
> Is to procure th' Opinion of his Wife,
> Spends all his dayes in Slavish fear,
> And makes a Burden of his Life.
>
> . . . .
>
> A Joviall Boy would break those hated chains,
> Would soon shake off the heavy yoke,
> Which has so long mens quiet broke,
> And bid adieu to all it's noisy pains;
> He'd scorn a Woman should an hind'rance prove,
> Or the least stop to an inviting joy,
> Nor would He contradict his Love,
> To please that weak inconstant Toy.[27]

The poem's attention seems to be on the rejection of the constraints of marriage, instead of the attractions of the rather hypothetical 'Joviall Boy': all the most emphatic language is directed against the 'hated chains' which make the husband's life a 'Burden', whereas the poem never brings the boy into focus. And in a different voice 'A Counter-counter-Satyr' redescribes the ideal of male relationships as pure and innocent companionship:

> Nothing more lasting Friendshipp can create,
> Than o're a kind Reviving Glass,
> To let pure inno'cent intercourses pass,
> And by those sweet Expressions tie
> Our Souls in Bonds of mutuall amity.[28]

The language here, the language of homosocial friendship, has a warmth which is missing from the lines in which the boy is supposed to provide ready pleasure as an alternative to a wife. Sexual interest in the boy seems rather gestural, part of a misogynist stance.

The assumption of homosexual interests among libertines is seen also in a number of satires on individuals. The 'Mock Song' continues by commenting on Lord Vaughan—the Vaughan who apparently

---

[27] John Chatwin, 'A Satyr against Sobriety', Bodl. MS Rawl. poet. 94, p. 38.
[28] Chatwin, 'A Counter-counter-Satyr to both the Foregoing', ibid., 43.

matched Sedley's exploits—that his 'long experiencd t-rs | Can work it self into any man's a-rs',[29] and this crude satire jars with that celebration of Corydon a few lines earlier, making the poem radically incoherent in its tone and attitude. Vaughan himself adopted a predictable libertine stance—amoral and irreligious—in a song attributed to him:

> There's no such thing as good or Evil,
> But that which do's please, or displease,
> There's no G-d, Heav'n, Hell, or a Devil,
> 'Tis all one to debauch, or to be Civil.[30]

Such an association of atheism and sodomy reappears in this account of the death of John Talbot in a duel at the hands of the Duke of Grafton:

> Duke parry's, & equips the Youngster through
> This deadly stroke ended the dreadfull Fight
> And now the Duke Bugger'd the *Sodomite*
> Such fatal Providence his hand did Rule
> He slew an Atheist to preserve a Fool.[31]

In another poem, the Earl of Rochester is said to have corrupted John Howe:

> How oft has *How* (by Rochester undone,
> Who sooth'd him first into Opinion
> Of being a Wit) been told that he was none?
> But found that Art the surest way to glide
> Not into's heart, but his well shap'd Backside:
> Not *Nobs*'s his Bum more adoration found,
> Tho' of't was sung, his was more white & Round.[32]

---

[29] 'Mock Song', MS Portland PwV 40, p. 156.

[30] Bodl. MS Firth c. 15, pp. 27–8. The spelling 'G-d' suggests that the copyist was uncomfortable about writing this thought.

[31] 'The Duel', dated 1685/6; BL MS Harley 7319, fol. 209ʳ; Crum W 255. For biographical details see *POAS* iv. 70 n., and for satirical comments on Talbot's sexuality see Dorset's 'A Faithful Catalogue of our most Eminent Ninnies' (ibid., 202). Talbot's brother, Charles, Earl of Shrewsbury, is referred to as 'that patient Bardash *Shrewsbury*' in 'Satyr. 1679', BL MS Harley 6913, fol. 61ʳ. Another homosexual rake whose death aroused interest was John Hoyle, friend and sometime lover of Aphra Behn. For Behn's poems on Hoyle see *LBM* 94–6; for satirical comments on Hoyle's sexuality see *POAS* iv. 213, v. 5; and for a letter supposedly written by Behn 'To Mr. *Hoyle, occasion'd by the Report of his too close Familiarity with young F—ws*, &c.' see *Familiar Letters of Love, Gallantry, And several Occasions*, 2 vols. (London, 1718), i. 38–9.

[32] 'Satyr On both Whigs and Toryes. 1683', Bodl. MS Firth c. 15, p. 146. 'Nobs' is

The syntax here is rather loose, but the lines appear to say that Rochester seduced Howe by flattering him about his abilities as a wit in order to make use of him sexually. Meanwhile, a woman writer, Jean Fox, in her verse letter 'Chloe to Sabina', takes over one of Rochester's literary voices in her imitation of his *Artemiza to Chloe* to complain that men are neglecting women in favour of boys:

> But to be thus by beardlesse foes undone
> Raw puny cocks whose spurs are not yet grown
> Sabina for my part for ever more
> I am resolv'd to shut up Eden door
> Where a strict guard still flameing in their eyes
> Shall stop mens passage to that Paradise.[33]

In these examples, whether voiced in the first person or presented as an observer's view of the libertine ethos, homosexual sex is basically exploitative or a substitute for sex with a woman; partners are reduced to sexual parts, and to bed one's page is a way of spiting women. More complex are the ways in which homosexual elements function in the work of the Earl of Rochester, where they exist in teasing relations with the authorial persona's dominantly heterosexual and homosocial interests. It is to his work that the remainder of this chapter is devoted.

ROCHESTER'S MALE RELATIONSHIPS

How is one to interpret those moments in Rochester's work when he turns aside from his concern with heterosexual desire and writes about erotic relations between men? Two uncertain boundary lines will feature in this discussion. The first is the familiar problem of the demarcation between the homosocial and the homoerotic. The second is a distinction between sex between two adult males on the one hand, and sex between a man and a boy on the other. Were these perceived as

---

presumably Nokes. For Howe see *The Surviving Works of Anne Wharton*, ed. G. Greer and S. Hastings (Stump Cross, 1997), 57–8. A satire attributed to Howe makes capital out of William III's interest in boys: see p. 180 above.

[33] 'Chloe to Sabina', ed. Gillian Manning from National Library of Ireland, Dublin, MS 2093 in *That Second Bottle: Essays on John Wilmot, Earl of Rochester*, ed. Nicholas Fisher (Manchester, 2000), 117–18. Jean Fox is unidentified. One song attributed to Rochester in some sources complains of the prevalence of sodomy, for few 'Dare put their Pricks in the Right Hole' (*Works*, ed. Love, 279), but this is entirely in the context of sex with women.

two separate phenomena, or as two aspects of the same desire; or were they perhaps not distinguished at all? When Rochester's poems evoke the sexual attractions of a 'boy' or a 'page', they never suggest his age, not even approximately. To some extent the words 'boy' and 'page' may be markers of social status and sexual role rather than of age. The present discussion will explore how sexual relations between men were presented in Rochester's writing, and how these texts were received and altered as they were circulated both in manuscript and in print. We should avoid trying to make these references coalesce centripetally into a coherent mode of subjectivity or a recognizable form of an individual's sexual desire; in the case of Rochester—more than with most writers—there is a strong centrifugal impulse, a desire to lose selfhood in a series of roles and masks and voices; to lose, particularly, that mode of coherent selfhood which is predicated upon narrative continuity. His poetry often disturbs such continuity through the fragmentation of experience into discrete moments which may be severed from any possible narrative by abrupt changes of argument or of register. We need to learn to read discontinuities which are formed locally, within texts, by unexpected fissures and contiguities, if we are to read the wider conceptual terrain which is formed around this subject.

Rochester's closest male friendship was with Henry Savile. In a letter dated 16 October 1677, Savile asks Rochester about a rumour concerning his latest escapade:

there has been such a story made concerning your last adventure as would perswade us grave men that you had stripd yourselfe of all your prudence as well as of your breeches which you will give a man leave to thinke impossible who knowes & admires your talents as much as I doe. After all if you have not caught cold and made yourselfe sick with your race, it is not one pinn matter for all the other circumstances of it though the same advantages have been taken of it heer that use to bee on any unseasonable pranke performed by your Lordship.[34]

As Savile notes, Rochester's behaviour has frequently been open to misconstruction, and an example of this is provided by Thomas Hearne's interpretation of this same episode: 'This Lord ... used sometimes with others of his companions to run naked, and particularly they did so once in Woodstocke park, upon a Sunday in the afternoon,

---

[34] *The Letters of John Wilmot Earl of Rochester*, ed. Jeremy Treglown (Oxford, 1980), 157.

expecting that several of the female sex would have been spectators, but not one appeared.'[35] Hearne interprets the episode as part of a habit ('used sometimes... to run naked'), as an act of sabbath-breaking, and as a form of exhibitionism which was designed to impress female spectators; but these women—who never appear in anyone's narrative—are merely part of Hearne's interpretation of Rochester's intentions. By supplying these absent women, Hearne makes this a story of homosocial play and heterosexually motivated display, which is certainly a comprehensible framework for the incident, but by no means the only possible reading.

Savile goes on to say:

without you the towne is soe dull that the Dutch men thinke themselves in Holland and goe Yawning about as if they were att home, for Gods sake come & helpe to entertain them for I am quite spent and can not hope to have my Spirits ever revived but by your Lordships Kindnesse and company of which I esteem one & love the other above all the happiness I have ever enjoyed.[36]

Should we hear a series of sexual innuendoes in 'entertain... spent... Spirits . . . revived', and in Savile's earlier reference to Rochester's 'talents'? If so, how are they directed—homosocially (sharing a self-deprecating joke with a male friend) or homosexually (making an erotic invitation to Rochester)? The problem of interpretation extends to the word 'Kindnesse', which had a wide semantic field from 'affectionate friendship' to 'sexual compliance'. What assumptions about likely behaviour between men, and what assumptions about epistolary idiom (at this date, and in this social circle) would we need to invoke in order to read this letter securely?[37]

[35] *Rochesteriana: Being Some Anecdotes Concerning John Wilmot Earl of Rochester*, ed. Johannes Prinz (Leipzig, 1926), 15.

[36] *Letters*, 157–8.

[37] When writing on 16 Jan. 1680 from Paris to his brother, George Savile, about the imminent arrival there of George's 18-year-old son, Henry Savile says: 'My nephew's coming over is the very best news I have heard since he went hence; his chamber shall be ready and clean sheets, with a promise to you that his priveledges in my house shall be only of that kind, and I will never force upon him any of those cruel enemys that come out of the cellar; but, as I know every young man must have a vice, I will not curb him in his inclinations to the sex; and be no otherwise a spy upon him or them, but to examine that all his tackling be sound, and to find good workmen to repair the breaches that may unfortunately happen; and truly I think I owe so much to the stallion of our family, abstracted from the personal kindness I have for him' (*Savile Correspondence: Letters to and from Henry Savile, Esq.*, ed. William Durrant Cooper, Camden

Rochester replied to Savile in a letter which is preserved only in a
printed text published in the reign of William III,[38] when standards of
public decency had changed—and when the questions which were
being raised about the new king's sexual interests made any reference
to sex between men a politically sensitive topic.[39] According to this
text, Rochester explains the adventure in these terms:

For the _hideous Deportment,_ which you have heard of, concerning _running
naked,_ so much is true, that we went into the River _somewhat late in the
Year,_ and had a _frisk_ for forty yards in the Meadow, _to dry ourselves._ I will
appeal to the _King_ and the _D._[uke] if _they_ had not done _as much;_ nay, _my
Lord-Chancellor,_ and the _Archbishops both,_ when they were _School-boys._

This explanation constructs the incident as an impeccably homosocial
occurrence, although the syntax mischievously allows us the image of
the King, the Duke, the Lord Chancellor, and the two Archbishops all
running naked through a meadow, until the sentence establishes this
as a hypothetical scene from childhood. Then Rochester reminds
Savile of an occasion in the previous year,

when _two large fat Nudities_ led the Coranto round _Rosamond's_ fair
Fountain, while the poor _violated Nymph_ wept to behold the strange decay
of _Manly Parts,_ since the Days of her dear _Harry_ the Second: _Pr-ck_ (tis con-
fess'd) you shew'd but little of, but for _A—_ and _B—ks, (a filthier
Ostentation! God wot!)_ you expos'd more of _that nastiness_ in _your two Folio
Volumes,_ than we _all together_ in our _six Quarto's._

This time, collective male nudity is presented both as grotesquely
unappealing and as a performance staged for a female audience (as
Hearne had imagined). These gestures of definition are perhaps
answers to a homosexual interpretation of the incident which is
implicit but never articulated in Savile's initial enquiry.

Society Publications 71 (London, 1858), 132–3). Here Savile's promise to examine his
nephew's 'tackling' is jocularly offered in the interests of ensuring the continuity of the
male line. Savile himself is not known to have married. In an earlier letter he had told
his brother: 'As for the pleasures that you tell me there are to be had in these parts, I con-
fess they would be very great ones to one that was not of my humour . . . as for ladyes,
the fairest cannot tempt me, for I am as rightly cut out for a batchelor as ever was man,
and therefore I am much obliged to nature that made me a younger brother' (2). The
tone and implications of this comment are, at this distance, irretrievable.

[38] _Familiar Letters: Written by the Right Honourable John late Earl of Rochester, And
several other Persons of Honour and Quality,_ 2 vols. (London, 1697), i. 41–2.

[39] For contemporary comments on William III's sexuality see pp. 172–83 above.

Rochester's letter then refers to Savile's request that he come to London to help entertain the Dutchmen who are in town with William of Orange, 'a thing I would avoid like killing *Punaises*,[40] the filthy savour of *Dutch-Mirth* being *more terrible*'. But, he says, 'the Prince of *Orange* is exalted *above 'em*, and I cou'd wish myself in Town to serve him in some *refin'd Pleasures*; which, I fear, you are too much a Dutchman to think of'. What might these '*refin'd Pleasures*' be? Given William's reputation for homosexual liaisons (whether this was justified or not is immaterial in this context—it suffices that there were already rumours around which Rochester could have heard[41]), are these the '*refined Pleasures*' which Rochester jokes about providing him with? Was this the reason why this letter was omitted when the collection of *Familiar Letters* was reprinted in 1699?

One has to remember how the letter continues: 'The best Present I can make at this time is the *Bearer*, whom I beg you to take care of, that the King may hear his Tunes, when he is easie and private, because I am sure they will divert him extreamly.' An implicit connection with the previous sentence is apparently being made, but as the sentence unfolds Rochester turns out to be offering the services of James Paisible not to William (or to Savile) but to Charles II, who is most unlikely to have been interested in this young Frenchman's services in anything other than a musical capacity. But Rochester's letter does manage to be suggestive about William of Orange within an impeccably polite phrasing which prevents the letter from being incriminatory should it fall into the wrong hands. This is a text which plays several different, teasing games with the reader, each of which is predicated upon the silent suggestion of sex between men.

Of a different tenor is the letter which Rochester wrote to Savile on 1 November 1679, when the latter was on an embassy in Paris:

The News I have to send, and the sort alone which could be so to you, are things *Gyaris & carcere digna*,[42] which I dare not trust to *this pretty Fool the Bearer*, whom I heartily recommend to your *Favour* and *Protection*, and

[40] Bed-bugs.

[41] French propaganda had spread allegations about William's homosexuality in 1673 (Stephen B. Baxter, *William III* (London, 1966), 111). Savile wrote to his brother in 1677: 'Here is Monsr Bentinck, a chief favourite to the Prince of Orange, come over yesterday to his Majty, but his business not publickly known' (*Savile Correspondence*, 59). The word 'favourite' in this period could, but need not, include a sexual implication: nothing untoward is being committed to paper here.

[42] 'Deserving [the penal colony of] Gyara and prison': a quotation from Juvenal, *Satires*, 1. 73.

whose Qualities will recommend him more; and truly if it might suit with your *Character*, at your times of leisure, to [make] Mr. *Baptist's* Acquaintance, the happy Consequence would be *singing*, and in which your *Excellence* might have a share not unworthy *the greatest Ambassadors*, nor to be despis'd even by a *Cardinal-legate*; the *greatest and gravest* of *this Court* of *both Sexes* have tasted his *Beauties*; and, I'll assure you, *Rome* gains upon us *here*, in *this point* mainly; and there is no part of the *Plot* carried with so much *Secresie* and *Vigour* as *this*. Proselytes, of consequence, are daily made, and my Lord *S*—'s Imprisonment is no *Check* to any.[43]

This time there can be no doubt as to the use which Savile is being invited to make of this second French servant.[44] But once again Rochester's text (at least, in so far as the *Familiar Letters* of 1697 preserves Rochester's original text) traces an intriguing connection between homosexual interests and political ones, linking two kinds of secrecy. This time the letter seems to suggest that the Roman Catholic community in London included a homosexual subculture—which is one explanation for the surprising ease with which Titus Oates was accepted into Catholic circles.[45] Another form of ambiguity resides in the phrase 'Proselytes, of consequence, are daily made': are these 'people made proselytes as a consequence of tasting Baptiste's beauties', or 'proselytes of great consequence in society'? And to what are these proselytes being converted—to Catholicism, or to sex with men? But the problem with this reading of the letter—taking it as a comment on current sexual practices in London society—is that it so obviously depends for its effect on giving a witty twist to the old commonplace associating Rome with sodomy. It is also a self-conscious rhetorical performance, and the quotation from Juvenal is in this respect perfectly apt. Once again, we are presented with a teasing, posing text, whose syntactical twists incite but ward off interpretation.

[43] *Familiar Letters*, i. 9–10. 'Lord *S*—' is Viscount Stafford, a Catholic imprisoned for his supposed part in the Popish Plot.

[44] Treglown suggests that Baptiste may subsequently have tried to blackmail Rochester on the basis of his homosexual interests, but this is no more than conjecture (*Letters*, 26, 243). One would like to know more about what prompted the letter from Rochester to Savile concerning the need to 'distinguish from' or 'comply with' certain pages and grooms of the King's Bedchamber (*Letters*, 113).

[45] See pp. 158–9 above.

SEX BETWEEN MEN IN ROCHESTER'S POETRY

Several of Rochester's poems refer to sex between men, and the texts of these were often altered during their transmission in manuscript and in print. The most curious case is the poem 'Love a Woman! y'are an Ass'. In the version which editors have agreed is closest to Rochester's original, it clearly fashions a stance which rejects erotic involvement with women in favour of the homosocial pleasures of the all-male drinking session, and, if necessary, the sexual pleasures provided by a page. The poem makes a clear distinction within this all-male milieu, for it is the adult friend who provides companionship and wit, and the page who supplies the sex:

Song.

Love a *Woman*! y'are an Ass,
'Tis a most insipid Passion,
To choose out for your happiness!
The idlest part of *Gods Creation.*

Let the *Porter*, and the *Groome*,
Things design'd for dirty *Slaves*,
Drudge in fair *Aurelias Womb*,
To get supplies for Age, and Graves.

Farewel *Woman*, I intend,
Henceforth, ev'ry *Night* to sit,
With my lewd well natur'd *Friend*,
Drinking, to engender *Wit*.

Then give me *Health, Wealth, Mirth*, and *Wine*,
And if busie *Love*, intrenches,
There's a sweet soft *Page*, of mine,
Does the trick worth *Forty Wenches*.

This is the text as it appears in the first printed collection of Rochester's poetry, the *Poems on Several Occasions by the Right Honourable, the E. of R——,*[46] a thoroughly disreputable edition which was published shortly after Rochester's death. The poem also survives in seven

---

[46] *Poems on Several Occasions by the Right Honourable, the E. of R——* ('Antwerp', 1680), 60–1; quoted from the facsimile of the Huntington Library copy published as *Rochester's Poems on Several Occasions*, ed. James Thorpe (Princeton, 1950); hereafter cited as *1680*.

manuscripts.[47] In four of these manuscripts its relationship to Rochester's other songs is odd, for although it is consistently associated with a group of thirteen songs and erotic poems which are probably by Rochester, it is detached from this sequence and placed by various manuscripts in different positions along with the song 'Amintor loved and lived in pain' (whose authorship is unknown), the obscene verses 'In the fields of Lincoln's Inn' (probably by Sir Charles Sedley), and the song 'As trembling prisoners stand at bar' (by Alexander Radcliffe).[48] So 'Love a Woman!' is found in a liminal position at the point where a coherent collection of poems securely attributable to Rochester dissolves into poems articulating a generally libertine ethos. The uncertainty which attends the position of this poem might be construed as evidence of uncertainty as to its authorship were it not that these poems are generally presented without attributions, and 'Love a Woman!' is included in the 1691 edition, which is not known to make any false attributions. So it may be the homosexual flourish in the final stanza which has caused it to be detached from the other pieces. The 1680 edition places it after the verses 'I rise at eleven', the quintessential description of a Restoration rake's day, which also includes a reference to sex with a page.[49] Evidently someone thought that this was an appropriate juxtaposition.

In 1685 a revised version of the 1680 collection was published by A. Thorncome, in which much of the explicit sexual language is bowdlerized. Thorncome's intervention extends to the complete eradication of the homosexual reference in this poem:

> Then give me Health, Wealth, Mirth and Wine,
> And if Busie Love intrenches,

---

[47] For information about MSS of Rochester see Peter Beal, *Index of English Literary Manuscripts*, ii. *1625–1700*, part 2. *Lee-Wycherley* (London, 1993), 225–87; and Rochester, *Works*, ed. Love, which includes a thorough collation of variant readings. Besides the MSS of this poem listed by Love, it also appears in the recently acquired BL MS Add. 73540.

[48] See Michael Brennan and Paul Hammond, 'The Badminton Manuscript: A New Miscellany of Restoration Verse', *English Manuscript Studies 1100–1700*, 5 (1995), 171–207. The two leaves preceding 'Love a Woman!' in MS Danchin have been torn out, so the context which that MS provides for this poem cannot be precisely established (Pierre Danchin, 'A Late Seventeenth-Century Miscellany: A Facsimile Edition of a Manuscript Collection of Poems, largely by John Wilmot, Earl of Rochester', *Cahiers Elisabéthains*, 22 (1982), 51–86). In BL MS Add. 73540 it appears within a group of Rochester's songs.   [49] See pp. 250–1 below.

> There's a sweet soft Love of mine,
> Does the trick worth forty Wenches.[50]

If this stanza still has some sort of point, the antithesis between 'Love' and 'Wenches' presumably now suggests a distinction between the poet's own girlfriend and the prostitutes who are less adept at 'the trick' than she is.

In the careful edition which Jacob Tonson published in 1691[51] the poem was at first set up in much the same form that it had taken in 1680, but as David Vieth pointed out, while the volume was being printed a cancel leaf was substituted which removed the final stanza.[52] This is more than an act of bowdlerization, for it creates a significantly different poem from the four-stanza version which readers had been used to up to that point, and which we now take for granted. It places the poem securely within the boundaries of homosocial companion-ship, putting any homosexual interests beyond the pale and drawing an invisible but firm line between homosocial and homosexual pleasures. The final turn of the poem now occurs on the idea that the engendering of wit is the only form of procreation for a sensible man, rather than the suggestion that sex with a page is the only form of sexual pleasure for a sensible man. The poem in this form is a pleasing and witty performance which would not have been out of place (at least in tone, if not in sentiment) in a volume by Lovelace or Waller.[53]

But it was not only printed editions which had problems with this final stanza. The manuscript transmission of Rochester's poetry was just as much subject to censorship by individual scribes and readers. In the manuscript owned by Pierre Danchin, the entire poem is heavily obliterated, so what one reader carefully copied out, a subsequent owner rejected as unacceptable. Moreover, those manuscripts which do preserve the poem show an interesting uncertainty at crucial points. The actual sexual act at which the page is so adept is variously called 'the trick', 'the feat', or 'the thing',[54] a set of variants which

---

[50] *Poems on several Occasions. Written by a late Person of Honour* (London, 1685), 49; hereafter cited as *1685*.

[51] *Poems, etc. On Several Occasions: With Valentinian; A Tragedy. Written by the Right Honourable John Late Earl of Rochester* (London, 1691); hereafter cited as *1691*.

[52] David M. Vieth, 'An Unsuspected Cancel in Tonson's 1691 "Rochester" ', *Papers of the Bibliographical Society of America*, 55 (1961), 130–3, at 131 n. 2.

[53] It is appropriately placed in *1691* alongside other love songs, coming between 'While on those lovely looks I gaze' and 'To this moment a rebel I throw down my arms'.

[54] 'Trick' in *1680*; 'feat' in MS Danchin; 'thing' in Nottingham University Library MS Portland PwV 40, p. 66.

cannot be explained palaeographically. As for the boy himself, he is either a 'sweet soft Page' (as the 1680 edition calls him) or a 'Soft Young Page' (in the 1691 edition before cancellation). The copyist of one manuscript[55] was evidently somewhat distracted by seeing the use of 'soft' to describe the page, and wrote the word in the previous line as well ('soft love' rather than 'busy love'). So the textual tradition reveals various forms of uncertainty and unease around the very point at which one has to conceptualize the male speaker's male lover, and the sexual act in which they engage.

Another poem which displays significant textual instability around a homosexual reference is 'The Disabled Debauchee', one stanza of which runs thus:

> Nor shall our *Love-fits Cloris* be forgot,
> When each the well-look'd *Link-Boy*, strove t'enjoy
> And the best Kiss, was the deciding *Lot*,
> Whether the *Boy* us'd you, or I the *Boy*.[56]

This is the text of the poem in the 1680 and 1685 editions; once again the 1691 edition was altered as it went through the press, and corrected copies omit this stanza, as do five of the manuscripts.[57] As in the case of the alterations to 'Love a Woman!' this has the effect of changing the poem's semantic field and consolidating the homosocial environment which it imagines. Actually, the second-person address to 'Cloris' here awkwardly disrupts the prevailing sense that this poem is spoken by the rake to his younger companions (who are addressed as 'you' in lines 18 and 47).[58] Some of the witnesses which do include this stanza alter the wording in ways which betray anxiety about what is being said. Two manuscripts have 'best Lov'd' for 'well-look'd', and although 'loved' is palaeographically a possible misreading of 'looked'

[55] MS Portland PwV 40.

[56] *1680*, 34.

[57] MS Tyrrell-Fisher, MS Rutland, Bodl. MS Eng. misc. e. 536, and BL MS Add. 73540 (not cited in *Works*, ed. Love) omit the stanza completely. In MS Tyrrell-Fisher the poem is dated 15 Feb. 1673, so this text comes from a point close to the poem's composition, not from a later milieu. Bodl. MS Eng. poet. e. 4 has the stanza number but omits the stanza itself. Six other manuscripts omit the lines as part of a larger excision, so that cannot be attributed specifically to sensitivity about homosexual sex. For information about variant readings see *Works*, ed. Love, 541.

[58] This raises the possibility that the stanza might be an interpolation. The early date of the text in MS Tyrrell-Fisher, which omits the stanza, might corroborate the suggestion that the stanza is a later addition, though other texts which are apparently from the 1670s do include it (e.g. Bodl. MS Don. b. 8).

it serves to remove the reference to the boy's beauty. Four manuscripts omit the word 'Boy' in the first line, a variant which might possibly be generated by a sensitivity to the niceties of metre, but which is more plausibly interpreted as a preference for imprecision. Three other manuscripts read 'sought' instead of 'strove', making the sexually motivated combat less vigorous. The two witnesses which read 'our deciding lot' instead of 'the deciding lot' make the game one which took place between the speaker and Cloris, thus blurring the obvious interpretation that each in turn kisses the boy, who then decides which of the two kisses was the best, and gives the winner a suitable reward.

Most strikingly, whereas the 1680 and 1685 editions print the last line of this stanza as 'Whether the Boy us'd you, or I the Boy', all but two of the manuscripts which record this line have not 'us'd' but 'fucked'.[59] The 1680 edition is not noted for its coyness, and happily prints 'fuck', 'fucking', and 'fuckt' elsewhere—albeit in heterosexual contexts. The manuscript tradition suggests that Rochester wrote 'fucked', and that whoever was responsible for *1680* (or for the copy-text which it was using) changed the word in this particular instance because it was too explicit a reference to homosexual intercourse. Nevertheless, the very imprecision of 'us'd' ironically creates a new field of meaning, a wider range of sexual possibilities than 'fuck'd'. Bodleian MS Don. b. 8 makes a confused attempt to deal with this point in a different way by removing the homosexual reference entirely and recording the last line as: 'Whether ye Boy you fucke, or you ye Boy.' Even the most careful student of Aretino's postures would have difficulty making sense of that distinction.

A similar act of censorship in *1680* is found in 'The Imperfect Enjoyment'. In the 1680 text we read:

> Stiffly resolv'd, twou'd carelesly invade,
> *Woman* or *Boy*, nor ought its fury staid,
> Where e're it pierc'd, a *Cunt* it found or made.[60]

Whereas *1680* reads '*Woman* or *Boy*', all but two of the extant manuscripts apparently read 'Woman or man'.[61] The consensus of manuscript witnesses points to Rochester having written 'man', and so once

---

[59] The exceptions are MS Portland PwV 40, which agrees with *1680*, and National Library of Ireland MS 2093, which replaces 'fucked' with 'kiss'd'.

[60] *1680*, 29.

[61] The exceptions are MS Portland PwV 40 (which once again agrees with *1680*) and Bodl. MS Add. B 106, which may derive from a printed text.

again the text has been rewritten in order to change the way in which sex between men is imagined, in this case transforming it from the encounter of two adults to what was apparently the less unacceptable paradigm of adult and boy.[62] A reading preserved in two manuscripts changes the graphic verb 'pierced' to the gentler 'pressed.'[63] The 1685 edition rewrites the lines even more drastically:

> Stiffly resolv'd, twou'd carelesly invade,
> Where it essay'd, nor ought its fury staid,
> Where e're it pierc'd, entrance it found or made.[64]

But one also has to ask whether this poem is, in any case, really interested in sexual relations between men. The reference is perfunctory, and the casual phrasing suggests that the gender of the partner is immaterial, though at the same time the line 'Where e're it pierc'd, a *Cunt* it found or made' makes it clear that the male body is no more than a convenient substitute for the female. There is in fact no trace here of homoeroticism, in the sense that there is no real responsiveness to the sexual attractions of the male body.

A rather different case is presented by the song variously entitled 'Nestor' and 'Upon his Drinking a Bowl'. This is an adaptation of a poem attributed to Anacreon (number 17 in Renaissance editions of Anacreon; now number 4 in the *Anacreontea*), with some touches added from a second (once 18, now 5).[65] Vulcan is asked to decorate the drinking bowl:

---

[62] The edns. by Keith Walker and David M. Vieth both take *1680* as their copy-text here, but both emend 'boy' to 'man' on the strength of the MS evidence. Love's eclectic text also prints 'man'. For the textual, grammatical, and sexual complexities produced by the variant readings at this point, see *Works*, ed. Love, 353–4.

[63] The Badminton and Gyldenstolpe MSS (*Works*, ed. Love, 518).

[64] *1685*, 29.

[65] There has been disagreement about the exact source of Rochester's poem (see Marianne Thormählen, *Rochester: The Poems in Context* (Cambridge, 1993), 16–19), but its ultimate origin lies in the two poems which modern scholars now print as nos. 4 and 5 of the *Anacreontea* (*Greek Lyric*, ii, ed. David A. Campbell, Loeb Library (Cambridge, Mass., 1988)). The Greek originals were first printed by Henri Estienne in *Anacreontis Teii Odae* (Paris, 1554), with a Latin translation. Such parallel texts continued to be available through the 17th cent., and Rochester probably used an edn. such as *Anacreontis et Sapphonis Carmina. Notas & Animaduersiones addidit Tanaquillus Faber* (Saumur, 1660). He was said by contemporaries to be proficient in the classical languages, but he seems to have also consulted Ronsard's adaptation, and possibly Stanley's.

> But carve thereon a spreading *Vine*,
>   Then add Two lovely *Boys*;
> Their Limbs in Amorous folds intwine,
>   The *Type* of future joys.
>
> *Cupid*, and *Bacchus*, my *Saints* are,
>   May drink, and Love, still reign,
> With *Wine*, I wash away my cares,
>   And then to *Cunt* again.[66]

In the first stanza Rochester sounds a note which has no exact precedent in the Greek text of *Anacreontea* 4:

> ποίησον ἀμπέλους μοι
> καὶ βότρυας κατ᾽ αὐτῶν
> καὶ μαινάδας τρυγώσας,
> ποίει δὲ ληνὸν οἴνου,
> ληνοβάτας πατοῦντας,
> τοὺς σατύρους γελῶντας
> καὶ χρυσοῦς τοὺς Ἔρωτας
> καὶ Κυθέρην γελῶσαν
> ὁμοῦ καλῷ Λυαίῳ,
> Ἔρωτα κἀφροδίτην.[67]

Instead, the image of the two boys seems to have come from *Anacreontea* 5:

> ὑπ᾽ ἄμπελον εὐπέταλον
> εὐβότρυον κομῶσαν
> σύναπτε κούρους εὐπρεπεῖς,
> ἂν μὴ Φοῖβος ἀθύρῃ.[68]

Here the κούρους εὐπρεπεῖς ('good-looking youths') have become the 'lovely *Boys*' of Rochester's poem, but in neither of the Anacreontic poems is there any precedent for the last two lines of the stanza, 'Their Limbs in Amorous folds intwine, | The *Type* of future joys'. That is Rochester's own imagination at work.

---

[66] *1680*, 57.

[67] *Anacreontea*, 4. 12–21: 'Put vines on for me with bunches of grapes on them and Bacchants picking them; put a wine-press and men treading it, the satyrs laughing, Loves all in gold, Cythere laughing together with handsome Lyaeus, Love and Aphrodite' (Loeb trans.).

[68] *Anacreontea*, 5. 16–19: 'Under a spreading leafy vine covered with bunches of grapes add handsome youths, unless Phoebus is playing there' (Loeb trans.).

Two of Rochester's contemporary admirers, Oldham and Lee, reacted to this poem in ways which suggest their disapproval of (or at least their lack of interest in) the homoerotic penultimate stanza. In 'An Ode of Anacreon Paraphras'd: The Cup' (1683), Oldham writes:

> Draw me first a spreading Vine,
> Make its Arms the Bowl entwine,
> With kind embraces, such as I
> Twist about my loving she.
> Let its Boughs o're-spread above
> Scenes of Drinking, Scenes of Love:
> Draw next the Patron of that Tree,
> Draw *Bacchus* and soft *Cupid* by;
> Draw them both in toping Shapes,
> Their Temples crown'd with cluster'd Grapes:
> Make them lean against the Cup,
> As 'twere to keep their Figures up:
> And when their reeling Forms I view,
> I'll think them drunk, and be so too:
> > The Gods shall my examples be,
> > The Gods, thus drunk in Effigy.[69]

Oldham has taken over Rochester's rhyme of 'vine' and 'entwine', but he makes it clear that to his imagination it is the vine which is entwined around the bowl, like the poet embracing his girl. Bacchus and Cupid are drawn in 'toping Shapes', leaning against the cup rather than mutually entwined, and serve as an encouragement to the poet to drink rather than make love. A second response to Rochester's poem may be traced in Nathaniel Lee's play *The Princess of Cleve* (staged 1682), in which Nemours says: 'the Fury of Wine and Fury of Women possess me waking and sleeping; let me Dream of nothing but dimpl'd Cheeks, and laughing Lips, and flowing Bowls, Venus be my Star, and Whoring my House, and Death I defie thee. Thus sung Rosidore in the Urn.'[70] Whether or not this is a direct allusion to this particular poem, Rochester's poetry generally, and his reputation, have been purged of any homoeroticism through the thoroughly conventional insistence on wine and women. And this care to dissociate Rochester from homoerotic pleasure is particularly remarkable since elsewhere in the

---

[69] 'The Cup', ll. 42–57.

[70] Nathaniel Lee, *The Princess of Cleve*, 3. 1. 129–33. The allusion is noted in John Wilmot, Earl of Rochester, *The Complete Works*, ed. Frank Ellis (Harmondsworth, 1994), 336.

play Lee makes Nemours express homosexual interests in conversation with his eunuch Bellamore.[71]

But homoeroticism is already displaced within Rochester's poem itself. In the final stanza Cupid and Bacchus, the gods of love and of wine, promise the satisfactions of drink and (as Rochester puts it with shocking crudity) '*Cunt*'. The movement between the last two stanzas presents a problem for the reader. One possible interpretation is that the two lovely boys turn out to be Cupid and Bacchus, and so the 'future joys' promised by these boys (which we thought were going to be the pleasures of homosexual sex) are defined instead as '*Wine*' and '*Cunt*'. An alternative reading is that the speaker's ideal world encompasses all these pleasures. So is Cupid an exclusive or inclusive symbol, the god of sexual pleasure in its various forms, or only of heterosexual pleasure? Does the gap between the stanzas mark a connection or a disjunction? There is also a shocking disjunction tonally as we move from the graceful sensuousness of the penultimate stanza to the graceless obscenity of the final line. This is a shock which several witnesses attempt to modify: *1691* and two manuscripts[72] read 'Love', which curiously has the inadvertent effect of keeping the homoerotic possibilities in play at the end of the poem. Some manuscripts make the ending return to drink ('And then to fill again') or to a named lover ('And then to Phill: again', Phill being a curiously androgynous name). All these changes, in their different ways, are responses to a perceived incoherence of tone and desire. So, if we think that the *1680* text is what Rochester wrote, how do we read the contrast between the homoerotic lyricism and the heterosexual crudity? The teasingly uncertain syntax and register through which this libertine milieu is constructed manage to offer the prospect of homoerotic pleasure without quite establishing it as part of the speaker's own fantasy.

Moreover, as Marianne Thormählen observes, the references to homosexual sex are conditional or unrealized:[73] the boys here are the type of future joys; the page is available if busy love entrenches, but we do not know that it will; the linkboy's decision is unknown, so we do not know whether the disabled debauchee ever did get to 'use' him. She makes this point in the context of showing that such a conditional mood and temporal displacement also generally characterize

---

[71] 1.1; 2.3.

[72] Bodl. MSS Eng. misc. e. 536 and Rawl. poet. 173, the latter perhaps copied from *1691*. For other variants see *Works*, ed. Love, 366, 536.

[73] Thormählen, *Rochester*, 22–3.

Rochester's descriptions of sex with women, but in the case of sex with men or boys there is a further grammatical distancing which can be observed. In 'Upon his Drinking a Bowl' the words 'I', 'me' and 'my' occur seven times, but not once in the stanza describing the boys: the speaker never explicitly owns this prospect. In 'Love a Woman!' the syntax changes at the end of the poem: after 'I intend . . . to sit . . . Drinking' and 'give me *Health, Wealth, Mirth,* and *Wine*', the first person singular retreats: 'There's a sweet soft *Page*, of mine | Does the trick'. In 'The Imperfect Enjoyment' it is the speaker's penis which is the grammatical subject, and the whole point of that poem, of course, is the way it functions independently of the speaker's desire.

These grammatical displacements of the speaker from the representation of sex between men contribute to forming the libertine pose. There is in some instances an epigrammatic shape to the lines—'Whether the boy fucked you, or I the boy'—which mark them as tendentious gestures. The persona which governs such utterances is presented in a convenient summary in the verses beginning 'I rise at eleven', which are part of the Rochester apocrypha, and actually precede 'Love a Woman!' in *1680*. The rake has been robbed by a prostitute, who has left him asleep:

> If by chance then I wake, hot-headed, and drunk,
> What a coyle do I make for the loss of my *Punk*?
> I storm, and I roar, and I fall in a rage,
> And missing my *Whore*, I bugger my *Page*:[74]

Again there is an epigrammatic punch to the line. This act seems to be produced more by anger and frustration than by desire, an assertion of power rather than an act of love. Indeed, *1685* rewrites the lines in just this spirit:

> I storm, and I roar, and I fall in a rage,
> And missing my Lass, I fall on my Page:[75]

Here 'fall on' could simply mean 'beat', with no sexual implications.

It is interesting, in the light of the grammatical caution of Rochester's own poems, that while the anonymous rake is made to dramatize himself quite freely here, the lines which have been quoted are not included when the verses are presented as part of an anecdote about Dorset and Rochester in a letter from Godfrey Thacker to the Earl of Huntington:

[74] *1680*, 60.   [75] *1685*, 48.

My Lord Buckhurst and Lord Rochester being in company, a suddaine Malancholly possest him Rochester inquiring the reason hee answered hee was troubled at Rochesters lude way of living, and in these verses over the leafe exprest it

> You rise at Eleaven
> And dine at two
> you get drunk at seaven
> And have nothing to doe
> you goe to a wentch but for feare of a clapp
> you spend in your hand or spue in her lapp.[76]

We cannot know whether Thacker omitted the lines about the page, or whether they were added when the verses were worked up for publication; but in any case it seems clear that they can prove acceptable as part of the mythology of the anonymous rake, but not as part of a narrative about named individuals.

Here again we meet a boundary. In other instances we noticed that a line of demarcation ran between sex with a boy and sex with a man: this was one of the boundaries which *1680* maintained. In the preparation of the 1691 edition there were evidently second thoughts about including the last stanza of 'Love a Woman!', and in its final form *1691* omits the homosexual references both in that poem and in 'The Disabled Debauchee'. Yet it prints 'Upon his Drinking a Bowl' in full, perhaps because there the reference forms an ecphrasis rather than part of a narrative. The manuscript tradition may have served as a convenient mode for the circulation of material which was too hot for printers to handle, but within that medium too there are many examples of censorship, revealing a range of sensitivities on this subject. It does not appear, however, that the manuscript tradition includes any evidence that Rochester's poems were altered to make them more explicit, as happened in the case of some Restoration satires.

One of the crucial differences between Rochester's references to heterosexual and to homosexual sex, is that while both are caught up in his endless posing (and in the reflexive commentaries which in turn expose those poses as egoistic fictions) homosexual sex is never included within a grammar of love, or a syntax of subjectivity; it belongs to epigram rather than narrative, and the isolated moments

---

[76] Huntington Library MS HA 12525; quoted from *The Poems of John Wilmot Earl of Rochester*, ed. Keith Walker (Oxford, 1985), 311.

which present it do not take on that extra dimension of existential contemplation which we find associated with reflection on erotic experience in Rochester's finest poems. There are two kinds of narrative silence in Rochester, two kinds of disjunction: one, which frames the homosexual references, marks them as part of a libertine mythology, and wards off autobiographical inferences; the other, found in heterosexual contexts, separates the present from the past and the future, and evokes absence as part of an acute act of self-awareness which calls into question the modes through which selfhood may be thought. Homosexual possibilities never function like that for Rochester. They form no part of the grounds for subjectivity.

That homosexual sex is supplementary, always a sign of something else, may be seen in the two plays with which Rochester is associated, *Sodom* and *Valentinian*. In the former, its frisson depends upon the reader sharing its essentially conservative assumption that sodomy is the ultimate form of transgression against society, nature, and God.[77] The play reduces the male body to members and orifices, and whatever else one might call it, it is hardly homoerotic, in that it shows little imaginative delight in the sexual attraction of the male body. Rochester's adaptation of Fletcher's *Valentinian* is more interesting in this respect, while still perhaps operating within the same conceptual framework as *Sodom*. In one of the passages which Rochester added, Valentinian reacts to the failure of his procurers to obtain for him Lucina, the wife of Maximus. He claims that her chastity is, in fact, one of the things which he most admires about her, and that he would have been disappointed if she had indeed yielded to his servants' persuasions. He then tells his servant Chilax:

> I'le play to night.
> You sawcy fool send privatly away
> For Lycias hither by the garden gate,
> That sweet fac'd Eunuch that sung
> In Maximus'es grove the other day
> And in my closet keepe him till I come.[78]

---

[77] I provide a brief discussion of *Sodom* in *LBM* 93–4, but the work is too puerile for extended commentary. Its authorship remains uncertain, though it is included in Rochester's *Works*, ed. Love.

[78] *Valentinian*, 2.2.170–7. Printed as *Valentinian: A Tragedy*. As 'tis Alter'd by the late Earl of Rochester (London, 1685). Quoted from *Works*, ed. Love, where it is entitled *Lucina's Rape or The Tragedy of Vallentinian*.

(It is curious that the fourth line here, which describes Lycias, is three syllables short: is something missing? Why should the text stumble over the description of the boy's attractions?) And when Valentinian has left, Chilax comments:

> 'Tis a soft Rogue, this Licias
> And rightly understood
> Hee's worth a thousand Women's Nicenesses.
> The Love of women moves ev'n with their Lust,
> Who therefore still are fond but seldome just.
> Their Love is Usury while they pretend
> To gaine the pleasure double which they lend.
> But a deare Boyes disinterested flame
> Gives Pleasure, and for meer love gathers Paine;
> In him alone fondnes sinceere does prove,
> And the kind, tender, naked boy, is Love.[79]

From this perspective, a boy will be a more satisfying lover because he receives no pleasure himself, acting out of pure affection for his partner, whereas women are always seeking (and faking) their own sexual gratification. This of course figures the boy once again as a replacement for a woman; and the comparison is made on an ostensibly logical, pragmatic basis, rather than being driven by any distinctive personalized desire.

After the death of Lucina, Valentinian and Lycias appear together in the final scene of the play, which opens with '*Vallentinian and the Eunuch discover'd on a Couch*'.[80] The Emperor says:

> Oh let me presse those balmy lips all day,
> And bath my Love-scorch't Soule in thy moist kisses;
> Now by my joyes thou art all sweete and soft,
> And thou shalt be the Alter of my Love;
> Upon thy Beautyes hourly will I offer
> And power out pleasure, a blest Sacrifice

---

[79] *Valentinian*, 2. 2. 178–88.

[80] Ibid. 5. 5. 0, *s.d.* In the production which was planned to take place *c.*1675–6 it was intended that Lycias would be played by Thomas Clark and Valentinian by Charles Hart (*The London Stage 1660–1800*, part 1. *1660–1700*, ed. William Van Lennep (Carbondale, Ill., 1965), 238). There is an intriguing echo in this casting of the roles which they took in Lee's *The Rival Queens* in 1677, when Hart played Alexander and Clark played Hephestion; even more intriguing is the fact that Hart and Clark also played Antony and Dolabella in Dryden's *All for Love* in the same year, which makes one wonder how that relationship was portrayed on stage (*London Stage*, 255, 265).

> To the deare Memory of my Lucina!
> No God nor Goddes ever was ador'd
> With such Religion as my Love shall be:
> For in the Charming Raptures of my Soule,
> Clasp't in thy Armes, I'le wast my selfe away,
> And Robb the Ruin'd World of their great Lord;
> While to the honour of Lucina's Name
> I leave mankind to mourne the Losse for ever.[81]

Although the speech opens with Valentinian showing some appreciation of Lycias' sensual attractions, it soon becomes clear that, as in the previous quotation, the boy's function is to replace the woman; more specifically in this case he provides a human altar on which Valentinian may make sacrifice to the memory of Lucina. Any embrace is but part of a ritual of regret for the absent woman, any worship offered is worship of her, and when Valentinian expires in the boy's arms it will not be in a climax of homosexual pleasure but in a self-destructive act of mourning.

Both these speeches are placed at a moment when the Emperor has been thwarted in his attempt to possess Lucina, and both use Lycias to chart a stage in the degradation of Valentinian. In the first example, he has just announced that he finds Lucina's chastity sexually exciting, and is going to alter his seduction strategy to incorporate this new realization. In the second, he is appropriating the memory of Lucina—over which he has no rights—and exploiting Lycias in a perverted ritual mourning. When the avengers break in to murder Valentinian they pay virtually no attention to Lycias: no one remarks on Valentinian's homosexual dalliance, and with good reason, because it is offered to us principally as a signifier of corruption. It is not made visible in and for itself, but functions metonymically as the sign of a larger category of deviance. Moreover, this is coupled with blasphemy, as Valentinian imagines all this as a religious ritual. In Rochester's imagination, then, the simulacrum of homosexual pleasure with a youth can appropriately function as a sign of a perverse and blasphemous heterosexual obsession. It is a way of conceptualizing sex between men which would surely have satisfied the most censorious Restoration divine.

[81] *Valentinian*, 5. 5. 1–14.

Conclusion

This book has looked closely at the detail of literary texts, at the implications of specific images, rhetorical figures, semantic fields, and literary allusions. It is in the detail, rather than in any grand theory, that we see the kinds of associations and dissociations through which seventeenth-century writers figured sex between men. Men who desire other men are linked with shepherds from classical pastoral, or with a variety of mythological figures—Adonis, Apollo, Ganymede, Narcissus—each of whom exemplifies a subtly different kind of desire or role. Such men are also linked, more polemically, with Turks, Italians, papists, and witches. In some texts friendship is eroticized, while in others a sexual element to friendship and comradeship is sharply denied. Definition and indefinition map out the potential spaces for homosexual desire, and for its punishment.

There is no unitary discourse either of homoeroticism or of sodomy in this period. Instead, this book has mapped a series of discontinuous micro-discourses which formed around particular texts or historical individuals. One such coalesces around Greek and Latin pastoral, another around the figure of Plato and Platonic love, though in both cases the classical signifier can be made to signify more than one kind of relationship. Shakespeare's *Sonnets* construct their own *ad hoc* discourse around the meaning of the poet's love for the youth, working through intratextual, self-referential redefinitions of its key terms. Marvell's poetry shapes teasing ambiguities through manipulations of the poetic persona and allusions to homoerotic pre-texts; though perhaps what we now take to be ambiguities would have been less ambiguous to his first readers, who knew their classical texts better, and would have seen more clearly than modern critics the homoerotic references braided across ostensibly heterosexual poems. To their first readers, these poems may even have flaunted their homoeroticism. Rochester's work incorporates homosexual interests as badges of the libertine, but carefully maintains some grammatical and rhetorical distance between them and the authorial first person; and Rochester's first editors intervened to tone down these poems for a wider readership. If these texts are creating potential spaces in Winnicott's sense,[1] invitations to play, some of the rhetorical uncertainties and complexities of these works—their elusiveness and allusiveness—may reveal an uncertainty over just how far their reader may be willing to enter into the game.

Micro-discourses also formed around political sodomites. These texts which satirized James I, Titus Oates, William III, and Andrew Marvell all responded to political anxieties which were specific to their historical moment, yet they share a common thread in resenting the inaccessibility of these figures. James and William are insulated by their minions from the advice of their subjects; Oates pursues his own trajectory of paranoid fantasy, impervious to argument and evidence; while Marvell makes himself an enigma, socially and politically as well as sexually. Not knowing how to reach or read these men creates resentment. And each, in his different way, has disturbed the social order. In each of these micro-discourses, miniature, localized sign-systems emerge, so that we soon acquire, for instance, an ear for the innuendoes about Marvell's supposed impotence and amphibious sexual interests.

In a society obsessed with knowing one's place, and with semiotic codes which enable one to read another's place (signifiers which range from clothing to coats of arms), sex between men inhabits various forms of utopia: mythologized pastoral, the half-secret spaces of the *Sonnets*, versions of Italy. There is not yet a recognizable urban geography within which sex between men can be located. In 1699, however, Ned Ward offered readers of *The London Spy* a satirical tour through the capital city, and when he came to the Royal Exchange, this was the scene which met his eyes:

We then proceeded and went on to the *Change*, turn'd to the Right, and Jostled in amongst a parcel of swarthy Buggerantoes, Preternatural Fornicators, as my Friend call'd them, who would Ogle a Handsome Young Man with as much Lust, as a true-bred English Whoremaster would gaze upon a Beautiful Virgin. Advertisements hung as thick round the Pillars of each Walk, as bells about the Legs of a Morris-dancer, and an Incessant Buz, like the Murmurs of the distant Ocean, stood as a *Diapason*, to our talk, like a *Drone* to a Bagpipe. The Wainescote was adorn'd with

---

[1] See p. 7 above.

Quacks Bills instead of Pictures; never an Emperick in the Town but had his Name in a Lacquer'd Frame, containing a fair Invitation for a Fool and his Money to be soon parted; and he that wants a dry Rogue for himself, or a Wet-Nurse for his Child, may be furnish't here at a minutes Warning. After we had Squeez'd our selves thro a Crowd of *Bumfirking-Italians* we fell into a throng of Strait-lac'd Monsters in Fur, and Thrum Caps with huge Logger-heads, Effeminate Wastes, and Buttocks like a Flanders-Mare, with Slovenly Mein, Swinish Looks, whose upper lips were gracefully adorn'd with T—d colour'd Whiskers, these with their Gloves under their Arm, and their Hands in their Pockets, were grunting to each other like hogs at their Pease; these my friend told me were the Water-Rats of *Europe*, who love no body but themselves, and Fatten upon the Spoiles, and build their own Well-fare upon the Ruin of their Neighbours.[2]

Ward's satirical picture of the Exchange suggests that the 'swarthy Buggerantoes' are easily recognized, and that this is one of their haunts—what we would now call a cruising ground. There is something un-English about them, as they are contrasted with a 'true-bred English Whoremaster' and associated with the '*Bumfirking-Italians*'[3] and the group of 'Strait-lac'd Monsters' with 'Effeminate Wastes, and Buttocks like a Flanders-Mare'. Their proximity to posters advertising quack medicines implies that there is something false about their activities too. (Sex between men is frequently figured as a parody of the real thing.) Perhaps they too can be bought, or are looking for trade; perhaps the 'dry Rogue' is a male prostitute. The text slides from one observation to another, implying guilt by association. This is both a rhetorically intoxicated fantasy and a description of an actual place: Ward's account of these monsters is not as grotesque as the pamphlets about Titus Oates, and is moving towards the delineation of a recognizable and inhabitable space in which observers may view this new race of men who seek sex with other men. It is a liminal text, on the edge of our period, and pointing towards an eighteenth-century world.

Chronology is problematic, and a teleological thesis untenable. Across the period, it is clear that there are certain major changes in the representation of sex between men: notably, lyrical homoeroticism almost disappears from English poetry, to be replaced by Marvell's games of hide-and-seek, and Rochester's rakish aggression and

---

[2] [Ned Ward], *The London Spy. For the Month of January, 1699* (London, 1699), 14.
[3] '*Bumfirking*' is from 'firk' to press hard or drive forward (*OED* firk 2), with an obvious play on 'fuck'.

insouciance. Potential spaces for homosexual love are erased from Shakespearian texts in the Restoration. But quite why the culture changed in this way is difficult to say. The homoerotic literary tradition is discontinuous: Barnfield reads Marlowe, Shakespeare reads Barnfield, but no homoerotic texts stem from Shakespeare's *Sonnets* until Tennyson and *In Memoriam*. Not only do these texts appear and disappear sporadically in time, they are themselves often atemporal, fashioning a kind of time which is not smoothly contiguous with the time of the reader. Marvell's poetry is temporally liminal, focused on the threshold between innocence and experience. Shakespeare's *Sonnets* are at war with Time for possession of the youth, a possession which is associated with the rarest of moments. Unlike Donne's *Songs and Sonets*, which are full of relics, Shakespeare's *Sonnets* preserve few souvenirs. There, memory and wish-fulfilment speak the same language.

These subtle and playful texts require an appropriate mode of reading which suspends the categories of modern sexuality and teases out the paradoxes and indirections through which a seventeenth-century man wrote of his love for another. So reading itself may be a tribute of love across time:

> O learne to read what silent love hath writ,
> To heare with eies belongs to loves fine wit.[4]

---

4 Shakespeare, Sonnet 23, ll. 13–14.

Bibliography

PRIMARY SOURCES

Where more than one edition of a work is listed, quotations are taken from the edition marked with an asterisk.

Manuscripts

Only those manuscripts which I cite at first hand are listed here, not those which are cited from printed sources.

Badminton House, Avon

MS FmE 3/12   Restoration poetry

Beinecke Library, Yale University

MS Osborn b. 111   Jacobite poetry

Bodleian Library, Oxford

MS Don. b. 8   Restoration poetry
MS Don. c. 24   Poems of Nicholas Oldisworth
MS Eng. misc. e. 536   Poems of the Earl of Rochester
MS Eng. poet. c. 51   Poems on the reign of William III
MS Eng. poet. d. 49   Poems of Andrew Marvell
MS Eng. poet. e. 4   Poems of the Earl of Rochester
MS Firth c. 15   Restoration political poetry
MS Malone 23   Poems on James I
MS Rawl. D. 361   Restoration political poetry
MS Rawl. poet. 94   Poems of John Chatwin
MS Rawl. poet. 159   Restoration poetry
MS Rawl. poet. 169   Restoration political poetry
MS Rawl. poet 173   Poems of the Earl of Rochester

British Library, London

MS Add. 22603   Poems on the reign of James I
MS Add. 22910   Letters of Sir Thomas Baines and Sir John Covell
MS Add. 23215   Letters of Sir John Finch and Lord Conway
MS Add. 23229   Poems on the reign of James I

MS Add. 29497	Poems on the reign of William III
MS Add. 29921	Poems of Sir Thomas Baines
MS Add. 73540	Poems of the Earl of Rochester
MS Egerton 923	Poems on the reign of James I
MS Harley 6913	Restoration poetry
MS Harley 7315	Poems on the reigns of James I and William III
MS Harley 7317	Restoration poetry
MS Harley 7319	Restoration poetry
MS Lansdowne 852	Poems on the reign of William III
MS Sloane 826	Poems on the reign of James I
MS Sloane 2717	Restoration political poetry
MS Sloane 3322	Allusion to Finch and Baines

Brotherton Collection, Leeds University Library

| MS Lt 55 | Restoration poetry |
| MS Lt q 38 | Restoration poetry |

Folger Shakespeare Library, Washington, DC

| MS V. a. 170 | Poems of Nicholas Oldisworth |

Nottingham University Library

| MS Portland PwV 40 | Restoration poetry |

Private Collection

| MS Tyrrell-Fisher | Poems of the Earl of Rochester |

Royal Society, London

| MS 32 | Poem on Andrew Marvell |

Printed Texts

Classical texts are cited from the editions in the Loeb Library, unless otherwise stated.

A Common-place-Book out of the Rehearsal Transpros'd (London, 1673).
A Dialogue Between a Yorkshire-Alderman and Salamanca-Doctor (London, 1683).
A Hue and Cry after Dr. T.O. (London, 1681).
A Hue & Crie after the Good Old Cause [London, 1659].
A Letany for St. Omers (London, 1682).
A Letter to the True Protestant Doctor, the Reverend Titus Oates (London, 1684).
A New Ballad, or, The True-Blew-Protestant Dissenter (London, 1682).
A New Ballad upon Dr. Oates his Retreat from White-Hall, Into the City (London, 1681).

ALEXANDER, NIGEL (ed.), *Elizabethan Narrative Verse* (London, 1967).

ANACREON, *Anacreontis et Sapphonis Carmina*, ed. Tanaquil Faber (Saumur, 1660).

—— *Anacreontis Teii Odae*, ed. Henri Estienne (Paris, 1554).

ATKINS, WILLIAM, 'A Relation of the Journey from St Omers to Seville, 1622', ed. Martin Murphy, *Camden Miscellany XXXII* (London, 1994), 235–8.

AUBREY, JOHN, *Aubrey's Brief Lives*, ed. Oliver Lawson Dick (Harmondsworth, 1972).

The Auricular Confession of Titus Oates to the Salamanca-Doctor, His Confessor (London, 1683).

BANKES, JOHN, *The Destruction of Troy* (London, 1679).

BARGRAVE, ROBERT, *The Travel Diary of Robert Bargrave Levant Merchant (1647–1656)*, ed. Michael G. Brennan (London, 1999).

BARKSTED, WILLIAM, *Mirrha the Mother of Adonis: or, Lustes Prodigies* (London, 1607).

BARNES, BARNABE, *Parthenophil and Parthenophe* (London, 1593), ed. Edward Arber in *An English Garner* (Birmingham, 1882), vol. 5.

—— *The Divils Charter: A Tragedie Conteining the Life and Death of Pope Alexander the Sixt* (London, 1607).

BARNFIELD, RICHARD, *The Complete Poems*, ed. George Klawitter (Selinsgrove, 1990).

BEHN, APHRA, *The Works of Aphra Behn*, ed. Janet Todd, 7 vols. (London, 1996).

BROWN, TOM, *The Salamanca Wedding: Or, A True Account of a Swearing Doctor's Marriage with a Muggletonian Widow in Breadstreet. London, August 18th 1693* (London, 1693).

BULLOUGH, GEOFFREY (ed.), *Narrative and Dramatic Sources of Shakespeare*, 8 vols. (London, 1957–75).

CAREW, THOMAS, *The Poems of Thomas Carew, with his masque Coelum Britannicum*, ed. Rhodes Dunlap (Oxford, 1949).

CAREY, HENRY, Viscount Falkland, *The History of the most Unfortunate Prince King Edward II* (London, 1680).

CARY, ELIZABETH, *Works by and Attributed to Elizabeth Cary*, ed. Margaret W. Ferguson (Aldershot, 1996).

CASAUBON, ISAAC, *Is. Casauboni Corona Regia. Id est Panegyricus Cuiusdam vere Aurei, Quem Iacobo I. Magnae Britanniae, &c. Regi, Fidei Defensori delinearat, Fragmenta* (London, 1615).

COWLEY, ABRAHAM, *Poems*, ed. A. R. Waller (Cambridge, 1905).

Cupid turn'd Musqueteer [London, 1683?].

DANCHIN, PIERRE (ed.), *The Prologues and Epilogues of the Restoration 1660–1700*, 7 vols. (Nancy, 1981–8).

DAY, JOHN, *The Ile of Guls* (London, 1606).

DEAN, J., *Oates's Bug- Bug- Boarding School, at Camberwell* (London, 1684).

DEKKER, THOMAS, *The Dramatic Works of Thomas Dekker*, ed. Fredson Bowers, 4 vols. (Cambridge, 1953–61).

DONNO, ELIZABETH STORY (ed.), *Elizabethan Minor Epics* (London, 1963).

DRAYTON, MICHAEL, *The Works of Michael Drayton*, ed. J. William Hebel, 5 vols. (Oxford, 1931–41).

Dr Oats's last Legacy's and his Farewel Sermon. He being sent for to be high Priest to the Grand Turk (London, 1683).

DRYDEN, JOHN, *The Poems of John Dryden*, ed. Paul Hammond and David Hopkins, in progress (London, 1995–).

—— *The Works of John Dryden*, ed. H. T. Swedenberg *et al.*, 20 vols. (Berkeley, 1956–)*.

DURFEY, THOMAS, *The Marriage-Hater Match'd* (London, 1692).

—— *The Royalist* (London, 1682).

Englands Parnassus, Compiled by Robert Allot, 1600, ed. Charles Crawford (Oxford, 1913).

F., E., *The History of the Life, Reign, and Death of Edward II . . . Written by E. F. in the year 1627* (London, 1680).

FAIRHOLT, FREDERICK W. (ed.), *Poems and Songs relating to George Villiers, Duke of Buckingham; and his Assassination by John Felton, August 23, 1628* (London, 1850).

Familiar Letters of Love, Gallantry, And several Occasions, 2 vols. (London, 1718).

FARMER, NORMAN K., Jr. (ed.), 'Poems from a Seventeenth-Century Manuscript with the Hand of Robert Herrick', *Texas Quarterly*, 16 (1973), 121–85.

F[ERGUSON], R[OBERT], *A Sober Enquiry into the Nature, Measure, and Principle of Moral Virtue* (London, 1673).

FRANZIUS, WOLFGANG, *The History of Brutes; or, A Description of Living Creatures*, tr. N. W. (London, 1670).

GERARD, JOHN, *The Herball or Generall Historie of Plantes . . .* very much enlarged and amended by Thomas Johnson (London, 1633).

GIOVANNI FIORENTINO, *Il Pecorone di Ser Giovanni Fiorentino* (Milan, 1558).

Gl'Ingannati degli Accademici Intronati di Siena, ed. J. P. (Edinburgh, 1943).

GOLDING, ARTHUR, *Shakespeare's Ovid: Being Arthur Golding's Translation of the Metamorphoses*, ed. W. H. D. Rouse (London, 1961).

GOODALL, CHARLES, *Poems and Translations, Written upon Several Occasions and to Several Persons. By a late Scholar of Eaton* (London, 1689).

GRANVILLE, GEORGE, *The Jew of Venice. A Comedy* (London, 1701).

Greek Lyric: Volume II, ed. David A. Campbell, Loeb Library (Cambridge, Mass., 1988).

HADFIELD, ANDREW (ed.), *Amazons, Savages, and Machiavels: Travel and Colonial Writing in English, 1550–1630: An Anthology* (Oxford, 2001).

HAMMOND, PAUL (ed.), *Restoration Literature: An Anthology* (Oxford, 2002).

HEAD, RICHARD, *The English Rogue Described in the Life of Meriton Latroon*

(London, 1665).

HEPWITH, JOHN, *The Calidonian Forrest* (London, 1641).

HERRICK, ROBERT, *The Poems of Robert Herrick*, ed. L. C. Martin (Oxford, 1956).

HICKERINGILL, EDMUND, *Gregory, Father Greybeard* (London, 1673).

HOBBES, THOMAS, *The Elements of Law Natural and Politic*, ed. J. C. A. Gaskin (Oxford, 1994).

HUBERT, FRANCIS, *The Poems of Sir Francis Hubert*, ed. Bernard Mellor (Hong Kong, 1961).

HUTCHINSON, LUCY, *Memoirs of the Life of Colonel Hutchinson*, ed. N. H. Keeble (London, 1995).

JAMES I, *Letters of King James VI and I*, ed. G. P. V. Akrigg (Berkeley, 1984).

JONSON, BEN, *Ben Jonson*, ed. C. H. Herford, Percy and Evelyn Simpson, 11 vols. (Oxford, 1925–52).

Laelia: A Comedy Acted at Queens' College, Cambridge Probably on March 1ˢᵗ, 1595, ed. G. C. Moore Smith (Cambridge, 1910).

LEE, NATHANIEL, *The Works of Nathaniel Lee*, ed. Thomas B. Stroup and Arthur L. Cooke, 2 vols. (New Brunswick, NJ, 1955).

[LEIGH, RICHARD], *The Transproser Rehears'd* (Oxford, 1673).

LEIGHTON, ALEXANDER, *An Appeal to the Parliament; or Sions Plea against the Prelacie* [London, 1628].

LEWKENOR, LEWIS, *A Discourse of the Usage of the English Fugitives by the Spaniard* (London, 1595).

LOVE, HAROLD (ed.), *The Penguin Book of Restoration Verse*, 2nd edn. (Harmondsworth, 1997).

LYLY, JOHN, *The Complete Works of John Lyly*, ed. R. Warwick Bond, 3 vols. (Oxford, 1902).

McCANN, MARIA, *As Meat Loves Salt* (London, 2001).

McCORMICK, IAN (ed.), *Secret Sexualities: A Sourcebook of Seventeenth and Eighteenth Century Writing* (London, 1997).

MACHIN, LEWES, 'Three Eglogs, The first is of Menalcas and Daphnis: The other two is of Apollo and Hyacinth', in William Barksted, *Mirrha the Mother of Adonis: or, Lustes Prodigies* (London, 1607).

MANUCHE, COSMO, *The Loyal Lovers: A Tragi-Comedy* (London, 1652).

MARLOWE, CHRISTOPHER, *Edward the Second*, ed. Charles R. Forker (Manchester, 1994).

—— *The Complete Poems and Translations*, ed. Stephen Orgel (Harmondsworth, 1971).

MARSTON, JOHN, *The Malcontent*, ed. George K. Hunter (London, 1975).

MARTIAL, *Martial in English*, ed. J. P. Sullivan and A. J. Boyle (Harmondsworth, 1996).

MARVELL, ANDREW, *Miscellaneous Poems. By Andrew Marvell, Esq;* (London, 1681).

MARVELL, ANDREW, *The Complete Poems*, ed. Elizabeth Story Donno (Harmondsworth, 1972).

—— *The Poems and Letters of Andrew Marvell*, ed. H. M. Margoliouth, 3rd edn. rev. Pierre Legouis and E. E. Duncan-Jones (Oxford, 1971)*.

—— *The Rehearsal Transpros'd and The Rehearsal Transpros'd The Second Part*, ed. D. I. B. Smith (Oxford, 1971).

Mercurius Dogmaticus, 4 (27 January–3 February 1648).

MILLES, ROBERT, *Abrahams Suite for Sodome. A Sermon Preached at Pauls Crosse the 25. of August. 1611* (London, 1612).

MILTON, JOHN, *Complete Shorter Poems*, ed. John Carey, 2nd edn. (London, 1997).

MOUNTFORT, WILLIAM, *Greenwich-Park* (London, 1691).

NASHE, THOMAS, *The Unfortunate Traveller and Other Works*, ed. J. B. Steane (Harmondsworth, 1972).

OLDHAM, JOHN, *Poems, and Translations* (London, 1683).

—— *The Poems of John Oldham*, ed. Harold F. Brooks and Raman Selden (Oxford, 1987)*.

OSBORNE, FRANCIS, *The True Tragicomedy Formerly Acted at Court*, ed. John Pitcher and Lois Potter (New York, 1983).

OTWAY, THOMAS, *The History and Fall of Caius Marius. A Tragedy* (London, 1680).

OVID, *Pub. Ovidii Nasonis Operum Tom. 2. Metamorphoseon Libri XV. Cum notis selectiss. Varior: studio B. Cnippingii* (Leiden, 1670).

—— *Shakespeare's Ovid: Being Arthur Golding's Translation of the Metamorphoses*, ed. W. H. D. Rouse (London, 1961).

—— *The Fable of Ovid Treting of Narcissus* (1560) in *Elizabethan Narrative Verse*, ed. Nigel Alexander (London, 1967), 27–32.

PARKER, SAMUEL, *A Reproof to the Rehearsal Transprosed* (London, 1673).

—— *Bishop Parker's History of his own Time*, tr. Thomas Newlin (London, 1727).

—— *Reverendi Admodum in Christo Patris, Samuelis Parkeri . . . De Rebus sui Temporis Commentariorum Libri Quatuor* (London, 1726).

PENMAN, BRUCE (ed.), *Five Italian Renaissance Comedies* (Harmondsworth, 1978).

PEPYS, SAMUEL, *The Diary of Samuel Pepys*, ed. Robert Latham and William Matthews, 11 vols. (London, 1970–83).

PERKINS, WILLIAM, *A Warning against the Idolatrie of the Last Times* (Cambridge, 1601).

Poems on Affairs of State: Augustan Satirical Verse, 1660–1714, ed. George deF. Lord *et al.*, 7 vols. (New Haven, 1963–75).

Poems on Affairs of State, From 1640. to the Present Year 1704, iii (London, 1704).

Poetical Recreations: Consisting of Original Poems, Songs, Odes, &c. With Several New Translations. In Two Parts. Part I. Occasionally Written by Mrs.

Jane Barker. Part II. By Several Gentlemen of the Universities and Others (London, 1688).

POPE, ALEXANDER, *The Twickenham Edition of the Poems of Alexander Pope,* ed. John Butt *et al.,* 11 vols. (London, 1939–68).

PRINZ, JOHANNES, *Rochesteriana: Being Some Anecdotes Concerning John Wilmot Earl of Rochester* (Leipzig, 1926).

PROUST, MARCEL, *A la recherche du temps perdu,* ed. Jean-Yves Tadié, Bibliothèque de la Pléiade, 4 vols. (Paris, 1987–9).

PURCHAS, SAMUEL, *Hakluytus Posthumus or Purchas His Pilgrimes,* 20 vols. (Glasgow, 1905).

R., B., *The Unfortunate Court-Favourites of England* (London, 1695).

Raree Show Or the True Protestant Procession ([London], 1681).

RAYMOND, JOAD, *Making the News: An Anthology of the Newsbooks of Revolutionary England 1641–1660* (Moreton-in-Marsh, 1993).

REEVES, BISHOP, 'Bodley's Visit to Lecale, County of Down, A.D. 1602–3', *Ulster Journal of Archaeology,* 2 (1854), 73–95.

ROCHESTER, JOHN WILMOT, EARL OF, *Complete Poems of John Wilmot, Earl of Rochester,* ed. David M. Vieth (New Haven, 1968).

—— *Familiar Letters: Written by the Right Honourable John late Earl of Rochester, And several other Persons of Honour and Quality,* 2 vols. (London, 1697).

—— *John Wilmot, Earl of Rochester: The Complete Works,* ed. Frank Ellis (Harmondsworth, 1994).

—— *Poems, etc. On Several Occasions: With Valentinian; A Tragedy. Written by the Right Honourable John Late Earl of Rochester* (London, 1691).

—— *Poems on Several Occasions by the Right Honourable, the E. of R—* ('Antwerp', 1680).

—— *Poems on several Occasions. Written by a late Person of Honour* (London, 1685).

—— *Rochester's Poems on Several Occasions,* ed. James Thorpe (Princeton, 1950).

—— *The Letters of John Wilmot Earl of Rochester,* ed. Jeremy Treglown (Oxford, 1980).

—— *The Poems of John Wilmot Earl of Rochester,* ed. Keith Walker (Oxford, 1985).

—— *The Works of John Wilmot Earl of Rochester,* ed. Harold Love (Oxford, 1999)*.

—— *Valentinian: A Tragedy. As 'tis Alter'd by the late Earl of Rochester* (London, 1685).

ROSS, ALEXANDER, *Mystagogus Poeticus* (London, 1647; 5th edn. 1672).

RYCAUT, PAUL, *The Present State of the Ottoman Empire* (London, 1667).

SAINTSBURY, GEORGE (ed.), *Minor Poets of the Caroline Period,* 3 vols. (Oxford, 1905–21).

S[ANDYS], G[EORGE], *Ovid's Metamorphosis Englished, Mythologiz'd, and Represented in Figures* (Oxford, 1632).

SAVILLE, HENRY, *Savile Correspondence: Letters to and from Henry Savile, Esq.*, ed. William Durrant Cooper, Camden Society Publications 71 (London, 1858).

Secret History of the Court of James the First, 2 vols. (Edinburgh, 1811).

Sh— Ghost to Doctor Oats. In a Vision, Concerning the Jesuits and Lords in the Tower (London, 1683).

SHAKESPEARE, WILLIAM, *An Excellent Conceited Tragedie of Romeo and Iuliet* (London, 1597).

—— *King Edward III*, ed. Giorgio Melchiori (Cambridge, 1998).

—— *King Lear: 1608 (Pied Bull Quarto)*, Shakespeare Quarto Facsimiles, 1 (London, 1939).

—— *Poems: Written by Wil. Shake-speare. Gent* (London, 1640).

—— *Shake-speares Sonnets Neuer before Imprinted* (London, 1609).

—— *Shakespeare's Sonnets*, ed. W. G. Ingram and Theodore Redpath (London, 1964).

—— *Shakespeare's Sonnets*, ed. Stephen Booth (New Haven, 1977).

—— *Shakespeare's Sonnets*, ed. Katherine Duncan-Jones (London, 1997).

—— *The Complete Works*, ed. Stanley Wells and Gary Taylor (Oxford, 1986).

—— *The Complete Works: Original-Spelling Edition*, ed. Stanley Wells and Gary Taylor (Oxford, 1986)*.

—— *The First Folio of Shakespeare: A Transcript of Contemporary Marginalia in a Copy of the Kodama Memorial Library of Meisei University*, ed. Akihiro Yamada (Tokyo, 1998).

—— *The Merchant of Venice*, ed. John Russell Brown (London, 1955).

—— *The Sonnets*, ed. Hyder Edward Rollins, 2 vols. (Philadelphia, 1944).

—— *The Sonnets and A Lover's Complaint*, ed. John Kerrigan (Harmondsworth, 1986).

—— *The Winter's Tale*, ed. J. H. Pafford (London, 1963).

—— *Twelfth Night*, ed. Roger Warren and Stanley Wells (Oxford, 1994).

SHIRLEY, JAMES, *Narcissus or the Self-Lover* (1646) in *Elizabethan Minor Epics*, ed. Elizabeth Story Donno (London, 1963), 325–51.

SMITH, WILIAM, *Intrigues of the Popish Plot Laid Open* (London, 1685).

Sober Reflections, or, a Solid Confutation of Mr. Andrew Marvel's Works, in a Letter Ab Ignoto ad Ignotum (London, 1674).

Sodom Fair: or, The Market of the Man of Sin (London, 1688).

SPENSER, EDMUND, *The Poetical Works of Edmund Spenser*, ed. Ernest de Selincourt and J. C. Smith, 3 vols. (Oxford, 1909–10).

STANLEY, THOMAS, *The Poems and Translations of Thomas Stanley*, ed. Galbraith Miller Crump (Oxford, 1962).

STOKES, EDWARD, *The Wiltshire Rant; or a Narrative wherein the most unparallel'd Prophane Actings, Counterfeit Repentings, and Evil Speakings of*

Thomas Webbe Late Pretended Minister of Langley Buriall, are Discovered (London, 1652).

S'too him Bayes (Oxford, 1673).

Strange and Wonderful News from South-wark, Declaring how a Sham Doctor got two Aldermen Students of the same University with Child. How they long'd for Venison, and what Ensued upon it (London, 1684).

STUBBE, HENRY, *Rosemary & Bayes* (London, 1672).

SULLIVAN, J. P., and A. J. BOYLE (eds.), *Martial in English* (Harmondsworth, 1996).

Sylvae: or, The Second Part of Poetical Miscellanies (London, 1685).

TATE, NAHUM, *The Ingratitude of a Common-Wealth: or, The Fall of Caius Martius Coriolanus* (London, 1682).

TATHAM, JOHN, *The Scotch Figgaries* (London, 1735).

TATIUS, ACHILLES, *Le Roman de Leucippé et Clitophon*, ed. Jean-Philippe Garnaud (Paris, 1991).

—— *The Loves of Clitophon and Leucippe* [tr. A. Hodges] (Oxford, 1638).

—— *The Most Delectable and Pleasaunt History of Clitiphon and Leucippe*, tr. W[illiam] B[urton] (London, 1597).

The Disappointed Marriage, or an Hue and Cry after an Outlandish Monster (London, 1733).

The Faithful Friends, Malone Society Reprint (Oxford, 1975).

The last Memorial of the Agent from the K. of Poland, to the Salamanca Dr. (London, 1683).

The Life of Edward the Second by the So-called Monk of Malmesbury, ed. N. Denholm-Young (London, 1957).

The Melancholy Complaint of D. Otes, of the Black Ingratitude of this present Age Towards Him (London, 1684).

The None-such Charles His Character (London, 1651).

THEOCRITUS, *The Idylliums of Theocritus with Rapin's Discourse of Pastorals*, tr. Thomas Creech (Oxford, 1684).

The Tryal and Conviction of Thomas Knox and John Lane, for a Conspiracy, to Defame and Scandalize Dr. Oates and Mr. Bedloe (London, 1680).

Titus' Exaltation to the Pillory, upon his Conviction of Perjury (London, 1685).

TOPSEL, EDWARD, *The History of Four-footed Beasts and Serpents* (London, 1658).

Troia Redeviva, or, the Glories of London Surveyed in an Heroick Poem (London, 1674).

Tyburn's Courteous Invitation to Titus Oates ([London], 1684).

The Petition of Themis against the Salamanca Fiend (London, 1684).

The Salamanca Doctor's Farewel [London, 1685?].

The Sodomite, or the Venison Doctor, With his Brace of Aldermen-Stags (London, [1684]).

Vaticinium Votivum: or, Palaemon's Prophetick Prayer (n.p., 'Anno Caroli

Martyris Primo' [i.e. 1649]).

VIRGIL, *Aeneas his descent into Hell*, tr. John Boys (London, 1661).

—— *Vergil: Eclogues*, ed. Robert Coleman (Cambridge, 1977).

W., C., *The Siege of Vienna, A Poem* (London, 1685).

WARD, NED, *The London Spy. For the Month of January, 1699* (London, 1699).

WELDON, SIR ANTHONY, *The Court and Character of King James. Whereunto is now added the Court of King Charles: Continued unto the Beginning of these Unhappy Times* (London, 1651).

WHARTON, ANNE, *The Surviving Works of Anne Wharton*, ed. G. Greer and S. Hastings (Stump Cross, 1997).

WHITE, JOHN, *The First Century of Scandalous, Malignant Priests* (London, 1643).

WITHER, GEORGE, *A Collection of Emblemes* (London, 1635).

Wit Restor'd in Severall Select Poems not formerly Publish't (London, 1658).

WYCHERLEY, WILLIAM, *The Plays of William Wycherley*, ed. Arthur Friedman (Oxford, 1979).

SECONDARY SOURCES

ABRAHAM, LYNDY, *Marvell and Alchemy* (Aldershot, 1990).

ADELMAN, JANET, *Suffocating Mothers: Fantasies of Maternal Origin in Shakespeare's Plays, 'Hamlet' to 'The Tempest'* (New York, 1992).

BAKER, DAVID, 'Cavalier Shakespeare: The 1640 *Poems* of John Benson', *Studies in Philology*, 95 (1998), 152–73.

BALDWIN, ANNA, and SARAH HUTTON (eds.), *Platonism and the English Imagination* (Cambridge, 1994).

BALDWIN, T. W., *On the Literary Genetics of Shakspere's Poems & Sonnets* (Urbana, Ill., 1950).

—— *William Shakspere's Small Latine & Lesse Greeke*, 2 vols. (Urbana, Ill., 1944).

BARKER, G. F. RUSSELL, and ALAN H. STENNING (eds.), *The Record of Old Westminsters*, 2 vols. (London, 1928).

BATE, JONATHAN, *Shakespeare and Ovid* (Oxford, 1993).

BAXTER, STEPHEN B., *William III* (London, 1966).

BEAL, PETER, *Index of English Literary Manuscripts*, ii. *1625–1700*, part 2. *Lee-Wycherley* (London, 1993).

BELLANY, ALASTAIR, '"Raylinge Rymes and Vaunting Verse": Libellous Politics in Early Stuart England, 1603–1628', in Kevin Sharpe and Peter Lake (eds.), *Culture and Politics in Early Stuart England* (Basingstoke, 1994), 285–310.

BERGERON, DAVID M., *King James and Letters of Homoerotic Desire* (Iowa City, 1999).

BINGHAM, CAROLINE, 'Seventeenth-Century Attitudes towards Deviant Sex', *Journal of Interdisciplinary History*, 1 (1971), 447–68.

BLY, MARY, *Queer Virgins and Virgin Queans on the Early Modern Stage* (Oxford, 2000).

BOITANI, PIERO (ed.), *The European Tragedy of Troilus* (Oxford, 1989).

BRAY, ALAN, 'Homosexuality and the Signs of Male Friendship in Elizabethan England', *History Workshop*, 29 (1990), 1–19.

—— *Homosexuality in Renaissance England* (London, 1982).

—— and MICHEL REY, 'The Body of the Friend: Continuity and Change in Masculine Friendship in the Seventeenth Century', in Tim Hitchcock and Michèle Cohen (eds.), *English Masculinities 1660–1800* (London, 1999), 65–84.

BREDBECK, GREGORY W., *Sodomy and Interpretation: Marlowe to Milton* (Ithaca, NY, 1991).

BRENNAN, MICHAEL, and PAUL HAMMOND, 'The Badminton Manuscript: A New Miscellany of Restoration Verse', *English Manuscript Studies 1100–1700*, 5 (1995), 171–207.

BROWN, SARAH ANNES, 'Ovid and Marvell's *The Nymph Complaining for the Death of her Faun*', *Translation and Literature*, 6 (1997), 167–85.

BRUMBLE, H. DAVID, *Classical Myths and Legends in the Middle Ages and Renaissance: A Dictionary of Allegorical Meanings* (London, 1998).

CAREY, JOHN, 'Reversals Transposed: An Aspect of Marvell's Imagination', in C. A. Patrides (ed.), *Approaches to Marvell: The York Tercentenary Lectures* (London, 1978), 136–54.

CHAMBERS, E. K., *The Elizabethan Stage*, 4 vols. (Oxford, 1923).

CLARE, JANET, *'Art Made Tongue-Tied by Authority': Elizabethan and Jacobean Dramatic Censorship* (Manchester, 1990).

CLARK, PETER, *The English Alehouse: A Social History* (London, 1983).

CLUBB, LOUISE GEORGE, *Italian Drama in Shakespeare's Time* (New Haven, 1989).

COGSWELL, THOMAS, 'Underground Verse and the Transformation of Early Stuart Political Culture', in Susan D. Amussen and Mark A. Kishlansky (eds.), *Political Culture and Cultural Politics in Early Modern England* (Manchester, 1995).

CORBALLIS, R. P., 'The Name Antonio in English Renaissance Drama', *Cahiers Elisabéthains*, 25 (1984), 61–72.

CRAWFORD, CHARLES, 'Richard Barnfield, Marlowe, and Shakespeare', *Notes and Queries*, 9th ser. 8 (1901), 217–19, 277–9.

CRUM, MARGARET, *First-Line Index of English Poetry 1500–1800 in Manuscripts of the Bodleian Library Oxford* (Oxford, 1969).

DANCHIN, PIERRE, 'A Late Seventeenth-Century Miscellany: A Facsimile Edition of a Manuscript Collection of Poems, largely by John Wilmot, Earl of Rochester', *Cahiers Elisabéthains*, 22 (1982), 51–86.

DAVIDSON, P. R. K., and A. K. JONES, 'New Light on Marvell's "The Unfortunate Lover"?', *Notes and Queries,* 230 (1985), 170–2.

DAVIS, J. C., *Fear, Myth and History: The Ranters and the Historians* (Cambridge, 1986).

DE GRAZIA, MARGARETA, 'The Scandal of Shakespeare's Sonnets', *Shakespeare Survey,* 46 (1994), 35–49.

DERRIDA, JACQUES, *De la grammatologie* (Paris, 1967).

DIGANGI, MARIO, *The Homoerotics of Early Modern Drama* (Cambridge, 1997).

DOVER, K. J., *Greek Homosexuality* (Cambridge, Mass., 1978, 2nd edn. 1989).

DRESEN-COENDERS, LÈNE (ed.), *Saints and She-devils* (London, 1987).

DUNCAN-JONES, E. E., 'Marriage of Souls', *London Review of Books* (7 Oct. 1993), 4.

DUNCAN-JONES, KATHERINE, *Ungentle Shakespeare* (London, 2001).

—— 'Was the 1609 *Shake-speares Sonnets* Really Unauthorized?', *Review of English Studies,* 34 (1983), 151–71.

EMPSON, WILLIAM, *Using Biography* (London, 1984).

ENTERLINE, LYNN, *The Tears of Narcissus: Melancholia and Masculinity in Early Modern Writing* (Stanford, Calif., 1995).

FISHER, NICHOLAS (ed.), *That Second Bottle: Essays on John Wilmot, Earl of Rochester* (Manchester, 2000).

FONE, BYRNE R. S., 'This Other Eden: Arcadia and the Homosexual Imagination', *Journal of Homosexuality,* 8 (1983), 13–34.

FOUCAULT, MICHEL, *L'Archéologie du savoir* (Paris, 1969).

—— *Histoire de la folie à l'âge classique* (Paris, 1972).

—— *Histoire de la sexualité,* i. *La Volonté de savoir* (Paris, 1976).

FRANCESCHINA, JOHN, *Homosexualities in the English Theatre: From Lyly to Wilde* (Westport, Conn., 1997).

GANTZ, TIMOTHY, *Early Greek Myth: A Guide to Literary and Artistic Sources,* 2 vols. (Baltimore, 1993).

GERARD, KENT, and GERT HEKMA (eds.), *The Pursuit of Sodomy: Male Homosexuality in Renaissance and Enlightenment Europe* (New York, 1989).

GILLESPIE, STUART, *Shakespeare's Books: A Dictionary of Shakespeare Sources* (London, 2001).

GOLDBERG, JONATHAN (ed.), *Queering the Renaissance* (Durham, NC, 1994).

—— *Sodometries: Renaissance Texts, Modern Sexualities* (Stanford, Calif., 1992).

GOUWS, JOHN, 'Nicholas Oldisworth and MS Don. c. 24', *Bodleian Library Record,* 15 (1995), 158–65.

GRANTLEY, DARRYLL, and PETER ROBERTS (eds.), *Christopher Marlowe and English Renaissance Culture* (Aldershot, 1996).

GRIEVE, M., *A Modern Herbal* (Harmondsworth, 1976).

HALPERIN, DAVID M., *One Hundred Years of Homosexuality* (New York, 1990).

HAMMOND, PAUL, 'Anonymity in Restoration Poetry', *The Seventeenth Century*, 8 (1993), 123–42.

—— 'Censorship in the Manuscript Transmission of Restoration Poetry', in Nigel Smith (ed.), *Literature and Censorship* (Cambridge, 1993), 39–62.

—— *Dryden and the Traces of Classical Rome* (Oxford, 1999).

—— 'Friends or Lovers? Sensitivity to Homosexual Implications in Adaptations of Shakespeare, 1640–1701', in Cedric C. Brown and Arthur F. Marotti (eds.), *Texts and Cultural Change in Early Modern England* (Basingstoke, 1997), 225–47.

—— 'James I's Homosexuality and the Revision of the Folio Text of *King Lear*', *Notes and Queries*, 242 (1997), 62–4.

—— *Love between Men in English Literature* (Basingstoke, 1996).

—— 'Marvell's Coy Mistresses', in *Re-constructing the Book: Literary Texts in Transmission*, ed. Maureen Bell *et al.* (Aldershot, n.d. [2001]), 22–33.

—— 'Marvell's Sexuality', *The Seventeenth Century*, 11 (1996), 87–123.

—— 'Rochester's Homoeroticism', in *That Second Bottle: Essays on John Wilmot, Earl of Rochester*, ed. Nicholas Fisher (Manchester, 2000), 46–62.

—— 'The King's Two Bodies: Representations of Charles II', in Jeremy Black and Jeremy Gregory (eds.), *Culture, Politics and Society in Britain, 1660–1800* (Manchester, 1991), 13–48.

—— 'Titus Oates and "Sodomy"', in Jeremy Black (ed.), *Culture and Society in Britain 1660–1800* (Manchester, 1997), 85–101.

HARRIS, TIM, *London Crowds in the Reign of Charles II* (Cambridge, 1987).

HENKE, ROBERT, *Pastoral Transformations: Italian Tragicomedy and Shakespeare's Late Plays* (Newark, NJ, 1997).

HIGHFILL, PHILIP H., JR., KALMAN A. BURNIM, and EDWARD A. LANGHANS, *A Biographical Dictionary of Actors, Actresses, Musicians, Dancers, Managers and other Stage Personnel in London, 1660–1800*, 16 vols. (Carbondale, Ill., 1973–93).

HILL, CHRISTOPHER, *The World turned Upside Down: Radical Ideas during the English Revolution* (London, 1972, 2nd edn. Harmondsworth, 1975).

HIRST, DEREK, and STEVEN ZWICKER, 'Andrew Marvell and the Toils of Patriarchy: Fatherhood, Longing, and the Body Politic', *ELH*, 66 (1999), 629–54.

HOWE, ELIZABETH, *The First English Actresses: Women and Drama 1660–1700* (Cambridge, 1992).

HUGHES, DEREK, *English Drama 1660–1700* (Oxford, 1996).

HUTSON, LORNA, *The Usurer's Daughter: Male Friendship and Fictions of Women in Sixteenth-Century England* (London, 1994).

KANTOROWICZ, ERNST H., *The King's Two Bodies: A Study in Medieval Political Theology* (Princeton, 1957).

KELLIHER, HILTON, *Andrew Marvell: Poet and Politician* (London, 1978).

KENYON, JOHN, *The Popish Plot* (London, 1972; Harmondsworth, 1974).

KNOWLES, JAMES, 'To "scourge the arse | Jove's marrow so had wasted": Scurrility and the Subversion of Sodomy', in Dermot Cavanagh and Tim Kirk (eds.), *Subversion and Scurrility: Popular Discourse in Europe from 1500 to the Present* (Aldershot, 2000), 74–92.

LANE, JANE (Elaine Dakers), *Titus Oates* (London, 1949).

LEGOUIS, PIERRE, *André Marvell, poète, puritain, patriote 1621–1678* (Paris, 1928).

LEISHMAN, J. B., *The Art of Marvell's Poetry*, 2nd edn. (London, 1968).

LEVINE, LAURA, *Men in Women's Clothing: Anti-theatricality and Effeminization, 1579–1642* (Cambridge, 1994).

LEWIS, CYNTHIA, ' "Wise Men, Folly-Fall'n": Characters Named Antonio in English Renaissance Drama', *Renaissance Drama*, 20 (1989), 196–236.

LOCKYER, ROGER, *Buckingham: The Life and Political Career of George Villiers, First Duke of Buckingham 1592–1628* (London, 1981).

LOXLEY, JAMES, 'Prepar'd at Last to Strike in with the Tyde? Andrew Marvell and Royalist Verse', *The Seventeenth Century*, 10 (1995), 39–62.

LOVE, HAROLD, *Scribal Publication in Seventeenth-Century England* (Oxford, 1993).

McFARLANE, CAMERON, *The Sodomite in Fiction and Satire 1660–1750* (New York, 1997).

McRAE, ANDREW, 'The Literary Culture of Early Stuart Libeling', *Modern Philology*, 97 (2000), 364–92.

—— *Unauthorized Texts: Satire and the Early Stuart State* (forthcoming).

MAHLER, ANDREAS, 'Italian vices', in Michele Marrapodi *et al.* (eds.), *Shakespeare's Italy: Functions of Italian Locations in Renaissance Drama* (Manchester, 1993; 2nd edn. 1997), 49–68.

MALLOCH, ARCHIBALD, *Finch and Baines: A Seventeenth Century Friendship* (Cambridge, 1917).

MAROTTI, ARTHUR F., *Manuscript, Print, and the English Renaissance Lyric* (Ithaca, NY, 1995).

—— 'Shakespeare's Sonnets as Literary Property', in Elizabeth D. Harvey and Katharine Eisaman Maus (eds.), *Soliciting Interpretation: Literary Theory and Seventeenth-Century English Poetry* (Chicago, 1990), 143–73.

MARRAPODI, MICHELE, *et al.* (eds.), *Shakespeare's Italy: Functions of Italian Locations in Renaissance Drama* (Manchester, 1993; 2nd edn. 1997).

MATAR, NABIL, *Turks, Moors, and Englishmen in the Age of Discovery* (New York, 1999).

MAULE, JEREMY, 'A New Poem by John Ford', *English Manuscript Studies 1100–1700*, 8 (2000), 137–59.

MAUS, KATHARINE EISAMAN, *Inwardness and Theater in the English Renaissance* (Chicago, 1995).

MELZI, ROBERT C., 'From Lelia to Viola', *Renaissance Drama*, 9 (1966), 67–81.

MILLER, JOHN, *Popery and Politics in England 1660–1688* (Cambridge, 1973).

MILLER, RACHEL, 'Physic for the Great: Dryden's Satiric Translations of Juvenal, Persius, and Boccaccio', *Philological Quarterly*, 68 (1989), 53–75.

MUIR, KENNETH, *Shakespeare's Sources*, i. *Comedies and Tragedies* (London, 1957).

NORMAND, LAWRENCE, ' "What Passions Call You These?": Edward II and James VI', in Darryll Grantley and Peter Roberts (eds.), *Christopher Marlowe and English Renaissance Culture* (Aldershot, 1996), 172–97.

NORTON, RICTOR, *Mother Clap's Molly House: The Gay Subculture in England 1700–1830* (London, 1992).

—— *The Homosexual Literary Tradition: An Interpretation* (New York, 1974).

ORGEL, STEPHEN, *Impersonations: The Performance of Gender in Shakespeare's England* (Cambridge, 1996).

OSBORNE, LAURIE E., 'The Texts of *Twelfth Night*', *ELH*, 57 (1990), 37–61.

PARKER, WILLIAM RILEY, *Milton: A Biography*, 2 vols. (Oxford, 1968).

PARTRIDGE, ERIC, *Shakespeare's Bawdy* (London, 1947; 3rd edn. 1968).

PATRIDES, C. A. (ed.), *Approaches to Marvell: The York Tercentenary Lectures* (London, 1978).

PEQUIGNEY, JOSEPH, *Such is my Love: A Study of Shakespeare's Sonnets* (Chicago, 1985).

—— 'The Two Antonios and Same-Sex Love in *Twelfth Night* and *The Merchant of Venice*', *English Literary Renaissance*, 22 (1992), 201–21.

POTTER, DAVID, 'Marlowe's *Massacre at Paris* and the Reputation of Henri III of France', in Darryll Grantley and Peter Roberts (eds.), *Christopher Marlowe and English Renaissance Culture* (Aldershot, 1996), 70–95.

RAY, ROBERT H., 'Marvell's "To his Coy Mistress" and Sandys's Translation of Ovid's *Metamorphoses*', *Review of English Studies*, 44 (1993), 386–8.

RAYLOR, TIMOTHY, *Cavaliers, Clubs, and Literary Culture: Sir John Mennes, James Smith, and the Order of the Fancy* (Newark, NJ, 1994).

RICKS, CHRISTOPHER, ' "Its own resemblance" ' in C. A. Patrides (ed.), *Approaches to Marvell: The York Tercentenary Lectures* (London, 1978), 108–35.

RIEBLING, BARBARA, 'England Deflowered and Unmanned: The Sexual Image of Politics in Marvell's "Last Instructions" ', *Studies in English Literature 1500–1900*, 35 (1995), 137–57.

ROCKE, MICHAEL, *Forbidden Friendships: Homosexuality and Male Culture in Renaissance Florence* (New York, 1996).

RUGGIERO, GUIDO, *The Boundaries of Eros: Sex, Crime, and Sexuality in Renaissance Venice* (New York, 1985).

SALINGAR, LEO, *Shakespeare and the Traditions of Comedy* (Cambridge, 1974).

SASLOW, JAMES M., *Ganymede in the Renaissance: Homosexuality in Art and Society* (New Haven, 1986).

SCHMITT, CHARLES B. (ed.), *The Cambridge History of Renaissance Philosophy* (Cambridge, 1988).

SCHNEIDER, BEN ROSS, 'Granville's *Jew of Venice* (1701): A Close Reading of Shakespeare's *Merchant*', *Restoration*, 17 (1993), 111–34.

SEDGWICK, EVE KOSOFSKY, *Between Men: English Literature and Male Homosocial Desire* (New York, 1985).

SENELICK, LAURENCE, 'Mollies or Men of Mode?', *Journal of the History of Sexuality*, 1 (1990), 33–67.

SERGENT, BERNARD, *L' Homosexualité dans la mythologie grecque* (Paris, 1984).

SHAHEEN, NASEEB, 'Shakespeare's Knowledge of Italian', *Shakespeare Survey*, 47 (1994), 161–9.

SHAPIRO, MICHAEL, *Gender in Play on the Shakespearean Stage: Boy Heroines and Female Pages* (Ann Arbor, 1994).

SHAPIRO, SUSAN C., ' "Yon Plumed Dandebrat": Male "Effeminacy" in English Satire and Criticism', *Review of English Studies*, 39 (1988), 400–12.

SHARPE, KEVIN, and PETER LAKE (eds.), *Culture and Politics in Early Stuart England* (Basingstoke, 1994).

SHAWCROSS, JOHN T., *John Milton: The Self and the World* (Lexington, 1993).

—— 'Milton and Diodati: An Essay in Psychodynamic Meaning', *Milton Studes*, 7 (1975), 127–63.

SKINNER, QUENTIN, *Reason and Rhetoric in the Philosophy of Hobbes* (Cambridge, 1996).

SMITH, BRUCE R., *Homosexual Desire in Shakespeare's England: A Cultural Poetics* (Chicago, 1991).

SMITH, NIGEL, ' "Courtesie is Fatal": The Civil and Visionary Poetics of Andrew Marvell', *Proceedings of the British Academy*, 101 (1999), 173–89.

SONINO, LEE A., *A Handbook to Sixteenth-Century Rhetoric* (London, 1968).

STAVES, SUSAN, 'A Few Kind Words for the Fop', *Studies in English Literature 1500–1900*, 22 (1982), 413–28.

STEWART, ALAN, *Close Readers: Humanism and Sodomy in Early Modern England* (Princeton, 1997).

STRAUB, KRISTINA, 'Actors and Homophobia', in J. Douglas Canfield and Deborah C. Payne (eds.), *Cultural Readings of Restoration and Eighteenth-century English Theatre* (Athens, Ga., 1995), 258–80.

SUMMERS, CLAUDE J. (ed.), *Homosexuality in Renaissance and Enlightenment England: Literary Representations in Historical Context* (Binghamton, 1992).

—— and TED-LARRY PEBWORTH (eds.), *Renaissance Discourses of Desire* (Columbia, 1993).

THOMAS, DAVID, and ARNOLD HARE, *Restoration and Georgian England, 1660–1788*, Theatre in Europe: A Documentary History (Cambridge, 1989).

THOMPSON, ROGER, *Unfit for Modest Ears* (London, 1979).

THORMÄHLEN, MARIANNE, *Rochester: The Poems in Context* (Cambridge, 1993).

TILLEY, MORRIS PALMER, *A Dictionary of the Proverbs in England in the Sixteenth and Seventeenth Centuries* (Ann Arbor, 1950).

Trumbach, Raymond, 'London's Sodomites: Homosexual Behavior and Western Culture in the Eighteenth Century', *Journal of Social History*, 11 (1977–8), 1–33.

—— *Sex and the Gender Revolution*, i. *Heterosexuality and the Third Gender in Enlightenment London* (Chicago, 1998).

—— 'Sex, Gender, and Sexual Identity in Modern Culture: Male Sodomy and Female Prostitution in Enlightenment London', *Journal of the History of Sexuality*, 2 (1991), 186–203.

—— 'Sodomitical Assaults, Gender Role, and Sexual Development in Eighteenth-Century London', *Journal of Homosexuality*, 16 (1988), 407–29.

—— 'Sodomitical Subcultures, Sodomitical Roles, and the Gender Revolution of the Eighteenth Century', *Eighteenth-Century Life*, 9 (1985), 109–21.

—— 'Sodomy Transformed: Aristocratic Libertinage, Public Reputation, and the Gender Revolution of the Eighteenth Century', *Journal of Homosexuality*, 19 (1990), 105–24.

Van Lennep, William (ed.), *The London Stage 1660–1800*, i. *1660–1700* (Carbondale, Ill., 1965).

Vendler, Helen, *The Art of Shakespeare's Sonnets* (Cambridge, Mass., 1997).

Venn, John, and J. A. Venn (eds.), *Alumni Cantabrigienses*, 4 vols. (Cambridge, 1922–7).

Vickers, Brian, *Returning to Shakespeare* (London, 1989).

—— *Rhetoric and Feeling in Shakespeare's 'Sonnets'* (Zürich, 1991), corrected reprint from Keir Elam (ed.), *Shakespeare Today: Directions and Methods of Research* (Florence, 1984), 53–98.

Vieth, David M., 'An Unsuspected Cancel in Tonson's 1691 "Rochester"', *Papers of the Bibliographical Society of America*, 55 (1961), 130–3.

Vinge, Louise, *The Narcissus Theme in Western European Literature up to the Early Nineteenth Century* (Lund, 1967).

von Maltzhan, Nicholas, 'Samuel Butler's Milton', *Studies in Philology*, 92 (1995), 482–95.

Williams, Craig A., *Roman Homosexuality: Ideologies of Masculinity in Classical Antiquity* (New York, 1999).

Williams, Gordon, *A Dictionary of Sexual Language and Imagery in Shakespearean and Stuart Literature*, 3 vols. (London, 1994).

—— *Shakespeare, Sex and the Print Revolution* (London, 1996).

Williams, Sheila, 'The Pope-Burning Processions of 1679–81', *Journal of the Warburg and Courtauld Institutes*, 21 (1958), 104–18.

Wilson, Jean, ' "Two Names of Friendship, but one Starre": Memorials to Single-Sex Couples in the Early Modern Period', *Church Monuments*, 10 (1995), 70–83.

Winn, James Anderson, *John Dryden and his World* (New Haven, 1987).

Winnicott, D. W., *Playing and Reality* (London, 1971).

Woolf, D. R., 'The True Date and Authorship of Henry, Viscount Falkland's

History of the Life, Reign, and Death of King Edward II', *Bodleian Library Record*, 12 (1985–8), 440–55.

ZIMMERMAN, SUSAN (ed.), *Erotic Politics: Desire on the Renaissance Stage* (London, 1992).

Index

This index includes literary treatments of historical characters, but not purely fictional or mythological characters. Modern scholars are included only when they are cited in the main text.

DATE DUE

DEC 2 7 2002			
MAY 1 5 2004			
GAYLORD			PRINTED IN U.S.A.